# Debating Worlds

# Debating Worlds

## *Contested Narratives of Global Modernity and World Order*

*Edited by*

DANIEL DEUDNEY, G. JOHN IKENBERRY, AND KAROLINE POSTEL-VINAY

OXFORD
UNIVERSITY PRESS

Oxford University Press is a department of the University of Oxford. It furthers the University's objective of excellence in research, scholarship, and education by publishing worldwide. Oxford is a registered trade mark of Oxford University Press in the UK and certain other countries.

Published in the United States of America by Oxford University Press
198 Madison Avenue, New York, NY 10016, United States of America.



Library of Congress Control Number: 2022950251

ISBN 978–0–19–767931–9 (pbk.)
ISBN 978–0–19–767930–2 (hbk.)

DOI: 10.1093/oso/9780197679302.001.0001

Paperback printed by Sheridan Books, Inc., United States of America
Hardback printed by Bridgeport National Bindery, Inc., United States of America

# Contents

*Acknowledgments* vii
*List of Contributors* ix

Introduction: Debating Worlds 1
*Daniel Deudney, G. John Ikenberry, and Karoline Postel-Vinay*

1. Angloworld Narratives: Race as Global Governance 28
*Duncan Bell*

2. The Rise and Fall of a Global Narrative: The Soviet Challenge to the Western World 58
*Michael Cox*

3. Pan-Islamic Narratives of the Global Order, 1870–1980 80
*Cemil Aydin*

4. The Enduring Dilemma of Japan's Uniqueness Narratives 115
*Kei Koga and Saori N. Katada*

5. Writing the Right: Radical Conservative Narratives of Globalization 143
*Jean-François Drolet and Michael C. Williams*

6. The Chinese Global in the Long Postwar: Narratives of War, Civilization, and Infrastructure since 1945 162
*Rana Mitter*

7. Narrating India in/and the World: Colonial Origins and Postcolonial Contestations 184
*Itty Abraham*

8. Inequality, Development, and Global Distributive Justice 211
*Jeremy Adelman*

9. The Great Schism: Scientific-Technological Modernity versus Greenpeace Civilization 236
*Daniel Deudney*

Conclusion: Many Worlds and the Coming Narrative Dilemma 271
*Karoline Postel-Vinay*

*Index* 285

# Acknowledgments

This volume is the outcome of several workshops held in Paris, Oxford, and Princeton. The editors wish to express their gratitude for their encouragement and generous support to the Policy Planning Department of the French Ministry for Europe and Foreign Affairs, Sciences Po Center for International Research, and Princeton Institute for International and Regional Studies.

# Acknowledgments

# Contributors

**Itty Abraham**, Professor, Arizona State's School of Futures and Innovation

**Jeremy Adelman**, Henry Charles Lea Professor of History and Director of the Global History Lab, Princeton University

**Cemil Aydin**, Professor, Department of History, University of North Carolina-Chapel Hill

**Duncan Bell**, Professor of Political Thought and International Relations, Fellow of Christ's College, University of Cambridge

**Michael Cox**, Emeritus Professor of International Relations and Founding Director of LSE IDEAS

**Daniel Deudney**, Professor, Department of Political Science, Johns Hopkins University

**Jean-François Drolet**, Reader in Politics and International Relations, School of Politics and International Relations, Queen Mary University of London

**G. John Ikenberry**, Albert G. Milbank Professor of Politics and International Affairs, Princeton University

**Saori N. Katada**, Professor, Department of Political Science and International Relations and Director of the Center for International Studies, University of Southern California

**Kei Koga**, Assistant Professor, Public Policy & Global Affairs, School of Social Sciences, Nanyang Technological University—Singapore

**Rana Mitter**, Professor of the History and Politics of Modern China, St Cross College, University of Oxford

**Karoline Postel-Vinay**, Professor, Center for International Research, Sciences Po Paris

**Michael C. Williams**, Professor, University Research Chair in Global Political Thought, Graduate School of Public and International Affairs, University of Ottawa

# Contributors

# Introduction

## Debating Worlds

*Daniel Deudney, G. John Ikenberry, and Karoline Postel-Vinay*

By the last decade of the twentieth century, the great questions of modernity seemed to be answered. With the collapse of the Soviet Union and global communism, the liberal democratic capitalist project seemed to be the only one left standing.[1] The liberal narrative of 1989 was symbolized by the fall of the Berlin Wall. Leonard Bernstein and Beethoven's "Ode to Joy" provided the soundtrack. The 1980s and 1990s were decades when the "liberal ideal" spread worldwide. China joined the World Trade Organization (WTO) and all the great powers—East and West—seemed to be converging and integrating as stakeholders into a single global liberal world order. After centuries of tumultuous conflicts and waves of globalization, it appeared that humanity was on the verge of achieving a worldwide shared understanding, a universal narrative, of how societies should operate—and a narrative of a jointly held brighter future.

Today, this universalistic narrative clearly rings hollow. The tectonic plates of the global distribution of power have shifted and the preeminence of the West is clearly on the wane. As the West recedes, the Rest have surged in power, bringing with them new stories of the global past and new directions for world order. China is rapidly emerging as a peer competitor of the United States, bringing with it a powerful new global narrative, emphasizing grievance and revision. A decade ago, new narratives of the so-called emerging powers—the BRICS—provided a narrative of global transformation. Political Islam also burst onto the global scene as a multifaceted transnational movement reshaping regional political order and geopolitical alignments. Its narrative centers on a civilizational religion, rejecting secular and Western ways of life. With the rapid advance of climate change—and the advent of the Anthropocene Age—there have arisen new narratives of global endangerment and dystopia, as well as new narratives of science, technology, and the

Daniel Deudney, G. John Ikenberry, and Karoline Postel-Vinay, *Introduction* In: *Debating Worlds*. Edited by Daniel Deudney, G. John Ikenberry, and Karoline Postel-Vinay, Oxford University Press. 
DOI: 10.1093/oso/9780197679302.003.0001

environment. Far from converging, fragmentation and contestation increasingly dominate debates over world order.

Challenges to the universalistic narrative have also erupted in the West. The high bastions of the advanced industrial democracies, the vanguard in the old narrative, have fallen on hard times. Economic decline of the working class, the financial crisis of 2008, the rise of extreme inequality, and renewed racial turmoil have all called into question the viability of the progressive liberal narrative in the United States and Europe. The new media environment of the internet has eroded civility and amplified grievances. With these setbacks, there has been a rise of right-wing and illiberal movements, organized around authoritarian parties and governments across the West. In Europe, the project of union has been undermined by Brexit. The spread and deepening of democracy have been challenged and reversed by rising ethno-centric and illiberal nationalism, especially in Poland and Hungary. In the United States, which had styled itself as the indispensable leader of the free world for the better part of a century, the election of Donald Trump was an abrupt shock and regression. Under the banner of America First, Trump actively undermined and subverted American multilateral leadership and global problem-solving. Across the world, the "third wave" of democratization rising after the Cold War has rapidly receded. With the growing power, self-confidence, and ideological assertiveness of authoritarians and even totalitarians, the future seems to be trending strongly against the universalization of Western liberal democratic modernity.

As the dominant narrative of the West has waned, a new plurality of narratives has emerged. Each of these narratives combines stories of the past with understandings of the present and attractive visions of the future. Competing narratives have always existed, but over the last several decades, narrative plurality and contestations have become increasingly salient. Given these new realities, a primary task for theorists of world order must be to map these narratives. This task requires an understanding of the key features of narratives, their origins, and their roles in struggles over world order. In short, narratives are an important part of all world orders, and no understanding of contemporary politics and the prospects for conflict and concord in the future can fail to take them into serious consideration.

The narratives prominent on the contemporary world stage are a volatile mix of components. Not only are they very different from one another, they are themselves internally heterogeneous and contested. They offer different understandings of the past, present, and future. Some are "pre-Western," predating the encounter with Western global modernity. Some are clearly Western in origin and character. And some are vigorously anti-Western. They also differ in regard to their scope. Some are regional and civilizational, without global aspirations. But others cast themselves as globally expansive and universally ambitious. They are defined in different degrees by their antagonism with their alternatives, ranging from essential indifference to vigorous hostility. Many view this new discursive plurality as a welcome liberation from the experience of an oppressive and unwanted hegemonic and imperial Western narrative of modernity.[2] One way or another, it is the interaction of these diverse narratives that will in some significant measure shape debates and struggles over world order in the decades ahead.

These narrative clashes have first-order, real-world implications. The essential feature of the contemporary global and planetary era is that all the parts of fragmented humanity are now embedded in a planet-wide mesh of cascading interdependences. In a rapidly globalizing and changing world system, beset with major global problems—ranging from nuclear war to pandemics to climate change—this vigorous dissensus casts a darkening shadow over humanity's future. This cacophony and strong contestation over the fundamentals of world order diminish humanity's capacity to avoid conflict and solve global problems of increasing magnitude.[3] Whatever the attractions of the past, of historical grievances, or disputes about preferred cultures and ways of life, and whatever their posture toward liberal and Western modernity, the fractious branches of the human world are all dependent on the competent global management of increasingly potent technologies and the onslaught of climate change.

In a world marked by clashing narratives, global cooperation is becoming precarious. Russia's invasion of Ukraine is a stark reminder that large-scale conflict, and even nuclear war, could be increasingly difficult to avoid. Beyond hard-power politics, what is at play in Russia's aggression, along with China's de facto support, is the volatile significance of global connectivity fueled by contradictory interpretations and stories. Global regulatory capacities are decaying, and so is the possibility of addressing global challenges such as climate change, pandemics, or the rise of extreme inequality. The Covid-19 sanitary crisis exposed yet again a fierce worldwide narrative contestation described by Josep Borrell, the European Union High Representative, as a "global battle of narratives"[4] that impacted the management of the crisis. In short, this new battle of narratives arrives just at the moment when humanity faces its greatest need yet for common understanding and collective action. Given these disturbing realities and trends, this volume is motivated by the hope that an improved mapping and understanding of these diverse narratives and their interaction can contribute to the reviving and reshaping of a universalistic project that is both truly universal, significantly pluralistic, and responsive to the imperatives of global problem-solving.

Our aim is to examine on their own terms many of the major narratives of global modernity and world order that have emerged and clashed across the past several centuries. As a first step toward this goal, the next section considers the character and importance of narratives in world politics. The following section examines the key feature of global modernity and Western liberalism about which the major narratives explored in this volume have been preoccupied. The final section introduces and overviews the historical cases.

## What Are Narratives in World Politics?

Narratives are stories that people tell themselves about the world they live in, their role in it, and what they should be doing. Narratives are a ubiquitous feature of the human world and play important roles in politics. This fact has been widely recognized. In recent years, extensive work on narratives has been pursued by scholars of both the humanities and social sciences. Narratives are a central focus for psychologists, theologians, and philosophers. Popular culture and politics are permeated with competing narrative constructions of many types and grades.

Looking across history, narratives have played often prominent roles in politics and international affairs. Narrative constructions play a powerful role in the founding of cities, religions, states, and empires. For all their profound differences, successful founders such as Moses, Mohammad, Madison, Hitler, and Lenin were storytellers as much as organizers. And in periods of great upheaval and challenge, leaders such as Napoleon, Lincoln, Bismarck, Franklin D. Roosevelt, and Churchill were successful in part because of their skill of articulating and reaffirming narrative stories of history, identity, and purpose. As the clash of narratives between Russia's President Putin, Ukraine, and the West reminds us, the battlefields of politics are as much narrative wars as clashes of arms.

At the most general level, narratives in world politics are "big stories." They are produced, as in any storytelling process, by individual or collective storytellers who assemble disparate events, data, and beliefs into a narrative form that makes sense of the past, the present, and the future.[5] Political narratives are accounts that mix empirical claims about the past and present with privileged values and preferred futures.[6] Narratives offer answers to the questions that all peoples ask: who we are, how did we get here, and where are we going? And they seek to address these questions in ways that orient actors toward political action, thus answering the perennial question: what is to be done?

Our focus is on a subset of political narratives that we call "narratives of the global." These are macro-stories that actors generate to make sense of their place in the long span of historical global development. Narratives of the global purport to explain how particular groups got to where they are, and where they are going on the world stage. Looking at macro-narratives of the global over the past several centuries shows many quite different narratives of the global. They include characterizations of relative power, the degree of interconnectedness, and ideas about the nature of global modernity. These narratives and the agendas that they support point toward specific world orders, patterns of authority, identity, and legitimacy. In world politics, narratives are deployed as calls for universal action or to help set international codes, norms, and rules. While always speaking to the whole, global narratives also embody the perspectives and experiences of particular peoples.[7] At the center of every narrative of the global is an actor—a people, a country, a movement, a religion, a civilization—whose interests and predicaments are the focus.

Narratives also have important performative aspects.[8] Their exponents make great efforts in embodying key narrative points in popular song, monumental architecture, commissioned art, and public ceremonies.[9] The key features are cast to be seen and emotionally captivating. For example, environmental narratives have typically entailed visual communication and collective performance, such as Al Gore's presentations of *The Inconvenient Truth* or Greta Thunberg's *Fridays for Future.*[10] Taken to the extreme, the public performance face of narratives not only can become the basis for special mass ceremonies, but also can be woven into texture of ordinary life in encompassing ways. Authoritarian governments, operating with the tools of unchecked state power, have produced total regimes that have sought to bring every aspect of life into conformity with what are deemed to be the edicts of their narratives. While most narratives of global modernity either do not have totalizing aspirations or have been unable to realize them, all have performative manifestations that are essential tools for recruitment and education and the mobilization of collective action on a large scale. The performativity of narratives has a naturalizing power. By combining political agendas and worldviews with emotional power and widely shared understandings and values, narratives are able to contain internal contradictions, discrepancies, and deviations and the inevitable gaps between the narrative storyline and real events.[11]

Finally, narratives have wide appeal and important impacts because they seek to respond to pressing and important actual situations and problems. When new problems arise and crises erupt, narrative revision and reformation frequently result. Big problems, major setbacks, and fundamental novelties compel actors to rethink their narratives. Threatening changes in circumstances require new ways of doing things and the mobilization of collective action, thus entailing the recasting of the narrative script. For example, when the Industrial Revolution brought scattered and low-skilled peasants into factories and cities, the pre-industrial agrarian narratives of *ancien régimes* were no longer adequate. To reclaim their political usefulness, narratives have to account for and incorporate, both discursively and politically, new actors and problems. As a result of this dynamic interplay between real-world problems and shared stories and understandings, narratives rise, fall, and evolve in major ways. Hence narratives succeed, fail, and change in significant measure as a result of their strengths and weaknesses in illuminating problems and predicaments and guiding actors in their problem-solving pursuits.

In sum, narratives are norm-infused cognitive maps that provide overarching stories of the past, present, and future in ways that frame and guide practical action and problem-solving at a societal—now increasingly global—scale. When the map in a narrative story ceases to capture important parts of reality, actions guided by the old map are unlikely to be responsive and can often be disastrous. Given these features of narratives, major rifts, common problems, and new directions can be identified across the global space of modernity. By looking at narratives in this way, an important dimension of world politics in the modern global era is illuminated.

## Studying Global Narratives

Within the humanities and social sciences, the study of narratives, or "narratology," has been extensively developed. The study of narratives is an integral part of literary studies and criticism.[12] The difference between a chronicle and a history is a narrative, and historians recognize themselves as storytellers. Advocates of "Big History" promote educational curricula in order to disseminate an appreciation of the temporal and special impacts of human agency.[13] Communication theorists study narratives.[14] Empirical social scientists study the role of narratives in society, economics, and politics.[15] Political scientists have identified the importance of narrative for institutions and collective action.[16] Political historians and analysts of elections study the role of clashing narratives in election campaigns and presidential policy-making.[17] Among international relations theorists, postmodernists and constructivists have explored the ways in which discourses and narratives permeate politics.[18] As scholars such as Thomas Risse, Nita Crawford, and Martha Finnemore have demonstrated, many of the great global struggles, such abolitionism and decolonialism, entailed the construction and wide dissemination of new stories that prominently feature moral arguments.[19] International relations (IR) theory has experienced a "narrative turn" inspired by subject-centered methodologies used in other disciplines, notably history.[20] The study of foreign policy-making has also analyzed the influential role of strategic narratives.[21]

A prominent tendency in thinking about narratives with wide influence has been the effort to subvert, debunk, and abandon narratives, and particularly grand narratives. The particular target of anti-narrative thinking has been the grand Enlightenment vision of human progress and liberation, and the various narratives and ideologies associated with it in late-modern politics. In the nineteenth century, a new hermeneutic of critique and suspicion of powerful social narratives was developed by many thinkers, especially Ludwig Feuerbach, Karl Marx, Friedrich Nietzsche, and Sigmund Freud. Their basic insight was that the organized ideas prevalent in society were essentially a sham—edifices of ideas designed to bolster the interests of powerful groups. Thus was born "critical theory," which entailed the systematic analysis of the reigning stories of modernity. This type of thinking was further developed by the members of the Frankfurt School in the interwar period, and then by postmodern anti-structuralists, most notably Jean-François Lyotard, Michel Foucault, and Jacques Derrida, who emphasized the unreliability of language and the ultimately arbitrary character of all human claims, including those offered by natural science.

In the later years of the twentieth century and beyond, this comprehensive posture of suspicion became vernacularized. On both the right and left, this debunking move has been increasingly absolutized and universally applied. In the face of this extensive radical suspiciousness, and amplified by the novel features of the internet-dominated information environment, facts have become suspect, disinformation rampant, and conspiratorial thinking widespread.[22] Critics of this powerful secular tendency, from the old left and right and center, question whether civil peace, democratic accountability, and the competent operation of government can be maintained without shared narratives and other common understandings, both empirical and normative.

Despite these debates, narratives are a distinctive social phenomenon, a composite mixture of different types of ideas, visions, theories, interpretations, and agendas. They draw from the past and they claim to embody something of prime importance from the past. They are constructed from selective social or "collective memories"[23] of the past, exaggerated facets of the past, and even largely imaginary renderings of the past.[24] In their most widely disseminated versions, narratives of the global offer selective histories, simplified in a story that can be widely grasped. They are also often associated with a grand political tradition such as liberalism, revolutionary socialism, or national statism. These narrative traditions have founding visionaries and thinkers, classical texts, complex lineages of arguments and debates, and interpretations of pivotal events.

Global narratives encompass both causal and normative claims. That is, they have accounts and theories about the way the world works, intermingled with normative claims about how the world should work. Integral to narratives of the global are political projects, ongoing programmatic efforts by leaders, activists, and movements working across time to realize their agendas. The narrative's sense of inheritance, lineage, and genealogy provides the foundation and legitimacy for shared beliefs about the past in order to inspire and direct mass action in chosen directions. Narratives also contain various futures, some vague and normative, others elaborate and specific. Among the many narratives that have existed across history, the limited set of narratives considered here have in common sweeping stories speaking to challenges and experiences of global modernity.

The concept of narrative has affiliations and overlaps with other important discursive concepts, most notably ideology, worldview, and cosmology. Different analysts define these concepts in different ways. Some view ideologies as ubiquitous across human experience, but others emphasize that the term dates to the period of the French Revolution, and others view political ideology as a distinctively late-modern discursive phenomenon.[25] However these terms are defined, the focus here is on large stories in global modern politics. Despite these analytic differences, there is general agreement that ideologies are confined to the sphere of politics, political economy, and social order. Narratives are also complexly related to the concept of worldview or *weltanschauung*. Worldviews are best seen as even more comprehensive than narratives and, like narratives, not solely confined to politics.[26] A prominent feature in worldviews is an understanding of the natural world, and indeed much of the theorizing of worldviews has emphasized the increasingly influential role of successive scientific revolutions. For many analysts, the shift from human pre-modernity to modernity has entailed a shift in worldview. In a less comprehensive scale, worldviews are thought to be a universal trait of human culture, psychology, and society. This way of thinking about worldviews opens the door to micro-sociological and therapeutic investigations. Another related ideational formation is cosmology, which is also at play in changing ways across history. In common Western analysis, cosmology refers to ideas and representations about the natural world at its largest scale.[27] From the beginning, cosmological analysis was focused on the sky, and it has been the project of astronomy to accurately grasp these realities. In part because of the profound revolutions in astronomy beginning with Copernicus and Newton, some recent analysists have used the term *cosmology* to indicate what previously was considered a worldview.

The actor-centric character of narratives means that narrative analysis must distinguish between four different types of investigations. On the one hand, there is the project of evaluating, assessing, and testing the truth content of the claims in the narrative and the project of constructing and modifying narratives in some significant way. On the other hand, are the projects—the focus of this volume—of providing genealogies of the content of the narratives, and explaining the roles and impacts that agents acting on the basis of narratives have had in world politics.[28] Consistent with these distinctions, the chapters in this volume are not attempts to test and evaluate the content of the narratives. Nor are the chapters attempts to construct or improve narratives. Rather, the chapters are genealogies and investigations of the impacts of agents articulating and acting out narratives. Thus, our task is not to provide new or improved liberal, Islamist, Marxist, civilizational, or other theories of global modernity and world order. Rather, the objective is to analyze the content, function, evolution, and impact of narratives of modern global world order as they have been defined and wielded by political actors across time and space.

## The West, Global Modernity, and Narratives of World Order

For several millennia prior to European-led globalization and its subsequent globalizing waves, much of humanity lived in societies ordered and guided by powerful and long-enduring narratives. These comprehensive narratives typically had a religious cosmology and ethical system at their core. These narratives commonly cast themselves as universal, but their actual sway was never more than regional (such as the Sino-centric "world under Heaven" or *tianxia*, or the Arab vision of Muslim community or *ummah*). They changed very slowly over time and they looked primarily to the past, and their vision of the future tended to be static. Their axial storyline was religious, incorporating natural, historical, and supernatural elements. While they were all quite parochial and particularistic, they also had important similarities in the types of agencies privileged and the problems they addressed.[29] These similarities reflected a fundamental basic similarity in material circumstance. They were agricultural societies in which elite stratification on the basis of domination had been crystallized into hierarchical political structures with elite rule cosmically hallowed. The vast majority of people in these societies were quite poor, chronically oppressed, and illiterate. The civilizations of the long agricultural-society millennia often borrowed from one another.[30] In some parts of the world they were in intimate and clashing relations, such as between Islam and Latin Christendom in the Mediterranean region. But the overall pattern of human civilization was marked by many worlds whose interaction at distance was severely restrained, perhaps most extremely in the isolation of the Aztec and Inca empires and civilizations from Eurasia. The narratives from these earlier civilizations have not disappeared during the modern global era, because they form the baseline against which modern civilization has interacted. They also still provide the narrative resources from which many contemporary global-scale peoples, societies, and movements are drawing and trying to keep alive and relevant.

As it is widely and inescapably recognized, the world began to radically change a half-millennium ago with the beginning of modernity and globalization. The wellsprings of this change were European innovations in technology and organization that revolutionized the production of violence and wealth. With new military and economic advantages, Europeans began expanding their reach and power on an unprecedented global scale. With their rapid mastery of ocean space, the Europeans began interacting aggressively with people scattered across global distances.[31] Fueled by capitalism and interstate rivalry, Europeans continued to rapidly innovate and grow in relative power, so that by the later nineteenth century, European empires and settler colonies dominated almost all the earth and almost all humanity.[32] From the standpoint of the peoples and societies who were conquered, dispossessed, enslaved, and killed, European globalization ranged from traumatic to catastrophic. The narratives of the vast majority of humanity, and particularly of the great pre-modern agricultural civilizations, were upended. As a result, the pattern of narrative development over the past several centuries has been necessarily responding to, and shaped by, the threats and opportunities of global modernity and European expansion.

Radical narrative disruption and innovation also occurred in the West throughout this period. Narrative contestation and evolution within the European-centered explosion of modernity was extensive and rapid. At its inception, European global modernity was a narrative revolution in cosmology, astronomy, and methods for acquiring knowledge. From the beginning, the prophets and thinkers of modern science anticipated that their new method of acquiring and accumulating usable knowledge about nature would permit those who possessed this knowledge to fantastically augment their military and economic capabilities. From the beginning, the modernity that originated in Europe was radically revolutionary in its implications for the foundational activities of human life and it also assumed universal spatial global application. By the Enlightenment of the eighteenth century, this narrative had spread through European-wide networks of scientists, engineers, and entrepreneurs, and it had started to realize its program with an outpouring of powerful and efficient machinery for factory production and massively more destructive weapons.[33] It was this explosion in technologies, techniques, and organizations that propelled the Europeans from their peninsular marginality to unprecedented global dominance.[34]

At the core of this new European civilization's dynamism was a widely dispersed network of knowledge acquirers, inventors, and explorers.[35] Of all the features of this European explosion, it is modern science and the pursuit of technological innovations that have proved to be the most universal and consequential. As these new technological possibilities emerged, European states, militaries, and business firms became increasingly adept at harnessing and stimulating these new paths to power and wealth.

Within the West, the ongoing revolution of modernity created profound turmoil, revolutions, counter-revolutions, and religious wars and ideological struggles, all accompanied by ferocious narrative contestation. The "new modern" posed fundamental challenges to the inherited pre-modern worldview in every dimension—cultural, economic, political, and social. Like its agricultural society siblings elsewhere, Latin Christendom offered a narrative that integrated everything. Culturally, the static and closed medieval worldview was challenged by a radical new cosmology that was purely secular, open-ended, dynamic, expansive, and innovative. The economic fabric of agricultural civilization was marked by subsistence production, class domination, and technological stagnation. This order was successively supplanted by market capitalism, production for the market, expanded trade, class mobility, and economic growth propelled by technological advance. In the political realm, traditional monarchies and feudal aristocracies based on inheritance and sanctioned by religion gave way to bureaucratic states, wider participation, meritocratic advancement, rational realpolitik, and enlightened despotism, and then to constitutional republican and liberal democratic rule. Modernity also brought societal revolution with rapid urbanization, new forms of class stratification, and an explosion of new professions, occupations, and educational institutions, elevating technical expertise in all realms of life.[36]

These changes were accompanied by vigorous narrative contestation and innovation, over both minor and fundamental questions. As these new powers and riches swelled Europe's role in the world, new European narratives of confidence and exceptionalism flourished. Initially, some located Europe's special role as rooted in Christian religion, with narratives of people divinely chosen and anointed.[37] But a wide array of triumphalist and exceptionalist European narratives were radically secular. They were all addressing the question of what made Europe so exceptionally successful. Some such narratives were civilizational, elaborated in economic, sociological, and anthropological stages of human development, starting with barbarism and savagery and culminating in European enlightened civilization. Another narrative was geographic, emphasizing the ways in which European climate and topography were uniquely stimulative of civilizational advance.[38] Related narrative explanations emphasized European political and economic freedom as the unique prerequisite for advance.[39] By the nineteenth century, when the machine products of the Industrial Revolution were so powerfully changing the world, European narratives of civilizational identity exalted technological progress itself as the definitive marker of European superiority.[40] Another narrative lineage of European superiority was racial, a view which became elaborately developed with the trappings of biological science and Darwinian-inspired evolutionary biology.[41] Despite these differences, these narratives of European superiority provided various justifications for European imperial and colonial expansion.

Among the narrative innovations in early modern Europe, perhaps the most novel cluster of ideas is centered on the freedom of individuals and a democratic vision of expanding wealth and power to include everyone in societies. Modern liberals and democrats not only championed the new modern, but also claimed to be its appropriate—even necessary—companion. Just as the intricacy of European scientific and technological knowledge exploded, so too political theorists generated a sophisticated array of freedom claims, arrangements to support freedom, and measures to liberate the oppressed and extend a thickening array of human rights to steadily widening communities of humans, starting inside nations but eventually extending universally. From the outset, the prophets and thinkers of both scientific and technological modernity and liberal democratic progressivism proclaimed that their new paths were comprehensively revolutionary and inevitably universal ways of realizing the most basic human aspirations. Both these scientific and freedom narratives of modernity were from their birth strongly future-oriented, illuminated by a rich tapestry of utopian end-states and progressive pathways.

As the modern period unfolded, a cluster of very influential ideas formed and reformed, a Western liberal narrative of global modernity and world order. Its first appearance at the edges in small mercantile city-states, scattered in the nooks and crannies of the European world, was a Renaissance revival and extension of ancient Roman republican ideas and ideals. With the success in England of the parliamentary party and the establishment of constitutional monarchy, the freedom narrative was further developed both ideologically and institutionally. Then the great democratic revolutions in America, France, and elsewhere marked the great spatial widening and broadening of the modern liberal democratic narrative and order. This emancipatory vision attracted the oppressed throughout Europe and its colonial extensions and across the world. By the nineteenth century, a core liberal democratic package had been assembled.[42] Its domestic parts combined constitutional government, rule of law, representative democracy, private property capitalism, civil society, and evolving protections for individual rights. Internationally and globally, the full project included anti-imperialism, national self-determination, the abolition of slavery, free trade, international law, disarmament and arms control, international community-building, and joint problem-solving.[43] If this path were realized, its advocates insisted, the overall human estate would be profoundly improved. The actual practices of Western states and peoples across the modern era often fell quite short of this progressive liberal democratic pathway. But this narrative has never been fully dominant, even in the West. It has been in continuous struggle with powerful and antagonistic illiberal, anti-democratic, imperialist, and racist ideologies and movements.[44] As a result, the overall impact of the West on the wider world has been a mix of liberal democratic and its complete antithesis.

Within the Western heartland of this explosive change, advancing modernization and rising liberal democracy evoked powerful counter-movements and narratives. As the juggernaut of modernity and democratization plowed relentlessly forward, counter-movements and resistances sprung up to contain, halt, or reverse it. The strongest Western opponent of the new civilization was the old religion, as the Roman Catholic Church tenaciously fought across centuries to combat secularism and the overthrow of traditional hierarchies. The feudal *ancien régime* in the countryside vigorously resisted the encroachments of modernity and challenges to its established privileges and power. A particularly stark version of these dynamics occurred in France, where the Enlightenment weakened, and the great revolution overthrew, a somewhat modernized medieval order that quickly reformed itself as a counter-revolutionary anti-modernism in the early nineteenth century.

Another counter-reaction was spawned by the discrepancies between the often-horrific socioeconomic conditions of the industrial working class and the ideals of the progressive liberation narrative. Out of this crucible, Karl Marx and other radical socialists fashioned an intellectually powerful and widely influential narrative of the modern in which capitalism and extreme individualism would be a passing stage on the road to a world of working-class hegemony and economic socialism. The fact that capitalism in its most illiberal and undemocratic form had become coercively globalized by the Europeans meant that the Marxist alternative-freedom narrative would have global appeal.

On the right, another counter-modern and anti-liberal democratic opposition centered their narrative of resistance on a cultivation of particularistic ethno-nationalism and elaborate racial ideologies and world orders. Also, on the right, autocracy and all-consuming state power were elaborately theorized and employed to resist political democratization and liberal individualism.[45] The right-wing counter-narratives offered visions to sustain European global supremacy while at the same time envisioning a world order in which Europe would jettison its universal and imperial aspirations and cultivate a particularistic and non-universal path in modernity.

Outside the West, fundamental narrative contestation and revision have taken place all over the world, as peoples in every corner of the globe sought to respond to the encroachment of European influence and the enormous efficacy of the new European ways. In some of the earliest cases of rebellion against the West, in North America and the Caribbean, the American and Haitian revolutionaries turned the universalistic narrative of liberation into a powerful tool to mobilize against European imperial rule.[46] In the densely populated and long-developed civilizations in Eurasia that the Europeans forcefully intruded themselves upon, various forms of collective defensive modernization became extensive.[47] For example, many in Japan and China initially thought they could import the power and wealth-producing technological innovations of the Europeans to bolster their capacity to resist European predations—without compromising their civilizational cosmologies, social systems, and political orders. But strategies of containing modernity typically proved infeasible as new technologies, such as railroads, steamships, telegraphs, and modern factory production, generated problems and created needs which the earlier civilizational maps and scripts were unable to meet.

As material modernization progressed, *ancien régimes* all over the world found themselves confronted by rising classes of merchants and workers and educated elites who carried not just Western technical skills but also Western ideals and political ideologies. For example, after several centuries of evolution, the Chinese civilizational narratives and world-order vision is an amalgam of imports—Marxist and socialist, economic capitalist, and Schmittian authoritarianism. As this has happened, the civilizational legacy of millennia of Mandarin civilization has been relegated to little more than decorative trimmings and the raw materials for yet another modern ethnocultural nationalism, albeit with an international outreach, especially in the Global South.[48] One of the most powerful exports from the West over the course of the past century has been the European nation-state. As anti-colonial, anti-imperial, and anti-racist thinkers and activists across the global European imperium sought to mobilize their populations to successfully rebel against and build the organizational capacities to sustain their independence and enlarge the wealth of their societies, Western models proved irresistibly attractive. In the wake of the great global expansion and rebellion, the narratives in all parts of the world are now amalgams in which indigenized European forms of modernity are predominant. This means that the pattern of narrative talking worlds is a novel mix of convergence and bricolage, and that the fault line of narrative contestation that occurred and is occurring in the West is now occurring, with various particularistic inflections, essentially everywhere.

## Road Maps and Chapters

The dominant narratives of the global have been written in the West. Echoing the historical advance of global integration, with its major nodes in Europe and North America, these narratives have taken different forms, organized around an array of recurring leitmotifs. They tend to tell the story of the Western global ascendancy, driven forward through the nineteenth and twentieth centuries by, variously, the protean forces of capitalism, industrialism, democracy, liberalism, nationalism, internationalism, imperialism, hegemony, civilization, liberal modernity, and great power politics. These have been stories of the "rise of the West," told as European, Anglo-American, and Western civilizational dramas.

This project seeks to step outside of these traditional Western parameters and highlight a wider array of narratives of the global—narratives of how different peoples, societies, and cultures have envisioned, shaped, and transformed the world in the modern era. It also aims at moving away from the monolithic image of the "West" to which "non-Western" or "de-centered" perspectives tend to refer, by showing the tensions and contestations that sustained divergent narratives of the global within the West. By gathering and juxtaposing these diverse stories, within and beyond the West, we hope to enrich the historical, conceptual, and contemporary ways in which we talk about the unfolding world system. Hence the core purpose of this volume is to look at the major narratives of the global that have tried to explain—since the nineteenth century until today—the meaning and consequences of an ever growing economic, political, and cultural interconnectedness on a global/planetary scale. What sorts of "orders" are out there? What are the big stories that existed alongside the dominant narratives of the global, and that we can go back to and expose? And what voices and strands of global thinking can we bring into the current debate?

The first two chapters discuss two narratives of the global that are intrinsically linked to the European experience: the narratives of Empire and of Revolution; respectively rooted in Great Britain and its territorial offsprings, and continental Europe and Russia. In Chapter 1, Duncan Bell analyzes the persistent narrative of global order that focuses on claims about the purported superiority of the "Angloworld"—a grouping of countries centered on Great Britain, the United States, Australia, Canada, and New Zealand. Originating in nineteenth-century British and American debates about the role of race and empire, it assumed new forms and a new terminology across the twentieth century. Today it has been articulated in a variety of contexts, above all the fierce debates about Brexit. Duncan Bell suggests that elites throughout the Angloworld have repeatedly articulated visions of an integrated geopolitical and economic unity, grounded in claims about a shared identity and political destiny, capable of playing a pivotal role in global affairs. At their most radical, such projects have imagined a form of global domination based on claims of racial superiority. After outlining the overlapping *fin de siècle* debates about the idea of Greater Britain and the possibilities of an Anglo-American (re)union, this first chapter traces the narrative through the twentieth century and into our own time. It delineates four models of world order rooted in claims about the Anglo world integration: Anglo-American, imperial-commonwealth, democratic unionist, and world federalist. It concludes with a discussion of post–Cold War accounts of Angloworld supremacy.

Across the English Channel, the European nineteenth century witnessed the production of various narratives of transnational revolution, accompanying the 1848 upheavals throughout the continent, and opening the way to the unfolding, in the early twentieth century, of a major script, written in the West and reinvented in Russia. As Michael Cox argues in Chapter 2, the Soviet Union created a singular narrative of its own that challenged Western notions of progress and modernity in very basic ways. Combining together threads drawn from Karl Marx, ideas developed by Vladimir Lenin, a significant set of easy-to-understand axioms outlined by Joseph Stalin, and latterly a range of new ideas about peace and the construction of socialism, put into practice by his various successors—including the last Soviet leader Mikhail Gorbachev—this narrative provided a ready-made road map of the past, an immensely powerful critique of the present, and a vision of a future which proved immensely attractive to millions of people for a good part of the twentieth century. Moreover, even if the USSR disintegrated, it left behind a set of ideas that continue to inform critical thinking about the liberal order and the contemporary international economy into the twenty-first century. The state with which this narrative was most closely allied might have gone; however, the narrative itself, shorn of some of its more dogmatic features, still shapes the discussion about the future of the world today.

The following two chapters explore narratives engendered by the encounter with European power in the late nineteenth century of two non-Western societies: the Muslim world and Japan. Neither are counter-narratives standing up against Western domination; rather, they provide alternative narratives of modernity aiming at mitigating the impact of Euro-centrism on the non-Western world. In Chapter 3, Cemil Aydin interprets modern Pan-Islamism as one of the contested narratives of the world order that is universalistic and modern in content rather than rejectionist and reactionary. Parallel to the development of Pan-African and Pan-Asian visions of the global, Pan-Islamic narratives emerged in the 1880s as a globalist response to the inequities of racialized Eurocentric imperial world order. Initially, the idea of trans-imperial Muslim solidarity proposed by Pan-Islamism aimed to give Muslims more rights within European empires and to assert the equality of existing Muslim states in international law while shadowing the Eurocentric narratives of history, progress and civilization. By examining the themes of Pan-Islamic discourse of the world order that emerged during the half century preceding the 1919 mobilization of Muslim intellectuals around the Paris Peace Conference, this chapter assesses the nature of world-making claims and demands on the international order made by Muslim intellectuals and publics. It also discusses the legacies, transformation, and diverse political utilization of Pan-Islamic narratives of the global order during the era of decolonization, Cold War, and the post-Iranian Revolution periods.

The narratives of modern Japan that Kei Koga and Saori Katada examine in Chapter 4, in a broader historical perspective, are almost a reverse symmetry of the Pan-Islamic story in the sense that they express, first and foremost, a constant obsession with national singularity. As a "liminal power," sitting on the edge of the Pacific, and located between the East and the West, the narrative of Japan on the international scene and within the global history of modernity has almost continuously been that of Japanese uniqueness. From the Meiji Restoration (1868) to Reiwa era (2019–), whether a rising power or a declining one, the rollercoaster-like historical trajectory of Japan never translated into a story aiming at universal significance. The dominant narrative of Japanese achievement has been that of the only Asian nation that had managed to modernize and militarize in the Western dominant world in the early 1900s, and an economic juggernaut in the 1980s that would forever preserve its unique post-1945 pacifist identity. Although Japan's successes as a Westernized modern power in the late nineteenth century and a "economic miracle" in the later part of the twentieth century have inspired reformist governments in Asia, the de facto Japanese model did not lead to the production of a narrative with a regional scope, yet alone a universal one. This inability to move beyond national uniqueness, Katada and Koga argue, has been an enduring dilemma for Japan's self-definition as a global actor.

Meanwhile, during the same long historical stretch that saw the planetary expansion of Western power, the rise of the narrative of global modernity, with its twin head trope of political and scientific progress, has been bitterly contested within Europe. Chapter 5, by Jean-François Drolet and Michael Williams, excavates the reactionary narrative response to the story of the liberal future that was shaped by this early intra-European contestation and that created a repertoire whose long-lasting political relevance is particularly salient today. Once considered an exhausted vestige of the past, the radical right has indeed re-emerged in the early twenty-first century as one of the most striking and in many eyes most troubling challenges to the contemporary world order. In "Writing the Right," Jean-François Drolet and Michael Williams trace the historical lineages of this resurging strand of radical conservatism. While these movements are often seen as "knee-jerk" reactions to globalization, the authors argue that today's radical right also has its own intellectual vanguard that mobilizes long-standing historical narratives and intellectual legacies to produce ideologically and emotionally powerful attacks on liberal institutions and rationalities of government. Only by taking these narratives seriously is it possible to come to terms with today's radical right and develop compelling and effective responses to it.

The next two chapters look at the post-1945 narrative trajectories of two major international actors, China and India, who decades before becoming the much-scrutinized members of the BRICS group, have been producing their own stories of the global, made of thick historical texture. In Chapter 6, Rana Mitter traces changing Chinese ideas of the "global" as expressed through evolving ideas of the place of China in world order. The chapter begins with Jiang Tingfu, one of the prominent thinker-bureaucrats of the postwar era, who sought to define a place for China in the Bretton Woods era. It then explores the way in which Communist China has generated a succession of visions of global order that are at times contradictory: Mao Zedong's idea of the Three Worlds, the Deng Xiaoping–era view of China as a country that would take a restrained role in the world, and the new embrace of the global in the twenty-first century as China has sought to create a discourse of itself as a global actor. The chapter then examines two major discourses in contemporary China that seek to portray it as a foundational member of global order. One is the idea of China as a "civilizational state" which draws on its longer historical trajectory to define its role in the present day. Another is the concept of China as a "postwar" state that stakes a claim to ownership of the post-1945 order because of its contribution to World War II. Rana Mitter highlights, overall, the protean nature of the Chinese narrative of the global while finding a constant factor: the search for a discourse that foregrounds China's role in the global order that is defined not just as a matter of power, but of moral standing in an anarchic world.

Moving to China's neighbor, Itty Abraham in Chapter 7 exposes an assemblage of narrative dynamics that complicates the standard account of India's self-portrait as player on the world stage; i.e., that of a postcolonial non-aligned leader turned into a realpolitik-inspired sovereign power. The liberal, secular, and anti-militarist legacy of Gandhi and Nehru has been superseded, according to this account, by the forces of conformity with hard materialist conceptions of power—a shift mapped easily onto the rise of an illiberal domestic social movement seeking to identify India as a Hindu majoritarian nation. Instead of a simple linear narrative of change from principled difference to aggressive conformity, Abraham proposes first that India's primary axis of reference to the world is still mediated through the idea of (a great) civilization. Both difference and conformity owe their origins to the colonial preoccupation with and debates over India's civilizational status. Furthermore, India's relations with the world have always been deeply ambivalent. Desire for and attraction with the international sit alongside popular outrage at the treatment of Indians abroad, subaltern cosmopolitanism jostles against elite insecurity. This ambivalence is the product of an unresolved tension between India as a global nation and India as a territorially bound international personality seeking recognition from international society. Indian "narratives of the global" are also shaped by diasporic experiences and imaginings (the global nation) that both trouble and inform the conceptions of scholars and intellectuals seeking to explain and join India with the world.

The last two chapters analyze narratives of the global over extensive spans of time and space that talk today to two major challenges for governments and governance in the twenty-first century: spiralling socioeconomic inequalities, on the one hand, and eruptive clashes of scientific technological imaginaries (affecting a range of issues from climate change to Covid-19 prophylaxis), on the other. Jeremy Adelman's Chapter 8 is a study of how people from what we now call the Global South developed a narrative about their place in the wider world economy as backward, underdeveloped, primitive versions of modern societies of what we would now call the West. An intellectual history of global economic integration seen from voices in the periphery, it surveys the landscape from the late nineteenth century to the late twentieth. The chapter makes three basic claims about narratives of integration: first, that the sense of being peripheral evolved into a critique of the world economy and claims for redistribution from the world's wealthy societies to the underdeveloped world as a way to "catch up." Along the way, there were varying degrees to which Latin American, African, and Asian thinkers narrated the source of their pathologies and justified consensual or confrontational means to change the global balance. This call for redistribution became a narrative for global justice, simultaneously a critique of capitalism (even if many voices wanted national capitalism) and a source of pressure for new institutions and policies. Second, this global vision of redistributive justice was the driving force behind the idea of development, from its origins in the 1930s to the first decade of the twenty-first century as a narrative about the capacity to engineer change and master time. Finally, development was for global distributive justice what welfarism and socialism were to the idea of national distributive justice. As such, the two had a coiled history from the 1880s, reaching something of a peak in the 1960s, and in simultaneous retreat ever since.

The spectacular advance of global integration in the late nineteenth century was sustained by and, dialectically, fed technological and scientific innovation that in turn triggered fundamental questions about the organization of societies. In Chapter 9, Daniel Deudney examines a great debate over technology and the Earth which has unfolded with increasing ferocity since the middle years of the twentieth century. He argues that contemporary discussions of the "clash of civilizations" based on cultural differences obscure the more important global dominance of a material civilization based on modern science and its technological applications. This material civilization has prevailed due to its superior capacity to generate wealth and power. But with the emergence of potent new super-technologies, such as nuclear weapons, and the "great acceleration" in human impacts on the biosphere, the assumptions, programs, and trajectories of scientific technological modernity (STM) and its world orders have increasingly been called into question. As clashes over technological choices and environmental impacts have become increasingly prevalent, discursive contestation has come to be marked by a new spectrum of technopolitical positions, stretching from Prometheans and techno-optimists at one end to Aquarians and Friends of the Earth at the other. This emergent axis of contestation has increasingly supplanted the older left-right configuration. The critics of STM also offer an alternative path of modernity, a "greenpeace civilization" or a "scientific-technological Earth modernity" (STEM). Clashes between these two modernities increasingly define politics at all levels and in all domains. As climate change worsens and the development and diffusion of potent violent technologies continues, this civilizational discursive clash will increasingly be central to all politics.

## Notes

1. Francis Fukuyama, *The End of History and the Last Man* (New York: Free Press, 1992).
2. Pankaj Mishra, *From the Ruins of Empire: The Revolt against the West and the Remaking of Asia* (New York: Picador, 2012)
3. For an overview of the quest for unifying worldviews responsive to global and planetary interdependence and vulnerability, see Jo-Anne Pemberton, *Global Metaphors: Modernity and the Quest for One World* (London: Pluto Press, 2001).
4. Josep Borrell, "The Coronavirus Pandemic and the New World It Is Creating," Brussels, March 24, 2020, eeas.europa.eu.
5. W. J. T. Mitchell, ed., *On Narrativity* (Chicago: University of Chicago Press, 1981).
6. Joseph Davis, ed., *Stories of Change: Narrative and Social Movements* (Albany: State University of New York Press, 2002). See also William Cronon, "A Place for Stories: Nature, History and Narrative," *The Journal of American History* (March 1992).
7. Charles Taylor, *Sources of the Self: The Making of the Modern Identity* (Cambridge, MA: Harvard University Press, 1989).
8. Narratives are not "just words," as John L. Austin pointed out in *How to Do Things with Words* (Oxford: Clarendon Press, 1962). See also Homi Bhabba, *Nation and Narrative* (London: Routledge, 1990) and Marina Grishakova and Marie-Laure Ryan, ed., *Intermediality and Storytelling* (Berlin: Walter de Gruyter, 2010).

9. David I. Kertzer, *Ritual, Politics, and Power* (New Haven, CT: Yale University Press, 1988).
10. See Stephen Daniels and Georgina H. Endfield, "Narratives of Climate Change: Introduction," *Journal of Historical Geography* 35 (2009): 215–222.
11. The sheer complexity of events, whether scientifically complex such as climate change or unfathomably multidimensional such as the triggering of a world war, often requires the performativity of narratives that offer the comfort of truth-likeness, or *vraisemblance*, as Roland Barthes defined it. See Stephen Bottoms, "Climate Change "Science" on the London Stage," *WIREs Clim Change* v3 (2012): 339–348; Hidemi Suganami, "Narratives of War Origins and Endings," *Millenium: Journal of International Studies* 26 (1997); and Roland Barthes, *Image-Music-Text* (New York: Hill and Wang, 1977).
12. Mitchell, ed., *On Narrativity*. The term "narratology" was coined by literary critic Tzvetan Todorov in 1969. See also Hayden White, *The Fiction of Narrative: Essays on History, Literature, and Theory, 1957–2007* (Baltimore, MD: Johns Hopkins University Press, 2010).
13. David Christian, *Maps of Time: An Introduction to Big History* (Berkeley: University of California Press, 2004).
14. Walter R. Fisher, *Human Communication as Narration: Toward a Philosophy of Reason, Value, and Action* (Columbia: University of South Carolina Press, 1987); and Mieke Bal, *Narratology: Introduction to the Theory of Narrative* (Toronto: Toronto University Press, 1985).
15. Barbara Czarniawska, *Narratives in Social Science Research* (London: Sage, 2004).
16. Frederick W. Mayer, *Narrative Politics: Stories and Collective Action* (Oxford: Oxford University Press, 2014); and Charlotte Linde, Chapter 26: "Narrative in Institutions," in Deborah Schiffrin, Deborah Tannen, and Heidi E. Hamilton, eds., *The Handbook of Discourse Analysis* (Oxford: Blackwell, 2001).
17. See Peter Hays Gries, *The Politics of American Foreign Policy: How Ideology Divides Liberals and Conservatives* (Stanford, CA: Stanford University Press, 2014).
18. See James Der Derian, *On Diplomacy: A Genealogy of Western Estrangement* (Oxford: Basil Blackwell, 1987); Nicholas Onuf, *World of Our Making* (Columbia: University of South Carolina Press, 1989); Friedrich Kratochwil, *Rules, Norms, and Decisions: On the Conditions of Practical and Legal Reasoning in International Relations and Domestic Society* (Cambridge: Cambridge University Press, 1989); and Kratochwil, *On Praxis: On Acting and Knowing* (Cambridge: Cambridge University Press, 2018).
19. Thomas Risse, "'Let's Argue!': Communicative Action in World Politics," *International Organization* 54, no. 1 (Winter 2000): 1–39; Nita Crawford, *Argument and Change in World Politics: Ethics, Decolonialization, and Humanitarian Intervention* (Cambridge: Cambridge University Press, 2002); and Martha Finnemore, *The Purpose of Intervention: Changing Beliefs about the Use of Force* (Ithaca, NY: Cornell University Press, 2003).
20. Geoffrey Roberts, "History, Theory and the Narrative Turn in IR," *Review of International Studies* (October 2006). For a comprehensive exploration of this

narrative turn, see Naeem Inayatullah and Elizabeth Dauphinee (eds.), *Narrative Global Politics: Theory, History and the Personal in International Relations* (London: Routledge, 2016).

21. Alister Miskimmon, Ben O'Loughlin, Laura Roselle, eds., *Forging the World: Strategic Narratives and International Relations* (Ann Arbor: University of Michigan Press, 2017).
22. Slavoj Zizek, *The Sublime Object of Ideology* (London: Verso, 1989); and Geoff Shullenberger, "Redpilling and the Regime," *The New Atlantis* 65 (Summer 2021): 3–14.
23. Maurice Halbwachs, *La mémoire collective* (Paris : Presses Universitaires de France, 1950); English translation: *The Collective Memory* (New York: Harper & Row, 1980).

    As Russia's invasion of Ukraine illustrates yet again, wars are also narrative production sites that function before, during, and beyond each conflict. See Valérie Rosoux, *Les usages de la mémoire dans les relations internationales* (Brussels: Bruylant, 2001); Jan-Werner Müller, ed., *Memory and Power in Post-War Europe* (Cambridge: Cambridge University Press, 2002); and Duncan Bell, ed., *Memory, Trauma and World Politics* (Basingstoke, UK: Palgrave Macmillan, 2006).
24. Eric Hobsbawm and Terence Ranger, eds., *The Invention of Tradition* (Cambridge: Cambridge University Press, 1983); and Hobsbawm, *Nations and Nationalism since 1780: Programme, Myth, Reality* (Cambridge: Cambridge University Press, 1981).
25. Michael Freeden, *Ideologies and Political Theory: A Conceptual Approach* (Oxford: Oxford University Press, 1996); and Lewis S. Feuer, *Ideology and Ideologist* (Piscataway, NJ: Transaction, 2010).
26. Peter J. Katzenstein, ed., *Uncertainty and Its Discontents: Worldviews in World Politics* (New York: Cambridge University Press, 2022).
27. Non-Western traditions provide a variety of conceptions of cosmology, and the Chinese one in particular conflates nature and politics. See, for example, Aihe Wang, *Cosmology and Political Culture in Early China* (Cambridge: Cambridge University Press, 2000); Richard Smith, *Mapping China and Managing the World: Culture, Cartography and Cosmology in Late Imperial Times* (London: Routledge, 2013).
28. For important studies in this tradition, see John M. Owen, IV, *The Clash of Ideas in World Politics: Transnational Networks, States, and Regime Change, 1510–2010* (Princeton, NJ: Princeton University Press, 2011); and Mark Haas, *The Ideological Origins of Great Power Politics, 1789–1989* (Ithaca, NY: Cornell University Press, 2005).
29. S. N. Eisenstadt, *The Political Systems of Empires: The Rise and Fall of Historical Bureaucratic Societies* (New York: Free Press, 1963); and John H. Kautsky, *The Politics of Aristocratic Empire* (Chapel Hill: University of North Carolina Press, 1983).
30. See William McNeil's critique of Samuel Huntington's civilizational historical narrative.
31. Alexander Anievas and Kerem Nişancıoğlu, *How the West Came to Rule: The Geopolitical Origins of Capitalism* (London: Pluto, 2015).

32. For the role of interstate rivalry in fueling innovation, see William McNeill, *The Pursuit of Power: Technology, Armed Force, and Society since A.D. 1000* (Chicago: University of Chicago Press, 1982); and Charles Maier, *Once Within Borders: Territories of Power* (Cambridge, MA: Harvard University Press, 2016).
33. See Barry Buzan and George Lawson, *The Global Transformation: History, Modernity and the Making of International Relations* (Cambridge: Cambridge University Press, 2015); C. A. Bayly, *The Birth of the Modern World, 1780–1914* (Oxford: Blackwell, 2004); Jurgen Osterhammel, *The Transformation of the World: A Global History of the Nineteenth Century* (Princeton, NJ: Princeton University Press, 2014); and David Landes, *The Unbound Prometheus: Technological Change and Industrial Development in Western Europe 1750 to the Present* (Cambridge: Cambridge University Press, 1969).
34. Among landmark historical accounts are William McNeill, *The Rise of the West: A History of the Human Community* (Chicago: University of Chicago Press, 1963); Carlo Cipolla, *Guns, Sails and Empires: Technological Innovation and the Early Phases of European Expansion, 1400–1700* (New York: Minerva Press, 1965); David Abernathy, *The Dynamics of Global Dominance: European Overseas Empires, 1415–1980* (New Haven, CT: Yale University Press, 2000); Daniel Headrick, *Power over Peoples: Technology, Environment and Western Imperialism 1400 to the Present* (New York: Oxford University Press, 2010); Kenneth Pomeranz, *The Great Divergence: China, Europe and the Making of the Modern World Economy* (Princeton, NJ: Princeton University Press, 2000); and Eric Jones, *The European Miracle: Environments, Economies and Geopolitics in the History of Europe and Asia* (Cambridge: Cambridge University Press, 1981).
35. Phillip Hoffman, *Why Did Europe Conquer the World?* (Princeton, NJ: Princeton University Press, 2015); Felipe Fernandez-Armesto, *Pathfinders: A Global History of Exploration* (New York: Norton, 2006). Joyce Appleby, *Shores of Knowledge: New World Discoveries and the Scientific Imagination* (New York: Norton, 2013); F. Lestringant, *Mapping the Renaissance World: The Geographical Imagination in the Age of Discovery* (Berkeley: University of California Press, 1994); Dane Kennedy, *The Last Blank Spaces: Exploring Africa and Australia* (Cambridge, MA: Harvard University Press, 2013); and Kennedy, *Reinterpreting Exploration: The West and the World* (Oxford: Oxford University Press, 2014).
36. This story is told by many scholars. See Maier, *Once Within Borders;* and Buzan and Lawson, *The Global Transformation.*
37. Anthony Pagden, *Lords of All the World: Ideologies of Empire in Spain, Britain and France, c. 1500–c. 1800* (New Haven, CT: Yale University Press, 1994); and David Armitage, ed., *Theories of Empire, 1450–1800* (Aldershot, UK: Ashgate, 1998).
38. J. M. Blaut, *The Colonizer's Model of the World: Geographical Diffusionism and Eurocentric History* (New York: Guilford, 1993).
39. John A. Hall, *Power and Liberties: The Causes and Consequences of the Rise of the West* (Berkeley: University of California Press, 1986); and Jerry Z. Muller, *The Mind and the Market: Capitalism in Modern European Thought* (New York: Knopf, 2002).

40. Michael Adas, *Machines as the Measures of Men: Science, Technology, and Ideologies of Western Dominance* (Ithaca, NY: Cornell University Press, 1989).
41. Philip D. Curtin, ed., *Imperialism* (New York: Walker, 1971), ch. 1, "The 'Scientific' Roots: Nineteenth Century Racism"; ch. 3, "The Application of Pseudo-Scientific Racism." On racial theories of Western—and Anglo-American—dominance, see Duncan Bell, *Dreamworlds of Race: Empire and the Utopian Destiny of Anglo-America* (Princeton, NJ: Princeton University Press, 2021).
42. See Helena Rosenblatt, *The Lost History of Liberalism: From Ancient Rome to the 21st Century* (Princeton, NJ: Princeton University Press, 2020); and James T. Kloppenberg, *Toward Democracy: The Struggle for Self-Rule in European and American Thought* (Oxford: Oxford University Press, 2016).
43. There is a large literature on the relationship between liberalism and empire. See Jennifer Pitts, *A Turn to Empire: The Rise of Liberal Imperialism in Britain and France* (Princeton, NJ: Princeton University Press, 2006); and Mehta's *Liberalism and Empire: A Study of Nineteenth-Century British Liberal Thought* (Chicago: University of Chicago Press, 1999). On anti-imperialism, see Jan C. Jansen and Jürgen Osterhammel, *Decolonization: A Short History* (Princeton, NJ: Princeton University Press, 2017); and William Roger Louis, "American Anti-Colonialism and the Dissolution of the British Empire," *International Affairs* 61, no. 3 (1985): 395–420. On self-determination, see Erez Manela, *The Wilsonian Moment: Self-Determination and the International Origins of Anticolonial Nationalism* (Oxford: Oxford University Press, 2009). On the rise of the discourse of human rights and abolition of slavery, see Gary Bass, *Freedom's Battle: The Origins of Humanitarian Intervention* (New York: Vintage, 2009). On international law, see Lauren Benton, *Rage for Order: The British Empire and the Origins of International Law, 1800–1850* (Cambridge, MA: Harvard University Press, 2018). On disarmament, see Andrew Webter, "The League of Nations, Disarmament and Internationalism," in Glenda Sluga and Patricia Clavin, eds., *Internationalisms: A Twentieth-Century History* (Cambridge: Cambridge University Press, 2017). On community-building, at least in the domain of security, see Karl Deutsch, *Political Community and the North Atlantic Area: International Organization in the Light of Historical Experience* (Princeton, NJ: Princeton University Press, 1957); and Emmanuel Adler and Michael Barnett, *Security Communities* (Cambridge: Cambridge University Press, 1998).
44. See Susan Pedersen, *The Guardians: The League of Nations and the Crisis of Empire* (Oxford: Oxford University Press, 2015).
45. See Jan-Werner Muller, *Contesting Democracy: Political Ideas in Twentieth-Century Europe* (New Haven, CT: Yale University Press, 2011).
46. For the classic study, see C. L. R. James, *The Black Jacobins: Toussaint L'Ouverture and the San Domingo Revolution* (London: Secker & Warburg,1938).
47. Philip D. Curtin, *The World and the West: The European Challenge and the Overseas Response in the Age of Empire* (Cambridge: Cambridge University Press, 2000).
48. Timothy Cheek, David Ownby, and Joshua A. Fogel., eds, *Voices from the Chinese Century: Public Intellectual Debate from Contemporary China* (New York: Columbia

University Press, 2019); Xu Jilin, translated from the Chinese and edited by David Ownby, *Rethinking China's Rise: A Liberal Critique* (Cambridge: Cambridge University Press); Sebastian Veg, *Minjian: The Rise of China's Grassroots Intellectuals* (New York: Columbia University Press, 2019). Also see Chris Alden and Daniel Large, eds., *New Directions in Africa-China Studies* (London: Routledge, 2019).

# 1

# Angloworld Narratives

## Race as Global Governance

*Duncan Bell*

### Introduction

On a chilly Tuesday in December 1999, Margaret Thatcher rose to deliver a speech in New York. Her hosts were the English-Speaking Union, founded in 1918 to promote cooperation between the "English-speaking peoples." She didn't disappoint her audience. The English-speaking world, she proclaimed, had a providential task to fulfill. "We take seriously the sanctity of the individual; we share a common tradition of religious toleration; we are committed to democracy and representative government; and we are resolved to uphold and spread the rule of law." Citing John Locke, Edmund Burke, and Thomas Jefferson, she recommended an alliance that would "redefine the political landscape" and ultimately transform "politically backward areas [by] creating the conditions for a genuine world community."[1]

Thatcher was far from the first to air such grandiose ideas. Indeed she was drawing on a proposal that the distinguished poet and historian Robert Conquest had sketched in a speech to the English-Speaking Union just a few months earlier. Conquest charged that existing international bodies, such as the United Nations and the European Union, had failed, and he insisted that a better alternative was required. He proposed an "Anglo-Oceanic" political association "weaker than a federation, but stronger than an alliance." This ocean-straddling institution would help bring peace to a violent planet.[2] In the first decade of the twenty-first century, this broad conception of the Anglosphere drew the attention of some senior politicians, including Tony Blair, Gordon Brown, and John Howard. Although the term "Anglosphere" was coined in the 1990s, the underlying idea can be traced back much further. If Thatcher was drawing on Conquest, Conquest was drawing in turn on a venerable tradition of thought that envisaged the "Anglo-Saxons" or

Duncan Bell, *Angloworld Narratives* In: *Debating Worlds*. Edited by Daniel Deudney, G. John Ikenberry, and Karoline Postel-Vinay, Oxford University Press. © Oxford University Press 2023. DOI: 10.1093/oso/9780197679302.003.0002

"English-speaking peoples" as a united community shaping global politics. Between the 1930s and 1950s, Winston Churchill had penned a four-volume *History of the English-Speaking Peoples* which weaved a golden Anglophone thread through a two-thousand-year story stretching from Julius Ceaser to the First World War.[3] This chapter refuses Churchill's invitation to travel to the ancient world, instead focusing on the long twentieth century. The Angloworld discourse emerged in the late nineteenth century, in the context of debates over the future of the British and American empires. It persisted through the twentieth century, waxing and waning in popularity.[4] In recent years it has played a potent role in offering British Euroskeptics an alternative to the European Union. Brexit, they have long hoped, would be followed by a reorientation to the Anglosphere.

This chapter offers a broad survey of Angloworld narratives across the long twentieth century, stretching from the Victorian era to the present. The opening two sections of the chapter explore overlapping elements of the *fin de siècle* Angloworld discourse. The first section focuses on the relationship between Britain and its colonial empire, while the following one turns to intersecting arguments over the future relationship between the empire and the United States. The third section traces the echoes of these debates through the twentieth century, discussing the interlacing articulation of imperial-commonwealth, Anglo-American, democratic unionist, and world federalist projects. Despite important differences between them, most versions of these grand supranational schemes were heirs of the earlier debates. In the final section I discuss contemporary accounts of Angloworld supremacy, looking at both neoconservative ideas about the Anglosphere and fantasies of post-Brexit Britian. While none of the most radical plans came to fruition, the evolving debate over the nature of the Angloworld formed a central element in the cultural construction of the "West," and highlights the extravagant hopes that have been invested in the "Anglo-Saxons" over the course of the twentieth century. It constitutes a prominent and durable narrative of global politics.

## Empire, Nation, State: On Greater Britain

Daniel Deudney has called the late nineteenth century the "global industrial period." The spread of the Industrial Revolution was a "primal development" for global politics, as new technologies intensified interactions across the planet, reshaping the material and imaginative contexts in which debates over the future took place. "As the scale and tempo of human affairs changed, a major and tumultuous reordering of large-scale political relationships and institutions seemed imminent and inevitable."[5] The thinkers of the time—the "industrial globalists"—proselytized a wide array of schemes for transcending the anarchic international system, including regional imperial structures, European union, the federation of the British Empire, and even the future development of a world state. Others advocated political associations based explicitly on racial or linguistic identity. Pan-Slavism, Pan-Asianism, Pan-Islamism, and Pan-Latinism all flowered in the shadow of geopolitical uncertainty, as thinkers throughout the world imagined new sources and modalities of political affiliation, legitimacy, and belonging.[6] The late Victorian and Edwardian debates about the Angloworld were an integral element of this more general discourse.

This period also saw the rearticulation of the global politics of race. In 1900, at the meeting of the Pan-African Congress in London, W. E. B. Du Bois predicted that the "problem of the twentieth century" would be "the problem of the color line."[7] Fears about racial contamination were rife. A civilizational dividing line was constructed between "white" peoples and others, resulting in the initiation of numerous exclusionary practices, including xenophobic immigration controls. This was a paradoxical process: "The imagined community of white men was transnational in its reach, but nationalist in its outcomes, bolstering regimes of border protection and national sovereignty."[8] Forms of transnational whiteness, Anglo-Saxonism foremost among them, were but an attempt to rethink the spatial configuration of global order. The "religion of whiteness," as Du Bois once termed it, catalyzed efforts to institutionalize racial supremacy within and beyond the borders of Europe and the Angloworld.[9] Those debating the future of the Angloworld insisted on carving out a space within the general identity of whiteness, establishing a stratified geo-racial imaginary. Usage of the term "race" was highly imprecise, but it typically designated a combination of cultural markers—historical mythscapes, habitus, shared language, cultural values, and political ideals—circumscribed by "whiteness." It constituted a biocultural assemblage.[10] The French, the Germans, the Russians, and the Hispanics were all considered inferior to the Anglo-Saxons. They in turn ranked higher on the scale of civilization than other non-white racial constellations populating the world outside the Euro-Atlantic zone and its diasporic outposts. In this conception of world politics, the basic ontological unit was race, and political institutions, including the state, were only of derivative importance. Such racial assumptions were articulated and defended routinely[11] in a variety of emerging academic disciplines, including political science.

The sweeping debate over the future of the British colonial empire was conducted under the sign of "imperial federation," while the assemblage of communities under discussion was frequently labeled "Greater Britain."[12] The debate formed a key building block in the ideological construction of the twentieth-century Angloworld. It was driven by two intersecting imperatives. Fear that British relative power was threatened by the rise of formidable states—notably Germany, Russia, and the United States—led many commentators to argue for the construction of a globe-spanning political association, encompassing Britain and its settler colonies in Australia, Canada, New Zealand, and (more ambivalently) South Africa, either to balance the new threats or to deter them from attempting to compete. These geopolitical concerns were reinforced by anxieties about the onset of democracy, with many imperial observers fearing that an expanding electorate would fail to recognize the importance of the empire, concentrating its energies on domestic reform. It was feared—prematurely as it turned out—that a democratic polity would invariably be anti-imperial. Creating a federal Greater Britain, while populating it in part through an accelerated program of "systematic" emigration from the "mother country," was thought to be one way of neutralizing these threats. Yet even some radical and liberal admirers of democracy saw benefits in imperial federation. For them, Greater Britain could simultaneously hasten the peaceful development of the international system and help to democratize Britain itself through the importation of progressive practices from the more egalitarian colonies.[13]

This recoding of space was amplified by widespread interest in the political technology of federalism. It was, Ernest Barker was later to write, the "note of the hour."[14] Federal structures were thought to offer a way of productively reconciling vast geographical expanse, political dynamism, and individual liberty, thus allowing the rescaling of political community. According to Hobson, great federal political communities would dominate the future, and it was thus essential to erect a "Pan-Saxon" one. As he proclaimed in *Imperialism*, "Christendom thus laid out in a few great civilizational empires, each with a retinue of uncivilized dependencies, seems to me the most legitimate development of present tendencies and one which would offer the best hope of permanent peace on an assured basis of inter-Imperialism."[15] Hobhouse, meanwhile, argued that imperial federation "is a model, and that on no mean scale, of the International State."[16] These arguments illustrate the two broad temporal logics that underpinned debates over Anglo-union deep into the twentieth century. In one of them, union represented the terminal point of future political development: the polity would take its place among other competing pan-racial or regional units. In the other, Anglo-union was figured as a transitional institutional formation, one that could serve as a template, catalyst, and leader of a future global political association.

A significant number of British unionists fantasized about the incorporation of the United States within an imperial federation, though most of them recognized that this was unrealistic (at least in the short term). Nevertheless, America played a crucial role in imperial discourse. First, it was regarded as a potential challenger to British supremacy, thus motivating the call for action. This was especially apparent in the wake of the McKinley Tariff of 1890, which incited the demand throughout Britain and its colonies for the creation of a system of imperial preference.[17] Second, the turbulent history of American-British relations, and in particular the War of Independence, preoccupied British imperial unionists, teaching them that the demands of colonial subjects had to be treated seriously. This meant granting them greater political autonomy. And finally, the United States demonstrated the power of federalism as a political technology by proving that individual liberty was compatible with vast geographical extent. This was welcome in an age in which it was commonly believed that the future belonged to huge omni-competent political units. Joseph Chamberlain, arch-federalist and Secretary of State for the Colonies, was far from alone in believing that "[t]he days are for great Empires and not for little States."[18] Size mattered.

The debates over Greater Britain generated hundreds of proposals, differing in ambition, detail, and rationale. Three general institutional models were discussed. The least ambitious was "extra-parliamentary" federation, wherein a group of distinguished individuals—organized as an imperial Advisory Council—would offer the British Parliament non-binding advice on imperial affairs.[19] A more constitutionally far-reaching model was "parliamentary federalism," in which the colonies were to send elected representatives to sit in Westminster. This had been a common exhortation since the late eighteenth century, though it was much less popular in the closing decades of the Victorian age. Finally, "supra-parliamentary federalism" connoted the formation of a sovereign federal chamber supervening on the individual political assemblies of the empire. This model followed the example, above all, of the United States.[20]

Not all advocates of Greater Britain proposed the creation of a vast federal polity. For many of them, the key to the future lay in the shared identity of the Anglo-Saxon race spread across the world, and they argued that further institutionalization was unnecessary—it either fell outside the scope of "practical politics" or it was counterproductive. Instead, they maintained that it was essential to nourish the existing connections. This was the course that the British government ultimately followed. Dilke and Goldwin Smith, both leading public intellectuals and critics of imperial federal schemes, extolled the superiority of the British "race" and promoted a vision in which the Anglo-Saxons, acting as a collective of independent states, would shape the future. They supported the independence of the British settler colonies, but as a means to the end of Anglo-unity, not its termination. For Dilke, the "strongest of arguments in favour of separation is the somewhat paradoxical one that it would bring us a step nearer to the virtual confederation of the English race."[21] Both of them also included the United States in their vision. The cultural-racial conception of "virtual confederation" proved the most enduring.

Arguments about both Greater Britain and Anglo-American union were premised on a cognitive revolution, a fundamental transformation in the perception of time and space. From the 1860s onward, new communications technologies radically altered the way in which individuals perceived the physical world and the sociopolitical possibilities it contained, spawning fantasies about the elimination of geographical distance that prefigure late twentieth-century narratives of globalization. H. G. Wells declared that "modern mechanism" had created "an absolute release from the fixed conditions about which human affairs circled." For J. R. Seeley, the leading intellectual of the imperial federalist movement, the "unprecedented facility of communication which our age enjoys seems to be creating new types of state."[22] A Greater British state was now realizable. Techno-utopianism underpinned arguments about the existence of a trans-planetary British political community. "When we have accustomed ourselves to contemplate the whole [colonial] Empire together and call it England," Seeley proclaimed, "we shall see that here too is a United States. Here too is a homogeneous people, one in blood, language, religion, and laws, but dispersed over a boundless space."[23] Previously viewed as immutable, nature was now open to manipulation, even transcendence.

All of these projects depended on claims about the common identity of the dispersed Anglo people(s).[24] The argument assumed two main forms. One insisted that the social ontological foundation of the people was *race*. They were, above all, Anglo-Saxon or members of the "English race." This view was compatible with (but did not entail) an argument that the populations of the individual colonies were coalescing into new nationalities, and that the United States already comprised a distinct nation. The other account accepted the centrality of race, but emphasized the idea of a singular *nationality*: the (relevant) population of Greater Britain was the British (or "English") nation writ global. Both conceptions sanctioned extensive discrimination. The indigenous populations of the settler colonies, and the vast majority of the people that Britain ruled over in the Caribbean, Africa, the Middle East, and Asia—and that the United States came to rule over in Hawaii and the Philippines—fell outside the scope of either account of the singular people.

The "nationality" view prevailed among late Victorian imperial thinkers. Seeley was only the most prominent to claim that "Greater Britain is homogenous in nationality."[25] During the Edwardian years, a multinational commonwealth vision began to eclipse the Seeleyean global nation-state. This position became increasingly popular over time, not least because it mirrored the views of the political elites in the colonies. Greater Britain morphed into a post-national (or multinational) political association. In 1905 W. F. Monypenny, a journalist with *The Times*, conceived of the colonial empire as a "world state" that "transcends nationality" while allowing separate nationalities to flourish within it.[26] The idea of an Anglo-Saxon commonwealth was central to the influential Round Table movement (founded in 1909–1910) because, as Lionel Curtis wrote in 1916, the colonies had acquired a "national consciousness of their own."[27] Both the nation-centric and the race-centric accounts, however, focused on an argument about the singularity of "the people."

The imaginative extension of the scope of the people was conjoined with an expansion of the compass of the public—of the set of individuals within the totality of the people regarded as politically significant. Arguments promulgating the unification of the British colonial empire (and also Anglo-America) embodied a claim about the existence or potentiality of an ocean-spanning public. This was a racially delimited precursor to the idea of a global public sphere. Indeed one of the most conceptually innovative features of the discourse, prominent especially in the early twentieth century, was the effort to inaugurate a system of Greater British imperial citizenship.[28] It is possible to view the Anglo-racial imaginary as an example of what Arjun Appadurai terms "translocal" affiliation—of an emergent cartography that escaped the topological imperatives of the modern territorially bounded nation-state.[29] As time and space were reordered, so it was increasingly argued that a strong sense of identity and belonging bound Britain and its colonial populations. However, whereas many of the examples explored by Appadurai are "counterhegemonic"—seeking to challenge extant power structures and sources of authority—the attempted reworking of "Anglo-Saxon" racial-national consciousness in the Victorian age was a hegemonic project, an effort to prolong British supremacy through novel articulations of political identity. It involved a double process of deterritorialization and reterritorialization.[30] The British polity was no longer to be conceived of as a small group of islands lying off the northwest coast of continental Europe (deterritorialization). Instead, it was to be seen as encompassing a vast range of territories in North America, the Pacific, and Southern Africa (reterritorialization). A similar geo-racial logic also helped underpin arguments about Anglo-American unity.

## The Reunion of the Race: On Anglo-America

The unity of the Angloworld was not preordained. For much of the nineteenth century, relations between the British Empire and the United States were antagonistic. Resentment about the colonial past, incessant disputes over the Canadian border, the bitter divide over the Civil War and its aftermath, pervasive cultural condescension from the British, and widespread Anglophobia in American public life: all fanned the flames of antipathy. Mutual suspicion was the norm. It was only during the last two decades of the century, and in particular during the late 1890s, that the animosity thawed. This "rapprochement"—and the subsequent creation of an Anglo-American security community—has long been the subject of intense scrutiny by diplomatic historians and international relations (IR) specialists.[31]

It was during the 1890s that the debate over Anglo-American union moved to the center of political debate. The Venezuelan boundary dispute (1895–1896) led to acrimonious exchanges between Washington and London, but it also prompted anguished commentators on both sides of the Atlantic to recoil from the prospect of war. Numerous proposals for Anglo-American union appeared. A range of new organizations fostered personal connections and build a sense of solidarity between like-minded members of the transatlantic elite. In February 1896 the "Anglo-American Union" was launched in London to agitate for an arbitration agreement.[32] It was followed by the Anglo-American Committee (1898), the Anglo-American League (1898), the Atlantic Union (1901), and the Pilgrims Society (1902). The clamor for racial unity was in part a result of America's new assertiveness, for although the United States had been engaged in imperial conquest since its founding, the annexation of Hawaii and the Spanish-American War (1898) signaled its first sustained burst of extra-continental imperial activity. This was seen as marking a new phase in American history: either a moment when the country assumed its predestined role as a great power, or when it betrayed the founding principles of the republic. Many observers on both sides of the Atlantic insisted that the British and Americans should be united, not divided, under conditions of global imperial competition. Arguments ranged from a minimalist position that simply encouraged deeper political and economic cooperation between the two "kindred" powers, through intermediate proposals seeking a formal defensive alliance, to maximalist plans for uniting the two countries in a novel transatlantic political community.

Plans for a formal alliance blended concerns over shared security interests with assertions about underlying cultural affinities. The British imperial commentator Arthur Silva White declared that schemes for a comprehensive political union were "at present impossible," but that there "remains but one expedient—an alliance, or accord, which would pave the way to concerted action in the future."[33] Yet many commentators were skeptical about such an alliance, either because they opposed closer connections in the first place, or because they thought it would instrumentalize (and potentially distort) a more fundamental form of unity. Alfred Mahan argued that it was vital to "avoid all premature striving for alliance, an artificial and possibly even an irritating method of reaching the desired end." Instead, he continued, "I would dwell continually upon those undeniable points of resemblance in natural characteristics, and in surrounding conditions, which testify to common origin and predict a common destiny."[34] A British military writer concurred, warning against the "artificial and temporary arrangements miscalled 'alliances,' which provide occupation for European chancelleries."[35] The "organic" bonds of "kinship" were sufficient. Fearful that talk about the Anglo-Saxons was dangerously triumphalist, Benjamin Harrison, the former US president, insisted that friendship was quite enough. "Are not the continuous good and close relations of the two great English-speaking nations—for which I pray—rather imperilled than promoted by this foolish talk of gratitude and of an alliance, which is often made to take on the appearance of a threat, or at least a prophecy, of an Anglo-Saxon 'paramountcy'?"[36] This was a prescient warning.

While few leading politicians endorsed institutionally radical plans for (re)union, many sang the praise of racial unity and supremacy. Theodore Roosevelt, for example, was keen to consolidate relations between the two main branches of the most "civilized" race on earth.[37] "It must always be kept in mind," he wrote in *The Naval War of 1812*, "that the Americans and the British are two substantially similar branches of the great English race, which both before and after their separation have assimilated and made Englishmen of many other peoples."[38] His multivolume *Winning of the West*, published first in 1889, opened with a famous chapter on "the spread of the English-speaking peoples" that tracked the historical continuities between Britons and Americans, and heralded their epochal role. "During the past three centuries," he boasted, "the spread of the English-speaking peoples over the world's waste spaces has been not only the most striking feature in the world's history, but also the event of all others most far-reaching in its effects and its importance." Forming a single race, they now held "in their hands the fate of the coming years."[39] Throughout his presidency he sought closer relations with the British Empire. In Britain, Joseph Chamberlain and Arthur Balfour (and later Churchill) were closely associated with ideas for Anglo-American unity, though like Roosevelt they held back from advocating formal political integration. "The Anglo-Saxon stock," Chamberlain proclaimed in Toronto in 1887, "is infallibly destined to be the predominant force in the future history and civilisation of the world," and Americans and Britons were "all of the same race and blood."[40] Balfour too hymned the glory of racial unity without committing to political integration. "I am nothing if not an apostle of the English-speaking world."[41] Many unionists, then, saw bold institutional solutions as either unrealistic (even if desirable) or as impediments to authentic racial union. Charles Dilke, a prominent liberal politician, discerned scant support in the United States for a "startling" departure from its isolationist tradition, but he reiterated the argument that he had made originally in *Greater Britain*, that the countries formed the "two chief sections of our race." "Common action will . . . be increasingly probable," he concluded, "but of permanent alliance there is as yet no sign."[42]

At the core of the Anglo-American vision lay a novel set of arguments that ruptured the isomorphic relation between state, citizen, and political belonging. Advocates of racial unity frequently decoupled the state from both citizenship and patriotism. Citizenship was reimagined as a political institution grounded ultimately in racial identity, not state membership. Dicey offered the most sophisticated elaboration of the idea of common citizenship, arguing in 1897 for "the extension of common civil and political rights throughout the whole of the English-speaking people." Rejecting the idea of a transatlantic (or imperial) federation, he insisted that "reciprocal" citizenship would be enough to secure permanent unity. The idea was, he averred, simply a return to a prior condition, for such a connection had existed before the Anglo-Saxon peoples were ripped apart by the War of Independence.[43] Patriotism, meanwhile, was also reconfigured as a form of allegiance owed, in the first instance, to the race. Arguments about "race patriotism"—a term usually associated with Balfour—circulated widely.[44] They implied that people were enmeshed in a concentric circle of belonging and affect, the outer (and most important) ring of which was the race.

Andrew Carnegie, the Scottish-born industrialist, argued repeatedly for racial fusion and the "reunion" of Britain and America. Carnegie dismissed the idea of an Anglo-American alliance as failing to grasp the far more important issues at stake. "Alliances of fighting power form and dissolve with the questions which arise from time to time. The patriotism of race lies deeper and is not disturbed by waves upon the surface." "[M]y belief," he declared, is that "the future is certain to see a reunion of the separated parts and once again a common citizenship." This federated "British-American Union" would constitute a "reunited state." Yet this vision was irreconcilable with imperial federation: the British had first to grant independence to their settler colonies, which would then be welcome to join the union as equal members.[45] Although perturbed by the South African War, and by the exuberant imperialism of the American administration, he never lost faith in the transformative potential of the Anglo-Saxon race.

Skeptics were quick to point to the empirical inadequacies of unionist plans. One of their main complaints focused on the pertinence of arguments about racial unity. America, they complained, was simply not an "Anglo-Saxon" lineal descendent of Britain. "There is," one critic observed, "no fundamental reason rooted in human nature by virtue of a community of blood and religion why Americans as a nation should regard England with instinctive sympathy and friendship."[46] Another stressed the multiethnic composition of the American population. "What about the descendants of French men, of Germans, of Slavs, and of Scandinavians, who do not admit Anglo Saxon superiority?" And what about the Irish or African-Americans?[47]

But such demographic arguments failed to register with the proponents of unity, not least because their conception of race was malleable (though still bounded by whiteness). In general, then, what marked the United States as an Anglo-Saxon country was its dominant political culture—its White Anglo-Saxon Protestant (WASP) institutions, values, and ideals. Pointing to his own Portuguese origins, John Randolph Dos Passos, prominent Republican lawyer and father of a famous son, celebrated the American polity as a machine for turning (European) immigrants into Americans, and thus into adherents to an Anglo-Saxon creed. The "foreign element," he argued, "disappears, almost like magic, in the bosom of American nationality."[48] "I believe," he boomed, "that the twentieth century is par excellence 'The Anglo-Saxon Century,' in which the English-speaking peoples may lead and predominate the world."[49] Carnegie, meanwhile, suggested that immigration had barely altered the racial composition of America: "in race—and there is a great deal in race—the American remains three-fourths purely British. . . . The amount of blood other than Anglo-Saxon or Germanic which has entered into the American is almost too trifling to deserve notice, and has been absorbed without changing him in any fundamental trait."[50] His equanimity about immigration was not widely shared—most who advocated Anglo-Saxonism supported racist immigration restrictions.[51] Moreover, skepticism about racial commonality did not preclude support for political union. The eminent Anglo-American archaeologist Charles Waldstein argued that the notion of "Anglo-Saxon" racial identity was both misleading and dangerous: "it opens the door to that most baneful and pernicious of modern national diseases, namely, Ethnological Chauvinism." Yet he was adamant that Britain and the United States shared enough features in common to constitute "one nationality," and he toasted the future creation of "a great English-speaking Brotherhood."[52]

Cecil Rhodes was another proponent of Anglo-American unity. At the heart of his vision lay an account of the fractured nature of history: its progressive course had been diverted by the catastrophic estrangement of the United States and Great Britain. This could only be put right if the two great institutional expressions of the race were reunited permanently. As a self-proclaimed "race patriot," Rhodes was largely agnostic about whether Britain or the United States should lead the Anglo-Saxons in fulfilling their destiny, suggesting that a "federal parliament" could rotate between Washington and London.[53] Rhodes's main practical contribution to the dream of global racial dominance was the establishment of the Rhodes Trust, endowed following his death in 1902 with the intention of strengthening bonds between the elites of the Angloworld, as well (initially) as Germany, that other Teutonic power. The radical journalist W. T. Stead agreed with his friend Rhodes that the "English-speaking race is one of the chief of God's chosen agents for executing coming improvement in the lot of mankind," and he utilized his position as a prominent author and editor to preach the gospel of Anglo-unity, seeking to "constitute as one vast federated unity the English-speaking United States of the World."[54] Like many of his contemporaries, Stead sensed a gradual intra-racial shift in the balance of power. In *The Americanization of the World*, he argued that the Americans had overtaken the British in most aspects of social and economic life, observed that Britain itself was slowly Americanizing, and determined that those ruling in London now faced a stark choice: ally with the United States in a grand project of earthly redemption, or become increasingly irrelevant as the empire slowly weakened and the settler colonies sought independence and looked to Washington for leadership. This was a cause for celebration: "there is no reason to resent the part the Americans are playing in fashioning the world in their image, which, after all, is substantially the image of ourselves."[55] American success was an expression of British power, institutions, and values. This was a common trope in British accounts of Anglo-America, with Dilke, for example, boasting that "[t]hrough America, England is speaking to the world."[56]

While many of the proposals for unity were motivated by pragmatic security concerns, an equally large number made drastic claims about the world-transforming potential of racial unity. The utopianism of this racial vision resided in the belief that if the United States and Greater Britain were properly aligned, the "Anglo-Saxon" race would help to bring peace, order, and justice to the earth. Carnegie argued that the "new nation would dominate the world and banish from the earth its greatest stain—the murder of men by men." Lyman Abbott, a prominent American Congregationalist theologian, dreamt of an Anglo century—even millennium. "[T]hese two nations, embodying the energy, the enterprise, and the conscience of the Anglo-Saxon race, would by the mere fact of their co-operation produce a result in human history which would surpass all that present imagination can conceive or present hope anticipate."[57] Rhodes once wrote: "What an awful thought it is that if we had not lost America, or even if now we could arrange with the present members of the United States Assembly and our House of Commons, the peace of the world is secured for all eternity!" In 1891, he predicted that union with the United States would mean "universal peace" within one hundred years. Stead agreed, envisaging that "war would by degree die out from the face of the earth."[58] This, then, was the promise of an Anglo-racial utopia.

## Anglo-America and Global Governance

During the twentieth century, proposals for supra-national political unions were divided among (at least) five models. One of them emphasized regional federation, and centered above all on combining the states of continental Europe. It was this vision that ultimately had the most practical effect, though only after the cataclysm of a genocidal war. The other four—which I will label imperial-commonwealth, Anglo-American, democratic unionist, and world federalist—placed the transatlantic British-American connection at the core of global order. All were descended, in part or wholly, from the earlier Angloworld projects. Some offered only minor modifications to earlier imperial schemes, while others pushed out in new directions. Perhaps most importantly, though, the majority of the interwar and mid-century projects regarded the "Anglo" powers as a nucleus or vanguard. And even those schemes that expanded beyond the institutional limits of the Angloworld were almost invariably liberal democratic and capitalist in form, and as such they exemplified, even embodied, the values and institutions on which the Angloworld was based, and over which its advocates claimed paternity.

The imperial-commonwealth model focused on the continuing role of the British Empire. During the Edwardian years and beyond, the Round Table and other British imperial advocacy groups continued to campaign on behalf of Greater British unity. The imperial federalist project reached its zenith during the First World War with the creation of an Imperial War Cabinet in 1917, which incorporated the prime ministers of the Dominions. This was the nearest the dream of a politically unified Greater Britain came to fruition. Yet the war also accelerated calls for further independence in the colonies. While the efforts of the imperial federalists did not go completely unheralded in the United States,[59] they found, perhaps ironically, a more receptive audience in continental Europe, with a number of them—notably Philip Kerr (Lord Lothian)—playing an important role in shaping the ideological foundations of European union.[60]

During the 1920s the balance of power continued to shift within the British Empire, and as the colonies were granted further autonomy they frequently came into conflict with London.[61] In the interwar period it became increasingly popular to reimagine the empire as the "British Commonwealth"—the two terms were often used interchangeably—and to see it either as a self-contained system capable of balancing other great political orders, or as the embryonic form of a future universal political system. Britain and its settler colonies remained at the center of the model, although India and other elements of the empire were sometimes allotted subordinate roles. In the second half of the twentieth century, following decolonization, the imperial-commonwealth vision morphed into a postcolonial international organization. Today it lingers on, a pale shadow of the hopes and dreams once invested in it.[62]

The Anglo-American model centered on the Anglo-Saxon—or "English-speaking"—peoples, and in particular on a British-American axis. Relations between London and Washington continued to strengthen in the wake of the late Victorian "rapprochement," and the alliance was cemented during the First World War when the United States joined the Franco-British cause in Western Europe. It remained close for the rest of the twentieth century, though not quite as close as many of its cheerleaders, then as now, like to boast. The First World War had a catalytic effect on American foreign policy discourse, spawning the development of a powerful, though often fractious, East Coast policy elite oriented toward greater American involvement in world politics, in cooperation (even alliance) with Britain.[63] During the interwar era a variety of institutions and informal networks were created to foster closer links between the United States and Greater Britain. They constituted an emergent epistemic community dedicated to emphasizing the importance of Angloworld global leadership. The Council on Foreign Relations in New York and the International Institute of International Affairs (Chatham House) in London served as institutional hubs of Angloworld thinking, in both its Anglo-American and British imperial-commonwealth articulations.[64] Such institutions, and the visions they articulated, were a target for E. H. Carr's 1939 polemic, *The Twenty Years' Crisis*. "For the past hundred years, and more especially since 1918," Carr observed, "the English-speaking peoples have formed the dominant group in the world; and current theories of international morality have been designed to perpetuate their supremacy and expressed in the idiom peculiar to them."[65]

While the 1920s saw constructive cooperation between Britain and the United States, relations during the 1930s were strained; it was only with the outbreak of war, and especially between 1940 and 1942, that the two powers were forced into a tight embrace.[66] During the second half of 1940, American policy planners even drew up plans for political reunion with Britain, though the idea was soon dropped.[67] Public interest peaked with the signing of the Atlantic Charter in August 1941, dedicated to the promotion of "certain common principles in the national policies of their respective countries on which they base their hope for the common world," though tension continued between London and Washington over the future of the British Empire. As American power increased, and it became clear that Britain would be a junior partner in any future relationship, so once again the dream of an Anglo-American order faded. Perhaps its last gasp can be found in Churchill's "iron curtain" speech in March 1946, in which he popularized the term "special relationship" and insisted that peace was impossible without "the fraternal association of the English-speaking peoples."[68] Like the contemporary Commonwealth, the "special relationship" in the postwar years was a weak imitation of the ideal that had inspired many British, and even a few American, commentators over the previous decades.

Another model envisioned the creation of a league (or concert) of democracies. Before 1945 this essentially meant a transatlantic union of the United States, Great Britain, and assorted western European countries. As such, it moved beyond the "racial" limits of the Angloworld. In the 1950s this idea sometimes mutated into an Atlanticist vision centered on the NATO countries. The most influential interwar democratic unionist vision was propounded by Clarence Streit, a journalist with the *New York Times*. In *Union Now*, he proposed a federation, on the model of the constitution of 1787, of the fifteen democracies of the Atlantic world. The union would serve three main purposes:

> (a) to provide effective common government in our democratic world in those fields where such common government will clearly serve man's freedom better than separate governments, (b) to maintain independent national governments in all other fields where such government will best serve man's freedom, and (c) to create by its constitution a nucleus world government capable of growing into universal world government peacefully and as rapidly as such growth will best serve man's freedom.[69]

He followed this up with *Union Now with Britain*, in which he argued that the creation of an Anglo-American union would guarantee the defeat of the Axis.[70] Streit's later work highlights the way in which the Cold War constrained the imagination of democratic unionists. The West, figured as an "Atlantic community"—a term first used by Walter Lippmann[71]—took center stage. In 1961 Streit published *Freedom's Frontier*, suggesting that the fifteen countries of NATO already constituted the nucleus of an immanent Atlantic federal state: "Atlantica."[72] This fed into a popular Atlanticist current of thought. Expressing a common view, Livingston Hartley, a former State Department official, demanded "the political integration of the Atlantic community, the citadel and the powerhouse of freedom."[73] For many, European union and Atlantic union went hand in hand, the development of the former helping to strengthen the viability of the latter.[74] For others, though, the creation of a European union threatened the more desirable goal of Atlantic union (just as it was seen by imperial advocates to threaten the ghostly remnants of the "kith and kin" dream). For Streit, avatar of Atlanticism, America needed to take the lead in creating a new order, "preferably teamed closely with Canada," while European integration threatened transatlantic division.[75]

The major difference between "Anglo" and "Democratic unionist" models concerns the identity claim on which they are based. The Anglo model is confined to a finite set of British diasporic communities; its potential spatial extent is bounded by a specific historical trajectory. It was a settler colonial vision of governance. A league of democracies is in principle more expansive, designating a community that shares a minimal set of political values and institutions, all of them hypothetically exportable. Yet in practice, at the heart of this picture were (and are) the Anglo-states. Moreover, the values and institutions associated with such a community—the architecture of liberal-democratic capitalism—were either implicitly or explicitly ascribed by contemporaries to the Anglo-American intellectual tradition. Once again, social science offered authoritative epistemic support. The empirical analysis and the normative affirmation of the Angloworld were high on the agenda of early postwar behavioral political science. Perhaps most notably the influential idea of a "security community" was forged in the crucible of Atlanticist politics. Pioneering political scientist Karl Deutsch argued, for example, that the North Atlantic security community was anchored in the most highly integrated states, namely the United States, Canada, and the United Kingdom.[76]

The final model was a universal world polity. Ideas about world government have percolated through the history of political thought, ebbing and flowing in popularity.[77] The 1940s witnessed an efflorescence of utopian political thinking, catalyzed by the old Kantian premonition that the route to perpetual peace would most likely wind its way through the valley of death; that a brutal war might, once and for all, force people to recognize the necessity of federation. Advocates of a global polity typically conceived of it as a long-term ideal rather than something within immediate grasp.[78] Nevertheless, many of them called for a federal institutional structure with an Anglo nucleus, while numerous advocates of democratic or Anglo-racial union saw their own more limited goals as temporary steps on the road to—and often agents in the creation of—a universal polity.

Perhaps the most famous advocate of the world state was H. G. Wells. In *Anticipations*, a bestseller published in 1902, he prophesized the emergence of a world state ruled over by a new techno-managerial class of "efficients"—the "kinetic men" of the future. The unification of the "English-speaking" peoples assumed a central role: they were to serve as pioneers of the world-state-to-come. By the year 2000 the English-speaking people would constitute a federal state, united by "practically homogenous citizenship," with its headquarters in the United States. They would govern all the "non-white states of the present British empire, and in addition much of the South and Middle Pacific, the East and West Indies, the rest of America, and the larger part of black Africa."[79] After the First World War, he continued to argue that a future world polity would result from the coagulation of regional and racial groupings.[80] Like most of his contemporaries, his account of a cosmopolitan world state never escaped the ethnocentric assumptions that had marked his earlier writings. Evolving through various iterations, his vision of a future global order was rooted in the purported superiority of the Western powers, and in particular the Anglo-Americans. He longed for the (re)union of the English-speaking peoples. In 1935, for example, he argued that "the commonsense of the world demands that the English-speaking community should get together upon the issue of World Peace, and that means a common foreign policy." It also meant economic unification, for "the world revival" would not materialize "unless we homologize the financial control and monetary organization of our world-wide group of people."[81] Wells exemplified the technocratic aspect of the world federalist project, even flirting with fascist methods during the 1920s and 1930s in order to help bring about a new global order.

World federalist thinking flourished in Britain and the United States in the 1940s and early 1950s, drawing in a wide array of intellectuals and politicians, from Albert Einstein and Aldous Huxley to Henry L. Stimson and John Foster Dulles. Campaigning organizations—notably the United World Federalists (1947)—were formed, politicians lobbied, newsletters and pamphlets circulated. Wendell Willkie's *One World* sold over two million copies.[82] Henry Usborne, a British Labour MP, created a Parliamentary Group for World Government and signed up over 200 MPs.[83] Under the leadership of its president, Robert M. Hutchins, the University of Chicago created a Committee to Frame a World Constitution.[84] House Concurrent Resolution 64, in 1949, proposed as a "fundamental objective of the foreign policy of the United States to support and strengthen the United Nations and to seek its development into a world federation." It secured 111 votes, including those of John F. Kennedy, Gerald Ford, Mike Mansfield, Henry Cabot Lodge, and Henry Jackson. The movement peaked in early 1950, with 150,000 members worldwide.[85]

In the shadow of the bomb, political realists had their own "one world" moment. John Herz and Hans Morgenthau, among others, argued that human survival demanded the creation of a world state, though both were skeptical of its plausibility.[86] The world federalist movement was stifled by the onset of the Cold War.[87] The dream of world federation struggled on, finding a variety of intellectual outlets, including the World Orders Model Project most closely associated with Richard Falk.[88] But it was an early victim of bipolar ideological confrontation. Though once a topic of mainstream concern for scholars, public intellectuals, journalists, and politicians, Thomas Weiss argues that today ideas about a global federal state are "commonly thought to be the preserve of lunatics."[89] Yet there are signs of a revival of interest in the idea, at least among scholars.[90] In IR, for example, Alexander Wendt and Daniel Deudney have offered theoretically sophisticated accounts of the plausibility, even inevitability, of a world state.[91]

The proponents of democratic leagues and world federation often drew inspiration from—and shared personnel with—the imperial federal movement. Lionel Curtis is a prominent example. An enthusiastic advocate of imperial and then world federalism over the course of five decades, his political thought was riddled with the tensions between universalism, Atlanticism, and imperialism.[92] Curtis's magnum opus, the sprawling politico-theological treatise *Civitas Dei*, posited that a federated British Empire could serve as a kernel and a model for a future universal commonwealth of nations, because of all extant political communities it offered the most appropriate space for human personality to find its fullest expression.[93] The most difficult stage in creating a world federal state was the first one; the "most experienced commonwealths" needed to show leadership. He identified the core of the global order in the union of Great Britain, New Zealand, and Australia.[94] The Second World War only reinforced his belief in the necessity of political transformation. In the early 1950s Curtis angrily denounced intellectuals for upholding the myth of sovereign statehood; they were, he charged, "responsible for the bloodshed of this century" and "answerable for the suffering, poverty, and death that millions are now facing."[95] Federation, with an Anglo core, was the only way to escape the killing machine. An arch Anglo-supremacist, Curtis was frequently hailed as one of the pioneers of the world federalist movement.[96]

A notable aspect of the debates over global order, in both the nineteenth and the twentieth centuries, was that the United States often served as a template for the future. Both American political experience and political philosophy were routinely cited as inspirational, even formative. Streit modeled his plan for an Atlantic union of democracies on the US Constitution. Indeed, he went so far as to call for a Federal Convention, similar to its namesake in Philadelphia in 1787, to deliberate over the desirability and potential form of a Transatlantic Union. This proposal gained the support of the Canadian Senate and dozens of US senators.[97] Twentieth-century British imperial federalists, meanwhile, regularly invoked the genius of the American founders, often interpreted through the prism of F. S. Oliver's *Alexander Hamilton*. Curtis, for example, was explicit about his debt to the Federalist Papers; they taught him, he recorded, about both the problem of political order and the best (federal) solution to it, fundamentally influencing his views over half a century of federalist agitation.[98] America was both model and motive. Indeed, many world federalist plans can be read as demanding the Americanization of the planet.

## The Return of the Anglosphere

While today there are few advocates of a global federal state outside of universities and think tanks, the vision of a "concert" or "league" of democracies has resurfaced in public life. "Democracy" has supplanted "civilization" as the defining feature in discourses of global governance. Democratic unionist arguments have been given a powerful boost by the popularity of theories of the "democratic peace," once again highlighting the complex entanglement of twentieth-century social science with projects for global order. This line of reasoning is directly descended from the mid-twentieth-century discourse. Michael Doyle, for example, identities Streit as the first modern commentator to point to "the empirical tendency of democracies to maintain peace among themselves."[99] Uniting liberal internationalists with neo-conservatives, the idea of a league of democracies has wide ideological appeal among members of the American political elite, even if it has resonated far less in Europe. Advisors to both Barack Obama and John McCain promoted the idea during the 2008 election campaign, and McCain endorsed it.[100] It has found its most systematic articulation in the Princeton Project on National Security, which proposes the creation of a global "Concert of Democracies" to institutionalize and ratify the "democratic peace."[101] In the Trump era, its future is uncertain.

Following the collapse of the Berlin Wall, elites throughout the West scrambled to develop workable visions of the coming post–Cold War era. Few in number at first, proponents of the Anglosphere argued that the settler colonies of the British Empire should reconvene to help steer the new world order. Proselytized by think tanks, public intellectuals, and politicians from the late 1990s onward, the idea was given impetus by Thatcher's endorsement. The calamity of 9/11 and the wars in Iraq and Afghanistan aroused further interest in the Anglosphere. George W. Bush, Tony Blair, and the conservative prime ministers of Australia and Canada, Stephen Harper and John Howard, all affirmed—with varying degrees of conviction—its importance as a source of global stability and leadership.

Advocacy of Anglo superiority has assumed different forms. One popular version, outlined in a bestselling book and a popular television series, is Niall Ferguson's paean to British imperial power, and the necessity of the American empire assuming the responsibility—the old "White Man's burden"—of hegemonic stabilizer and civilizing agent.[102] Other widely discussed proposals have emanated from the American businessman James Bennett and the British historian Andrew Roberts. Echoing earlier discussions about the world-historical function of the telegraph, Bennett contends that the internet can serve as a medium through which the geographically scattered but culturally and politically aligned members of the "Anglosphere" can come into closer communion, and act together for the planetary greater good.[103] He sees this as both desirable and necessary, given the likely development of other competing network "spheres"—Sino, Luso, Hispano, and Franco. He concludes that the inherited political and economic traditions of the Anglosphere mean that it is uniquely equipped to thrive in the coming century. Roberts, meanwhile, seeks to pick up where Churchill finished his own bombastic history of the English-speaking peoples.[104] Rather than advocating formal union, he outlines a vision, grounded in a hubristic reading of twentieth-century history, in which the English-speaking peoples are united by "common purposes" and in defeating waves of totalitarianism, today exemplified by Islamic fanaticism. Superior political institutions mean that when they act in unison, the whole world benefits. Roberts's vision of the English-speaking peoples is limited to the United States, the United Kingdom "and her dependencies," New Zealand, Canada, and Australia, as well as the British West Indies and Ireland—though of the latter two, the first is largely ignored while the second is routinely assailed for failing to live up to the standards set by others. Reproducing earlier arguments about race patriotism, Roberts decenters the state: the ontological foundation of his argument is a singular people, while the political units of this singularity play a secondary function. "Just as we do not today differentiate between the Roman Republic and the imperial period of the Julio-Claudians when we think of the Roman Empire, so in the future no one will bother to make a distinction between the British Empire-led and the American Republic-led periods of English-speaking dominance."[105]

Most such arguments assert the powers of shared culture, traditions, and interests, saying little about new overarching political institutions. They envisage a "virtual confederation." But the vision of an institutionalized Anglo-union has not disappeared completely. As we have seen, Conquest and Thatcher called for one. Like Roberts, Conquest was driven in part by a sense of anger at the duplicity of British politicians signing up to European integration, and thus betraying their true kin in the dominions and across the Atlantic. Since the first decade of the twenty-first century, following the lead of Thatcher, a stream of Tory Euroskeptics hailed the Anglosphere as the natural home of Britain, and a preferable alternative to the European Union. This discourse played a central role in the elite campaign for Brexit.[106] Indeed some leading Brextiers now support a warmed-over version of imperial federation, CANZUK (Canada, Australia, New Zealand, and the United Kingdom).[107] James Bennett wrote the first programmatic proposal, *A Time For Audacity*. He conceives of the CANZUK Union—which he also calls the "Commonwealth Union" and the "Commonwealth Federation"—as a "political federation having the character of a state, consisting of Canada, Australia, New Zealand, and the United Kingdom, and possibly other Commonwealth Realms."[108] The idea has been developed by Roberts has taken up the cause, declaring that the "heroic" Brexit vote cleared the ground for a "new federation based upon free trade, free movement of peoples, mutual defence, and a limited but effective confederal political structure." Channeling Churchill, he decreed that CANZUK would constitute the "third pillar" of Western civilization, standing proudly alongside continental Europe and the United States. "It would be easily the largest country on the planet, have a combined population of 129 million, the third biggest economy and the third biggest defence budget."[109] CANZUK, then, would be far more than a loose group of friendly nations bound by shared values and norms; it would instead constitute a vast political community.

The last 150 years, then, have seen the elaboration of numerous projects to unify or coordinate the scattered polities of the Angloworld. Each phase has also been predicated on hyperbolic claims about the power of new communications technologies to transform the nature and scope of political association. Highly ambitious institutional visions of formal political union have been accompanied by more modest proposals for strengthening existing connections and fostering close cooperation. All of these varied projects, however ambitious, have been based on claims about translocal identity and belonging. They have insisted that the members of the Angloworld share much in common—a language, a history, a set of values, political and economic institutions, and a destiny. Initially projects for a new Anglo century based on British imperial federation, the focus switched to the Anglo-American relationship. Proposals for a league of democracy, Atlantic union, even world federalism were heirs of this Anglo discourse, not discrete and incompatible models of global order. They emerged from the earlier imperial-racial debates, and many of the proposals for transcending the existing system were similar in form and ambition to the projects for Angloworld imperium. To chart the "growth of nations," Tocqueville once wrote, it is imperative to remember that they carry with them "some of the marks of their origin."[110] The same is true of projects of global governance.

## Notes

This essay is an updated and modified version of an earlier piece, "The Project for a New Anglo Century: Race, Space and Global Order," published in Peter Katzenstein, ed., *Anglo-America and Its Discontents: Civilizational Politics beyond East and West* (London: Routledge, 2012), 33–56.

1. Thatcher, "The Language of Liberty," December 7, 1999, http://www.margaretthatcher.org/document/108386.
2. Conquest, *Reflections on a Ravaged Century* (New York: Norton, 2000), 225. A few years later he argued that an "Anglosphere Association" would become "a centre of hope in the world . . . round which peace, cooperation and democracy can develop." Conquest, *The Dragons of Expectation: Reality and Delusion in the Course of History* (New York: Norton, 2004), 221–235.
3. Churchill, *A History of the English-Speaking Peoples*, I–IV (London: Cassell, 1956–1958).
4. For the term "Angloworld," see James Belich, *Replenishing the Earth: The Settler Revolution and the Rise of the Angloworld* (New York: Oxford University Press, 2009).
5. Deudney, *Bounding Power: Republican Security Theory from the Polis to the Global Village* (Princeton, NJ: Princeton University Press, 2007), 215, 219. See also Barry Buzan and George Lawson, *The Global Transformation: The Nineteenth Century and the Making of Modern International Relations* (Cambridge: Cambridge University Press, 2015).
6. On "pan" schemes, see Musab Younis, "'United by Blood': Race and Transnationalism during the Belle Époque," *Nations and Nationalism* 23, no. 3 (2017): 484–504; Cemil Aydin, *The Politics of Anti-Westernism in Asia: Visions of World Order in Pan-Islamic and Pan-Asian Thought* (New York: Columbia University Press, 2007); Sebastian Conrad and Dominic Sachsenmaier, eds., *Competing Visions of World Order: Global Moments and Movements, 1880s–1930s* (Basingstoke, UK: Palgrave, 2007).
7. Du Bois, "To the Nations of the World" (1900) in *Writings by W. E. B. Du Bois in Periodicals Edited by Others*, ed. Herbert Aptheker (New York: Kraus-Thomson, 1982), I:10–11.
8. Marilyn Lake and Henry Reynolds, *Drawing the Global Colour Line: White Men's Countries and the International Challenge of Racial Equality* (Cambridge: Cambridge University Press, 2008), 4.
9. The phrase is from Du Bois, "The Souls of White Folk," in Herbert Aptheker, ed., *Writings by W. E. B Du Bois in Periodicals Edited by Others* (New York: Kraus-Thomson, 1982), II:26.
10. See here Duncan Bell, *Dreamworlds of Race: Empire and the Utopian Destiny of Anglo-America* (Princeton, NJ: Princeton University Press, 2020), ch. 1.
11. Jessica Blatt, *Race and the Making of American Political Science* (Philadelphia: University of Pennsylvania Press, 2018); Robert Vitalis, *White World Order, Black Power Politics: The Birth of American International Relations* (Ithaca, NY: Cornell University Press, 2015); Erroll Henderson, "The Revolution Will Not Be Theorised: Du Bois, Locke, and the Howard School's Challenge to White Supremacist IR Theory," *Millennium* 45, no. 3 (2017): 492–510.
12. I expand on the argument in this section in Duncan Bell, *The Idea of Greater Britain: Empire and the Future of World Order, 1860–1900* (Princeton, NJ: Princeton University Press, 2007).
13. The idea of importing reform from the colonial periphery was prevalent in wider social reform debates: Daniel Rodgers, *Atlantic Crossings: Social Politics in a Progressive Age* (Cambridge, MA: Harvard University Press, 2000).

14. Barker, *Political Thought in England, 1848–1914* (London: Williams & Norgate, 1915), 181. See also Henry Sidgwick, *The Development of European Polity*, ed. Eleanor Sidgwick (London: Macmillan, 1903), 439.
15. Hobson, *Imperialism: A Study* [1902] ed. Philip Siegelman (Ann Arbor: University of Michigan Press, 1997), 332.
16. Hobhouse, *Liberalism*, ed. J. Meadowcroft (Cambridge: Cambridge University Press, 1994), 116. Note that Hobson later abandoned his support for imperial federation.
17. Marc-William Palen, "Protection, Federation and Union: The Global Impact of the McKinley Tariff upon the British Empire, 1890–94," *Journal of Imperial and Commonwealth History* 38 (2010): 395–418; P. J. Cain and A. G. Hopkins, *British Imperialism, 1688–2000* (London: Routledge, 2002), ch. 7.
18. Chamberlain, *The Life of Joseph Chamberlain* [1902] ed. J. L. Garvin and J. Amery (London: Macmillan, 1968), 177.
19. E.g., Marquis of Lorne, *Imperial Federation* (London: Swan Sonnenschein, 1885).
20. E.g., Francis de Labillière, *Federal Britain, or, Unity and Federation of the Empire* (London: S. Low, 1894).
21. Dilke, *Greater Britain, A Record of Travel in English-Speaking Countries during 1866 and 1867* (London: Macmillan, 1898), II:157.
22. Wells, *Anticipations of the Reaction of Mechanical and Scientific Progress upon Human Life and Thought* [1902] (Mineola, NY: Dover, 1999), 38, 44; Seeley, *The Expansion of England* (London: Macmillan 1883), 62.
23. Seeley, *The Expansion of England*, 158–159.
24. For further details, see Duncan Bell, *Reordering the World: Essays on Liberalism and Empire* (Princeton, NJ: Princeton University Press, 2016), ch. 7.
25. Seeley, *The Expansion of England*, p. 49.
26. Monypenny, "The Imperial Ideal," in Charles Goldman, ed., *The Empire and the Century: A Series of Essays on Imperial Problems and Possibilities* (London: John Murray, 1905), 23, 27.
27. Curtis, *The Problem of Commonwealth* (London: Macmillan, 1916), 68; cf. Jeanne Morefield, *Covenants without Swords: Idealist Liberalism and the Spirit of Empire* (Princeton, NJ: Princeton University Press, 2004).
28. Daniel Gorman, *Imperial Citizenship: Empire and the Question of Belonging* (Manchester: Manchester University Press, 2006).
29. Appadurai, "Sovereignty without Territoriality," in Patricia Yaeger, ed., *The Geography of Identity* (Ann Arbor: University of Michigan Press, 1996).
30. Ibid., 54.
31. For recent accounts, see Srdjan Vucetic, *The Anglosphere: The Genealogy of a Racialized Identity in International Relations* (Palo Alto, CA: Stanford University Press, 2011); Charles Kupchan, *How Enemies Become Friends: The Sources of Stable Peace* (Princeton, NJ: Princeton University Press, 2012), ch. 3.
32. "The Anglo-American Union," *Review of Reviews* 13 (1896): 364–365. For a useful case study, see Stephen Bowman, *The Pilgrims Society and Public Diplomacy, 1895–1945* (Edinburgh: Edinburgh University Press, 2018).

33. White, "An Anglo-American Alliance," *North American Review* 158 (1894): 492–493; see also Walter Besant, "The Future of the Anglo-Saxon Race," *North American Review* 163 (1896): 129–143.
34. Mahan and Charles Beresford, "Possibilities of an Anglo-American Reunion," *North American Review* 159 (1894): 554.
35. G. S. Clarke, "Imperial Responsibilities a National Gain," *North American Review* 168 (1899): 141.
36. Harrison, "Musings upon Current Topics II," *North American Review* 172 (1901): 354. On the history of the concept of the "English-speaking peoples," usage of which originated in the 1870s and peaked during the early decades of the twentieth century, see Peter Clarke, "The English-Speaking Peoples before Churchill," *British Scholar* 4 (2011): 199–231.
37. On Roosevelt's increasingly positive attitude toward Britain, see William Tilchin, *Theodore Roosevelt and the British Empire: A Study in Presidential Statecraft* (London: St. Martin's, 1997).
38. Roosevelt, *The Naval War of 1812* (New York: G. P. Putnam, 1900 [1882]), I:59. On Roosevelt's racialized vision of political order, see Thomas Dyer, *Theodore Roosevelt and the Idea of Race* (Baton Rouge: LSU Press, 1980).
39. Roosevelt, *The Winning of the West* (New York: Collins, 1889), I:17, 21.
40. Chamberlain, "The Mild Sovereignty of the Queen" [1887] in Chamberlain, *Foreign and Colonial Speeches* (London: Routledge, 1897), 6.
41. Blanche Dugdale, *Arthur James Balfour* (London: Hutchinson, 1936), II:401.
42. Dilke, "An Anglo-American Alliance," *Pall Mall Magazine* 16, no. 65 (1898): 37, 38.
43. Dicey, "A Common Citizenship for the English Race," *Contemporary Review* 71 (1897): 458.
44. On Balfour's "race patriotism," see Jason Tomes, *Balfour and Foreign Policy: The International Thought of a Conservative Statesman* (Cambridge: Cambridge University Press, 1997), chs. 2–4; Duncan Bell, "Beyond the Sovereign State: Isopolitan Citizenship, Race, and Anglo-American Union," *Political Studies* 62, no. 2 (2014): 418–434.
45. Carnegie, "Americanism versus Imperialism," *North American Review* 162 (1899): 5–6; Carnegie, *A Look Ahead* (Edinburgh: Darien Press, 1893), 9; Carnegie, "The Venezuelan Question," *North American Review* 162 (1896): 132.
46. Mayo Hazeltine, "The United States and Great Britain," *North American Review* 162 (1896): 597.
47. John Fleming, "Are We Anglo-Saxons?" *North American Review* 153 (1891): 254.
48. John Randolph Dos Passos, *The Anglo-Saxon Century and the Unification of the English-Speaking People*, 2nd ed. (New York: G. P. Putnam, 1903), 101, 104.
49. Dos Passos, *The Anglo-Saxon Century*, vii.
50. Carnegie, *A Look Ahead*, 9.
51. For details, see Lake and Reynolds, *Drawing the Global Colour Line*.
52. Charles Waldstein, "The English-Speaking Brotherhood," *North American Review* 167 (1898): 225, 230, 238.

53. Rhodes, *The Last Will and Testament of Cecil J. Rhodes*, ed. W. T. Stead (London: Review of Reviews, 1902), 73.
54. Stead, *The Americanization of the World* (New York: Review of Reviews, 1901), 100, 397.
55. Ibid., 2.
56. Dilke, *Greater Britain*, 318.
57. Carnegie, *A Look Ahead*, 12–13; Abbott, "The Basis of an Anglo-American Understanding," *North American Review* 166 (1898): 521.
58. Tourgée, "The Twentieth Century Peacemakers," *Contemporary Review* 75 (1899): 886–908; Rhodes, *Last Will and Testament*, 73, 66; Stead, *The Americanization of the World*, 435. For more on the utopian argument, see Duncan Bell, "Before the Democratic Peace," *European Journal of International Relations* 20, no. 3 (2014): 647–670.
59. E.g. William Roy Smith, "British Imperial Federation," *Political Science Quarterly* 36 (1921): 274–297; George Burton-Adams, *The British Empire and a League of Peace: Suggesting the Purpose and Form of an Alliance of the English-Speaking Peoples* (New York: G. P. Putnam, 1919).
60. John Kendle, *Federal Britain: A History* (London: Routledge, 1997), ch. 6; Andrea Bosco, "Lothian, Curtis, Kimber and the Federal Union Movement (1938–1940)," *Journal of Contemporary History* 23 (1988): 465–502; Michael Burgess, *The British Tradition of Federalism* (London: Leicester University Press 1995), Pt. III; John Turner, ed., *The Larger Idea: Lord Lothian and the Problem of National Sovereignty* (London: Historians' Press, 1988).
61. Margaret MacMillan, "Isosceles Triangle: Britain, the Dominions, and the United States at the Paris Peace Conference of 1919," in Jonathan Hollowell, ed., *Twentieth-Century Anglo-American Relations* (Basingstoke, UK: Palgrave, 2001), 1–25.
62. Timothy Shaw, *Commonwealth: Inter- and Non-state Contributions to Global Governance* (London: Routledge, 2008); Philip Murphy, *The Empire's New Clothes: The Myth of the Commonwealth* (London: Routledge, 2018).
63. Priscilla Roberts, "The Anglo-American Theme: American Visions of an Atlantic Alliance, 1914–1933," *Diplomatic History* 21, no. 3 (1997): 333–364.
64. Nicholas Cull, "Selling Peace: The Origins, Promotion and Fate of the Anglo-American New Order during the Second World War," *Diplomacy and Statecraft* 7 (1996): 1–28; Priscilla Roberts, "The Transatlantic American Foreign Policy Elite: Its Evolution in Generational Perspective," *Journal of Transatlantic Studies* 7 (2009): 163–183; Inderjeet Parmar, "Anglo-American Elites in the Interwar Years: Idealism and Power in the Intellectual Roots of Chatham House and the Council on Foreign Relations," *International Relations* 16 (2002): 53–75; Paul Williams, "A Commonwealth of Knowledge: Empire, Intellectuals and the Chatham House Project, 1919–1939," *International Relations* 17 (2003): 35–58.
65. Carr, *The Twenty Years' Crisis, 1919–1939: An Introduction to the Study of International Relations* (Basingstoke, UK: Palgrave, [1939] 2001), 74.
66. David Reynolds, *The Creation of the Anglo-American Alliance, 1937–41: A Study in Competitive Co-operation* (London: Europa, 1981); Reynolds, "Roosevelt, Churchill, and the Wartime Anglo-American Alliance, 1939–45," in William Roger Louis and Hedley Bull, eds., *The "Special Relationship": Anglo-American Relations since 1945* (Oxford: Clarendon, 1986).

67. Stephen Wertheim, *Tomorrow, the World: The Birth of U.S. Global Supremacy* (Cambridge, MA: Harvard University Press).
68. Robert Rhodes James, ed., *Winston S. Churchill: His Complete Speeches, 1897–1963* (New York: Chelsea House, 1974), 289. Churchill advocated a common citizenship between Britain and the US. See Henry Butterfield Ryan, *The Vision of Anglo-America: The US-UK Alliance and the Emerging Cold War, 1943–1946* (Cambridge: Cambridge University Press, 1987), ch. 3; Richard Toye, *Churchill's Empire: The World That Made Him and the World He Made* (London: Macmillan, 2010), 240.
69. Streit, *Union Now: A Proposal for a Federal Union of the Democracies of the North Atlantic* (New York: Harper, 1938), 2.
70. Streit, *Union Now with Britain* (London: Jonathan Cape, 1941).
71. Lippmann, *US Foreign Policy* (Boston: Hamilton, 1943), 83.
72. Streit, *Freedom's Frontier: Atlantic Union Now* (New York: Harper, 1961).
73. Hartley, *Atlantic Challenge* (New York: Dobbs, 1965), 92.
74. Robert Strauz-Hupe, James Dougherty, and William Kintner, *Building the Atlantic World* (New York: Harper & Row, 1963).
75. Streit, "Atlantic Union," *Annals of the American Academy of Political and Social Science* 288 (1953): 8. While Streit routinely talked of uniting "all democracies," he also stressed "Atlantic Union," thus leaving unclear the role of the non-Atlantic parts of Greater Britain.
76. Karl Deutsch et al., *Political Community and the North Atlantic Area* (Princeton, NJ: Princeton University Press, 1957); see also Bruce Russett, *Community and Contention: Britain and America in the Twentieth Century* (Cambridge, MA: MIT Press, 1963).
77. Derek Heater, *World Citizenship and Government: Cosmopolitan Ideas in the History of Western Political Thought* (Basingstoke, UK: Palgrave, 1996); Jens Bartelson, *Visions of World Community* (Cambridge: Cambridge University Press, 2009).
78. Jo-Ann Pemberton, *Global Metaphors: Modernity and the Quest for One World* (London: Pluto, 2001); Wesley Wooley, *Alternatives to Anarchy: American Supranationalism since World War II* (Bloomington: Indiana University Press, 1988).
79. Wells, *Anticipations*, 146.
80. Wells, *The Outline of History* (London: Waverley, 1920).
81. Wells, *The New America, the New World* (London: Macmillan, 1935), 24.
82. Dulles, *War, Peace, and Change* (New York: Harper, 1939); Willkie, *One World* (New York: Cassell, 1943). See here Samuel Zipp, *The Idealist: Wendell Wilkie's Wartime Quest to Build One World* (Cambridge, MA: Belknap, 2020).
83. Joseph Preston Baratta, *The Politics of World Federation*, 2 vols. (Westport, CT: Praeger, 2004), 162–164.
84. Hutchins et al., *Preliminary Draft of a World Constitution* (Chicago: University of Chicago Press, 1948); cf. G. A. Borgese, *Foundations of a World Republic* (Chicago: University of Chicago Press, 1953). See here Or Rosenboim, *The Emergence of Globalism: Visions of World Order in Britain and the United States, 1939–1950* (Princeton, NJ: Princeton University Press, 2017), ch. 6.
85. Thomas Weiss, "What Happened to the Idea of World Government?" *International Studies Quarterly* 53 (2009): 258; John Preston Baratta, "The International Federalist Movement," *Peace & Change* 24 (1999): 342

86. Craig Campbell, *Glimmer of a New Leviathan: Total War in the Realism of Niebuhr, Morgenthau and Waltz* (New York: Columbia University Press, 2003); Deudney, *Bounding Power*, ch. 8. Rens van Munster and Casper Sylvest, *Nuclear Realism: Global Political Thought during the Thermonuclear Revolution* (Abingdon, UK: Routledge, 2016).
87. Baratta, *The Politics of World Federation*.
88. Falk, *A Study of Future Worlds* (New York: Free Press, 1975). Falk drew on Louis Sohn and Grenville Clark, *World Peace through World Law* (Cambridge, MA: Harvard University Press, 1958).
89. Weiss, "World Government?," 258.
90. Luis Cabrera, "World Government," *European Journal of International Relations* 16 (2010): 511–530.
91. Wendt, "Why a World State Is Inevitable," *European Journal of International Relations* 9 (2003): 491–542; Deudney, *Bounding Power*.
92. On his life and religious views, see Gerald Studdert-Kennedy, "Christianity, Statecraft and Chatham House: Lionel Curtis and World Order," *Diplomacy & Statecraft* 6 (1995): 470–489; Deborah Lavin, *From Empire to International Commonwealth: A Biography of Lionel Curtis* (Oxford: Oxford University Press, 1995). See also Rosenboim, *Globalism*, 107–114.
93. Curtis, *Civitas Dei*, 3 vols. (London: Macmillan, 1937).
94. Curtis, "World Order," *International Affairs* 18 (1939): 309; cf. Curtis, *Civitas Dei*, III. Curtis also expressed admiration for Streit's alternative Atlanticist plan: Curtis, "World Order," 310; Curtis, "The Fifties as Seen Fifty Years Hence," *International Affairs* 27 (1951): 273–284.
95. Curtis, "The Fifties," 284.
96. E.g., Streit, "Lionel Curtis," *Freedom & Union* 10 (1956): 10.
97. Streit, "Atlantic Union"; Curtis, "The Fifties," 275–276.
98. Oliver, *Alexander Hamilton* (London, 1906); Curtis, "World Order," 302–307. Deudney's fascinating discussion of republican security in *Bounding Power* is also modeled on American experience.
99. Doyle, "Liberalism and World Politics," *American Political Science Review* 80 (1986): 1162 n2; cf. Ikenberry, *After Victory: Institutions, Strategic Restraint, and the Rebuilding of Order after Major Wars* (Princeton, NJ: Princeton University Press, 2001), 178–179. See also Bell, "Before the Democratic Peace."
100. McCain, "An Enduring Peace Built on Freedom," *Foreign Affairs* 86 (November/December 2007): 19–34.
101. John Ikenberry and Anne-Marie Slaughter, *Forging a World of Liberty under Law*, Princeton Project on National Security, 2006, last accessed July 22, 2011, http://www.princeton.edu/~ppns/report/FinalReport.pdf, 7.
102. Ferguson, *Empire: How Britain Made the Modern World* (London: Penguin, 2004).
103. Bennett, *The Anglosphere Challenge: Why the English-Speaking Nations Will Lead the Way in the Twenty First Century* (Lanham, MD: Rowman & Littlefield, 2004). For the wider context, see Andrew Mycock and Ben Wellings, eds., *The*

*Anglosphere: Continuity, Dissonance and Location* (Oxford: Oxford University Press, 2019).

104. Roberts, *A History of the English Speaking Peoples since 1900* (London: Weidenfeld & Nicholson, 2010).
105. Ibid., 381.
106. Michael Kenny and Nick Pearce, *Shadows of Empire: The Anglosphere in British Politics* (Cambridge: Polity, 2018), ch. 6.
107. Duncan Bell and Srdjan Vucetic, "Brexit, CANZUK, and the Legacy of Empire," *British Journal of Politics and International Studies* 21, no. 2 (2019): 367–382. The basic idea (and acronym) can be traced to the 1960s.
108. Bennett, *A Time for Audacity: New Options beyond Europe* (Washington, DC: Pole to Pole, 2016).
109. Roberts, "CANZUK: After Brexit, Canada, Australia, New Zealand and Britain Can Unite as a Pillar of Western Civilisation," *Daily Telegraph*, September 13, 2016.
110. Tocqueville, *Democracy in America*, 13.

# 2

# The Rise and Fall of a Global Narrative

## The Soviet Challenge to the Western World

*Michael Cox*

### Introduction

> *"We live in a permanent "battle of narratives" about the issues that determine our future.*[1]

In one of his lesser remembered works, published in 1946, the English historian E. H. Carr reminded his readers that the Soviet Union, which had emerged more powerful than ever from World War II, should be thought of less as a military threat to Western Europe, and more as a political and economic challenge to which the West should now respond in an imaginative and intelligent fashion.[2] As Carr went on to point out, the Soviet Union had already had a massive impact on the West since the revolution of 1917, and no doubt would continue to do so in the years ahead. He also added that there was little chance of this particular challenge disappearing from the stage of history any time soon. Western policymakers would be well advised therefore not to base their policies on what he saw as the illusion that communism was so flawed as a system that it was doomed to fail. It had survived Western intervention between 1918 and 1920. It had implemented three Five Year Plans in the 1930s. It had then gone on to defeat Nazi Germany between 1941 and 1945. And by the end of World War II it controlled half of Europe, had important relations with increasingly powerful communist parties around the world, and would soon have another ally in the shape of communist China. Its survival was thus guaranteed.

Nor was this Carr's view alone. In fact, the Cold War which followed presupposed that whatever else happened, the system against which the West and the United States were now pitted would endure—as it most obviously

Michael Cox, *The Rise and Fall of a Global Narrative* In: *Debating Worlds*. Edited by Daniel Deudney, G. John Ikenberry, and Karoline Postel-Vinay, Oxford University Press. 
DOI: 10.1093/oso/9780197679302.003.0003

did for the next forty years or so, defining the contours of American foreign policy, reshaping its economy, impacting its politics, legitimizing its many alliances, and leading it into making several rather disastrous interventions into what after 1952 came to be known the "Third World."[3]

Yet against all expectations, including one must suppose that of Carr (who died in 1982), something called Soviet communism did come to an end, leaving most scholars confused, policymakers searching for new strategies, and the West celebrating a victory it had never really planned for. But something else ended, too: namely, the idea that there was, or could any longer be, a viable alternative to what was on offer in the West. In fact, as the world began to look forward to a new world order without a "clear and present danger," many began to wonder whether or not they may have gotten the Soviet Union completely wrong?[4] As a symposium organized by specialists on post-communist Russia much later pointed out, "the collapse of socialist regimes during 1989–1991 profoundly affected the conditions of knowledge production about the former socialist countries."[5] It certainly did. After all, for over four decades, nearly everybody of note had assumed that what the West had been facing was a most serious challenge. As late as 1983, Reagan was even calling the USSR an "evil empire" bent on world domination.[6] But the speed with which Soviet power imploded seemed to suggest that this once mighty empire stretching across eleven time zones, with its massive natural resources, may have been nothing more than a house of cards, almost a "flash in the pan," as one ex-Sovietologist put it.[7] Indeed, one of the odder features of the debate occasioned by the end of the Cold War and the collapse of the USSR was that having failed almost completely to predict these seismic events, many writers now started to talk as if it had all been inevitable![8]

The task I have set myself in this chapter is not so much to discuss what happened between 1989 and 1991 and why we failed to anticipate it, but rather try to explain how a system that disappeared so rapidly, with barely a shot being fired in its defense, nevertheless managed to construct a narrative that seemed both credible and coherent to so many people for so long. It is easy to say that those who advanced or accepted this construction were misguided or misinformed. Nevertheless, in its own way the Soviet Union told a story about itself which led whole generations to see something worthwhile about what many at the time believed was the greatest experiment of modern times.[9] Critics could easily argue (and did) that it was all an "illusion."[10] But this hardly explains the appeal of a system which for all its faults and weaknesses was still able to challenge liberal notions of economic progress and western visions of the "good life" for a good part of the twentieth century. Indeed, until Gorbachev entered the scene in 1985 and finally upset everything with his brand of "new thinking," this narrative, which stressed both the enormous strides which the USSR had made at home and the contribution it had made to international peace abroad, proved immensely attractive to many millions of people around the world.

But what exactly was the Soviet narrative? In what follows I have tried to unpack what by any measure was a complex amalgam of sometimes quite contradictory ideas. The discussion begins with what was central to this narrative: Marxism and its later iterations in a Stalinized form of "Leninism." It also looks at the enormous changes brought about in the USSR as a result of industrialization and global war. We will also explore the meaning of the Cold War and why escape from it proved so difficult for the USSR. We will in turn look at the USSR's "forgotten successes" through the 1950s and 1960s before examining what happened in the 1980s when the system (and with it the narrative it had created) fell apart.

Finally, the chapter will examine the not insignificant legacy of the Soviet narrative. As we shall argue, even if the Soviet system is no more, part of the anti-American and anti-Western discourse it championed until 1989 continues to shape the global discourse. Indeed, with the competition between Russia and China on one side, and the liberal West on the other, fast taking shape in the shadow of war in Ukraine, that narrative has taken on an increasingly significant form. The USSR may be no more; however, some of the ideas it spawned before it left the stage of history still live on.

## From Marx to Stalin

> *Marxism explained all the hitherto inexplicable questions and problems, and brought into a strictly scientific and logical system the solution to these questions, which were thus raised to the level of a truly scientific theory.*[11]

It has often been remarked that realists feel intellectually comfortable when it comes to talking about power, but have very little understanding of ideas and the power of ideas. This in part might help explain why realists never completely understood what drove the USSR other than the most basic aim of achieving security in an insecure world. Material capabilities are what matter when it comes to understanding the foreign policy of nations, not ideology, according to realists. Indeed, according to the most influential postwar realist of all, Hans J. Morgenthau, we should avoid looking at what he termed "philosophic or political sympathies" when understanding what nations do.[12] Interests, not beliefs, shaped and shape the politics among nations, including by definition the politics of both the Soviet Union and the United States after World War II.

Yet trying to explain the Soviet Union without some reference to Marxism is about as useful as trying to understand the Papacy without Catholicism. Indeed, like Catholicism (but without a belief in the hereafter or God), Marxism was a powerful belief system which even before Lenin and the Russian revolution had attracted thousands to its banner.[13] Whether Marx was "the greatest living thinker" of all time is no doubt something his many critics would wish to contest.[14] Nonetheless, they could hardly deny his achievement which, following nearly fifty years of intense study interspersed with short bursts of revolutionary activity from Brussels to Paris, allowed him to construct something close to a worldview. This united a critical political economy of capitalism, an argument for revolution, a theory of history which purported to show that capitalism was but a mere staging post on the road to socialism, and finally, some rough and ready vision of what socialism itself might look like. There has been much discussion of course as to what Marx meant by socialism; and not surprisingly, Soviet theoreticians in particular always liked to stress that because Marx was not a "utopian" he never laid down a blueprint as to what the future socialist society might look like. But as Bertell Ollman has shown, one can in fact piece his ideas together, and it is clear that Marx's vision of a future society bears only a formal resemblance to what finally came into being in the Soviet Union.[15]

Indeed, almost from the moment the Bolsheviks took power in 1917, they were constantly having to defend what they were doing against the charge—invariably leveled against them by others on the left—that they were deviating from the basics of Marxism. Even taking power in a backward country where the working class were in a minority seemed to run against Marxist teaching. A few years on and the Soviet leadership was confronted with yet another dilemma: how to justify the idea of "socialism in one country" without appearing to abandon the idea of world revolution. Translating the idea of socialism in one country into a material reality then caused even further ideological readjustment as the regime embarked on a course which transformed the economy but at a massive human cost. Finally, as Stalin imposed his iron grip on society through the 1930s, the regime was compelled yet again to explain away the fact that as the USSR moved closer to what they claimed was becoming a classless socialist society, the state was becoming ever more repressive.[16]

Soviet leaders were nothing if not adept in adjusting their own narrative to the new reality and where necessary simply eliminating all those—Trotsky here being the most famous—who persisted in questioning the "general line."[17] There was little that could not be rationalized away. Thus if the USSR in the 1930s was becoming more unequal rather than less, then this, it was argued, was but a temporary measure on the road to creating a new society in which all would one day become equal.[18] If the main enemy in earlier times had been "great Russian chauvinism" but now became "petty bourgeois nationalism," then again this was a necessary step on the road to establishing an even stronger Soviet Union.[19] And if the state was becoming ever more "vigilant" (to use a favorite Soviet term), then the reason it was doing so was not because the Communist Party of the Soviet Union (CPSU) was hostile to democracy—indeed, many of its foreign supporters even insisted the Constitution of 1936 was possibly one of the most democratic in the world[20]—but because the first workers' state was surrounded (or more precisely encircled) by enemies on all sides.[21] In fact, precisely because it was living in such a hostile international environment in which war by the West against the first workers' states remained an ever-present possibility, the USSR really had no choice other than to take the firmest political measures at home. No doubt, one day, when the whole world had become socialist, there would be no need for such measures and the state may at last be able to "wither away," as Marx and even Lenin suggested it might. But in the meantime the "enemies of the people," as Stalin preferred to call his opponents, would have to be tracked down and "liquidated."[22]

Yet none of these various gyrations appeared to dampen down support for the USSR. Even so, one still confronts something that at first sight seems bizarre: the fact that as the Soviet Union became more authoritarian and its policies more brutal, the more successful it seemed to be in winning new foreign converts to the cause. There is by now a vast literature on what some have called "fellow traveling" and others a latter-day form of "pilgrimage" in which very large numbers of otherwise critical Western intellectuals looked for, and seemed to discover in the Soviet system everything their own societies lacked.[23] Of course, not every writer subscribed to the idea that the USSR was a "new civilization" in the making; and many who once did, soon "saw the light" and went on to become the most vocal (and often the most effective) opponents of the system.[24] However, many were won over, though in some cases less out of a commitment to revolutionary politics themselves (think here of Fabians like the Webbs and H. G. Wells) and more because of the contrast they saw between the great economic strides being made in the USSR after 1930, and the collapse of economic hope in the West brought about by the Great Depression. With millions queuing up for outdoor relief in one "camp" and enthusiastic workers straining their all to build a new society in the other, it was hardly surprising that the Soviet Union, with its sense of collective purpose, was able attract new admirers from far and wide. Long before the USSR had embarked on its first Five Year Plan, the American writer Lincoln Steffens was already claiming (in 1919) that he had seen the future and "it works."[25] A few years on, with capitalism now going through what many believed was its death throes, how much easier it was for a lost generation to look for answers in the new socialist utopia.[26] As one of the more talented propagandists for the USSR put it at the time, while the "body" of American capitalism was being eaten alive by "an incurable cancer that will eventually destroy it," the workers in Russia were taking control of their destiny.[27]

If for some *bien pensant* writers and journalists the Soviet Union represented the future and capitalism the past, for others, supporting the USSR may have had less to do with pictures of happy workers and even happier collective farmers and more with the international situation. Hitler's rise to power and the threat which the new Nazi Germany posed to its neighbors (not to mention to thousands of its Jewish citizens) may have been of little concern to those on the right who preferred Hitler to Stalin. However, it did cause many people in the West to view the Soviet Union in a more favorable light. Moreover, as the threat of Nazism increased, the more it looked as if the USSR was the only state standing in Germany's way. Nor were Soviet propagandists slow in trying to deploy the new global conjuncture to their own advantage. Indeed, for a while, it very much seemed as if Soviet Russia was the main, possibly the only European country prepared to stand up to Hitler. Thus while the British prime minister Neville Chamberlain was discussing how to carve up Czechoslovakia with Hitler in 1938, Moscow was trying to build a popular front with like-minded anti-fascists; and while the democracies remained committed to the policy of nonintervention and neutrality during the Spanish Civil War—while Luftwaffe's Condor Legion and Italy's Aviazione Legionaria set about destroying the ancient Basque city of

Guernica—the USSR sent in materiel and weapons to help the republicans defend themselves against Franco. Ultimately, such gestures could no more save Spain than the idea of collective security could thwart Hitler. Indeed, the idea itself finally collapsed under the weight of its own contradictions—no Western state after all was prepared to ally itself with a power whose official worldview was rooted in Marxism, while the USSR (forever suspicious of the West's intentions) decided by 1939 to neutralize the Nazi threat by making a controversial Pact with Germany. Justified in classically Leninist terms of exploiting the "contradictions within the imperialist camp," the move may have had the short-term advantage of keeping the Nazi threat at bay. However, it did so at a very high price in terms of its own prestige. Nor in the end did the strategy work, and in June 1941 the "imperialist" power with which it had in effect been allied for nearly two years finally turned against it in what quickly turned into the most barbaric war in history.[28]

## World War to Cold War

> [*The*] *world view of Stalin and the Stalinist elite . . . was an ideologized Leninist concept of the outside world.*[29]

As we have shown, every twist and turn in Soviet policy up to, and even including, the disastrous Nazi-Soviet Pact invariably had to be justified (and was) in formal ideological terms. In this Marx and Engels were of little use.[30] Far more important by far was Lenin and what after 1924 went under the official heading of "Leninism." Lenin of course had never used the term, and a number of more critical figures in the Communist Party (when it was still possible to raise such questions) not only wondered what "Leninism" was supposed to mean, but were astounded that one of the least theoretically equipped members of the Bolshevik leadership bestowed upon himself the mantle of being Lenin's one true interpreter. But what exactly was it? The answer was clear, at least it was to Stalin, who first outlined the new operational code in 1924 in a series of lectures delivered at Sverdlovsk University. Stalin was certainly no stylist. However, in his less than scintillating prose he stressed that Leninism was not merely Marxism applied to Russian conditions, but was rather a higher form of Marxism that came into being in what Stalin called the epoch of imperialism, war, and "proletarian revolution," the first of which had taken place in the USSR in 1917.[31]

As Lenin also went on to point out, the fact that the revolution had survived at all was largely down to the failure of the capitalists to unite. Even so, the goal of Western leaders—whether they were conservatives like Churchill or liberals such as Wilson—remained what it had always been: that is, the destruction of the Soviet system. The democracies had aimed to do this after 1918, and now—years after Lenin had passed from the scene—is what Nazi Germany was attempting to do once more in what the USSR came to define (and still refer to) as the "Great Patriotic War." Yet not only did the USSR survive on both occasions, but by 1945 was emerging as one of the world's two great powers. Victory in turn not only justified the harsh measures that had been taken in the 1930s; perhaps even more important, it only confirmed what many of the Soviet Union's many friends had been claiming for years: that planning actually worked. Nor were Soviet propagandists shy in making the comparison between what had happened in World War I when pre-revolutionary Russia had been roundly defeated by Germany, and World War II when the Soviet Union had triumphed against an even more formidable enemy. "The spirit of the great Lenin" and the inspired political leadership of Stalin may have set the nation on the road to victory, as Soviet propaganda of the time declared. But it was the new socialist order which, more than anything else, made victory possible. As Stalin put it in a speech in 1946, "the war was something of an examination" which our new "Soviet social system" had not only "passed." It had also proved that our socialist system was "a better form of organization of society than any non-Soviet social system."[32]

Nor was this particular lesson lost on the rest of the rest of the world, where socialist-style planning (though not Soviet-style politics) seemed to hold many attractions for several advanced countries coming out of the war,[33] as well as for the new elites who would soon be leading their countries toward independence from colonial rule.[34] A number of classical liberal writers were clearly worried about what they believed was this dangerous trend. Indeed, one in particular—Hayek—even penned an extraordinarily influential polemic warning that the world was on the road to a new form of "serfdom," synonymous in his view not just with the USSR as such (which Hayek studiously avoided mentioning) but the more general transition from the liberal idea of political and economic freedom toward a society organized around "centrally directed economic activity." Supported outside the USSR by what Hayek liked to call "the totalitarians in our midst" (which incidentally also happened to include E. H. Carr) the future, he concluded, looked decidedly threatening. Which of the two conflicting ideas—individualism or collectivism—would triumph remained an unknown. However, one thing was clear. The only true "progressive policy" had to be based on a "policy of freedom" which placed the individual at its center.[35]

Hayek of course said very little, almost nothing at all, about the looming clash between the United States and the USSR. Yet in an important way his underlying thesis that the world stood at a crossroads, with one sign pointing to "freedom" and another to its opposite, does help us situate and give meaning to the conflict which ensued. More often than not cast as the expression of a competition between two rising powers by realist scholars of international relations (IR),[36] it is critical not to forget the degree to which the Cold War was in a more fundamental sense a competition between two stories and two opposed ways of thinking about the future of the world. In fact, when Truman went before Congress in March 1947 and called upon the US to come to the aid of Greece, he did so not in strategic terms or by invoking the balance of power, but by painting the conflict there in almost Hayekian terms of a much broader conflict between "two ways of life."[37] Significantly, too, when the US drew up its grand strategy in NSC-68, it cast the relationship in much the same way—that is, not as a straightforward rivalry between two superpowers with different material capabilities (though that was not ignored), but instead as an almost existential clash between two polar opposite civilizations, one with a fundamental purpose "to assure the integrity of our free society which is founded upon the dignity and worth of the individual," and the other with a fundamental design to enslave and destroy the free world.[38]

The Cold War in turn gave rise to two completely different narratives about which of the two systems was most responsible for having caused the breakdown of relations in the first place. Thus, on the one side, the West took it as an almost indisputable truth verging on the status of an orthodoxy, that the underlying reason for the clash was the USSR and its desire to destroy the West and Western institutions. There were of course different ways of explaining Soviet behavior, with at least one rather influential US policymaker insisting that the Soviet Union was by far and away the weaker party which kept the conflict alive largely for domestic purposes. However, Kennan's call for a more nuanced understanding was quickly pushed to one side by those who wanted a black-and-white story to tell, and that story took it as read that Soviet aggression made the conflict inevitable and containment necessary.[39]

Naturally enough, Soviet writers adopted a rather different position. Stalin, they argued, was keen to accept the new status quo in Europe; the United States, on the other hand, was not.[40] In fact, through the vehicle of the European Recovery Program and other active measures, it attempted to "change the results of World War II."[41] Nor in purely power terms was the USSR in a position to challenge the US after World War II. Thus whereas the United States had emerged from the war with its economic and military position much enhanced, the Soviet Union was in a parlous state, with its economy shattered and its people exhausted.[42] Even Western intelligence (to which Moscow had a great deal of access at the time) assumed that it would take the USSR at least a decade to recover. The United States, on the other hand, was in a position to reshape the world in its own image. Indeed, the alarmist, but popular, idea then widespread in America, that the Soviet Union was bent on world domination, was, it was argued, a much more accurate description of US foreign policy in the postwar period than it was of the USSR, which, as ever, remained committed to peace.[43]

What then, it was asked, was driving US foreign policy? Here opinion differed, but only somewhat. Certain individuals may have mattered, and certainly the death of Roosevelt and his replacement by the "Man from Missouri" Harry Truman accelerated the downward trend in US-Soviet relations after the war. But being sound Marxist-Leninists trained in the Leninist school of anti-imperialism, it was structures which mattered far more, and no structure mattered as much as US capitalism. Building upon a then common view—one even held by certain American economists for a while[44]—the United States, they argued, had emerged from the war with a mighty machine of production but with insufficient domestic capacity to absorb the surplus. There was in effect only one solution to this particular conundrum: imperialism, or in terms that even some American radical writers would recognize, an open door policy that would give the US ready access to foreign markets, thus ensuring that its highly dynamic economy could keep on growing.[45] This of course was not a problem facing the USSR. As Khrushchev later pointed out, thanks to the USSR's socialist system where the "home market was unlimited," and where there were no classes or social groups "interested in profiting by war" (a side swipe here at the US military-industrial complex), the USSR had no need to pursue an expansionist policy of conquest. The United States, on the other hand, had no alternative but to do so, leading, as in the end it was bound to, to increased instability and the ever-present danger of war.[46]

## The Limits of Peaceful Coexistence

> *From its very inception [in 1917] the Soviet state proclaimed peaceful coexistence as the basic principle of its foreign policy. It was no accident that the very first state act of the Soviet power was the decree on peace, the decree on the cessation of the bloody [world] war.*[47]

Having what they considered to be a superior understanding of the dynamics of world politics did not, however, change facts on the ground; and what these told Soviet leaders was that even if the USSR was in a much more powerful position than it had ever been before, the "correlation of forces" still told against it. Moreover, in its various attempts to shift that balance after 1947, it only managed to make matters worse. Thus its efforts to slow down Europe's recovery by launching a series of politically inspired strikes in effect helped legitimize the Marshall Plan. Creating the so-called *Cominform* in 1947 then made it appear as if there were a serious Soviet threat to Europe. Attempting to force the Western powers out of West Berlin only made the case for NATO that much stronger. And giving the green light to the North Koreans in 1950 only ended up justifying an American military buildup. Indeed, not only did these somewhat desperate efforts unite the West, they also placed the USSR in an even more disadvantaged position. As a result, it was forced to step back from its earlier militant stance in favor of a policy of peaceful coexistence—one which later came to be associated with the name of Stalin's successor, Nikita Khrushchev.[48]

Of course, as long as Stalin remained at the helm, insisting that war between the imperialist countries was inevitable, it was almost impossible to open any kind of meaningful dialogue with the West.[49] But with his death in 1953, followed by a settlement over Korea, accompanied in turn by a partial "thaw" in the USSR itself, the way now looked to be open for a serious reduction of tensions. With nuclear war an ever-present danger and the West now keen to ensure that instability in Eastern Europe did not spill over into something wider,[50] Khrushchev made a very determined effort to win over public opinion in the West by playing the "peace card." As he put it in one of his two most significant speeches delivered at the 20th Congress of the CPSU in 1956—the other was his "Secret" speech denouncing Stalin—there was no reason (as he later argued in the house journal of the US foreign policy establishment) why "different social systems" could not coexist peacefully.[51]

In important and significant ways, Khrushchev's hope that the two opposing systems could find ways of avoiding a direct military conflict turned out to be extremely well founded. In 1963, following the Cuban missile crisis, Washington and Moscow opened up a "hot line" designed to facilitate communication between the US president and the Soviet premier. In 1968 the Nuclear Non-Proliferation Treaty was signed. The first SALT agreement and the ABM Treaty were agreed to four years later. The Threshold Test Ban Treaty was then passed in 1974. And then, in 1979, SALT II was negotiated, though never entered into force. Certainly if one of the purposes of diplomacy was to make sure the Cold War remained "cold," then the conscious efforts by both superpowers turned out to be immensely successful in managing an ever-escalating arms race.[52]

Nonetheless, arms control alone, no more than frequent high-level meetings between leaders, could overcome the rivalry between the two competing systems. Stalin's death may well have been welcome. But as the archives show, it did not reduce Western suspicion of Soviet intentions. Even Khruschev's call for "peace" caused great consternation in the West, where it was assumed that his purpose was either to lower the West's guard, or, following his successful 1959 visit to the United States, to improve the Soviet Union's image abroad.[53] Nor did steady economic growth or scientific breakthroughs on the part of the USSR do anything to allay Western suspicions. The modest but real increases in Soviet living standards may have helped enhance its "soft power" appeal, as did the great successes it achieved, first by launching Sputnik in 1957, and four years later when Yuri Gagarin became the first man in space. But their overall result was to set the alarm bells ringing in the West. In fact, the more successful the Soviet Union appeared to be in the economic and technological spheres, the more of a challenge it became. As the then director of the CIA openly confessed, if the Soviet economy continued to grow at the rate it had been doing in the 1950s, the United States would be confronting "the most serious challenge" it had ever faced in peacetime.[54]

There was in addition another equally important reason why the West and the Americans remained as suspicious as they did, and this focused on the increasingly important role the USSR was beginning to play in the new Third World. Khrushchev might have talked the language of coexistence. But it soon became clear that this did not involve the Soviet Union accepting the status quo, especially in a part of the world where the West was at its most vulnerable: in its former colonial possessions. Here the USSR had some ready-made advantages. Most obviously, it had never been a colonial power outside its own Eurasian "heartland." For a number of very good reasons (including terms of imprisonment) many of the new rulers in Africa and across Asia were hostile to their former overlords. Moreover, many felt they saw a way out of poverty and underdevelopment not by adopting Western-style capitalism (most unfashionable until the 1980s), but rather by going for socialist economic strategies in which the state, rather than the market, would play the central role.[55] The Soviet Union also had another weapon in its ideological armory: V. I. Lenin, whose savage attack on imperialism back in 1916 played especially well to the anti-colonial movement,[56] as did his speech in 1920 at the Second Congress of the Comintern, where he called upon communists to support the struggle of all the oppressed peoples suffering under the heel of colonialism.[57] Now, in the long postwar period, it was possible to turn Lenin's call into a reality, from Egypt and India in the 1950s, and then on to Vietnam, Central America, and even southern Africa in the 1960s and 1970s.[58]

Yet perhaps the biggest obstacle standing in the way of any far-reaching rapprochement was not just the USSR's support for various struggles on the periphery, but the more fundamental difference between the two social systems themselves—one defining itself as being broadly liberal and the other not.[59] Conservatives might well have been the USSR's more intransigent enemies. However, it was the postwar liberal order organized on the basis of open markets, open societies, and liberal economics which posed the greatest problem (and potential threat) to a state whose very existence had been defined in terms of opposing all three. It was hardly surprising, of course, that whereas Soviet leaders like Brezhnev managed to get on well with conservative realists like Kissinger and Nixon, they found the liberal Carter a much more difficult proposition.[60] Indeed, having rather foolishly signed up to the Helsinki Accords of 1975 in the vain hope that this would legitimize their control over Eastern Europe, they soon discovered that it led to quite the opposite. The part played by the Accords in accelerating change in the Soviet bloc has been the subject of much debate among scholars looking for more novel ways of explaining the end of the Cold War. But there can be little doubt that by providing a legally recognized basis which East European dissidents were then able to refer to, this went some way in weakening Soviet control within its own "backyard."[61]

## Gorbachev Changes the Narrative

*Between 1985 and 1991, the foundation of Soviet foreign policy changed from a Marxist-Leninist view of inevitable conflict between capitalism and socialism to an idealist vision of cooperation between states in solving global problems.*[62]

One of the many ironies of the history of the Cold War is that until the end of the 1970s, it was not the USSR which appeared to be in long-term decline, but rather the United States.[63] Even a few years into the Reagan presidency, the notion that the sun was slowly setting on the American empire was a view which, if the huge popularity of Paul Kennedy's book was anything to go by, continued to command a great deal of support.[64] Yet as we know, history did not quite work out like that. The USSR gradually, and then more rapidly disappeared from the international stage, while the liberal West went on to win what Francis Fukuyama in his much quoted (and much misunderstood) article of 1989 believed was a massive ideological victory over its collectivist rival.[65]

The question then arises, when did this all begin? Here the consensus seems to be that even though it took a Gorbachev to alter the debate about the Soviet role in the world,[66] many of the changes that came about under him had been long in gestation.[67] After all, it was not Gorbachev who had initially challenged the Stalinist system, but Khrushchev. Nor was he the first to question the efficacy of the planned economy. This particular honor had fallen to Khrushchev's successor, Nikolai Kosygin, in 1965. Soviet foreign policy had also come under critical scrutiny long before 1985. As a number of Soviet writers had already pointed out, it was all very well flying the revolutionary flag in the Third World, but such interventions, they noted, were extraordinarily costly and contributed little or nothing to Soviet security. It also made any kind of stable relationship with the United States virtually impossible.[68]

Nor did more recent developments in the communist camp provide much room for comfort either. China remained as hostile as ever to its onetime friend and ally. A number of leading communist parties in Western Europe—most obviously in Italy and Spain—were beginning to distance themselves from Moscow. And the situation in Eastern Europe remained challenging, to say the least. Indeed, not only did the USSR derive little comfort from hanging on to its many unruly dependencies there; having gotten into enormous debt with the West during the 1970s, many of them had become something of an economic liability too.[69] Finally, to add to this long list of woes, the USSR was embroiled in an unwinnable war in Afghanistan, which its many enemies, from radical jihadists to the United States, were exploiting with cruel and ruthless efficiency.[70]

Thus when Gorbachev took over the leadership in 1985 there was already a sense among most, if not all, of the Soviet elite that something would have to give.[71] The economy was beginning to slow down. An even bigger material gap was beginning to open up between the Soviet Union and the capitalist West. Life expectancy for men was falling. Chronic illness due to excessive alcohol consumption was on the rise. Revenues from oil sales were falling. And Soviet agriculture remained in the doldrums with little to recommend it to anybody else in the world. In fact, compared to US agriculture it was positively primitive. As one expert on the subject asked in 1982, "how was it possible" for the Soviet Union, with just as much arable land per head of the population as the United States, being unable to feed its own people, "whereas U.S. agriculture not only supplies" its own population "with one of the richest diets in the world, but in addition supplies more food for export than any other country" in the world?[72]

In many respects, therefore, Gorbachev entered office at a critical moment in the history of the USSR, made all the more critical perhaps by the fact that in at least two Western countries—the United States and Great Britain—two powerful leaders, in the shape of Reagan and Thatcher, were waging a confident ideological war against all manifestations of socialism, including the variety which existed in the Soviet Union. No doubt the system itself could have limped on in its own inefficient way. Most of its Russian citizens, after all, seemed to be content enough with their lot, so long as the regime delivered the basic necessities like a regular job (however badly paid), an apartment (however cramped), and an annual holiday organized through their work unit. There was certainly little evidence that when Gorbachev took over, the country was unstable or about to collapse.[73] Indeed, there is a whole school of thought which insists that the main reason the USSR finally disappeared from the world's stage was not because it was in terminal economic decline, or could not compete militarily with the United States, but rather because Gorbachev indulged in all sorts of ill-thought-out initiatives which may have reassured the West about the USSR's benign intentions, but which in the end only caused the whole system of Soviet power (including that in Eastern Europe) to implode.[74]

Still, it is difficult to think that history would have played out much differently once Gorbachev set about trying to redefine the Soviet relationship with the rest of the world while gradually abandoning the narrative which had carried the USSR along for decades. Whether what came into being as the new narrative was any more credible or coherent than that which was now being jettisoned is highly doubtful. Certainly Gorbachev himself never appeared to have a very clear idea of his own of what he was seeking to achieve or even how he would bring it about. However, once he began to tinker with the system at home and started talking of building something as vague as a "common European home" within an "interdependent world based on common values," then it was highly unlikely if not impossible (and here paraphrasing the great Irish poet William Butler Yeats) for "the centre . . . to hold." Whether or not in the end the system was defeated by its rivals, brought down by its own contradictions, committed suicide, was unable to resist the siren call of the market, or simply fell apart by accident, will no doubt be debated by scholars for many years to come. One thing, though, is clear: without a positive story to tell itself and the world, the USSR simply could not go on.[75]

## Conclusion: Legacies

*The past is never dead. In fact, it is not even past.*[76]

Lastly, it is perhaps worth reflecting on the legacy of the Soviet Union and the global narrative it constructed over most of its lifetime. Obviously the Soviet system is no more, while Marxism itself seems to have been superseded by all manner of other intellectually appealing "isms." Nevertheless, many of the ideas and beliefs once propagated by the USSR have not all been consigned into that proverbial dustbin of history as Reagan (and even Fukuyama) once predicted they would be. China, for one thing, still refers to itself as a "socialist" country led by a Communist Party, guided by Marxism-Leninism. Indeed, two hundred years after the death of Marx in 2018, the People's Republic of China—now the second-largest economy in the world—not only paid for a new statue of Marx to be erected in his hometown of Triers in Germany, but President Xi JinPing himself talked of Marx as being the greatest thinker of all time (even while independent Marxist critics were at the same time being arrested for making the case for "real" socialism in China!).[77]

China also appears to have learned a great deal from the old USSR, including a distrust of the West, an active hostility toward the United States, and since the war in Ukraine began in early 2022, a deep suspicion of NATO. Even a cursory glance through its current propaganda evokes memories of the past, with crude images of "Uncle Sam" looking to dominate the world beyond its borders, while doing little to address the many issues it faces at home.

Nor should we ignore the potpourri of ideas now being put forward by Putin in Russia (and with ever greater ferocity since Moscow launched its "limited military operation" against Ukraine). None of what he says can in any way be defined as Marxist or Leninist in formal terms. If anything, Putin seems to draw more inspiration from Russian imperial history of the eighteenth century than he does from Lenin in the twentieth. But in spite of that, Putin has over the years developed a narrative of his own—fiercely anti-American and hostile to nearly everything Western—which borrows heavily (albeit selectively) from his Soviet predecessors. It is also one which seems to appeal to a good number of people both inside and outside of Russia as well. Even Stalin, it would seem, now finds favor in the Putin narrative, not as a communist but as a great leader who transformed Russia and turned it into a great power (something Putin himself is now seeking to do).[78] Perhaps even more crucial is his appeal to Russian patriotism and the role Russia in particular played between 1941 and 1945 in defeating German Nazism. It is not accidental, of course, that in justifying his war against Ukraine he has sought to show a direct line between Russia's anti-Nazi role in World War II and what he claims Russia is seeking to do to its Ukrainian neighbor today.

Finally, though there are few people in the world today who would wish to see a return of anything resembling a Soviet model of socialism—including, of course, Putin himself—it would seem that a very large number of younger people in the West—even in the United States—are now discovering that liberalism and liberal capitalism do not have all the answers. Certainly since the crisis of 2008 the mood has definitely shifted, and few if any seem to be confident that either unfettered markets or liberal economics have all the answers to the challenges facing a post-pandemic world.[79] Thirty years ago, liberalism looked to have won the battle for the future, while socialism looked to be utterly discredited. As memories fade and new generations make their voices heard, it would appear that new narratives are already being written by those who have grown up without the Soviet Union either inspiring them—as it may have done once—or just as likely, warning them not to exchange the certainties of the present for an unknown and unknowable future.

## Notes

1. Quote from Joseph Borrell, The High Representative for Foreign Affairs and Security Policy. In Rosa Balfour, "Against a European Civilization: Narratives about the European Union," *Carnegie Europe*, April 6, 2021.
2. E. H. Carr, *The Soviet Impact on the Western World* (London: Macmillan, 1946).
3. See Campbell Craig and Fred Logevall, *America's Cold War: The Politics of Insecurity* (Cambridge, MA: Harvard University Press, 2009).
4. Michael Cox, "Why Did We Get the End of the Cold War Wrong?," *British Journal of Politics and International Relations* 11, no. 2 (2009): 161–176.
5. "Writing a Global History of Soviet Socialism: Geopolitics, Knowledge, Experience," *NYU, Jordan Center for the Advanced Study of Russia*, April 17, 2021.
6. Ronald Reagan's famous speech was delivered on March 8, 1983, to a meeting of the National Association of Evangelicals in Orlando, Florida. Interestingly, in the same speech he also argued (a few years before it happened) that "communism" was "another sad, bizarre chapter in human history whose last pages even now are being written."
7. See Arch Getty, "The Future Did Not Work," *The Atlantic*, March 2000. https://www.theatlantic.com/magazine/archive/2000/03/the-future-did-not-work/378081/.
8. For a range of assessments about the end of the Soviet system, see Michael Cox, ed., *Rethinking the Soviet Collapse: Sovietology, the Death of Communism and the New Russia* (London and New York, 1998).
9. David L. Hoffman, "The Greatest Socialist Experiment? The Soviet State in International Context," *Slavic Review* 76, special issue 3 (Fall 2017): 619–628.
10. Francois Furet, *The Passing of an Illusion: The Idea of Communism in the Twentieth Century* (Chicago: University of Chicago Press, 1999).
11. Andrei Y. Vyshinsky, *The Law of the Soviet State* (New York: Macmillan, 1948), 8.
12. Quoted from his second principle on realism reprinted in Hans J. Morgenthau, *Politics among Nations: The Struggle for Power and Peace*, 5th edition, revised (New York: Alfred A. Knopf, 1978), 4–15.
13. See Gary Steenson, *After Marx, Before Lenin: Marxism and Socialist Working Class Parties in Europe 1884–1914* (Pittsburgh: University of Pittsburgh Press, 1991).
14. The reference to Marx was made in a speech delivered by Frederick Engels at Marx's funeral in Highgate Cemetery London on March 17, 1883.
15. Bertell Ollman, "Marx's Vision of Communism: A Reconstruction," *Critique* 8, no. 1 (1977): 4–41.
16. Robert V. Daniels, *The Conscience of the Revolution: Communist Opposition in Soviet Russia* (Cambridge, MA: Harvard University Press, 1960).

17. For a critical assessment of Leon Trotsky's critique of Stalinism, see Hillel Ticktin and Michael Cox, eds., *The Ideas of Leon Trotsky* (London: The Porcupine Press, 1995)..
18. See Moshe Lewin, "Society and the Stalinist State in the Period of the Five Year Plans," *Social History* 1, no. 2 (1976): 139–175.
19. Veljko Vujacic, "Stalinism and Russia Nationalism; A Reconceptualization," *Post-Soviet Affairs* 23, no. 2 (April 2007): 156–183.
20. See Sidney and Beatrice Webb, *Soviet Communism: A New Civilisation*, 2 volumes (New York: Charles Scribner's Sons, 1936).
21. See James Harris, "Encircled by Enemies: Stalin's Perceptions of the Capitalist World," *Journal of Strategic Studies* 30, no. 3 (2007): 513–545.
22. The classic analysis of the purges remains Robert Conquest, *The Great Terror: A Reassessment* (Oxford: Oxford University Press, 1968).
23. For a discussion of fellow traveling written from the critical left, see David Caute, *The Fellow Travellers: The Intellectual Friends of Communism* (New Haven, CT: Yale University Press, 1988); and from the right, see Paul Hollander, *Political Pilgrims* (New York: Oxford University Press, 1981).
24. See the influential collection of ex-communist "confessions" brought together in Richard Crossman, ed., *The God That Failed: A Confession* (New York: Harper Brothers, 1949).
25. Cited in Peter Hartshorn, *I Have Seen the Future: A Life of Lincoln Steffens* (Berkeley, CA: Counter Point, 2011).
26. Eugen Lyons, *Assignment in Utopia* (New York: Harcourt, Brace, 1938).
27. The reference to "cancer" was made by the American writer and communist Joseph Freeman. It is cited in *Investigation of Un-American Propaganda Activities in the United States, 1938–1944* (Washington, DC: USGPO). Freeman's very positive observations on the working class in the USSR can be found in his *The Soviet Worker: An Account of the Economic, Social and Cultural Status of Labor in the USSR* (New York: Liveright, 1932).
28. For two very different discussions of the Soviet role in the 1930s, see Jonathan Haslam, *The Soviet Union and the Struggle for Collective Security in Europe 1933–1939* (New York: St. Martin's Press, 1984), who holds the UK and France responsible for the failure of collective security, and Jiri Hochman, *The Soviet Union and the Failure of Collective Security, 1934–1938* (Ithaca, NY, and London: Cornell University Press, 1984), who is far more critical of the USSR.
29. Evan Mawdsley, "World War II, Soviet Power and International Communism," in Norman Naimark, Silvio Pons, and Sophie Quinn-Judge, eds., *Cambridge History of Communism* (Cambridge: Cambridge University Press, 2017), 15–27.
30. The USSR did, however, publish the works of Marx and Engels through Progress Publishers based in the USSR. The fullest collection of their work, though, was brought out by Lawrence & Wishart, who held the copyright for the Marx Engels Collected Works. Between 1975 and 2004, Lawrence & Wishart published fifty volumes of the works of Marx and Engels in English. These covered the period 1835–1895. The volumes contain all the written works of Marx and Engels, including formerly unpublished manuscripts and letters.

31. J. V. Stalin, *Foundations of Leninism* [1924] (Moscow: Foreign Languages Publishing House, 1953)..
32. J. V. Stalin, "Speech Delivered by J. V. Stalin at a Meeting of Voters of the Stalin Electoral District, Moscow," February 9, 1946 (Moscow: Foreign Languages Publishing House, 1950).
33. On the British experience with planning after World War II, see Stephen Brooke, "Problems of Socialist Planning: Even Durbin and the Labour Government of 1945," *The Historical Journal* 34, no. 3 (September 1991): 687–702.
34. On the influence of Soviet style planning on the first leader of independent India, see A. I. Tchitcherov, "Jawaharlal Nehru and Socialism," *World Affairs* 3, no. 1 (June 1994): 64–70.
35. F. A. Hayek, *The Road to Serfdom* (London: George Routledge & Sons, 1945).
36. Thus, according to William C. Wohlforth: "The Cold War was caused by the rise of Soviet power and the fear this caused in the West." See his "Realism and the End of the Cold War," *International Security* 19, no. 3 (Winter 1994–1995): 96.
37. A copy of Truman's March 12 speech, which soon acquired the status of a "doctrine," can be found at https://avalon.law.yale.edu/20th_century/trudoc.asp.
38. NSC-68, which was drawn up in 1950, was finally declassified by Henry Kissinger in 1975. For the original, see https://digitalarchive.wilsoncenter.org/document/116191.pdf?v=2699956db534c1821edefa61b8c13ffe.
39. I discuss Kennan's understanding of the Soviet system in my "Requiem for a Cold War Critic: The Rise and Fall of George F. Kennan," *Irish Slavonic Studies* 11 (1990–1991): 1–35.
40. See Michael Cox and Caroline Kennedy Pipe, "The Tragedy of American Diplomacy: Rethinking the Marshall Plan," *Journal of Cold War History* 7, no. 1 (Winter 2005): 97–134.
41. Quote from Maryna Bessonova, "Soviet Perspectives on the Cold War and American Foreign Policy," in Lee Trepanier et al., eds., *Comparative Perspectives on the Cold War* (Krakow: AFM Publishing House, 2010), 44.
42. The imbalance of power between the USSR and the United States after World War II is outlined in detail in Melvyn P. Leffler's definitive study, *A Preponderance of Power: National Security, the Truman Administration and the Cold War* (Stanford, CA: Stanford University Press, 1993).
43. The USSR was very active in promoting "peace" through various front organizations, including the World Peace Council (WPC). The Council was founded in 1950 to promote peace campaigns around the world in order to oppose "warmongering" by the United States. Some of its early and more famous supporters included W. E. B. Du Bois, Paul Robeson, Howard Fast, Pablo Picasso, Louis Aragon, Jorge Amado, Pablo Neruda, György Lukacs, Renato Guttuso, Jean-Paul Sartre, Diego Rivera, Muhammad al-Ashmar, and Joliot-Curie.
44. In 1943, Paul Samuelson wrote that were we "to wind up the war effort in the greatest haste . . . then there would be ushered in the greatest period of unemployment and industrial dislocation which any economy has ever faced." "Full Employment after the War," in S. E. Harris, ed., *Postwar Economic Problems* (New York: McGraw Hill, 1943).

45. See, for example, *William Appleman Williams*: *The Tragedy of American Diplomacy* (Cleveland, OH: World Publishing, 1959).
46. Nikita S. Khrushchev, "On Peaceful Coexistence," *Foreign Affairs* 38, no. 1 (October 1959): 3.
47. Ibid.
48. Marshall Shulman, *Stalin's Foreign Policy Reappraised* (Cambridge, MA: Harvard University Press, 1963).
49. Stalin's discussion on the inevitability of war between the capitalist countries (though significantly not between the socialist states and the capitalist camp) can be found in *Bolshevik* 18 (September 1952): 1–50. Reprinted in *Pravda*, October 3, 1952, 2–5, and October 4, 1952, 2–4. Accessed at http://soviethistory.msu.edu/1947-2/cold-war/cold-war-texts/stalin-on-the-inevitability-of-war-with-capitalism/.
50. See Zbigniew Brzezinski and William E. Griffith, "Peaceful Engagement in Eastern Europe," *Foreign Affairs* (July 1961).
51. The best study on Soviet foreign policy thinking is still Margot Light, *Soviet Theory of International Relations* (Brighton: Wheatsheaf, 1988).
52. For an early classic examination of the issue, see Hedley Bull, *The Control of the Arms Race* (New York: Frederick A. Praeger, 1965).
53. See Rósa Magnúsdóttir, "'Be Careful in America, Premier Khrushchev!': Soviet Perceptions of Peaceful Coexistence with the United States in 1959," *Cahiers du Monde Russe* 47, no. 1–2 (January–June 2006): 109–130.
54. The head of the CIA, Allen Dulles, sounded the alarm as early 1958: "If the Soviet industrial growth rate persists at 8 or 9 per cent per annum over the next ten years as is forecast . . . the gap between our two economies by 1970 will be dangerously narrowed." Quoted in Mark Trachtenberg, "Assessing Soviet Economic Performance during the Cold War: A Failure of Intelligence," *Texas National Security Review* 1, no. 2 (March 2018): 81.
55. See W. W. Rostow's rebuttal of the Soviet position in his controversial, but much discussed study, *Stages of Economic Growth: A Non-Communist Manifesto* (Cambridge: Cambridge University Press, 1960).
56. See V. I. Lenin, *Imperialism, The Highest Stage of Capitalism* (1916) in *Lenin's Selected Works*, Vol. 1 (Moscow: Progress, 1963), 667–766.
57. Michael Cox, "The *National and Colonial* Questions: The First Five Years of the Comintern, 1919–24," *Searchlight on South Africa* 4, no. 1 (1990): 33–43
58. See Fred Halliday, *Cold War, Third World: An Essay on Soviet-US Relations* (London: Hutchinson Radius, 1989).
59. G. J. Ikenberry, "Liberalism and Empire: Logics of Order in the American Unipolar Age," *Review of International Studies* 30, no. 4: 609–630.
60. See "Carter and Human Rights, 1977–1981." Office of the Historian. Foreign Service Institute, United States Department of State.
61. See Daniel C. Thomas, "Human Rights Ideas, the Demise of Communism and the End of the Cold War," *Journal of Cold War Studies* 7, no. 2 (Spring 2005): 110–141.
62. Deborah Welch Larson and Alexei Shevchenko, "New Thinking and the Revolution on Soviet Foreign Policy," *International Organization* 57, no. 1 (Winter 2003): 77.

63. Michael Cox, "Whatever Happened to American Decline? International Relations and the New United States Hegemony," *New Political Economy* 6, no. 3 (2001): 311–340.
64. Paul Kennedy, *The Rise and Fall of the Great Powers* (New York: Random House, 1987).
65. Francis Fukuyama, "The End of History," *National Interest* (1989).
66. See Jeff Checkel, "Ideas, Institutions, and the Gorbachev Foreign Policy Revolution," *World Politics* 45, no. 2 (January 1993): 271–300
67. Archie Brown, ed., *The Demise of Marxism-Leninism in Russia* (New York: Palgrave Macmillan, 2004).
68. Elizabeth K. Valkenier, *The Soviet Union and the Third World: An Economic Bind* (New York: Praeger, 1983).
69. See Peter Summerscale, "Is Eastern Europe a Liability to the Soviet Union?," *International Affairs* 7, no. 4 (Autumn 1981): 585–598.
70. Rodric Braithwaite, *Afgantsy: The Russians in Afghanistan, 1979–1989* (London: Oxford University Press, 2013).
71. For the most systematic critique of the Soviet economy written from a Marxist perspective, see Hillel Ticktin, *Origins of the Crisis in the USSR: Essays on the Political Economy of a Disintegrating System* (Armonk, NY: Myron Sharpe, 1982).
72. Karl Eugen-Wadekin, "Soviet Agriculture's Dependence on the West," *Foreign Affairs* 60, no. 4 (Spring 1982): 882.
73. In one of his many influential studies on the late USSR, Seweryn Bialer not only cautioned against thinking that the Soviet system was teetering on the edge, but went into great detail describing what he saw as the USSR's many sources of stability. See his *Stalin's Successors; Leadership, Stability and Change in the Soviet Union* (Cambridge: Cambridge University Press, 1980).
74. Still the best study on Eastern Europe in 1989 is Jacques Levesque, *The Enigma of 1989: The USSR and the Liberation of Eastern Europe* (Berkeley: University of California Press, 1997).
75. There is by now vast literature on Gorbachev and Gorbachev's role. The best (and the most sympathetic) study is probably by Archie Brown, *The Gorbachev Factor* (Oxford: Oxford University Press, 1996).
76. William Faulkner, "Requiem for a Nun," Act 1, Sc. 3, 1951.
77. Palden Sonam, "No Place for Real Marxists in China," *The Diplomat* (October 6, 2018).
78. There is now vast body of work on Putin and "Putinism." The most insightful on the relationship between Putin's concept of Russia and Stalinism is David Satter, *It Was a Long Time Ago, and It Never Happened* (New Haven, CT: Yale University Press, 2012).
79. Lydia Saad, "Socialism as Popular as Capitalism among Young Adults in the U.S.," *Gallup*, November 25, 2019.

# 3

# Pan-Islamic Narratives of the Global Order, 1870–1980

*Cemil Aydin*

On May 17, 1919, three Indian Muslim leaders met the US president Woodrow Wilson in Paris to make a case for the preservation of the Ottoman caliphate in Istanbul, and for the national self-determination of Muslim-majority Turkey.[1] The claims made by Aga Khan, Abdullah Yusuf Ali, and Sahibzada Aftab Ahmad Khan on behalf of what they called "the last remaining Muslim power in the world" might appear to represent a distinctly Muslim vision of the global political order and a unique approach to international politics derived from their religion, but such a conclusion would be mistaken. The Indian Muslims made their case for Turkish independence by appeals to the universalist narrative of rights for all, irrespective of race and religion, particularly to Wilson's fourteen points for peace. There was also a British imperial narrative apparent in the conversation, as the Indian Muslim delegation emphasized their sacrifice as soldiers in the British imperial forces fighting and defeating the German-Ottoman alliance as a basis of their demands. Edwin Montagu, Secretary of State for British-ruled India, arranged the meeting because he believed that the British Empire, as the largest Muslim empire in the world, had a moral responsibility to listen to the Indian Muslim case for the sovereignty of Ottoman Turkey. All three Muslim leaders were loyal subjects of the British Crown, seeing no contradiction in their political allegiance to the British king and spiritual ties to the Ottoman caliph. Several Indian Hindu leaders joined the meeting, making clear their solidarity with their fellow Indian Muslims, which was best represented by their active participation in the Pan-Islamic Khilafat movement.[2] Last but not least, there was a European narrative implicit in the meeting, as Indian Muslims were criticizing how Europe expelled and discriminated against the Ottomans because of Christian prejudice toward Muslims, and were urging Europeans to now treat post-Ottoman Turkey with dignity. From the

Cemil Aydin, *Pan-Islamic Narratives of the Global Order, 1870–1980* In: *Debating Worlds*. Edited by Daniel Deudney, G. John Ikenberry, and Karoline Postel-Vinay, Oxford University Press. © Oxford University Press 2023. DOI: 10.1093/oso/9780197679302.003.0004 perspective of Turkish leaders, Indian Muslim mobilization on their behalf was helping them to gain their sovereignty as a state belonging to the club of European empires and nations.

Historians approach grand narratives such as the clash of civilizations theory with suspicion, and rightly so.[3] This conversation at the Paris Peace Conference in 1919 invalidates some of the most prominent grand narratives about an eternal clash between Islamic and Western/Christian political visions and civilization. Bernard Lewis's influential essay in *The Atlantic* magazine, "The Roots of Muslim Rage" (1990), which became the basis of Samuel Huntington's popular work, *The Clash of Civilizations and the Remaking of World Order* (1996), argued:

> In the classical Islamic view, to which many Muslims are beginning to return, the world and all mankind are divided into two: the House of Islam, where the Muslim law and faith prevail, and the rest, known as the House of Unbelief or the House of War, which it is the duty of Muslims ultimately to bring to Islam. . . . The struggle between these rival systems [of the Islamic world and Christendom] has now lasted for some 14 centuries. It began with the advent of Islam, in the 7th century, and has continued virtually to the present day. It has consisted of a long series of attacks and counterattacks, jihads and crusades, conquests and reconquests.[4]

In spirit and substance, the meeting of the Indian Muslim leaders with Woodrow Wilson in 1919 contradicts every single claim by Lewis and Huntington about the eternal clash of political values between Islamic and Western civilizations. It does, however, still illustrate a Pan-Islamic narrative of the world order that emerged in the half century that preceded this meeting in a complex and interdependent imperial world. Closely related to Pan-Africanism and Pan-Asianism, Pan-Islamism emerged in the 1880s as a response to denial of equal rights to Muslims due to unequal power relations in the racialized Eurocentric imperial world order. Pan-Islamist narratives reached their peak political mobilization from the Paris Peace Conference of 1919, when the Muslim delegations meeting with Wilson occurred, and the Lausanne Treaty of 1923. Turkey benefited from Pan-Islamic global support at the Lausanne Treaty negotiations, yet decided to abolish the spiritual Ottoman Caliphate in March 1924. The Pan-Islamic narrative framework persisted in new political projects and struggles for rights throughout the rest of the twentieth century. While rejecting the simplistic account of an Islamic view of politics in the racialized notions of clash of civilizations, we should take Pan-Islamism seriously as one of the modern contested narratives of the world order that is globalist and humanist in content, and which has inspired the political mobilization and arguments of many political actors, as seen in the conversation between Indian Muslim delegation and Woodrow Wilson.[5]

The first half of this chapter will describe the genealogy and formation of the Pan-Islamic narratives of the global order from the 1870s until the aftermath of World War I. The chapter will then discuss the geopolitical uses of the power of the Pan-Islamic narratives by different state and non-state actors for about a century from the 1880s to the 1980s.

## Problem Space of the Muslim Narrative in the Racialized Eurocentric World

The origins of the contested but connected narratives of the world order go back to the second half of the nineteenth century, when all regions of the world became tightly linked and entangled by European imperial rule that justified itself with a narrative of Europe's civilizational superiority. It is in that context that publics and leaders of various Asian and African societies had to engage with the rapidly globalizing set of Eurocentric ideas about history, civilization, progress, and race. This engagement should not be seen as an emulation, clash, or synthesis between two (or three or four) systematic, monolithic, and rigid civilizations. What is today considered as European, Islamic, African, or Asian civilization did not precede this late-nineteenth-century process of imperial globalization linked by steamship, telegraph, railways, and printing presses. In fact, all of the civilizational narratives became co-constituted in conversation with each other, in the context of unequal economic, political, and cultural power relations characterized by racialized European empires. There was no shared Pan-Islamic narrative of the world order, or idea of Islamic civilization, preceding the nineteenth-century hegemony of the European empires or Eurocentric imperial world.

Pre-nineteenth-century geographic, historical, and political imaginations in Muslim societies were fractured and diverse, and did not constitute a single dominant narrative that is in engagement with any other master global narrative. In terms of the planetary narratives that exist today, the most powerful one was the nineteenth-century universalist European claims of superiority in civilization and progress, even if this universalist claim was coupled with ideas of racial exclusion and colonial violence. Europe's civilizing mission or claim to religious and racial superiority aimed to generate additional soft power to legitimate and secure Europe's already existing military and geopolitical power. Counter-narratives of modernity and civilization that Muslim, African, and Asian intellectuals produced in conversation with the master European narrative may retrospectively look naive: multiple new civilizational narratives of Asia, Islam, and Africa aimed at producing novel universalist arguments about their history, culture, and race in order to gain rights in an era when Europe's geopolitical power was overwhelming. Was it possible to curb racism and tame colonialism by simply talking back against the European master narrative of the superiority of Western civilization, and or by showing the moral hypocrisy of universalist European claims to justice, morality, and peace? Could Ukrainians under Russian assault in 2022, for example, just talk back against Putin's historical claims of Russian civilization, or expose Eurasianist justification for Russian imperialism to gain their freedom? In the context of the peak of European hegemony in the world in late nineteenth century, however, we see simultaneous formulations of apologetic modernity on behalf of Asians, Africans, and Muslims, as if intellectuals of those societies believed that they should first dispel the racial stigma attached to them by colonial hegemons with new narratives to prepare the foundations for their equality and emancipation.

It is mistaken to assume that Muslims were united throughout history with a view of the world primarily shaped by religious texts, and that they became divided due to European colonialism or nationalism. On the contrary, it was only at the peak of European colonial hegemony in the early twentieth century that we see the emergence of a contemporary modern narrative of the victimhood and humiliation of the Muslim world, and arguments for pan-Islamic solidarity. Throughout the millennium from the ninth to the nineteenth century, Muslim societies were ruled by multiple kingdoms, sultanates, and empires, many of which were in conflict with each other. There was a cultural connectivity among Muslim societies facilitated by a network of schools, legal practices, sufi orders, religious rituals such as the pilgrimage to Mecca, and trade, but none of the Muslim dynasty ruled empires behaved like the Soviet Union and Communist China, following sharia rules like communist bureaucrats were trying to follow Stalinist ideology or Mao's *Red Book*. Muslim political experiences were not stagnant and uniform, and they changed dramatically from the early rise of the Muslim faith practices in the seventh century to the nineteenth century. There were already secular visions of politics formulated by the bureaucrats of Umayyad and Abbasid caliphates from the eighth to the eleventh century, and the temporal power of the sultans overshadowed the religious notions of the caliphate as successor to the Prophet Muhammad.

In 1814, at the end of the Napoleonic wars in Europe, more than two dozen disparate Muslim kingdoms in Eurasia and Africa did not constitute a vision of a united Muslim world in solidarity, as they did not share a narrative of the world order. Even though there were observers critical of the injustices and violence of European rule over Muslim populations of Asia and Africa before the mid-nineteenth century, the major response to the expansion of the power of European empires in Muslim societies was not solidarity in the name of the Muslim *ummah*. Instead of forming a single Muslim narrative, there were reformulations of an earlier cosmopolitan hybrid legitimacy of Muslim dynasties in a set of ambitious self-strengthening reforms in Tunis, Egypt, Ottoman Turkey, and Persia. Initially, it was the European colonial epistemology that marked millions of individuals from Eastern Europe to West Africa, to Egypt to India and China, as primarily Muslim, racializing them by ascribing a set of characteristics to their religion, and becoming suspicious of their solidarity and unity against European colonial rule.

In the early nineteenth century, Greek nationalists became the first successful actors to use a Eurocentric notion of civilization successfully to gain political intervention by great powers against the Ottoman Empire. Even though the Ottoman Empire could be justified to suppress the Greek revolt according to the imperial norms of the Congress of Vienna, there was an overly politicized use of the term "civilization" ascribed to Greeks, and "barbarism" ascribed to the Ottoman Muslim elites so that the rules of the Congress of Vienna could be broken in favor of Greek nationalists. When the Greek war of independence ended, the Ottoman Empire, which ruled over more Christian Greeks than the Kingdom of Greece in the 1830s, reasserted their imperial cosmopolitanism, and appointed an ethnically Greek bureaucrat (Musurus Efendi) as the first Ottoman ambassador to Athens, while insisting on their membership in the European concert of empires that emerged after the Congress of Vienna. Soon after the Greek revolution, the Ottoman elite themselves decided to benefit from the political power of the discourse of civilization in its military confrontation against Egypt. By depicting the Egyptian Muslim ruler as African and less civilized, the Ottoman government managed to gain the support of England and Russia, and weakened the pro-Egyptian public opinion in France. The 1839 Ottoman proclamation of radical reforms relied on the Eurocentric notion of civilization, and aimed at bolstering the security and legitimacy of the Ottoman polity as a member of the European club of empires.

From this imperial perspective, the Indian rebellion against British hegemony in India in 1857 should not be seen as an Islamic or Pan-Islamic revolt against Christian modernity or imperialism. In the 1857 rebellion, Muslim and Hindu rebels collaborated, both declaring a holy war against the British, but not against each other. There were also large groups of Muslims and Hindus who collaborated with the British rule, and after the defeat of the rebellions, Muslims populations and elites found ways to imagine their empowerment and peace under the rule of Queen Victoria, as many Christians and Jews in Iraq and Palestine could accept the rule of a reformist Muslim sultan in Istanbul. During the nineteenth century, Indian Muslims began to show greater respect to the Ottoman Empire's Sunni rulers, but this was not because of their belief in a clash of civilizations. On the contrary, Ottoman rulers were respected partly because they were allies of the British Empire and a member of the European club of civilized empires, while giving equal rights to Christians, appointing them as ministers and bureaucrats.

The Pan-Islamism narrative of civilization, history, and world order, similar to other forms of pan-nationalisms, started with the formulation of an intellectual counter-narrative of civilization and modernity in response to a set of questions and problems created by European imperial hegemony, in affirmation of the equal right of Muslims. In the late-nineteenth-century imperial context, citizenship or subjecthood in an empire or a state was not sufficient to claim rights for the majority of individuals, because they were categorized as belonging to an inferior culture and civilization, and therefore not worthy of a full set of rights. When colonized populations asked for rights equal to those of white Christian metropole residents or white settlers, their requests were denied on the basis of their race and religion. Muslims in French colonies, for instance, could not become equal citizens because practicing their religious law would render them ineligible for equality. As Muriam Haleh Davis notes about French-ruled Algeria in late nineteenth century,

> being Muslim was not a question of individual belief or religious practice—and even conversion to Christianity did not attenuate the effects of these legal structures. This suggests that discrimination against Muslims was not necessarily . . . a function of what one believes but rather operated in a

similar fashion to racism, which is based on unchangeable physical features ("what one is").[6]

The last quarter of the nineteenth century witnessed the extraordinary level of interconnectivity among different Muslim publics across Eurasia and Africa. More individuals who were Muslim began to travel in steamships, or wrote and read articles in Muslim journals published cheaply in new printing technologies, receiving instant news via globalized telegraph networks. Thus, Muslim publics began to discuss and debate a set of problems they faced across different imperial spaces, such as Russian-ruled Europe and Central Asia, British-ruled Indian Ocean, French-ruled North Africa, and Dutch-ruled Indonesia, in the context of shared patterns of racialization of Muslims. While European empires were marking Muslims as a backward global community requiring European colonial rule, they were also allowing Muslim intellectual and political elites to interact and talk to each about their common problems and predicament, and talk back against colonial claims of Muslim inferiority. Thus, the late-nineteenth-century Muslim narrative of the world order reflected a kind of re-regionalization of the globe. The most overwhelming period of the Western hegemony in the world also became the peak of inter-Asian, inter-Muslim, and inter-African/African American connections. Thus, the intellectual networks that created the imagination of the Muslim world became co-constituted by the problem space of European colonial rule and its intellectual hegemony.

Muslim intellectuals were aware of the constructed nature of new European categories of Islam's "Oriental inferiority" and uncivil nature, and had objections to them, but many felt the need to utilize the civilizational and geopolitical conceptual categories that they encountered in Europe in these polemics and rebuttals. For example, Ottoman intellectuals read in European writings and heard from their European counterparts that the Ottomans did not belong to Europe in terms of culture, religion, civilization, and race. Ottoman elites and intellectuals who were engaged with European-inspired self-strengthening reforms realized the negative implications of these categorizations. It is worth quoting Gladstone's remarks on the Ottoman Empire, in the context of the Ottoman suppression of the Bulgarian insurrections of 1876, when the Ottomans and the British empires were still in alliance against Russia. These remarks were aimed at encouraging Britain's decision to undo its alliance with the Ottomans, and help Bulgarian independence or support Russia against Ottomans:

> Let me endeavour very briefly to sketch, in the rudest outline, what the Turkish race was and what it is. It is not a question of Mahometanism simply, but of Mahometanism compounded with the peculiar character of a race. They are not the mild Mahometans of India, nor the chivalrous Saladins of Syria, nor the cultured Moors of Spain. They were, upon the whole, from the black day when they first entered Europe, the one great anti-human specimen of humanity. Wherever they went, a broad line of blood marked the track behind them; and, as far as their dominion reached, civilization disappeared from view.[7]

The Ottoman intellectuals responded to Gladstone's accusations of barbarism and inferiority with counter-arguments by insisting that they were also part of the civilized European club of empires, or that Islamic and European values of progress were not incompatible. Ottoman Muslim elites felt the need to defend Islam against the Orientalist stereotype that it is a religious tradition that teaches anti-rational fanaticism to its followers.[8] For that reason, Ottoman intellectuals were especially concerned about Ernest Renan's speech that Islam is an impediment to science and rationality, and wrote refutations against him. Namık Kemal, famous for his statement that "Europe Knows Nothing about the Orient," accused Ernest Renan's Islamophobic thesis of "being full of delusions born of total ignorance, . . . in his outright attacks against Islam."[9] It was clear that Muslim reformers and publics perceived Renan's arguments as an attempt to justify denial of their rights in French colonies and beyond.[10] When William Muir wrote about the barbarism of Muslims because of the original delusions of Muhammad in 1860, or when William Hunter wrote about the innate unreliability of the Muslim subjects of the queen in India because of their political fanaticism in 1871, reformist Muslim intellectuals had to respond because these ideas impacted their rights and claims within European empires.

Thus, Pan-Islamism partly emerged as a counter-narrative against European imperial Islamophobia, and became instrumental in the formation of anti-colonial counter-public opinion, which was seen as necessary to demand political rights within existing empires and in the international domain. Muslim intellectuals attended Orientalist congresses in Europe to counter the discourses of their inferiority promulgated by European scholars.[11] In fact, critique of European Orientalism was always seen as essential for the defense of the rights of Muslims. Late Ottoman Pan-Islamist and author of the poem that became the Turkish national anthem, Mehmet

Akif Ersoy (1873–1936), praised Muhammed Abduh's critique of French Orientalist denigration of Islam as a necessary act to defend the rights of Muslims under French colonial rule: "To fight against Monsieur Hanotaux and defend the rights of millions of Muslims in the Western Islamic world is more of a good deed than centuries of futile piety."[12] Abduh wrote detailed refutations of the Islamophobic writings of Gabriel Hanotaux (1853–1944), the former minister of Foreign Affairs of France, who saw Islamic faith as a threat to French colonial rule and Western civilization due to its innate characteristics.

Muslim critique of European "civilizing mission ideology" often included the contradictions between noble ideals and violent practices. A Pan-Islamic Russian Muslim, Abdurreşid Ibrahim, narrates a conversation with a French traveler on a train in Russia: when the French person criticized that Russian behavior toward Muslims was uncivilized and unjust, İbrahim responded by saying,

> When there is might, there is no question of rights and truth. You French people treat Algerians like animals, insult their religion, and violate their human rights. If "civilized" nations like France are guilty of such a degree of injustice, oppression, and lack of clear consciousness, what can we expect from the Russians?[13]

The Pan-Islamic narrative was often about rights claims: Al-Afghani became a champion of the argument that

> Westerners [*gharbiyun*], despite their altruistic claims, are not trying to improve life in the East [*shark*] or to preserve the rights of Easterners, but to prolong the denial of these rights. The Westerners say their presence in the East is needed to safeguard Christian and other minorities and to teach liberty, but these are deceptive claims.[14]

Some of the earlier formulations of a global Muslim narrative of history and civilization may seem very harsh to Muslim practices and failures in the face of European colonialism. But even self-critique ended up contributing to the formation of modern Pan-Islamic identity. For example, in the 1870s, Jamaluddin al-Afghani blamed Muslim societies for creating the conditions for their colonization and humiliation at the opening of Istanbul University, both to explain why these societies had lost their rights under the hegemony of unjust European laws, and to offer a solution: reform and revival.

> My brothers, Arise from the sleep of neglect. Know that the Islamic people were [once] the strongest in rank, the most valuable in worth. . . . Later this people sank into ease and laziness. . . . Some of the Islamic nations came under the domination of other nations. The clothes of abasement were put on them. The glorious *milla* [nation] was humiliated.[15]

This self-condemnation and critique allowed for arguments for women's rights as essential for the self-improvement of Muslim societies in the struggle to gain their rights, as seen in a speech Al-Afghani gave in Egypt, Alexandria. "It is impossible to emerge from stupidity, from the prison of humiliation and distress, and from the depths of darkness and ignominy as long as women are deprived of rights and ignorant of their duties. . . ."[16] Pan-nationalist thought encouraged and facilitated a great outburst of demands for rights for Muslim, African, and Asian women, often from within a discourse of double critique: female intellectuals and their male supporters criticized the colonial and racist discourse that the lack of women's rights within their society was a sign of the inferiority of their civilization, while simultaneously criticizing the patriarchal customs and interpretation of religions that prevented women from holding full rights.[17]

Articulation and defense of rights through the languages of civilization, history, religion, and race ended up epistemologically reformatting Muslim intellectual heritages, re-coding them in a set of terms, concepts, and concerns that were palatable to their imagined Western audience. Those Muslim intellectuals who were dealing with the same set of questions and problems, such as stigmatization of their religion, Social Darwinist claims of lagging behind and decline, and racialization, produced narrative features in the content of the Pan-Islamic discourse of civilization from the 1880s to the 1920s, which still shape much of contemporary transnational Muslim thought. In addition to the secular idea of Islamic civilization,[18] Pan-Islamic intellectual networks built a plot of humiliation of Muslims by Western hegemony, in contrast to past glories, expressing a will to redeem the Muslim world's dignity in the future. They also created a historical consciousness of an eternal Muslim world–Christian West conflict, which was not historically accurate.

In short, the modern Muslim narrative of the globe did not emerge as a result of a contemplative process where intellectuals had the luxury to form a congress and share interpretations of the complex processes of empire, racialization, and globalization. It was shaped over half a century from the 1880s to the 1920s in a highly politicized context, with incremental changes, with the purpose to claim rights for discriminated Muslim populations either under European imperial rule, or in international law. Yet, there is clearly a gradual shift that is eventually looking like a silent revolution, a dramatic paradigm change. By the early twentieth century, the experience of imperial globalization fostered the emergence of a basic theme and outline, such as the story of a shared history of all Muslims societies in the world, distinct from European Christians, Hindus, and Chinese, and the trope of a golden age and decline, as well as the idea of the unjust/unfair treatment and humiliation of Muslim societies by European colonial powers.

## Reforming the Imperial World through the Power of Narratives

Narratives of the world are not political ideologies, but they can shape, motivate, and justify political formations, and they may have elected affinities with a set of political perceptions. Initially, the power of the Pan-Islamic narrative was aiming to reform and cure a globalizing imperial world order afflicted with different forms of racial discrimination and exclusions. All kinds of actors could utilize this narrative for their political projects and claims of rights in different locations.

Some Europeans who influenced the formation of Muslim narratives of the globe were sympathetic to a kind of Muslim empowerment as a tool of European imperial interests. In 1883, Wilfred Blunt wrote *The Future of Islam*, an influential book arguing that the Ottoman Empire would eventually be expelled from Europe due to Western Islamophobia and that Europe's crusading spirit would turn Istanbul into a Christian city. Blunt also claimed that the British Empire, supposedly lacking the hatred of Muslims that the Austrians, Russians, and French had, can become the protector of the Islamic world, which does not have any political leadership. In patronizing and imperial ways, Blunt seemed to care about the future of Muslims and their rights, and imagined an Islamic world in Asia under the protection of the British queen.[19]

Pan-Islamic as well as Pan-Asian and Pan-African civilizational narratives were never anti-Western. On the contrary, in terms of their normative content, they were affirming as well as universalizing many of the proclaimed universal values such as self-determination, racial equality, citizenship rights, and equality under law. Pan-Islamists believed in and advocated for the fair implementation of international law and establishment of international organizations such as the League of Nations that will not make a discrimination between white Christians and non-white populations.

None of the Pan-Islamists advocated for the isolation of Muslim societies, either from non-Muslim Asians and Africans, or from the West. In fact, their narrative of world history posited that humanity benefited from each civilization's contribution and from the interconnectivity of cultures, religions, and races. Their objection was mainly to the white supremacist interpretation of this global history of cultural contact and exchange, as Pan-Islamists did not see human diversity as a proof of the superiority of Western civilization and the white race. Thus, the postcolonial emphasis on the cultural authenticity of Islamic faith and or the national sovereignty of Muslim-majority countries was not originally intended to call for a return to a mythic past or even to deny the experience of Westernization of the globe. Here, the main concern was to find a fair and inclusive process of norm globalization, asking that the rules and values that will govern the post-racist world should include contributions from all civilizations and races. This was done through their constant demands to improve international law and international institutions to provide mechanisms extending justice and fairness to all populations across the world. Those calling for non-racist global norms and institutions did not initially advocate the end of imperial rule everywhere. In fact, some imagined that European empires could be reformed according to universal notions of justice and equality to accommodate pan-nationalists' demands and claims for rights. Yet in the aftermath of the Russo-Japanese War, there was a growing demand to end the era of empires in Asia. Halil Halid's book on Pan-Islamism concludes: "There is room for all desirable strangers in this hospitable continent of Asia, but empire-making by outsiders is henceforth forbidden."[20]

In this discursive strategy, there was still a commitment to the idea of the universal progress of world civilization. There was also a hope of addressing European public opinion in order to generate pressure to end colonialism. For example, Muhammad Barakatullah, who published the magazine *Islamic Fraternity* in Tokyo in 1911, hoped to convince an imagined European reader when he wrote the following about the Dutch colonial rule in Java:

> We do not desire to make political capital out of the unfortunate situation and hold the Dutch nation to the contempt of the civilized world. Our object in giving publicity to this account [of the barbarity of Dutch rulers in Indonesia] is simply to appeal to the conscience of the Dutch people that they may realize the enormity of the evil perpetrated by their representatives in the East Indies under the inhuman and barbarous system, or want of system, called government which they have sanctioned to exist in their possessions in the Indian Archipelago.[21]

It is because of the racial equality claims of the competing narratives of the global order in early twentieth century that the Russo-Japanese War of 1905 became interpreted as a proof of the fallacy of racial hierarchies in the world, and strengthened the persuasive power and confidence in critiques of Eurocentric ideas by Pan-Islamic, Pan-African, and Pan-Asian intellectuals. Indeed, the Japanese victory contributed immensely to the reconsideration in the scientific literature on race at the 1911 Universal Races Congress, an event that indicated the global impact of the ideas and critiques of non-Western intellectuals.[22]

Shukri al-Asali, a Syrian member of the Ottoman Parliament, expressed this vision of Asians and Africans gaining their collective rights in relation to Europe in internationalist language in 1911:

> The East Awakened . . . we have not yet reached the middle of the century but . . . Asia has become like Europe today . . . moving with Europe and America in the way of progress and success by the end of the twentieth century. Perhaps this lifeblood (patriotism) will creep into the Negroes of Africa and the peoples of Zanzibar and the Congo and Morocco in the beginning of this next century. . . . After that you will see each people ruling itself by itself, and ending the greedy ambitions of the Western nations. Perhaps that depends on the result of uniting the peoples of Asia before (the West's) ambitions. Thus an international court will be established and will solve problems. . . . Attention would be diverted away from wars, and if there were wars, they would be economic wars and boycotts.[23]

It is from this half-century background of Pan-Islamic narratives of global order that we can make sense of their mobilization after World War I: the extraordinary excitement surrounding the universalist proclamations of Woodrow Wilson and Vladimir Lenin, as well as at the Paris Peace Conference and the League of Nations, was not because Muslims were suddenly inspired by the prophetic visions of white saviors, but because they saw this as the fulfillment of their own demands.[24] At the same time, disappointment with the League due to the perpetuation of European imperial violence toward populations in Africa and Asia further empowered pan-nationalist mobilization and moral claims in the 1920s. When Indian Muslims in the Pan-Islamic Khilafat movement wrote telegrams to the League of Nations in September 1925 advocating for the rights and freedoms of Muslims in the Rif region of Morocco who were resisting Spanish colonial aggression, they highlighted both their Muslim sensibilities and universal notions of rights that they assumed they shared with the principals of the League:

> We Musalmans of Delhi, India's historic capital, assembled in Jami Masjid or Cathedral Mosque after Friday Service to offer prayers to almighty God for success of our Rifi brothers against despoilers of their freedom declare that while we repose our trust in God alone, eyes of entire Muslim World and of East are fixed upon League of Nations today and they desire to ascertain if League is to be guardian of rights and liberties of mankind and righteous instrument of peace or merely confederacy of big three or four among Christian powers of Europe for robbing weak nonchristian and eastern nations and peoples through unrighteous war and exploitation of their freedom and resources.[25]

## Coupling Geopolitical Power with the Power of Civilizational Narratives

Different actors of pan-nationalist narratives have reached a common realization that they cannot achieve their goals by simply shaming the European public through an exposition of colonial violence or by appealing to international law and universal values. As Chinese leader Sun Yat-Sen eloquently summarized in his speech on Great Asianism in Kobe in 1924, "But to rely on benevolence alone to influence the Europeans in Asia to relinquish the privileges they have acquired in China would be an impossible dream. If we want to regain our rights, we must resort to force."[26]

As the chapters on China and India in this volume show, competing Asian narratives of the global order can be appropriated by different state and imperial actors. Every time an actor appropriates and utilizes a grand narrative claim, it refashions it for a particular political purpose, and this may end up tarnishing the universalist moral claims of each narrative as kingdoms, states, empires, or even international organizations may also betray some of the values of each civilizational universalism.

Pan-Islamic narratives of the global order emerged in a truly inter-imperial context in the late nineteenth century, but at some point, the Ottoman Empire symbolized the hopes of the colonized Muslims in Asia and Africa, while pragmatically using this Pan-Islamic sympathy in its demands to belong to Europe as an equal imperial member. Until the eve of World War I, the Ottoman government presented the caliphate title of their monarch as a spiritual sovereign of the Muslim populations partly to bolster a geopolitical alliance with the British against Russia. The utilization of the Pan-Islamism for radical and revolutionary diplomacy in Asia and Africa can be traced back to the response to the 1911 Italian invasion of the Ottoman North African province. Ottoman territorial losses after the Italian invasion of the Ottoman province of Libya in 1911 led to broader public opinion mobilization across Muslim societies from India to West Africa. Italian actions were a clear violation of international law, yet European powers did not intervene to censure Italians and defend the legal rights of the Ottomans in international law. Indian Muslims mobilized to pressure London to intervene on the Ottoman side against Italian violation of international norms, arguing that Britain, as the largest Muslim empire in the world, had a moral responsibility to help the Ottomans. A manifesto issued by Muslim students in Edinburgh quoted this line from Turkish newspaper before asking Muslims to collect donations to strengthen the Ottoman navy: "treaties are concocted by European powers to mislead and cheat, to be torn up and jettisoned whenever necessary."[27] It was during this period that Ottoman military forces were identified as the last army of Islam, a slogan that would be repeated during World War I.[28]

During the Ottoman mobilization against Italy, Ottoman elites argued that the survival and strength of the Ottoman Empire were linked to the future of Islam and the Muslim world. Presenting inter-imperial wars as a clash between civilization and races was a common way to perceive, interpret, and narrate international affairs during the first two decades of the twentieth century. The Balkan Wars of 1912–1913 further confirmed the Ottoman elite's conviction that the policy of utilizing international law to defend their empire had not worked. Following two years of bitter fighting which witnessed the displacement of a large Muslim population from the Balkans to the Ottoman interior, as well as a series of massacres, the Ottoman state was forced to cede almost all of its European territories to the coalition of the Balkan states.[29] This event was perceived within European conservative circles as a necessary expulsion of barbaric Muslim Turks from civilized Europe, and there was an excitement among broader European publics during the Bulgarian military assault on the Ottoman capital city of Istanbul that the city could be returned to its former Christian identity.[30] European sympathy for the massacres committed by Christians against the Muslim population in the Balkans led to a Pan-Islamic perception that there was a new "Christian crusade" of Europe against the Muslim world and that Ottoman Turkey had to consider new policies.

The Balkan Wars demonstrated the significance of the states that gained independence from Ottoman rule, such as Greece, Serbia, Bulgaria, and Montenegro, in building the clash of civilizations narrative, as they justified their wars with the claims that Muslim Ottomans cannot have any sovereignty in the sacred Christian lands of Europe. The sense of disappointment with the failure of Ottoman elites to appeal to European international law to defend their sovereignty and presence in Balkans was articulated by Celal Nuri, a Young Turk intellectual, writing on racial politics of international law on the eve of World War I in a book titled *International Law from Our Perspective*:

> There is not one, but two, kinds of international law. One for us, and one for them, the Europeans. Europe's morality and consciousness is [*sic*] also not one but two. One never feels empathy with our suffering and catastrophe. [In reference to watching lions tearing apart the human beings in ancient Rome], there is some Roman blood in the veins of every European . . . if you scratch the skin of any European today, you could discover a crusader under it.[31]

Despite Ottoman elites' disillusionment with the failures of their strategy to defend sovereignty through European international law, however, until the eve of World War I, the Ottoman government refrained from promotion of an anti-imperialist and anti-European notion of the caliphate and

Pan-Islamism. The Ottoman elites could utilize several other narratives for its legitimacy, such as the ideal of civilized empire, or the law of nations in Europe. But, when the Ottoman government joined World War I on the side of the German Empire, both the Ottoman and German leaders decided to pragmatically benefit from the moral claims and power of Pan-Islamic public opinion and narratives, and declared holy war against Allied empires in November 1914. The Ottoman call for geopolitical jihad invited colonized Muslims to revolt against British, French, and Russian empires on behalf of the caliphate, while simultaneously articulating the necessity of respecting the sovereignty of every nation or kingdom, including Persia and Afghanistan. Muslims under French, Russian, and British rule rejected this Ottoman call for holy war, and served their empires as soldiers. We should here note that the notorious Ottoman jihad proclamation was announced in the context of a firm formal alliance with the German Empire, seen as a sign of the Ottoman Empire's belonging to the European club of empires. Thus, Ottoman policies during World War I illustrate how a medium power can utilize multiple narratives simultaneously by synthesizing them, arguing that they belong to Europe and uphold true international law, while declaring European empires in Asia as vicious and bankrupt. Ottoman use of the caliphate as a tool of warfare during World War I increased anti-Ottoman racialization in Europe as well as in America, with Ottomans depicted as "terrible Turks" representing the worst militaristic aspects of Islam.

After the defeat of the Ottoman-German campaign in World War I, ironically, Pan-Islamism continued to be used for revolutionary diplomacy more effectively by former Young Turk leaders and Turkish nationalists in the context of the Bolshevik Revolution and the rise of Wilsonianism.[32] The Bolshevik Revolution gave the earlier socialist narrative of the world a stronger state support. The Bolsheviks promoted a non-civilizational universalist narrative based on class struggle. But in early stages of the Revolution, from 1918 to 1922, Bolshevik leaders themselves hoped to benefit from the revolutionary potential of the Pan-Islamic critique of European imperialism, and claimed to speak on behalf of oppressed Muslims and Orientals, allying with World War I era Ottoman leaders who were in exile in Europe after the defeat.

An official Ottoman government memorandum at the Paris Peace Conference claimed a majority Turkish rule in Anatolia according to Wilsonian principles, while still bolstering this claim with arguments for the civility of Muslims and Islam's compatibility with European values. This

Ottoman memorandum was rejected by the great powers with a thesis that Ottoman Muslim leaders exhibited uncivilized and un-European Asiatic behavior, and thus were undeserving of self-determination. With a similar Eurocentric argument of civilization, the British Empire encouraged and authorized the Greek Kingdom's invasion of western Turkey in May 1919. Article 142 of the Treaty of Sèvres that ended the Allied powers' war with the Ottoman Empire, signed in August 1920, described the Ottoman state as a terrorist state, reaffirming an anti-Muslim narrative of European civilizational superiority.

It is in this context of the Greek invasion of Anatolia and the Sèvres treaty that Muslim elite of the Ottoman Empire tried to leverage Pan-Islamic narratives, with Bolshevik support, in their struggles against the Allied plans to divide Ottoman territories from 1919 to 1923. Therefore, the Pan-Islamic ideal of Muslim solidarity was meant to aid the Turkish war of independence. Former Ottoman leaders (Enver, Talat, and Cemal) established links with Moscow and Berlin, as well as Tehran, Ankara, and Kabul, to remake Asia based on the principles of Muslim awakening and liberation, and the notion of self-determination based on both Wilsonian principles and the Bolshevik Revolution.[33] It is in this context that Indian Muslims, with support from Hindu nationalists, created an extraordinary mobilization under the banner of the Khilafat movement in support of the Turkish war of independence. Indian Muslim leaders condemned the Sèvres Treaty as a violation of all the moral principles of world order and the promises made to them by the British. Khilafat movement leader Muhammed Ali was in France when the Sèvres Treaty was announced, and he made the following speech:

> Is there any shameless Turk in this assembly or at Versailles or in Constantinople or even in the camp of Mustafa Kamal who is prepared to sign this treaty, then tell him as we have told Lloyd George and the Viceroy of India—we at least will not accept this treaty. . . . If you look at this question from our religious point of view this treaty is unacceptable to us, and remember there are more than 300 million Musalmans in the world, in India, Turkey, Algeria, Morocco, Asia Minor, Egypt and Central Asia, whose religious obligations are being disregarded in this treaty. Again there are distinct pledges which had been given to us and which have got to be respected by you and by England. If they are disregarded today remember you who are a banking nation . . . that a dishonoured cheque is not accepted twice. We ask for no gratitude for anything that we may have done for France or

> England but I say this to you that if the Indian soldiers knew that after their defense of France and of England and after victories of Mesopotamia (Iraq) and Palestine, not British victories but Indian victories, if they had known that this would be the kind of treaty that would result from their victories, they would not have come to your aid in those dark hours of October 1914.[34]

It is with this Pan-Islamic support from the Khilafat movement both financially and morally, and with Bolshevik encouragement, that the Turkish war of independence defeated the British-supported Greek forces in Anatolia, canceled the Sèvres Treaty, and renegotiated a new peace as a victorious military power. This background should help us understand why the Turkish national delegation at the Lausanne Treaty negotiations that created the peace in the post-Ottoman Middle East during 1922–1923 can exhibit a commitment and reinterpretation of European international law or European notions of sovereignty and nationhood, while appealing to the collective power of the Muslim world and the East against Western hegemony. This commitment to belong to Europe and discourses of representing the discriminated yet awakening Muslim world were seen as complementary by Ottoman elites, not contradictory. The Lausanne delegation, thus, continued to utilize a hybrid mix of different narratives of the Ottoman elite in interpreting and solving their problems: the twentieth-century Ottoman claim of leadership in the Muslim world was an extension of its investment in Eurocentric global governance and laws, and, ironically, the so-called Caliphate Pan-Islamism aimed to correct, tame, and reform the norms of the European law of nations, which was seen as prejudiced toward Ottomans due to "Eastern question" diplomacy. Similarly, Pan-Islamist discourses that peaked from the 1911 Italian invasion of Libya to the Lausanne negotiations of 1923 were part of a problem of unequal treatment of Ottomans in parallel to the unequal treatment of Muslim populations in colonial empires of Asia and Africa, and did not mean a rejection of European laws and order. Thus, both the late Ottoman elites and the delegation that represented the Ankara government at Lausanne could see a Muslim modernist critique of European islamophobia, Pan-Islamic notions of clash of civilizations, as well as a universalist language of sovereign equality of their state in international law, as complementary to each other, not contradictory. As Turkish Foreign Minister Tevfik Rüştü Aras confided in Joseph Grew, US ambassador to Turkey, "Europe had repeatedly ejected Turkey by the door, but Turkey had invariably returned through the window." Furthermore, Aras made known his conviction that "Turkey was and always would be essentially European," although it was declined to be so.[35] It is important to note that, even though Turkish nationalists benefited from Pan-Islamic mobilization in India, there was no alternative to the European-centered international order for the new Turkey or the Ottoman Empire in 1923.

The Turkish nationalist government's use and utilization of Pan-Islamic narratives and support in its negotiation with the Allied powers and in securing its achievements of the Lausanne Treaty illustrate a crucial aspect of the relationship between narratives and state powers. Each state, in trying to own a particular civilizational narrative, inevitably revises the narrative for its geopolitical purposes, and what was done by Turkey can be seen in the way Iran, Egypt, Saudi Arabia, or Pakistan used Pan-Islamism in the twentieth century. When these countries leveraged their limited geopolitical power by utilizing the narrative power of Pan-Islamism, they also faced the risks of a small or medium geopolitical power using a global narrative. Some grand narratives to remake the unequal world with promises of justice to oppressed or discriminated societies can also be a burden for medium or large state actors who cannot deliver the emancipatory promises due to their limited military and economic might.

The post-Ottoman Turkish Republic decided to recalibrate and refashion the political implications of both Pan-Islamic and Western civilizational narratives after they secured the sovereignty of their borders at Lausanne in 1923. Turkish nationalists perceived and presented their diplomatic achievements as a re-inclusion of their state back into Europe, after more than a half century of struggle against racial treatment and unequal international law.[36] According to the new Turkish national narrative, the world order that excluded the Ottomans from 1856 to 1914, and eventually included the Republic in 1923 with recognition of legal equality (sovereignty without capitulations), was the same European imperial world order. Founders of the Turkish Republic presented their achievement as the fulfillment of their right to self-determination as Muslim Turks in Anatolia in 1923, but they were not imagining a decolonized world without civilizational hierarchies or empires. After all, the Arab populations of the Ottoman Empire were subjected to a mandate regime justified by claims of their inferiority in civilization, and racialized empires continued in Asia and Africa. Thus, despite their full sovereignty without extraterritorial laws or unequal treaties as assured with the Lausanne Treaty, the leaders of the Turkish Republic still felt they could face exclusion due to religious or racial difference. At that point, instead of continuing the late Ottoman attempt to prove that Muslims deserved respect, rights, and equality, the Turkish government changed its cultural diplomacy approach by promoting an idea that Turks are European and white.

During the interwar period from the 1924 abolishment of the caliphate to the end of World War II in 1945, Pan-Islamic critiques of the imperial world order continued to be shared publics and leaders of colonized Muslim societies. But the narrative gradually became reinterpreted in light of the new norms of nationalism, self-determination, and Westernization. After the last Ottoman caliph was sent into exile in March 1924 by the Turkish Parliament, the Turkish government initiated a set of radical Westernization reforms to empower the new Republic's domestic stability and international legitimacy. During the interwar period, the delegitimization of Western colonial rule became stronger, while Pan-Islamic narratives merged closely with multiple nationalist movements and imaginations, from Egypt and India to Indonesia. Within the diversity of political experiences, the main Pan-Islamic networks became active within the British Empire, especially around the concerns for the destiny of Palestinian Muslims under the threat of a British mandate working to implement Zionist projects. It was in Jerusalem that the most successful interwar-era Pan-Islamic Muslim world conference was held in 1931. Turkish, Persian, and Afghan governments did not send representatives to this Pan-Islamic congress in Jerusalem, as it was hosted by a nongovernmental body with the aim of dealing with religious issues of Muslims under colonial rule. But Arab-Indian Muslim activists who gathered in Jerusalem in 1931 continued to articulate a vision of imperial and post-imperial world order that gives Muslim populations equality, dignity, and sovereignty.

The interwar-era imperial world order made modest norm adjustment through the League of Nations, accepting several Muslim-majority countries as equal members without the stigma of unequal treaties. At the end of this seemingly chaotic interwar period, the Axis empires revived the political imagination of the Pan-Islamic narrative by adopting the Muslim world's liberation from Allied empires as part of their war propaganda. Throughout World War II, Mussolini's Italy, Hirohito's Japan, as well as the Soviet Union, Great Britain, and the United States, also formulated their own special propaganda and plans regarding the Muslim world, trying to gain favor in public opinion to harness the political power of Muslim populations, which were still seen as united in religious and political outlook. All the Axis empire propaganda toward the Muslim societies reflected an awareness of the dominant Muslim narratives of the global order that Muslims have been unfairly discriminated and colonized by modern Europe, which claimed to civilize them but instead imposed on Muslims a modern version of white Christian supremacy. Because Axis empires had promised independence and emancipation for colonized Muslim societies, the new United Nations–based international order also had to appeal to norms of self-determination and allow the entrance of Muslim-majority countries as equal members.

## Muslim Narratives of the Global in the Post-Imperial World

In the decade from the end of World War II until the Bandung Conference of 1955, most of the Muslim-majority societies in the world gained their independence. At the Bandung gathering of African and Asian nations, fourteen out of thirty participating countries were of a Muslim majority (Afghanistan, Egypt, Indonesia, Iran, Iraq, Jordan, Lebanon, Libya, Pakistan, Saudi Arabia, Syria, Sudan, Turkey, Yemen).[37] It is important to note that this gathering of the official representatives of the new Muslim-majority nations, in a Muslim-majority city, was a third-world internationalist one under the leadership of secular nationalists, embracing a Afro-Asian narrative of the global order, not an explicitly Pan-Islamic one. Even though anti-colonial Muslim leaders tried to create their own independent nation-states, the speeches at the Bandung Conference reflected the legacies of earlier Pan-Islamic (as well as Pan-Asian) critiques and demands about the imperial world order, and delegates emphasized the significance of their Muslim or Asian identities.[38] In fact, African American socialist intellectual and journalist Richard Wright wrote about "the Color Curtain" as being more important for Asian and African leaders than the "Iron Curtain" of the Cold War when he witnessed the traces of Islamic, Asian, and African narratives of the global order in various speeches at the Bandung Conference. In the year of the Bandung Conference, a journal named *Progressive Islam*, published in Amsterdam by young Muslim intellectuals in the English language, started their commentary on colonialism and racism with this paragraph:

> In the last issue, we have dealt with the traits of colonialism and their rationalization put forward by the colonial powers. The traits were the following: the colour line, the political control of the colony by the colonizing

> power, the economic dependence of the colony on the colonizing country, the appallingly low standard of social service, and the lack of contact between the ruling power and the natives of the colony. These traits were respectively rationalized by the following ideas: the superiority of the white race, the incapability of the colony for self-rule, the incapability of the natives to exploit economically the country, the financial insufficiency of the government, and the culturally and intellectually lower position of the natives. In this issue, we are presenting the refutation of all these rationalized ideas.[39]

From the perspective of the Bandung moment in the mid-1950s, redemptive nationalism, coupled with self-modernization projects, may look like an end of history for political imaginations about Muslim societies. It seems as if Muslims could resolve their problems with the imperial and racial world order of the preceding century by gaining sovereignty and independence as nation-states and as members of the United Nations. Egypt, Iran, Turkey, Syria, Lebanon, India, and Saudi Arabia were founding members of the United Nations in 1945, with Afghanistan, Yemen, Pakistan, and Indonesia joining the UN by 1950. Yet, behind and beyond the process of nation-state formation in Muslim-majority countries, there were still influences of the late-nineteenth-century Pan-Islamic narratives of the global order in terms of seeing this process as a correction of the injustices done to the Muslim world, and in terms of expecting the UN system to remedy past and present injustices. In that sense, the Pan-Islamist story of the world order was affirming some of the new international institutions and norms while continuing to present the decolonization process as an incomplete project of full emancipation and equality.

The partitions of India and Palestine both contributed to the persistence of a distinct Muslim discontent and narrative of the new world order centered at the United Nations. There was a temporary Muslim solidarity at the UN General Assembly in opposition to the partition of Palestine in November 1947, but that unity was not sustained in the aftermath of the vote. There were 13 voting members, out of 56 total members of the UN at that point, that voted against the partition plan, and 10 of these were Muslim-majority countries (Afghanistan, Iran, Iraq, Lebanon, Pakistan, Saudi Arabia, Syria, Yemen, Turkey, and Egypt). India also supported this Muslim bloc of 10 UN member states. The British Empire, still wielding large Muslim populations under its rule, chose abstention in that vote, together with several other countries with significant Muslim populations—namely China, Yugoslavia, Thailand, and Ethiopia—which illustrates the perceived impact of the symbolism of the Palestine question to interwar-era Pan-Islamic public opinion.[40] Upon the recognition of Israel as a member of the UN, and as a sovereign country, Turkey and Iran recognized the state of Israel. In fact, throughout the Cold War, Muslim-majority countries took contradictory positions in opposite Cold War camps, some advocating an alliance with the US, and others with the Soviet Union. Highly symbolically, for example, NATO member Turkey did not vote in favor of the resolutions supporting Algeria's right to self-determination, due to its prioritizing of Turkish-French relations over its ties to Algeria. Turkish diplomats were aware of the historic ties between Algeria and Turkey, as well as the respect shown by Algerians to Mustafa Kemal Atatürk, who was hailed as a great nationalist Muslim hero. Yet, Turkish diplomats felt the need to align their national interests as a NATO member with the French government's arguments and position.[41]

Postcolonial era Muslim leaders and intellectuals tried to reform and remake the world order while accepting the reality of the nation-state-based UN system as the main normative framework. As the broader decolonization of Muslim societies from World War I until the 1970s lasted about four decades, there was a tendency to see this process almost as a jigsaw puzzle over a map of the world. The emergence of a post-imperial world of independent nation-states was almost complete by the mid-1970s, with the emergence of about forty Muslim majority-state members of the UN General Assembly. Because of the ongoing struggle for independence by Palestinians and others, however, the process seemed incomplete. There was a conviction that with norm-producing internationalist solidarity of Third World-ism, socialist internationalism, Pan-Arabism, and Pan-Africanism, the Palestine question could also be solved.

Muslim decolonization and nationalist modernization projects created an altered problem space for postcolonial Muslim political leaders and elites, and favored the adoption of new narratives of the global that de-emphasized the earlier obsession with Muslim identity and civilizational essence. Yet, this refashioning of a narrative of the global without a focus on Muslim identity seemed to upset the traditional terms of Western Orientalists and international relations scholars. These intellectuals, like their forebears for at least a century, tended to bundle all Muslims into a single geopolitical, racial, and religious group and to explain their politics primarily by reference to their shared religion. By the early 1960s, however, it had come to seem even to this group as though Islam was unimportant in world politics dominated by secular nationalisms and internationalisms as well as the strategic exigencies of the Cold War. When the Duke University Committee on International Relations held an interdisciplinary conference on Islam and international relations in 1963, in the aftermath of Algerian independence and at the peak of Cold War rivalries, the twenty-six participating scholars could not agree on what role Islam played in global politics. According to a book collecting papers from the symposium, "Most of the principal speakers maintained that Islam is actually of quite limited significance in shaping the attitudes and behavior of Muslim states in international relations today, but others differed sharply and few were prepared to dismiss its relevance altogether."[42] Indeed, symposium participants not only paid attention to policy differences among majority-Muslim countries but also rejected essentialist generalizations about Islam and the Muslim world. When the political scientist Dankwart Rustow quoted Bernard Lewis's 1953 claim of affinity between Islam and communism because both "profess a totalitarian doctrine, with complete and final answers to all questions on heaven and earth," and both harbor the "aggressive fanaticism of the believer"—the utterly different content of these beliefs being apparently insignificant—he did so in order to challenge and dismiss Lewis's argument.[43] The place of Muslim identity in world politics was, at this point, so multifaceted that it was no longer possible to maintain narratives of unitary Pan-Islamism as both European and Muslim intellectuals had in the 1878–1924 period.

Another kind of intellectual debate cropped up in academic circles as decolonization proceeded into the early 1970s, as some scholars wondered if Muslim's faith in the *ummah* was compatible with the reality of fifty nation-states.[44] In practice, this was an idle concern, as independent nation-states fulfilled the political and theological demands of many Muslims. Historically, it is even more irrelevant, as Muslims were never politically united during the previous millennium. Nationalism, socialism, and liberalism seemed to replace imperial-era Muslim narratives with new master narratives of nationalism and Cold War, even though they could accommodate the persistence of transnational Muslim identities, whether applied to politics, historical consciousness, charities, religious organizations, tourism, education, sports, or popular culture.

The rapid process of decolonization altered the problem space of the imperial-era Pan-Islamic narrative, and there emerged multiple new and compelling reinterpretations and new narratives. For example, from the late 1950s to 1967, Jean Paul Sartre's existentialism became the most influential and popular philosophy in the postcolonial Arab countries. Sartre's leftist philosophy of engagement was empowering the Arab intellectuals who believed that late development of the Arab societies was caused by colonial hegemony and capitalism, and that new Arab generations can work together, in solidarity with other progressive people, to create the new Arab nations, free from all kinds of political, economic, and social subjugations. The success of the Algerian war of independence, which was supported by the European left as well as global Third World and socialist blocs from China and Indonesia to Brazil, gave hope that with similar global solidarity and freedom-oriented ideologies, all Arab societies could gain their emancipation and attain economic prosperity and development.[45]

From 1945 to mid-1975, the older forms of Pan-Islamic narratives of the global order faded away, and were replaced with new paradigms, but certain themes and aspects of this narrative never completely disappeared. It seemed as if some of the ideas of old Pan-Islamic civilizational narratives were lurking behind the big geopolitical narratives of the Cold War and decolonization. The popularity of Arnold Toynbee's (1889–1975) ideas about world history of civilizations, for example, became a means to refashion older Muslim narratives of the global order in the postcolonial Cold War context.[46] Toynbee's historical framework depicting Islamic civilization as one of the last surviving world civilizations resisting the materialist and destructive aspect of Western civilization appealed to different ideological currents in the postcolonial Middle East and Islamicate societies for diverse reasons. Especially intellectuals who were later called Islamists, due to their critique of Westernizing reforms initiated by nationalist regimes of Turkey, Iran, or Egypt, embraced Toynbee's world historical model because this model allowed them to offer a critique of Eurocentrism and secular nationalism at the same time. For example, Turkish Islamist Sezai Karakoç relied on Toynbee's ideas in formulating an Islamic revival as an alternative to both socialism and capitalism. In its Islamist version, a Toynbean model of modern world history reduced the Cold War versions of the US- or the Soviet Union-promoted model of modernity to a product of Western Christian civilization. Beyond that, this association of modernity with Western civilization tied all the dark sides of modern times (colonialism, destructive wars, corruption of Third World political elites) to Western hegemony. According to some utopian Muslim readers of Toynbee, however, one could escape from the decadence of the secular modernism of the contemporary West to a synthesis of the good aspects of modernity and Islamic civilization. Different Muslim intellectuals from various political orientations in the 1970s imagined solutions to the problems of the postcolonial world by returning to or resurrecting Islamic civilization, but they seemed like a minority opinion in relation to nationalist, socialist, and liberal Muslim narratives of that period.

## Late Cold War Geopolitical Rivalries and Refashioning of a New Pan-Islamic Narrative

Given the appeal of nationalist, socialist, liberal, or Cold War narratives of the world order among Muslim majority societies from 1945 to 1975, the re-emergence of an imperial-era Pan-Islamic narrative about an unjust international order discriminating against Muslims in the late Cold War period needs closer examination. If there were injustices in the international order, various forms of internationalism, ranging from Third World alliance to socialist solidarity, were promising to fix and reform this system. Yet, various Cold War rivalries and perceived failures of postcolonial nationalist claims of salvation of oppressed Muslims encouraged a new version of the Pan-Islamic narrative of the world order.

Saudi Arabian King Faisal played a crucial role in refashioning the legacy of imperial-era Pan-Islamic narratives of the world order to serve the interest of his Kingdom. Faisal established a transnational network of Muslim organizations around himself, primarily to bolster Saudi Arabia's legitimacy against the challenge of Nasserism, while encouraging an interstate solidarity of Muslim nations to deal with shared problems, such as the Palestinian question. The Cold War Pan-Islamism project promoted by Saudi Arabia gained some level of appeal in Muslim publics in other countries in the mid-1970s, especially after the 1973 Arab-Israeli War, leading to the expectation that a Muslim solidarity could create enough global pressure to solve the Palestinian question.[47] Especially after the disillusionment with the Camp David Accords, a vocal group began to advocate that the postcolonial project of remaking the world order to give Muslim populations dignity and equality failed, and what Muslim populations need is a geopolitical and civilizational solidarity across the globe to achieve their full redemption from the legacy of colonial humiliation. In the aftermath of the Iranian Revolution and the Soviet invasion of Afghanistan, the 1980s witnessed a resurgence of a new Pan-Islamic narrative of the global that looks similar to the late-nineteenth-century imperial-era narratives, but that is radically different in content.

How could the historical narratives of the Muslim world's unjust colonization by the Christian West be revived so rapidly in the postcolonial context of the Cold War? Part of the reason for this easy revival of the narrative was the fact that the early twentieth-century Muslim narrative of humiliation by the imperial West became a foundational trope of various Arab, Persian, Turkish, Malay, and Indonesian nationalisms, which was then transcribed in school textbooks as part of the story of national awakening. Because the ancient regime of the postcolonial nation-states, namely European empires, relied on the story of Western civilization and the white man's burden, anticolonial nationalism embraced a counter-narrative of Islamic civilization to intellectually ground its claims of national freedom.

The Cold War–era revival of the Pan-Islamic civilizational narrative was not an idea planned in Mecca by King Faisal and other Saudi leaders and disseminated to the rest of the Muslim societies. There were many other actors interested in a new solidarity of the Muslim world in an age of nationalism desperately looking for a Muslim great power, a Muslim leader, or a sponsor. Moreover, a UN-based vision of Muslim solidarity in international affairs to bring justice to their causes was not necessarily anti-American in its earlier Cold War version and assumed a working relationship with both the United States and the Soviet Union by uniting a passive Muslim world. For example, on the eve of the 1967 War between Israel and the Arab states, Pakistan's Jamaat-i Islami published several of Mawdudi's speeches on the *Unity of the Muslim World*. The introduction to this book by Khurshid Ahmad encapsulates the UN-based vision of the international politics of Muslim unity:

> Muslims today constitute one-fifth of the Human race. Muslim states in the U.N. go to make up about one-fourth of its total membership. Africa is the Muslim continent, 60 percent of its population believes in the Unity of God and the Prophethood of Muhammad (peace be upon him). Muslim countries contain huge quantities of some of the most important minerals and economic resources of the world. The racial and physical stock of their populations is one of the best in the world. They possess the great ideology of Islam, which can lead mankind out of its contemporary crisis, generated by the conflict of Godless, amoral and lop-sided ideologies of Communism and Secularism. And despite all this, Muslims have no effective voice in

> the world affairs. They have become passive camp-followers of others. Imperialist powers of the East and the West are active in their lands. Their basic problems remain unattended, what to say [*sic*] of their solution. Palestine bleeds. Kahmiris groan. Turkish Cypriots cry. Eritrian Muslims are being crushed. Nigerians are being subjected to sabotage from within. Somalians grumble and protest. But all these voices of agony and anguish fall on deaf ears. Problems are becoming more and more aggravated. [The] Situation is worsening and we, the six hundred and fifty million Muslims stand bewildered and aghast, helpless spectators of our own ruin. This is a paradox and we must wriggle ourselves out of this unhappy state of affairs. The answer to this situation is that the Muslims must sincerely remodel their individual and collective life in accord with the principles of Islam and pool their resources to play their rightful role in the world. It is through Islamic Revival and Islamic Unity that we can change the course of events and fulfil our tryst with destiny. Mualana Maududi has called the Muslim World, particularly its thinking elements, to this strategy.[48]

In detail, however, this book, published before the 1967 War, cannot predict a revival of the geopolitical claims over the Pan-Islamic narrative in the 1980s. Critiques of cultural Westernization of postcolonial nation-states and a call for the revival of authentic Islamic traditions, in response to the crisis of the Cold War–era world order, turned into a new utopian ideology after the Iranian Revolution in 1979.[49] The Cold War refashioning of the Pan-Islamic narrative shows that contested narratives are never insular, as they constantly allow cross-pollination of ideas, concepts, and frameworks. Muslim narratives during the Cold War, for example, embraced and appropriated ideas from both the US-led capitalist and the Soviet-led socialist blocs, calling the West exploitative, imperialist, and godless. Islamist slogans during the Cold War described the twentieth century not as a century of enlightenment and freedom, but as a century of continuous exploitation, ignorance, and violence. There was also something temporal about this Islamist discourse in that the critique of nationalism increased after the perceived failure of the postcolonial Asian and African states to remake the world as a more egalitarian space. Without this perceived failure of the promises of postcolonial nationalism, socialism, and liberalism to remake the world, Islamist narrative would not be able to attract advocates.

When a Christian Zionist set fire to the pulpit of the third most sacred site for Muslims in Jerusalem in August 1969, King Faisal bin Abdulaziz bin Saud of Saudi Arabia called for a summit of leaders of Muslim-majority countries. Held that year on September 25 in the Moroccan capital of Rabat, the summit brought together Iran's shah, Turkey's foreign minister, Pakistan's prime minister, and many other leaders. It was the first gathering of representatives from independent countries in the name of Muslim-world solidarity. Just a few years earlier, an event of the sort probably would not have attracted such high-placed officials. During the 1965 Arab Summit, King Faisal had proposed a meeting of global Muslim leaders, but in the heyday of Egyptian president Gamal Abdel Nasser's secular nationalism, plans for a meeting of only Muslim leaders never got off the ground. Events change minds, though, creating space for new politics. In this case, it was military defeat in 1967, when Nasser and his allies tried to liberate Palestine, along with the humiliation and sense of urgency brought about by the 1969 arson, that altered the political context. Secular nationalist Muslim leaders came to recognize common problems facing Muslim populations divided across national boundaries and accepted the Saudi king's invitation.

A new political project of Pan-Islamic solidarity became a function of the contingent political struggles of the 1970s. One set of intellectual and geopolitical conditions fostered a climate of opinion receptive to King Faisal's pan-Islamic initiatives, and another redirected that pan-Islamism to more radical goals after the 1973 Arab-Israeli War. The tensions were inescapable after Camp David, where Egypt was seen as abandoning the project of redeeming the humiliation of Muslims by agreeing to a separate peace with Israel and shutting out the Palestinians, whose cause had become essential to pan-Islamic thought. The unexpected and unthinkable 1979 Islamic Revolution was born of this resurgent geopolitical pan-Islamism and also complicated it. Asserting his own claim to leadership of the Muslim world, Imam Khomeini articulated many pan-Islamic grievances concerning humiliating Western imperialism and US hegemony in the Middle East. He and his followers dissolved the shah's alliance with Israel and the United States and turned over the Israeli embassy to the Palestine Liberation Organization. Sometimes, narratives that may look puritanical and religious can be a product of the cross-pollination of ideas, without an acknowledgment of the source. Khomeini's depiction of the US as a Great Satan appropriated all the postcolonial narratives of neo-imperialism and a narrative of the clash between Islam and the West, and appealed to publics who were disappointed with the perceived (and real) "hypocrisy" of the Western powers in late Cold War period. There were many socialist and Third World anti-imperialist narratives in Khomeini's seemingly Muslim narrative. Iran financed projects committed to pan-Islamic geopolitical solidarity, effectively competing with the sponsorship role the Saudis had embraced under Faisal. Yet, Khomeini's Iran and its regional rival Saudi Arabia both privileged the national interest of their states. More importantly, Iran's competition with Saudi Arabia devolved into sectarianism and led to a battle of divergent visions of the Muslim world up to the present. When multiple medium-power state actors tried to own and use the Pan-Islamic narrative, they ended up further dividing the political projects of this narrative, ironically creating new divisions among Muslims despite the rhetorical appeal of imagined Muslim unity.

## Conclusion

As Charles Kupchan argued, the early twenty-first-century international order is moving away from a Euro-American (or Western)-centered one to a multi-centered system, which he describes as *No One's World*.[50] Current claims of a multicentered world have led to a debate on the relevance of different civilizations in the new structures of world order, assuming that the national powers of Russia, India, China, South Africa, Iran, and Brazil have their own alternative values in relation to the US and Europe. The multicentered order of the early twenty-first century may seem deceptively similar to the civilizational divisions of the world, but current divergences about global values do not stem from a civilizational continuity, of traditions of non-Western societies surviving a century-long Eurocentric global hegemony. What we consider and describe today as regions and civilizations, with their own competing interpretations of world events and values, emerged in late nineteenth century as a result of the narrative formations about the Western white world, the Muslim world, Asia, and Africa, rather than stubborn continuities in civilizational traditions. In that sense, multiple narratives of the global order in contemporary times had shared and interlinked origins in the long nineteenth-century struggle over rights within imperial systems.

Pan-Islamic civilizational narratives, similar to Pan-African and Pan-Asian narratives, defeated the idea of white supremacy in international law and global political governance, helped decolonize the world, and contributed to the formation of several international institutions simply by challenging the master narrative of the colonizing West. The political order of the earth, and rights of human beings across Asia and Africa, changed dramatically over a century from the last quarter of the nineteenth to the last quarter of the twentieth century, partly due to the power of the competing narratives of humanity, modernity, and global order. But this modern counter-narrative of civilization needs historicization to show its genealogy, purpose, and political implications. Otherwise, we may end up reproducing conservative civilizational essentialism of one kind against another. Offering historical genealogy of each narrative may help to denaturalize and desacralize them, and invite all of us to rethink the political purposes of each narrative, thus encouraging upholders of different narratives to communicate with each other.

## Notes

1. Foreign Relations of the United States, Paris Peace Conference, "Stenegrophic Notes of a Meeting Held at President Wilson's House in the Place des Etat-Unis, Paris, on Saturday, May 17, 1919, at 4.30 pm.; for Pan-Asian mobilization during Japan's race equality proposal, see Cemil Aydin, *Politics of Anti-Westernism in Asia* (New York: Columbia University Press, 2007).
2. Vanya Vaidehi Bhargav. "A Hindu Champion of Pan-Islamism: Lajpat Rai and the Khilafat Movement." *The Journal of Asian Studies* (2022): 1–17.
3. Samuel P. Huntington, "The Clash of Civilizations?" *Foreign Affairs* 72, no. 3 (1993): 22–49; Francis Fukuyama, *The End of History and the Last Man* (London: Penguin Books, 1992).
4. Bernard Lewis, "The Roots of Muslim Rage," *Atlantic Magazine* (September 1990), https://www.theatlantic.com/magazine/archive/1990/09/the-roots-of-muslim-rage/304643/.
5. For the exceptionalist argument, see Shadi Hamid, *Islamic Exceptionalism: How the Struggle over Islam Is Reshaping the World* (New York: St. Martin's Press, 2016); Michael Cook, *Ancient Religions, Modern Politics: The Islamic Case in Comparative Perspective* (Princeton, NJ: Princeton University Press, 2014).
6. Muriam Haleh Davis, "Incommensurate Ontologies? Anti-Black Racism and the Question of Islam in French Algeria," *Cultural Constructions of Race and Racism in the Middle East and North Africa / Southwest Asia and North Africa (MENA/SWANA)* 10, no. 1 (Spring 2021).
7. W. E. Gladstone, *Bulgarian Horrors and the Question of the East* (New York: Lovell, Adam, Wesson, 1876), 8.
8. For examples of Ottoman intellectual response to racialized Europaan discourse on Ottoman inferiority, see Zeynep Çelik, ed., *Europe Knows Nothing about the Orient: A Critical Discourse from the East (1872–1932)* (Koç University Press, 2021).
9. Çelik, ed., *Europe Knows Nothing about the Orient*, 93. This quote is from the translation of Namık Kemal's "Refutation of Renan."

10. Numan Kamil Bey, "Vêritê sur l'Islamisme et l'Empire Ottoman," in *Prêsentêe au X. Congrês International des Orientalistes a Geneve* (Paris: Imprimerie de Charles Noblet et Fils, 1894).
11. Carter Vaughn Findley, "An Ottoman Occidentalist in Europe: Ahmed Midhat Meets Madame Gulnar, 1889," *American Historical Review* 103, no. 1 (1998): 15–49. For speakers defending Islam and the Ottoman Empire at the Chicago World Parliament of Religions, see Umar F. Abd-Allah, *Muslim in Victorian America: The Life of Alexander Russell Webb* (Oxford: Oxford University Press, 2006).
12. Mehmet Akif Ersoy, "Hasbihâl," *Siratı Müstakim* 3, no. 91 (20 Mayıs 1326 [June 2, 1910]): 222–223.
13. Abdurreşid İbrahim, *Alem-i Islam ve Japonya'da Intişari Islamiyet* [The Muslim World and the Spread of Islam in Japan] (Istanbul: Ahmed Saki Bey Matbaası, 1912), 88.
14. Afghani, quoted in Nikki Keddie, *Sayyid Jamal Ad-Din "Al-Afghani": A Political Biography* (Berkeley: University of California Press, 1972), 399. Shark [East] and Gharb [West] became established terms by the early 1880s in both Arabic and Ottoman writings.
15. Pankaj Mishra, *From the Ruins of Empire: The Intellectuals Who Remade Asia* (New York: Farrar, Straus and Giroux, 2012), 78–79.
16. Mishra. *From the Ruins of Empire*, 94.
17. For Pan-Islamic debates on Muslim women's rights, see Ansev Demirhan, " 'We Can Defend Our Rights By Our Own Efforts': Turkish Women and the Global Muslim Question, 1870–1935," unpublished PhD thesis, University of North Carolina, Chapel Hill, 2020. See also B. Molony and K. Uno, eds., *Gendering Modern Japanese History* (Cambridge, MA: Harvard University Press, 2008).
18. Katerina Dalacoura, "'Islamic Civilization' as an Aspect of Secularization in Turkish Islamic Thought," *Historical Social Research* 44, no. 3 (2019): 127–149.
19. Wilfrid Scawen Blunt, *The Future of Islam* (London: Kegan Paul, 1882).
20. Halil Halid, *The Crescent versus the Cross* (London: Luzac, 1907), 240.
21. Barakatullah, *Islamic Fraternity* 2, no. 2 (May 15, 1911).
22. Robert John Holton, "Cosmopolitanism or Cosmopolitanisms? The Universal Races Congress of 1911," *Global Network* 2 (April 2002): 153–170. For a recent reassessment of the London Universal Races Congress of 1911, see the special Forum section in *Radical History Review* 92 (Spring 2005): 92–132.
23. Renee Worringer, *Ottomans Imagining Japan: East, Middle East, and Non-Western Modernity at the Turn of the Twentieth Century* (Basingstoke, UK: Palgrave Macmillan, 2014), 57, quoting from Shukri al-Asali, "Nazra Fi'l Shark (A Glance to the East)," *al-Muqtabas* (July 25, 1910).
24. Erez Manela, *The Wilsonian Moment: Self-Determination and the International Origins of Anticolonial Nationalism* (Oxford: Oxford University Press, 2007).
25. The telegram, sent to the president of the League of Nations from Delhi on September 19, 1925, carries the signature of Muhammed Ali, editor of *Comrade Magazine* and leader of the Congregation. From the League of Nations Archives (original text in English). United Nations Library & Archives, Geneva, "Dossier concerning various requests for League intervention in the Riff war." File number R591/11/41612/12861.

26. For the text of Sun Yat-Sen's Great Asianism Speech in Kobe, see Marius Jansen, *The Japanese and Sun Yat-sen* (Cambridge, MA: Harvard University Press, 1954).
27. Jonathan Conlin and Filiz Yazıcıoğlu, *Plaid Panislamism: The Edinburgh Declaration of 1911* (forthcoming 2022).
28. Yahya Kemal Beyatlı, a celebrated Turkish poet, described the armies of the Turkish war of independence as "the Last Army of Islam" in a poem published on August 26, 1922.
29. Justin McCarthy, *Death and Exile: The Ethnic Cleansing of Ottoman Muslims, 1821–1922* (Princeton NJ: The Darwin Press, 1995), 135–164.
30. After about six months of negotiation, during which a second Balkan War occurred, the Treaty of London, signed on May 30, 1913, ended the Balkan Wars. With that treaty, Turkey ceded most of its territory in Europe.
31. Celal Nuri, *Kendi Noktai Nazarimizdan Hukuk-i Düvel* [International Law from Our Point of View] (Istanbul: Osmanlı Şirketi Matbaasi, 1911), 5.
32. Andrew Orr, "'We Call You to Holy War': Mustafa Kemal, Communism, and Germany in French Intelligence Nightmares, 1919–1923," *The Journal of Military History* 75 (2011): 1095–1123.
33. Alp Yenen, "The Other Jihad: Enver Pasha, Bolsheviks, and Politics of Anticolonial Muslim Nationalism during the Baku Congress 1920," in T. G. Fraser, ed., *The First World War and Its Aftermath: The Shaping of the Middle East* (London: Gingko Library Press, 2015), 273–293.
34. Noor Mohammed Khalid, "The Treaty of Lausanne: Role of Indian Muslims," quoted from A. C. Niemeijer, *The Khilafat Movement In India: 1919—1924*, 101 at: https://turkvehint.org/2019/12/mohammed-ali/the-treaty-of-lausanne-role-of-indian-muslims/#_edn7 (accessed on March 15, 2022).
35. From Joseph C. Grew to the Secretary of State, Desp. 463, August 29, 1928. For the broader context of Tevfik Rüştü Aras's European-oriented diplomacy, see Dilek Barlas and Serhat Güvenç, "Turkey and the Idea of a European Union during the Inter-war Years, 1923–39," *Middle Eastern Studies* 45, no. 3 (2009): 425–446.
36. Mehmed Cemil Bilsel, *Cemiyet-i Akvam, Suret-i Teessüsü, Mahiyeti, Vezaifi, Teşkilatı, Misakı* (1340; repr. Istanbul, Turkey, 1924); Mehmed Cemil Bilsel, *Lozan* (Istanbul, Turkey, 1933).
37. Matthieu Rey, "Fighting Colonialism versus Non-Alignment: Two Arab Points of View on the Bandung Conference," in Natasa Miskovic, Harald Fischer-Tine, and Nada Boskovska, eds., *The Non-Aligned Movement and the Cold War* (London: Routledge, 2014), 163–183.
38. Richard Wright, *The Color Curtain; A Report on the Bandung Conference*. Foreword by Gunnar Myrdal (Cleveland: World Pub., 1956).
39. *Progressive Islam* 2, no. 5 (December 1955): 1.
40. On the Palestine Vote at the United Nations in 1947, see WOR Collection (Library of Congress). United Nations Vote for Palestine Partition. 1947-11-29.
41. For Turkey's vote at the UN against Algerian claims, see Şinasi Sönmez, "Cezayir Bağımsızlık Hareketinin Türk Basınına Yansımaları (1954–1962) [Turkish Press Coverage of the Algerian War of Independence]," *ZKÜ Sosyal Bilimler Dergisi*, Cilt 6, Sayı 12 (2010): 289–318.

42. J. Harris Proctor, ed., *Islam and International Relations* (New York: Frederick A. Praeger, 1965), vii.
43. Dankwar Rustow, "The Appeal of Communism to Islamic Peoples," in J. Harris Proctor, ed., *Islam and International Relations* (New York: Frederick A. Praeger, 1965), 40–60, 41–42. Rustow quotes from Bernard Lewis, "Communism and Islam," in Walter Z. Laqueur, ed., *The Middle East in Transition* (New York: Praeger, 1958), 302.
44. James P. Piscatori, *Islam in a World of Nation-States* (Cambridge: Cambridge University Press, 1986); Abdullah Ahsan, *Ummah or Nation? Identity Crisis in Contemporary Muslim Society* (Leicester, UK: Islamic Foundation, 1992).
45. Yoav DiCapua, *No Exit: Arab Existentialism, Jean-Paul Sartre, and Decolonization* (Chicago: Chicago University Press, 2018).
46. For good biographies of Arnold Toynbee, see W. McNeill, *Arnold Toynbee: A Life* (Oxford: Oxford University Press, 1990) and M. Perry, *Arnold Toynbee and the Crisis of the West* (Washington, DC: University Press of America, 1982).
47. Gerald De Gaury, *Faisal: King of Saudi Arabia* (Louisville, KY: Fonts Vitae, 2007).
48. S. Abul A'la Maududi, *Unity of the Muslim World* (Lahore: Islamic Publications, 1967). The Introduction by Khurshid Ahmad was signed February 17, 1967.
49. Maryam Jameelah, *Islam versus the West* (Lahore: Mohammad Yusuf Khan Publishers, 1962).
50. Charles Kupchan, *No One's World: The West, the Rising Rest, and the Coming Global Turn* (New York: Oxford University Press, 2012).

# 4

# The Enduring Dilemma of Japan's Uniqueness Narratives

*Kei Koga and Saori N. Katada*

## Japan: Between the East and the West, between Prominence and Obscurity

Japan has long promoted its own uniqueness narratives, and it is an interesting and illustrative case of competing narratives on modernity and world order. The country sits in the edge of the Pacific as a "liminal power," particularly based on several factors: its position between the East and the West, its changing material capabilities, as well as its ambivalent social status through the nineteenth and twentieth centuries, as Japan's international power status has arched dramatically. Japan has transitioned from a small power in the Far East during the Meiji era, to a rapidly rising one in the early nineteenth century, to an economic great power in the Cold War era, to a relatively declining power in Asia in the post–Cold War era. Throughout these 150 years from the Meiji Restoration (1868) to the Reiwa era (2019–present) and despite its repeated rise to prominence—on some occasions inspiring other non-Western nations, and at other times oppressing the nations in the region—Japan has never managed to establish either a consistent or universal narrative for its place in the world.

In this chapter, we argue that Japan has faced an enduring dilemma of its own uniqueness narratives. On the one hand, Japan went through intense periods of assimilation in the forms of Westernization after country-opening in the late 1800s and the post–World War II US occupation and democratization pressure, when the country was in a weak position. On the other hand, when Japan gained power and prominence, it tended to promote a narrative of its unique characteristics and was not able to utilize its assimilated universal values to lead. In a way, Japan was not able

Kei Koga and Saori N. Katada, *The Enduring Dilemma of Japan's Uniqueness Narratives* In: *Debating Worlds*. Edited by Daniel Deudney, G. John Ikenberry, and Karoline Postel-Vinay, Oxford University Press.
 DOI: 10.1093/oso/9780197679302.003.0005

to deploy its own "narrative of the global" that would "call for universal action or to help set international norms and rules."[1] We identify such a trend at the times of the interwar *Tenno-sei* (imperial system) narrative and the *nihonjinron* boom during the 1980s. This boom (uniqueness) and bust (assimilation) narrative cycle has swung to the side of assimilation in the twenty-first century during the time of Japan's relative weakness, where Japan has capitalized on international contribution and support of the rules-based order. The Japanese narratives of its success as the only Asian nation that had managed to successfully modernize and militarize in the Western dominant world in the early 1900s, or as a peaceful economic juggernaut in the 1980s, had only a limited impact on global norm-setting. That is because these narratives posed by Japan have failed to generalize the country's liminal existence and experiences, and never fed into a useful universal narrative of the global.

After this introduction, this chapter consists of four sections. First, the chapter discusses our theoretical framework to examine the motivation behind a country's global narrative, where we argue how global narratives are closely related to its power, social status, and aspired state goals. In such a context, Japan's narratives fluctuated based on where the country stood in the global pecking order. The second section outlines Japan's changing power status from the late 1800s into the 2020s by focusing on its economic power and military power relative to the other major powers. This section also establishes periodization of Japan's 150-year modern history based on its relative position in the world. The third section examines fluctuating global narratives narrated by Japan in these four clearly delineated historical periods: (a) assimilation narrative of the post-Meiji Restoration era; (b) uniqueness narrative of the 1930s into the 1940s; (c) assimilation narrative of the immediate postwar period; and (d) uniqueness narrative of the 1970s through the early 1990s as Japan was at the height of its economic power. Following this long-term historical analysis of Japanese narratives, the fourth section explains how Japan's contemporary narrative of "Free and Open Indo Pacific" fits in the assimilation narrative as Japan is faced with a rising China as Japan's own economy declines. Finally, we conclude with implications of our analysis to understanding Japanese history and its place in the world, as well as how our analysis contributes theoretically to examining dynamics of contested global narratives.

## Japan in the Global Narrative of Modernity and World Order

Global narratives are an important conceptual tool for states to identify their respective social status and to nurture state identity.[2] We view that finding a social status in the world helps clarify how a state is perceived by the world and what social role it is expected to play. By setting a state identity, narratives shed light on national goals to which the state aspires in the world. Moreover, such a narrative provides a political tool for the state to justify its international actions and to persuade the domestic audience to follow its leadership. This is particularly important under the Westphalian international system, where the states are considered sovereign and, without enforcement by a world government, international norms, rules, and law are contested.

At the same time, under this international system, the state has power to manipulate its global narrative in order to shape its domestic worldview and define a course of actions that the state needs to take in the world. In so doing, the state can instigate nationalism and mobilize domestic support for its foreign policy. This is particularly useful when the state attempts to challenge the existing international order. Also, if the state effectively gains international support for its global narrative, it will likely gain an opportunity to project its social values and worldviews as "universal" values and views at the international level.

A proper understanding of the world order and social location become imperative for a state's survival. Without such an understanding, the state will be vulnerable to external and internal pressures, incapable of appropriately managing those pressures that make the state susceptible to collapse. If such a narrative deviates from the actual international order or does not consider the configuration of power relationship among great powers, the state would likely face negative consequences, at worst a war, under the Westphalian system. Therefore, global narratives are closely related to its power, social status, and aspired state goals.

Japan is a unique case in this context. As discussed in the following sections, Japan's power and social status have significantly fluctuated since 1868, when Japan's modern regime emerged after the country was forced to open itself to the world. From 1868 to 1945, Japan climbed the international social ladder to become Asia's foremost major power, but after its defeat in the Pacific War by challenging the Western-dominated regional order in

Asia, Japan under the unconditional surrender began to be fully incorporated into the US-led international order. During the Cold War, Japan became a world economic power under the Yoshida Doctrine that generated rapid economic growth from the 1960s and 1970s, yet its military capabilities were significantly limited constitutionally, legally, politically, and socially. In the post–Cold War era, Japan's economic capabilities faced a gradual decline, while being unable to fully relax its constraints on the military, and eventually lost its world second economic power status to China in 2010.

Given such fluctuation, Japan's narrative has not been consistent throughout these distinct periods. During certain periods, when being a small power, Japan tends to emulate the global narratives of the Western great powers and follow their modus operandi. During these periods, the discourse of Japan's own uniqueness becomes less prominent, and rather, such a uniqueness can be seen as a sign of inferiority and a precarious factor that would risk Japan's state survival. For example, if the world order is significantly shaped by imperial expansion and actions or is based on such international principles as democracy and human rights, Japan will follow suit. Japan accepted in the late nineteenth century the dichotomous worldviews between "civilized" and "uncivilized" that the West invented, as well as the Western discourse of "free world" or "advanced democracy" and "anti-communism" during the Cold War.[3] This diplomatic posture is understandable because it would be least likely to provoke the West and would ensure the country's own survival under the West-dominated Westphalian system. As a small power, Japan was unlikely to have agency or power in challenging and shaping the existing global narratives in a significant way. Instead, accepting the status quo for the time being, Japan concentrated on increasing its power and social status, so that it could be a major player in shaping international order.

In other periods, when being seen as a major power, Japan's global narrative shifts to emphasize its national/cultural uniqueness. Such uniqueness includes Japanese ecology, culture, homogeneity, ideology, and social structure.[4] During these periods, Japan tends to attribute its material and ideational success to its unique characteristics of Japanese-ness, often manifested in *nihonjinron* (theories about the Japanese). The core argument of this *nihonjinron* emphasizes that Japanese uniqueness cannot be easily imitated by non-Japanese. A corollary of this uniqueness logic is that since Japan's ability cannot be emulated by others, Japan takes a distinctive path to success and inevitably attains a higher social status in the world. This logic is useful to eschew a responsibility to become a fully "responsible" great power that actively shapes international order by providing public goods. At the same time, while being implicitly isolationist, such a uniqueness narrative can also satisfy national pride by positively distinguishing Japan from the rest of the world. Consequently, Japan did not consciously aim to universalize its social values and worldview and to shape international rules, norms, and principles, even when Japan had sufficient power to do so.

Japan's fluctuating narratives also reflect Japan's liminality. For example, Befu talks about *nihonjinron* in contrast to a reference group of the West since the Meiji Restoration.[5] That is, when the Japanese discuss *nihonjinron* positively, Japan is a proud unique power. When it is cast in a negative light, Japan tries to adjust to more universalistic values, and modernity dominates. *Nihonjinron* of the 1940s to 1960s repudiates Japan's uniqueness, where "[u]niqueness thus became a code word applied to exotic phenomena whose attractiveness lay precisely in the way they gave lively contemporary witness to a world and life style transcended by the mark of time and progress in the West."[6]

The potential reasons that Japan tends to conduct such a pattern in adopting global narratives are twofold. One is that even during its ascent in power, Japan still felt that it did not have sufficient capabilities to become a global power or hegemon that can create a dominant global narrative. Since the Meiji Restoration, Japan's "reference groups" or "significant others" have consistently been the West—Europe and the United States—which has predominantly formulated and reformulated international order.[7] Therefore, Japan had a narrow objective of creating a narrative that could justify its detachment from the West or the United States. To this end, Japan focuses on East Asia as its own safe space, which it considered was less contentious to control because the region does not entirely define the world order led by the West. This "safe space" came in the forms of the "Greater East Asia Co-Prosperity Sphere" prior to World War II, and preserving Japan's economic primacy in the region without taking military responsibilities under the Yoshida Doctrine during the Cold War period.

The other reason is that Japan tends to be satisfied with a non-great-power status that can conform to the existing international norms, rules, and principles. Obviously, Japan's foremost strategic priority during the early Meiji period was to consolidate its state sovereignty for survival, while it could not afford to aspire to be a global power. However, precisely for this reason, Japan was able to concentrate on strategizing how to protect itself, rather than satisfying its nationalism with its growing social status during its ascent of power by such means as the provision of *nihonjinron*. In other words, Japan did not have to reinterpret or re-examine the global narrative that the West constructed. Japan's approach to maintaining the existing international order, social values, and worldview is not necessarily the same as the one pursued by the West or the United States. Nonetheless, with the use of the same global narrative, Japan could attain absolute material and ideational benefits, such as economic cooperation and the status of a "reliable state" for the West in aspiring to the same international objectives. Furthermore, as long as Japan saw the system as fair and equal for its interests, it would not oppose the given global narrative and would accept its social location in it.

With this theoretical framework, the following section discusses how Japan's material capabilities and global narratives are correlated by examining the trend of Japan's military and economic capabilities and the shifts in the global narrative in Japan from the Meiji era to the post–Cold War era. With these findings, we will analyze the emerging narrative of Japan's Indo-Pacific in the twenty-first century.

## The Fluctuating Power of Japan: From the Meiji Restoration to the Reiwa Era

The Japanese economy and its military power, the basis on which the Japanese leaders and public construct the country's narratives, have fluctuated over the course of a century and a half since the country's opening to the world in the 1850s through the 2020s. Although Japan saw development of commercial capitalism during the Edo period (1600–1867) with establishment of a national market, price system, and financial infrastructure,[8] Japan's economic size remained small compared to any of the Western powers in the late 1880s.[9] Prior to World War II, Japan's rapid economic catch-up started in the 1910s into the 1940s, with some setbacks in the late 1920s (Figure 4.1).

During the Meiji period, Japan engaged in two wars, the Sino-Japanese War (1894–1895) and the Russo-Japanese War (1904–1905), both of which brought Japan victory and prestige. By the time of Japan's triumph against Russia, Japan had managed to reverse all the unfair treaties imposed by the West during the early Meiji period, and gained territories, including the concession of Taiwan (1895), South Sakhalin (1907), and later the annexation of the Korean Peninsula (1910). The size of the Japanese military (army and navy) expanded dramatically prior to and during these two wars, and so did

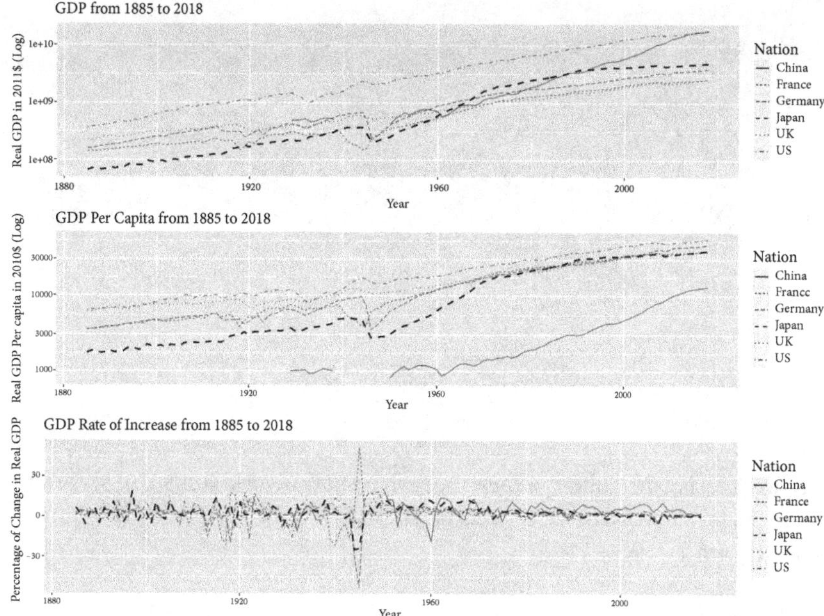


**Figure 4.1.** The size and growth of the Japanese economy relative to other powers: 1885–2018.

Source: UN national accounts statistics (mpd2020) and Total Economy database for 2008–2016.

Standardization: for GDP (1st graph) and GDP per capita (2nd graph): the *y* axis is on log 10; for GDP rate of increase, no log is applied; GDP = population. *GDP per capita. GDP rate of increase = GDP of n year/GDP of n–1 year) –1; GDP pc: real GDP per capita in 2011 USD.

the government expenditure (Figure 4.2). With these efforts, the Japanese military and naval weapons production achieved self-sufficiency by the eve of World War I.[10] Industrialization, particularly in the heavy industries such as steel production and shipbuilding, expanded rapidly, along with investments in infrastructure in railways, roads, irrigation, and phone lines.[11] From 1914 to 1918, Japan's industrial production expanded five times, and exports, more than three times, turning Japan's perpetual balance-of-payments deficit into a comfortable surplus.[12]

By the end of World War I in 1918, the West began to consider Japan as one of the major powers worthy of being invited to international summits, along with the United States, the United Kingdom, France, and Italy. Meanwhile, Japan's rapid ascent provoked concerns among the West, contributing to the Washington Naval Conference of 1921–1922, where Japan's naval power was restricted to 60 percent of those of the US or the UK. After experiencing a difficult economic downturn in the 1920s and sensing both political and economic spaces, which had supported Japan's internationalism, closing

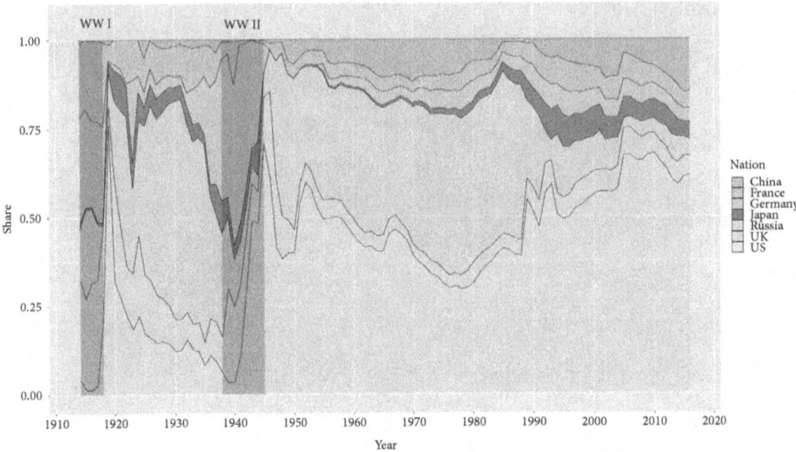


**Figure 4.2.** Japan's military expenditure share in the world: 1885–2018.
Source: Military Expenditure, The Correlates of War Project.
Units: Thousands of current USD.

in, Japanese foreign policy shifted its course with the 1931 Manchurian Incident. With the rise of militarism domestically, Japan's expansionism into Asia began in the 1930s as a way to the "final war to end all wars,"[13] surrounding Asia with the beginning of the Second Sino-Japanese War from July 1937, and cumulating in the Pacific War with Japan's Pearl Harbor attack in December 1941.

These wars proved futile. Japan unconditionally surrendered to the Allied Powers in August 1945, with the country in total ruins. With an estimated 3 million Japanese, both military and civilian, dead, and the industrial capacity contracted by 30 percent from the peak of the war, Japan suffered several years of economic hardship under the US occupation. The Japanese economy was plagued by triple-digit hyperinflation from 1946 through 1949, and at one time the country was concerned about its ability to feed its population. To tame such inflation, the occupation force implemented the so-called Dodge line (severe economic contraction policy) in March 1949. Before the real impact of such deflationary policy was felt in Japan, the Korean War (1950–1953) started, and the associated massive military procurement saved the Japanese economy and triggered the first postwar economic boom in Japan, with above 10 percent annual GDP growth (Figure 4.3).

By the time Japan regained its independence in 1952, its economic boom had already started. During the twenty years between 1951 through 1971,

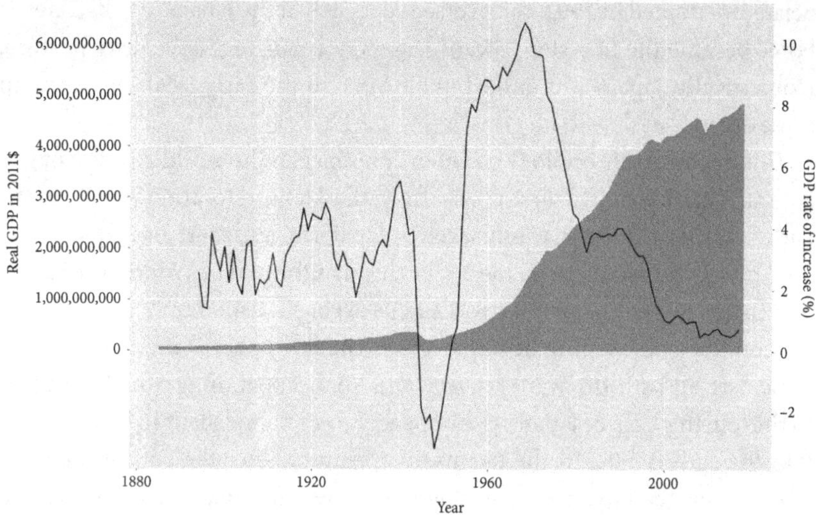


**Figure 4.3.** Rate of Japan's GDP increase: 1885–2018.

Source: UN national accounts statistics (mpd2020) and Total Economy database for 2008–2016. Standardization: for GDP (area), the left *y*-axis is on log 10; for GDP rate of increase, no log is applied on the right *y*-axis; The solid line represents 10-year-average (simple moving average) rate of increase.

the Japanese nominal GDP grew at an annual average rate of 14.5 percent (real GDP grew 9.4 percent). Japan's balance of payments turned positive, and the Japanese economy, which had long suffered from dollar shortage, started to accrue trade surplus vis-à-vis the world. Meanwhile, the Japanese security policy was constrained under the US-drafted peace constitution, and its own self-limiting measures in the context of the Cold War, such as the one-percent GDP ceiling for military expenditure and no-nuclear weapons principles. Japan became the second largest economy in the world after the United States in 1968, and kept this status until it was taken over by China in 2010. Even with the self-imposed military expenditure to one percent of the country's GDP, the Japanese military expenditure also showed robust growth along with the size of its economy (Figure 4.2).

Finally, multiple shocks shifted, albeit gradually, Japan's place in the world starting in the early 1990s. The Cold War, which in countless ways served to benefit Japan, ended undeniably with the collapse of the Soviet Union in 1991. This coincided with the first Gulf Crisis, where Japan was exposed to heightened pressure to contribute to global security challenges with their "boots on the ground." With the Peace-Keeping Operation (PKO) legislation belatedly adopted in 1992, the overseas dispatch of the Japanese Self-Defense Force became the first step toward Japan's normalizing its security posture. Domestically, Japan's economic bubble burst in the early 1990s, ushering in three decades of slow to no growth (Figure 4.3).

This historical chronology of Japan's presence in the world consists of five contrasting phases. The first phase, from the Meiji restoration (1868) to the end of Taisho era (1926), was marked by Japan's meager start and rapid catch-up. The second phase, from the 1930s through the end of World War II, was dominated by Japanese militarism and its expansionism into Asia, leading to the country's devastating defeat in 1945. The third phase, another catch-up time starting with the war recovery and US occupation, gradually leading to the fourth phase of Japan's rise of peaceful economic giant from the 1970s into the early 1990s. In the twenty-first century, after the end of the Cold War and plagued by economic stagnation, the fifth phase has given rise to Japan's Indo-Pacific strategy, which capitalizes on Japan's push for the rules-based order and increased security efforts in support of regional and global public goods.

## Japan's Global Narratives: Assimilation versus Uniqueness

### From the Meiji Restoration to Taisho

Japan's global narratives have been largely constructed since the Meiji Restoration in 1868, after the country was forced to open the country by America's "gunboat diplomacy." Prior to opening, Japan significantly limited its foreign interaction for a 264-year *sakoku* (closed economy) period. As it faced new regional challenges, Japan closely observed the imperial quest in Asia and analyzed the structure of the world system, so that it could appropriately gauge its own social location and understand what role it should play. From the Japanese leaders' perspective, they saw how Western imperialism largely dominated Asia, as these Western powers ruthlessly divided the traditional suzerain state, China. China then was diplomatically marginalized by a series of unequal treaties with Britain and France after the First and Second Opium Wars. The traditional tributary system China had constructed in Asia no longer reflected the regional reality, and the Western imperialists dominated the region, with other Asian countries seen as weak states that lost their political and social autonomy.

In this environment, Japan's assimilation imperative kicked in. Japan saw itself as a small state, which had yet to consolidate its statehood, short in military and economic capabilities, and lacking diplomatic relations with major powers to ensure its state sovereignty. These perceived vulnerabilities reflected Japan's understanding of the world; Japan needed to enhance its military and economic capabilities, to amend unequal treaties, and to build a nation-state under the Japanese sovereign system. Subsequently, Japan sought to consolidate internal social and political cohesion, and thus Japan established a state system under the *tenno-sei* (imperial system). Under this system, the emperor was sovereign, and according to the "imperial sovereignty" defined by the 1889 Meiji constitution, the Japanese nation's rights were given by the emperor.[14] This differed from "state sovereignty," although the Japanese legal norm began to question such an interpretation from the 1900s. At the same time, another imperative task that Japan needed to fulfill was to strengthen its economy and military, so that it could conduct a more effective diplomacy vis-à-vis the West. Therefore, under the banner of *Fukoku Kyohei* (Rich Nation, Strong Army), Japan concentrated on industrialization and building its army and navy on the basis of Western models.[15] With the rapid growth of economic and military capabilities, Japan made diplomatic efforts to revise unequal treaties.[16]

During this time, the most controversial debates regarding Japan's foreign policy in the 1870s and 1880s was over Korea. Japan's vulnerability came from a weak Korea, which might be overrun by China or Russia, and which would directly threaten Japan. The controversy, then, was whether Japan should preemptively dominate or align with Korea to counter the Western powers. Meanwhile, Korea, under the same imperialist pressure from the Western powers as Japan, also had similar debates that Japan had at the time of the Meiji Restoration, yet such debates were never settled. In fact, Korea's traditional political and social affiliation with China divided the country, which invited interventions from both China and Japan. In 1890, Prime Minister Yamagata Aritomo established two important strategic concepts, the "line of sovereignty" and the "line of interest."[17] The former signified the state's border, while the latter was the areas surrounding the line of sovereignty, and Yamagata advocated that the line of interest included Korea, a strategy which resulted in the Sino-Japanese war in 1894–1895. Yet, the point here was that these countries struggled to find a solution to the management of external pressures in Asia.

From a broader strategic perspective, Japan's treatment of Korea was closely related to its debate over Japan's policy direction in its global narrative, whether Japan should align with Asian states to counter the Western threats or accept the Western-led global order and aim to become a great power in Asia.[18] In 1885, Fukuzawa Yukichi published a famous op-ed called *datsu-a ron* ("On Leaving Asia") in the *Jiji shinpo* newspaper, stating that it was imperative for Japan to assimilate Western civilization to survive and prosper, rather than resisting it.[19] This logic was more effectively spread by newspaper columnist Suzuki Kentaro in 1887 under the name of *datsu-a nyu-o* ("On Leaving Asia, Entering West").[20] That said, to preserve Japanese characteristics, *wakon-yosai* ("Japanese spirit with Western learning"), also became popular terminology in the Meiji period. In short, Japan considered that Asian and Japanese civilizations were capable of resisting external powers, and for successful negotiations of treaty reforms, Japan began to consider it important to emulate the Western civilization, the attitude which was well-illustrated by the conclusion of the Anglo-Japan alliance in 1902 to counter Russian threats.

After the 1895 Sino-Japanese War and the 1905 Russo-Japanese War, Japan climbed the ladder of global power ranking, being recognized as the rising regional power in Asia, and it inspired other non-Western nations as the only country that had defeated a Western power. Its efforts to assimilate itself into Western international politics continued while Japan aimed to secure its sphere of influence in Asia. However, Japan's rising status did not necessarily reflect its major power privilege to receive material and economic benefits. For example, after the Sino-Japanese war, the Triple Intervention by Russia, Germany, and France prevented Japan from the returns promised in the Treaty of Shimonoseki in the form of the Liaodong Peninsula accession. In the post-Russo-Japanese War, the Treaty of Portsmouth was not concluded in complete favor of Japan despite its victory. This was because Japan nearly exhausted its financial and military resources and did not have sufficient capabilities to continue the war. As a result, Japan renounced war reparations under the motto of *gashin shotan* (enduring hardships for the sake of future vengeance), which caused public dissatisfaction leading to a massive public demonstration in 1905 called the Hibiya incendiary incident.[21]

The democratization process in Japan diversified domestic opinions, and thus global narratives, and this trend continued in the 1910s. There was, however, a common understanding in the international relations surrounding Japan that was shared among Japanese decision-makers—its sphere of influence in Manchuria. During this period, Japanese leaders debated over "the line of interests" in the context of Western imperialism and the extent to which Japan should draw strategic lines in Asia to contain Western influence. In particular, Japan's primary objectives continuously focused on Korea, but this line also expanded to Manchuria. After Japan ensured its control over Korea by its 1910 annexation, Japan began to closely negotiate with the Western great powers over its "special interests" in China in order to strategically avoid provoking them. This is because leaders such as Yamagata Aritomo from the Privy Council of Japan, Inoue Kaoru from the House of Peers, and Prime Minister Kato Taka-aki understood that Japan had yet to attain sufficient power to counter the West by itself.[22]

At the same time, Japan attempted to make the most of relative retrenchment by the Europeans after the 1890s to secure its sphere of influence in Asia. Japan made some gains on this front. In 1905, President Theodore Roosevelt privately told a Japanese diplomat, Kaneko Kentaro, that Japan should adopt an "Asian Monroe Doctrine." This discussion was kept private because such an idea would raise concerns from European states, including the United Kingdom, France, and Germany, regarding their influence in Asia. This Japan-US tacit agreement led to the conclusion of the Lansing-Ishii Agreement in 1917, by which the United States recognized Japan's "special interests" in China, particularly in Manchuria.[23] In the context of World War I, the Japanese government secretly inflicted "twenty-one demands" on China in 1915, which included Japanese control over China's finances. When the information about these demands were leaked, international criticism against Japan's unilateral approach heightened, and the Japanese government had to reduce the twenty-one demands to thirteen.

Furthermore, there emerged a gradual interpretation gap in the concept of the "Monroe Doctrine" between the United States and Japan. On the one hand, the United States reinterpreted the doctrine during the 1910s. While the United States consistently prevented European countries from intervening in South America, the United States no longer aimed at politically dominating and controlling the region based on regular colonial practices. Instead, respecting their sovereign rights, the United States aimed at granting more political autonomy to the South American countries. On the other hand, Japanese interpretation was still based on the traditional colonial practices, in which Japan considered it justifiable to annex Manchuria.[24] Obviously, there was a debate over whether Japan should continuously grant China independence or eventually annex it; however, in terms of Manchuria, the leaders supported the annexation.[25] Even the foremost Japanese internationalist at that time, Shidehara Kijuro, who had long insisted on the importance of international cooperation in the 1920s, implicitly supported this position.[26]

After World War I, the Japanese government recognized a change in the international order led by the United States and accepted the League of Nations in 1918. While Japan's policy to pursue amicable relations with the Western powers continued, Japan also kept pursuing its "special interests" in China and attempted to annex the Shandong peninsula that had been occupied by Germany prior to the war. In response, US and British interventions, as well as rising Chinese anti-Japanese nationalism, prevented Japan from achieving this goal.[27] Furthermore, the international rejection of Japan's "Racial Equality Proposal" at the 1919 Paris Peace Conference made Japan realize that it was not considered a full-fledged member among the Western great powers, even though Japan steadily became a recognized regional power in Asia.[28] At this point, Japan's narrative was bifurcated, based on whether a shift in international order was generally better for Asia and the world. This split was also reflected on the debates over Japanese foreign policy regarding whether to engage in international cooperation or to pursue its own national interest at the cost of international isolation.

As Japan attained international status with increasing military and economic capabilities, its social dissatisfaction gradually grew because of the persistent inequality in major power privileges between Japan and the West. In this context, international cooperation with the West in a new international order based more on self-determination and regional autonomy resonated with Japan's vision, and the political leaders tended to accept this new reality. Such acceptance of the new international system led Japan to support reluctantly the agreements concluded by the 1922 Washington Conference that included the quota of Japan's naval power relative to other great powers.[29] Accepting this system, Japan further sought international cooperation under the so-called Shidehara diplomacy and following the Western imperial legal and political norms to administer colonies;[30] yet it also aimed at increasing Japan's social rank and capabilities.

That said, there was a growing narrative gap between Japan and the West with regard to a new international order. Despite the emerging norms of anti-imperial practice, Japan still considered that it would be able to detach and control Manchuria as long as Japan ensured an open-door policy and independence of the rest of China. At this time, Manchuria's territory and natural resources became more important not only geopolitically but also socially for Japan because of its over-population problem. Internationally, the existing racial and social hierarchy, the Western control over Asia, and emerging block economies in the post-1929 Great Depression increased Japan's desire for enhancing regional autonomy in Asia. Accordingly, there was growing dissatisfaction among the military because of the international agreements under the Washington system that limited Japan's capabilities. This tension led to the May 15 Incident in 1931, where Japanese naval officers assassinated Prime Minister Inukai Tsuyoshi.

## Rise of Japan's Militarism: 1930s and 1940s

In this context, it was the Manchurian Incident in September 1931, when a part of the South Manchuria Railway line near Mukden was reportedly detonated by the Chinese, which triggered a total shift in Japan's global narrative, from embracing the Western global order to one that challenged this order. The incident was, however, staged by personnel of Japan's Kwangtung Army, who aimed to give political and military cover for the Japanese army and to gain public support for invading Manchuria.[31] In 1932, Japan established Manchukuo under its puppet regime to control the region and pursued regional hegemony. This move accelerated Japan's isolation from the community of the Western great powers, particularly after Japan withdrew from the League of Nations in protest against its investigation of the Manchuria Incident by the Lytton Commission in 1933. Japan's dominant narrative shifted to a tone that condemned the existing Western-dominated, international order as unfair and called to establish *to-a shin chitsujo* ("New East-Asian Order").[32] There was no consensus as to how to achieve such a new order, with possible strategies including re-negotiations with the West, particularly the United State, over the colonial territories.[33]

With increased social status and power, Japan emphasized its uniqueness in its new narrative during the 1930s and 1940s in challenging the existing international order in Asia. Under the strong political influence of the Japanese army and navy, Japan's narrative resurrected the characteristics of *tenno-sei*. In this hierarchical social system, Japan used Asianist arguments that Japan had abandoned during the Meiji era—aligning with Asian states to rebuild a regional order in Asia. The reversal of Japan's narrative was evident in the revival of *tenno-sei* discourse. From the 1900s to the 1920s, Japan reversed its original interpretation of the Meiji Constitution and accepted a Western legal norm, under which the Japanese emperor was located on the top of Japan's state system. This was called *tenno-kikan-setsu* and was based on the concept of the nation-state under the Westphalian system. Two decades later, the uniqueness narrative changed the discourse on the status of the emperor back to *tenno-shuken-setsu,* which advocated that the sovereignty belonged to the emperor under the Meiji Constitution. This narrative became dominant with the government statement called *kokutai myocho seimei* (the government statement of clarification) that officially rejected *tenno-kikan-setsu.* As the military began to dominate the political sphere, the range of Japan's global narrative forcibly narrowed to its political and social uniqueness that self-compelled Japan to take the lead in nurturing the regional order in East Asia.

This type of narrative solidified between 1938 and 1940. The first official policy outline toward an East Asian regional order stated by Prime Minister Konoe Fumimaro was *to-a shin chitsujo kensetu no seimei* ("Statement on the Construction of a New East Asian Order").[34] This statement was Japan's "unshakable" national policy direction to align with Manchuria and China in order to maintain East Asian stability through the establishment of international justice in the region, collective self-defense, new culture, and integrated economies, based on the Japanese spirit.[35] In 1940, the second Konoe administration adopted *kihon kokusaku yoko* ("Basic Outline of National Policy"), which was based on *hakko ichi-u* that aspired to a peaceful world under the Japanese emperor.[36] While aiming to control Asia as a regional hegemon, Japan reinforced this narrative to justify its military expansion. Such military dominance also shaped its domestic governance system, including the establishment of the Ministry of Greater East Asia in 1942, which argued that "no diplomacy" was needed in Greater East Asia as their relationship across the region was not one based on nation-states, but came in the form of a family, headed by Japan.[37]

In sum, the period from the 1920s to the 1940s illustrates Japan's growing power, reflecting a change in its narrative. As its international status rose, Japan advocated for racial equality, which could in the contemporary context be considered a universal value. The idea was, nonetheless, inconsistent with the Western powers' international order at the time. The national sentiment and the Japanese military expressed their dissatisfaction with Japan's status in the world. At the same time, Japan's power in the East Asian regional context stood out enough to shape a regional order and aimed to attain primacy, although Japan had been far from a match with global powers, such as the United States and the United Kingdom. Under this circumstance, Japan began to detach itself from the Western international order and to establish its own regional order from the 1930s by emphasizing its own unique national characteristics. This lasted until Japan reached the disastrous end of its military expansion with the defeat in the Pacific War in 1945.

## Post–World War II Americanization

The nation's defeat and its unconditional surrender to the Allied forces in August 1945 ushered in Japan's universal narrative of modernity under occupation and close collaboration with the United States, as well as its approach to working with American-led international order.

Japan's postwar reform was to take up once again a modernization project, which started at the early Meiji and failed during the 1930s and 1940s.[38] One channel of such reform was imposed on Japan by the postwar US occupation that started in the summer of 1945. The Supreme Commander for the Allied Powers, General Douglas MacArthur, once noted that "measured by the standards of modern civilization, they [the Japanese] would be like a boy of twelve as compared with our development of forty-five years."[39] Based on such assumptions, the US occupation engaged in Japan's "reforms" so that the country would "grow up" in the image of American democracy and modernity. During the nearly seven years of US occupation, when the Japanese public was still in a state of shock with a sense of powerlessness, the strong force of Americanization, on the one hand, and the domestic desire to be accepted as a member of international society, on the other, led the way.[40] As Japan gained independence in 1952 after the 1951 San Francisco Peace Treaty, Japan's diplomatic vision largely followed the US lead in the volatile region, as it lost pre-war vision.

Constrained by its past belligerent actions and the US-drafted Constitution, as well as a "culture of anti-militarism,"[41] the Yoshida Doctrine, with an emphasis on economic recovery and growth under the US security umbrella with very limited arms, became the principal narrative of how postwar Japan would re-engage with the world.[42] In the Cold War context, the Japanese government was also eager, despite domestic popular pushback, to engage in an alliance with the United States.

By the second half of the 1950s, Japan's foreign policy narrative incorporated new developments of the time, such as an increased number of newly independent nations and non-aligned movements, as Japan itself successfully joined the United Nation in 1956. This was also the time of heightened Cold War tensions. As such, Japan's global narrative emphasized universalism and solidarity with Asia and the West. For instance, in Japan's first Diplomatic Blue Book, published in 1957, the Japanese government announced three pillars of Japan's diplomacy as "UN-centered diplomacy," "maintenance of Japan's position as a member of Asia," and "cooperation with the free world." These three principles constituted Japan's narrative of peaceful diplomacy and support of democracy in the conflicted world.[43] Such narrative appeared, however, quite inconsistent with the political facts on the ground, as the Kishi government (1957–1960) engaged in revision of the US-Japan Security treaty without democratic debates and despite massive protests against its conclusion.

## In the 1970s and 1980s

Japan's miraculous economic success that kicked off in the 1950s became abundantly visible in the 1970s after Japan's ascent as the second largest economy in the world in 1968. The country's economy continued to grow, though at a slower pace than the first high-growth period, even after the devastating oil shocks of the 1970s. In the context of the "economic miracle" experienced by Japan, the new global narrative emphasizing its uniqueness came to the forefront. Such a narrative covered both the security and economic sides of Japan's uniqueness, as it was publicized to the global community.

On the security side, the narrative depicted Japan as a unique pacifist nation. Japan's pacifism was an inescapable product of both the stigma arising from the defeat in World War II and the country's fear of getting entrapped in the Cold War, but the term *heiwa kokka* was often narrated to assert Japan's uniqueness as different from the rest of the region and beyond. As Japan's economic rise became a certainty and hot wars subsided in Asia in the early 1980s, the Japanese government began to stress the country's unique foreign policy of pacifism. The narrative was that Japan, unlike other great economic powers, would not transform itself into a military power, and such deliberate choice was a "historically unprecedented experiment" (*shijo ruirei o minai jikken)* that would "contribute to peace, stability, and development for the world."[44] This special role that Japan was playing during this period led another prime minister, Miyazawa Ki'ichi, to note that this "experiment" was "the first of its kind in human history."[45] Hence, this pacifist stance placed Japan in an "unrealistic and abnormal" state, which incurred domestic pushback and pressure from the United States, demanding that Japan share more of the security burden.[46] All, nonetheless, constituted a unique approach to national security.[47]

Japan also described the country's miraculous economic success under the uniqueness narrative. The special characteristics of Japan's business practices and institutions, from "Japan Inc."[48] to the flying geese pattern of development with Japan as the lead goose, became broadly accepted ways to explain Japan's economic rise.[49] Widely discussed by the so-called Japan revisionists in Western journalism and academia, the uniqueness of the Japanese economy became the core of US-Japan tension from the 1970s to the early 1990s.[50] Inheriting economic nationalism, blended with the Meiji slogan of *wakon yosai*, the Japanese government and businesses globally promoted the superiority of Japanese economic practices, ranging from government guidance of industrial policies, Japanese-style corporate governance including *keiretsu*, to quality manufacturing production (*monozukuri*). The country's strategy of "embedded mercantilism" of aggressive export promotion and domestic protectionism was also justified as the fate of a country without natural resource endowment.[51] All these economic accomplishments constituted a principal symbol of national pride[52] and economic nationalism.[53]

To promote Japan's unique contribution, Prime Minister Nakasone Yasuhiro (1982–1987) emphasized, in his 1986 speech at the Diet, that Japan should revisit its unique civilization, and away from Western assimilation, to contribute to the world:

> In our zeal to assimilate foreign cultures and ideas, we have sometimes been derelict in our duty to help the rest of the world benefit from our Japanese ideas and cultural heritage. There is a new need today to make a major effort to explain Japan overseas and to assist other peoples wanting to know more about Japan. Prerequisite to this, we must be able to look objectively at our own civilization and make an effort to know ourselves better.[54]

The Japanese uniqueness narrative during this period was also in prominent display as Japan resisted US pressure toward economic liberalization and deregulation. The Japanese government and business leaders used often-mocked excuses of Japan's idiosyncrasies to fend off market-opening demands.[55] Furthermore, as the Japanese government resisted economic liberalization through foreign pressure (*gaiatsu*) throughout a series of US-Japan trade conflicts in the 1980s into the 1990s, it invoked the common narrative of the "black ship" metaphor for Japan's unique society, pried open by a foreign power.[56]

During this period, the Japanese government was keen on promoting the Japanese economic model, as represented by the publication of the book *East Asian Miracle* by the World Bank, funded by the Japanese government, and high-profile debates that Japan's aid practitioners had with Western donors on economic development strategy.[57] Nonetheless, the Japanese promoters of the Japan model did not universalize the model into a global narrative that could turn Japan's historical experience into a shared understanding.

In sum, Japan's economic rise as a unique pacifist power has invited a popularity of *nihonjin-ron*. The focus of Japan's narrative at the height of Japanese economic power was the special character of Japanese culture, social structure, psychology, and identity that allowed Japan to rise from the ashes and achieve significant prosperity without relying on military means. Partly as a way to search for its collective identity,[58] and partly to establish a "broadly based ideological stance for Japan's nationalism," *nihonjin-ron* widely applied to multiple aspects of Japan's success.[59] One example is the application of *ie* (interdependent and vertically connected Japanese family system) society onto Japan's organized capitalism and management system.[60]

## Value-Based Diplomacy and Indo-Pacific Narrative in the Early Twenty-first Century

How do we assess Japan's emerging narrative in the twenty-first century? With the continued domestic economic challenges one decade after the bursting of the Japanese financial bubble in the early 1990s and facing stark uncertainty in the post–Cold War era, Japan's global narrative began once again to draw closer to universalism. In fact, the perception that Japan failed to fully contribute to the 1990–1991 Gulf War traumatized Japan and propelled it to proactively make an international contribution through the United Nations. Such a narrative was not consolidated, but the debates intensified over the types of international contributions that Japan could make.[61] Among them,

Japan took the initiative to disseminate the concept of "human security" to the world that highlighted "human" rather than "state" in terms of international security from the early 1990s, which closely related to "universal values" such as human rights and democracy.[62] By the first decade of the twenty-first century, after the shocks of both the Asian financial crisis (1997–1998) and the 9/11 terrorist attacks on US soil (2001), Prime Minister Koizumi Jun'ichiro (2001–2006) kicked off the so-called value-based diplomacy (*kachi no gaiko* or *kachikan gaiko*). His 2002 speech in Singapore insisted that Japan include liberal democracies such as Australia and New Zealand in Japan's "expanded East Asia" efforts. During this time, the Japanese government advocated democratic values, human rights, and rule of law in all the ASEAN + 3 declarations.[63] Such a shift was solidified under the first Abe government (2006–2007) where, led by Foreign Minister Aso Taro, the 2007 version of the Diplomatic Blue Book stated, "a new pillar of Japanese diplomacy [adding to the three from 1957 discussed above] involves placing emphasis on *universal values* such as freedom, democracy, fundamental human rights, the rule of law, and the market economy and creating an Arc of Freedom and Prosperity [emphasis added by the authors]."[64]

At the same time, the narrative and politics of value-based diplomacy have embodied ambivalence based on both domestic and foreign policy. Domestic support for this narrative was not widespread in the early 2000s. After Prime Minister Abe Shizo stepped down in September 2007, the foreign ministry's emphasis on the universal value faded away, and some criticisms also emerged against the way that Abe and Aso were masking over Japan's totalitarian past and war history in their efforts to revise Japan's historical narrative to "break away from the postwar regime" (*Sengo regimu kara no dakkyaku*). In relation to Asia, the ambivalence came from the fact that the Japanese government continued to be hesitant about imposing these values on its neighbors in the context that these values are either "pie in the sky" or a dangerous interventionist proposition. This consideration aimed to avoid backlash from regional states in the Indo-Pacific (particularly those which are not democratic states, such as Brunei, Cambodia, Laos, Myanmar, and Vietnam), and Japan remained ambiguous regarding the extent to which it would push the universal values in the region.[65]

As the overwhelming power and influence of China became undisputable in the 2010s, Japan's value-based diplomacy returned under Prime Minster Abe's second term (December 2012–September 2020). This time, the Japanese narrative became more concrete and policy-oriented, with introduction of the Free and Open Indo Pacific (FOIP) concept during the Sixth TICAD (Tokyo International Conference on African Development) conference in 2016. In his speech, Prime Minister Abe emphasized that "Japan bears the responsibility of fostering the confluence of the Pacific and Indian Oceans and of Asia and Africa into a place that values freedom, the rule of law, and the market economy, free from force or coercion, and making it prosperous."[66] This FOIP strategy was overlaid on top of value-based diplomacy, with Japan's regional projects ranging from mega-free trade agreements such as the Trans-Pacific Partnership and infrastructure investment initiative in the form of Partnership for Quality Infrastructure Investment, both of which emerged during the course of the 2010s. The Japanese government's narrative utilizes and supports existing and US-led rules-based international order as a way to shape and consolidate regional order.[67] At the same time, this narrative has allowed Japan to create value-coalition to counter China's aggressive behavior, especially around the important sea-lanes such as the South China Sea.[68]

In sum, Japan's FOIP initiative, aiming to maintain and enhance the existing rules-based international order, emerged at the time when Japan was facing imminent decline. This initiative has also aimed to counter China's rise and its assertive behavior in the region. In the twentiy-first century, as China began to promote its own global narrative challenging the dominant Western narrative of the past 100 years, Japan's assimilation narrative insists on the preservation of US- and Western-dominated order.

## Conclusion

As a liminal power located in Asia in a world dominated by the West, Japan's global narrative has swung between its aspirations to become a model student of modernity, following Western values, and its insistence on its uniqueness. When the country's power was at its height, in the 1930s to the early 1940s and once again in the 1980s, the Japanese narrative emphasized the country's unique features as the foundation of its success. Thus, while non-Western states often considered the "Japan model" as an alternative to the Western model and emulated it, such as an export-oriented economy, these models were not intentionally created by Japan, and even if so, Japan considered that such a model would be unique and difficult to be perfectly emulated.

Meanwhile, the Japanese global narrative was and currently is in support of so-called universal values, which are most of the time promoted by the West. The ironic enduring dilemma for Japan, a country which would have been a robust candidate that could promote alternative non-Western values at the height of its power, was that it was never able to promote a global narrative that others could follow and support. To some extent, this tendency of Japan has allowed the "Anglosphere" order promoted by the United States and the United Kingdom to endure longer, with Japan's assimilation narrative to bolster their version of universal values.[69] Furthermore, the new challenge emerging from Russia's invasion of Ukraine in 2022 during the period of Japan's weakness will draw Japan even closer to the democracies of Europe.

With these analyses, we can draw three main theoretical implications. First, power status matters in the shaping of a state's global narratives. This seems like an obvious claim. Nonetheless, power status is a useful tool for a state to recognize its position in the world. Such recognition in turn shapes its global narrative, which also manifests what future status it aspires to. For Japan, when its power status was low at the beginning of the Meiji era and in the immediate postwar period, its global narrative was assimilated into the dominant one constructed by the great powers. On the other hand, as Japan increased its material capabilities, it aimed to climb up the international social ladder to become one of the shapers of international order. Through the difficulty it experienced in this process, however, the existing power structure became the target of a diplomatic struggle for social equality in the international community. The dominant means to relieve such a struggle was to emphasize national uniqueness, which became embedded in Japan's global narrative. Therefore, power status and a state's relative power within it foster characteristics of one's global narrative.

Second, it is unlikely that a state's global narrative is altered overnight. Rather, social irregularity that a state constantly perceives, such as injustice and inequality, lays a firm foundation for such a change. For example, the accumulation of domestic political dissatisfaction vis-à-vis the international order of that time led Japan to establish its own sphere of influence in Asia—the Greater East Asian Co-Prosperity Sphere—in the 1930s and the 1940s. The persistence of unequal treatment and racial discrimination among the West-dominated international community that the Japanese leaders perceived tipped the scale among a wide divergence of foreign policy opinions within Japan to harden its strategic posture against the West. Moreover, in the postwar period, it was an "irregular" power status—an economic great power without military capabilities—that propelled Japan to emphasize its uniqueness, deviating from the rest of the international community in the 1970s–1980s. It is important to identify what social irregularity and sense of injustice a state embeds in its narrative, because a clash between such a narrative and the existent global ones could even lead a state to engage in a war.

Third, the dynamics of global narratives become an essential element in understanding the process of peaceful power transition. As often discussed by power transition theorists, power transition in the nuclear age would likely happen through normative contestations between the system leader and a challenger, and not by a hegemonic war.[70] Since international norms and rules are generally embedded in and legitimized by global narratives of the international community, one's narrative and changes in its narrative become important variables to measure the likelihood of a state's intended challenge against the existing international order. This is what Mitter analyzes in the case of China and its strategy of discourse power.[71] It is worth noting, however, that a narrative change does not automatically lead a state to be confrontational. In fact, Japan's narrative changes occurred in both the 1930s–1940s and the 1970s–1980s, but their outcomes were different—the former ended with the Pacific War, and the latter made Japan seek a "unique" social role as a peaceful nation that it could play in the international community. Therefore, there are variants of narrative changes that could facilitate peaceful power transition. While such a topic is outside the scope of this chapter, Japan's cases illuminate the fact that examining the causes and processes that lead to changes in narratives contributes to advancing a theoretical framework of power transition.

In the contemporary world where we see a variety of emerging powers construct their respective narratives to tell the story about the world and their rise, Japan's example provides an intriguing illustration of the implicit status hierarchy, which established a benchmark of global norms and constrained a rising power's space to construct its narrative. The importance of such interaction should not, therefore, be underestimated.

## Notes

1. Deudney, Ikenberry and Postel-Vinay, Introduction to this volume.
2. Social status, role, and identity (and their changes) are discussed in role theory in the international relations literature, but such literature does not generally relate to

a study of narrative except for a few. See Cameron Thies, "Role Theory and Foreign Policy," *Oxford Research Encyclopedia of International Studies* (2010), https://doi.org/10.1093/acrefore/9780190846626.013.291; Leslie Wehner and Cameron Thies, "Role Theory, Narratives, and Interpretation: The Domestic Contestation of Roles," *International Studies Review* 16, no. 3 (2014): 411–436; Wali Aslam, Leslie Wehner, Kei Koga, Janis van der Westhuizen, Cameron Thies, and Feliciano de Sá Guimarães, "Misplaced States and the Politics of Regional Identity: Towards a Theoretical Framework," *Cambridge Review of International Affairs* 33, no. 4 (2020): 502–526.

3. Tadashi Anno, "Kachi gaiko no rekiteki haike: nihon gaiko no retorikku ni miru fuhenn shugi to tagenn shugi [Historical Background for Value-Based Diplomacy: Universalism and Pluralism]," Japan Forum on International Relations, Report on Energizing Japan's Diplomacy Based on Value-Based Diplomacy (2014), 13–15.
4. Harumi Befu, "Nationalism and nihonjinron," in *Cultural Nationalism in East Asia: Representation and Identity* (1993), 107–135, especially 108–116.
5. Ibid., 125.
6. Peter N. Dale, *The Myth of Japanese Uniqueness* (London: Taylor & Francis, 1986), 205.
7. Befu, "Nationalism and nihonjinron"; and Kei Koga, "The Evolution of Japan's 'Misplacement': From the Meiji Restoration to the Post-Cold War Era," *Cambridge Review of International Affairs* 33, no. 4 (2020): 572–587.
8. Yasukazu Takenaka, "Endogenous Formation and Development of Capitalism in Japan," *The Journal of Economic History* 29, no. 1 (1969): 141–162.
9. In 1885, Japan's per capita GDP (at 2011 price) was $1,729, only half that of Germany or France and a quarter of the United States (data source: Our World in Data, https://ourworldindata.org/economic-growth).
10. Manjari Chatterjee Miller, *Why Nations Rise: Narratives and the Path to Great Power* (Oxford: Oxford University Press, 2021), 73.
11. Kenichi Ohno, *Tojokoku Nippon no Ayumi: Edo kara Heisei made no Keizai Hatten* [The Path Traveled by Japan as a Developing Country: Economic Growth from Edo to Heisei] (Tokyo: Yuhikaku, 2005).
12. Masataka Kosaka, "The Showa Era (1926–1989)," *Daedalus* 119, no. 3 (Summer 1990): 27–47.
13. Ibid., 34.
14. "The Constitution of the Empire of Japan (Meiji Constitution)," February 11, 1889, https://www.ndl.go.jp/constitution/e/etc/c02.html.
15. From the 1870s through the 1880s, the Japanese army was modeled after the French and Prussian armies, while the naval training was conducted with the help of British officers. Emily O. Goldman, "Cultural Foundations of Military Diffusion," *Review of International Studies* 32, no. 1 (2006): 69–91.
16. Ministry of Foreign Affairs of Japan, "Shiryo to kaisetsu" [Data and Explanation], December 14, 2018, https://www.mofa.go.jp/mofaj/ms/da/page25_001749.html.
17. Aritomo Yamagata, "Shisei hoshin enzetsu" [Policy Speech], December 6, 1890, https://worldjpn.grips.ac.jp/documents/texts/pm/18901206.SWJ.html.
18. Yuichi Sasaki, *Teikoku nihon no gaiko 1894–1922* [Diplomacy of Imperial Japan 1894–1922] (Tokyo: Tokyo University Press, 2017).

19. Yukichi Fukuzawa, "Datsu-A Ron: On Leaving Asia," *Jiji Shino*, March 16, 1885, https://www.asianstudies.org/publications/eaa/archives/lesson-plan-on-leaving-asia-primary-source-document./
20. Maruyama Masao and Techo no Kai, *Maruyama Masao Wa Bunshu* 4 [Anthology of Masao Maruyama, No. 4] (Tokyo: Misuzu Shobo, 2009), 2–56.
21. Takeshi Horikawa, 6.
22. Ryoju Sakurai, "Dainji Okuma naikakuki niokeru gaikoseisaku no shoso" [Aspects of Foreign Policy during the Second Okuma Cabinet], *Kokusai Seiji* [International Politics] 139 (2004): 62–64.
23. Daiki Kusano, "Nichibei daito to chiikiteki kokusai Chitujo no Rensa" [The Rise of Japan and the United States and the Linkage between their Regional Orders], *Kokusai Seiji* [International Politics] 183 (2016): 36–37.
24. Ibid., 37–38.
25. Sakurai, "Dainji Okuma naikakuki niokeru gaikoseisaku no shoso," 67–68.
26. Toshihiro Nishida, "Shidehara Kijuro no kokusai ninshiki" [Shidehara Kijuro's Perspective on International Relations], *Kokusai Seiji* [International Politics] 139 (2004): 100.
27. Ibid., 97.
28. Masaki Matsu-ura, "Shimaguni, soshite rikuno teikoku kara umi no teikoku e" [Island State from Land Empire to Maritime Empire], *Kokusai Seiji* [International Politics] 139 (2004): 108.
29. Kusano, "Nichibei daito to chiikiteki kokusai Chitujo no Rensa," 38.
30. Miller, *Why Nations Rise*, 77.
31. For example, see "Mukden incident (18 September 1931)," in Anne Kerr and Edmund Wright, eds., *Dictionary of World History*, 3rd ed. (Oxford: Oxford University Press, 2015).
32. Kusano, "Nichibei daito to chiikiteki kokusai Chitujo no Rensa," 39–40.
33. Jun'ichiro Shoji, "'Shokuminchi sai bunnkatsu ron' to nihon" ["Colonial Readjustment" and Japan: In Pursuit of a New World Order], *Kokusai Seiji* [International Politics] 139 (2004): 125–143.
34. "O-A shin chitujo kensetsu no seimei" [Statement on the Construction of a New Regional Order in East Asia], November 3, 1938, https://www.jacar.archives.go.jp/aj/meta/listPhoto?LANG=default&BID=F2006092114573424545&ID=M2006092114573624563&REFCODE=B02030031600.
35. Ibid.
36. The Konoe Cabinet, "Kihon Kokusaku Yoko (Kakugi Kettei)" [Basic Outline of National Policy (Cabinet decision)], July 26, 1940, https://rnavi.ndl.go.jp/politics/entry/bib00254.php.
37. Hirozumi Abe, "Fashizumu gaiko no ronri to kokusai ninshiki" [Logic of Fascism Diplomacy and International Recognition], *Kokusai Seiji* [International Politics] 51 (1974): 121–122. For the development of the concept, the Greater East Asia Co-Prosperity Sphere, see Jeremy Yellen, *The Greater East Asia Co-Prosperity Sphere: When Total Empire Met Total War* (Ithaca, NY: Cornell University Press, 2019).

38. Carol Gluck, Chapter 3, "The Past in the Present," in Andrew Gordon, ed., *Postwar Japan as History* (Berkeley: University of California Press, 1993), 64–96.
39. U.S. Senate, 82nd Congress, 1st session, Committees on Armed Services and Foreign Relations, Military Situation in the Far East (Washington, DC: GPO, 1951), 310–311.
40. Akira Iriye, *Shin Nihon no Gaiko: Chikyuka Jidai no Nihon no Sentaku* [New Japanese Diplomacy: Japan's Choice in the Globalizing Era] (Tokyo: Chuko shinsho 1000, 1991), 51.
41. Thomas Berger, "From Sword to Chrysanthemum: Japan's Culture of Anti-Militarism," *International Security* 17, no. 4 (1993): 119–150.
42. Kenneth B. Pyle, *The Japanese Question: Power and Purpose in a New Era* (Washington, DC: American Enterprise Institute), 1996.
43. Ministry of Foreign Affairs, "Wagakuni no Gaiko Kinkyo" [Our Country's Diplomatic Updates], available online: https://www.mofa.go.jp/mofaj/gaiko/bluebook/1957/s32-contents.htm.
44. From Prime Minister Fukuda's speech on August 17, 1977, which constituted Japan's Fukuda Doctrine charting Japan's relationship with Southeast Asia. The text of full speech is available at: https://worldjpn.grips.ac.jp/documents/texts/docs/19770818.S1J.html.
45. Kenneth Pyle, *Japan Rising: The Resurgence of Japanese Power and Purpose* (New York: Public Affairs, 2017), 267.
46. Karl Gustafsson, Linus Hagström, and Ulv Hanssen.,"Long Live Pacifism! Narrative Power and Japan's Pacifist Model," *Cambridge Review of International Affairs* 32, no. 4 (2019): 502–520, see 503.
47. See also Bhubhindar Singh, "Japan's Security Policy: From a Peace State to an International State," *Pacific Review* 21, no. 3 (2008): 303–325.
48. The term "Japan Inc." was coined by Kaplan; Eugene Kaplan, *Japan: The Government-Business Relationship: A Guide for the American Businessman*, Vol. 2 (US Bureau of International Commerce, 1972), and others characterized Japan in similar ways; James C. Abegglen, *The Strategy of Japanese Business* (Cambridge, MA: Ballinger, 1984); Michael L. Gerlach, *Alliance Capitalism: The Social Organization of Japanese Business* (Berkeley: University of California Press, 1992).
49. Kaname Akamatsu, "A Historical Pattern of Economic Growth in Developing Countries," *The Developing Economies* 1 (1962): 3–25; Walter Hatch and Kozo Yamamura, *Asia in Japan's Embrace: Building a Regional Production Alliance* (Cambridge: Cambridge University Press, 1996); Walter Hatch, *Asia's Flying Geese: How Regionalization Shapes Japan* (Ithaca, NY: Cornell University Press, 2011).
50. The "gang of four" of Japan revisionism were Chalmers Johnson (University of Berkeley professor, author of *MITI and the Japanese Miracle*), Clyde Prestovitz (trade negotiator in the Reagan administration), James Fallows (journalist, *Atlantic Monthly*), and Karel van Wolferen (Dutch journalist).
51. T. J. Pempel, *Regime Shift: Comparative Dynamics of the Japanese Political Economy* (Ithaca, NY: Cornell University Press, 1998); Kanishka Jayasuriya, "Embedded Mercantilism and Open Regionalism: The Crisis of a Regional Political Project," *Third World Quarterly* 24, no. 2 (2003): 339–355.

52. Mayumi Itoh, *Globalization of Japan: Japanese Sakoku Mentality and US Efforts to Open Japan* (New York: Palgrave Macmillan, 2000).
53. Derek Hall, "Japanese Spirit, Western Economics: The Continuing Salience of Economic Nationalism in Japan," *New Political Economy* 9, no. 1 (2004): 79–99.
54. Speech by Prime Minister Yasuhiro Nakasone to the 104th Session of the National Diet on January 27, 1986, https://www.mofa.go.jp/policy/other/bluebook/1986/1986-appendix.htm.
55. The examples are abundant, including the type of snow that was not suited for the use of American skis, or Japanese people's intestines being too long to digest American beef.
56. Hall, "Japanese Spirit, Western Economics."
57. For example, Kenichi Ohno and Izumi Ohno (eds), *Japanese Views on Economic Development: Diverse Paths to the Market* (London: Routledge, 1998).
58. Dale, *The Myth of Japanese Uniqueness*.
59. Befu, "Nationalism and nihonjinron," 107.
60. Yasusuke Murakami, "Ie Society as a Pattern of Civilization," *The Journal of Japanese Studies* 10, no. 2 (Summer 1984): 279–363.
61. For example, Ichiro Ozawa, *Nihon kaizo keikaku* [Blueprint for a New Japan] (Tokyo: Kodan-sha, 1993); Masayoshi Takemura, *Chi-isaku tomo kirari to hikaru kuni nihon* [Japan, a Small but Shining Country] (Tokyo: Kobun-sha, 1994).
62. Akiko Fukushima, "Human Security and Japanese Foreign Policy," in *International Conference on Human Security in East Asia* (Seoul: Korean National Commission, 2003), 121–167, https://unesdoc.unesco.org/ark:/48223/pf0000136506.
63. Ken Jimbo. "In Search of Value in Japanese Diplomacy: Revisiting Value-Oriented Diplomacy and the Arc of Freedom and Prosperity," *Keio SFC Journal* 18, no. 1 (2018): 62–83, see 76.
64. Ministry of Foreign Affairs, Gaiko Seisho 2007, 2.
65. Giulio Pugliese, "Kantei Diplomacy? Japan's Hybrid Leadership in Foreign and Security Policy," *The Pacific Review* 30, no. 2 (2017): 163.
66. Address by Prime Minister Shinzo Abe at the Opening Session of the Sixth Tokyo International Conference on African Development (TICAD VI), August 27, 2016, https://www.mofa.go.jp/afr/af2/page4e_000496.html.
67. Kei Koga, "Japan's "Indo-Pacific" Question: Countering China or Shaping a New Regional Order?" *International Affairs* 96, no. 1 (2020): 49–73, especially p. 50.
68. Anno, "Kachi gaiko no rekiteki haike," 15.
69. Duncan Bell, "Angloworld Narratives: Race as Global Governance," Chapter 1 in this volume.
70. For example, see Randall Schweller and Xiaoyu Pu, "After Unipolarity: China's Visions of International Order in an Era of U.S. Decline," *International Security* 36, no. 1 (2011: 41–72.
71. Rana Mitter, "The Chinese Global in the Long Postwar: War, Civilization, and Infrastructure since 1945," Chapter 6 in this volume.

# 5

# Writing the Right

## Radical Conservative Narratives of Globalization

*Jean-François Drolet and Michael C. Williams*

Narratives are stories—stories through time; stories about time. They are tales of infinite progress, eschatological prophecies of movement toward an ultimate—sometimes apocalyptic—end; visions of circular time and eternal return; or narratives of decay and decline, albeit sometimes with chances of redemption and renewal. Narratives are also, of course, much more than recountings. They are processes of emplotment. In them, time and tale combine to produce narrative effects and affective responses. Irony and tragedy have both been used in this way in the study of world politics, usually in opposition to visions of progress.[1]

In this chapter, we examine the sweeping historical and global narrative of radical conservatism. Once considered a moribund relic of the past, the radical Right has emerged in the past decade to pose a fundamental challenge to prevailing liberal and mainstream conservative visions of politics, both domestic and international. While these movements are often seen as splenetic reactions to globalization, we argue that today's radical Right also contains a systematic and sustained philosophic enterprise that over several decades developed a narrative of globalization that could equip a renewed radical Right with an analytic, strategic, and affective foundation for its return to political prominence, and even power.

The radical Right presents an immense challenge to attempts at clear definition, never mind synthetic appraisal. Yet this diversity should not prevent us from examining the ways in which the global figures in its thinking. Narratives of the global provide a particularly revealing way of doing this, since they help to bring to light the intellectual lineages and narrative structures that, along with its international intellectual networks, provide a degree of international coherence and direction to these disparate movements.[2] In what follows, we use the label "New Right" to designate the

Jean-François Drolet and Michael C. Williams, *Writing the Right* In: *Debating Worlds*. Edited by Daniel Deudney, G. John Ikenberry, and Karoline Postel-Vinay, Oxford University Press. © Oxford University Press 2023.
DOI: 10.1093/oso/9780197679302.003.0006

intellectual vanguard that has been at the helm of this ideological project since the 1970s. This New Right takes many forms and expressions in different countries. In Europe, the historical origins of the New Right are generally traced back to the French *Nouvelle Droite* established in 1968 by Alain de Benoist, Dominique Venner, and other militant right-wing intellectuals associated with the *Groupement de recherché et d'etudes pour la civilisation européenne* (GRECE). Its agenda took shape on the back of the multiple ideological realignments spawned by the cultural revolutions and economic crises that shook so many Western societies at the time. The Nouvelle Droite developed strong counterparts in Italy (*Nuova Destra*) and Germany (*Neue Rechte*) in the 1970s, and subsequently in several other countries across Western and Eastern Europe.[3]

In North America, the radical conservative politics of the New Right has been promoted actively in recent years by cultural enablers such as Greg Johnson, Michael O'Meara, Jared Taylor, Kevin MacDonald, Richard Spencer, and other ideological entrepreneurs gravitating around the publishing and media platforms of the Alt-Right, the North American New Right, and other agents of white nationalism. The New Right in the United States is also closely related to the development of the "paleoconservative" movement, led by intellectuals such as Paul Gottfried, Sam Francis, Thomas Fleming, and Mel Bradford, which sought to counter the growing influence of the neoconservative and neoliberal strains of conservatism that were also often designated as the "New Right" in the United States and the United Kingdom at the time.[4] Although relatively unknown in the mainstream media and largely ignored in academic circles, this anti-establishment strain of radical conservatism has provided intellectual ammunition to a wide range of agents and ideological forces challenging the prevailing liberal order, nationally and internationally, since the end of the Cold War, including the Tea Party, the Alt-Right, and "Trumpism."[5]

Narratives of the global are a key dimension of this intellectual and political project. The New Right seeks to do more than analyze the world: it seeks to change it. Narrative mobilization is an important part of this strategy. In it, ideology, political theory, and evocative accounts of the sweep of history and detailed analyses of present situations are woven together in a re-description of the world. These accounts seek to provide narrative framings that mobilize specific social groups. Indeed, they seek to allow these groups to see themselves *as groups* and to mobilize them as such: narrative and mobilization are complementary.

Our analysis proceeds in three parts. First, we explore the location of the contemporary New Right within longer historical narratives on the right. These narratives relate the modern epoch as one of decline, not of progress. In particular, the global expansion and dominance of the post-Enlightenment West masks the fact of its gradual decay—decay inextricable from globalization itself. In the second section, we examine how this declinist narrative has been adopted and adapted by the New Right over recent decades. This is not just a question of producing new studies, editions, translations, and commentaries in order to expose new generations of readers to well-known, forgotten, or previously unpublished texts. It is also a conscious strategy of countercultural hegemony seeking to shape the identity, collective self-understanding, and agenda of the New Right by constructing its own intellectual history and lineages. Here, meta-historical visions of the "enemies of the enlightenment"[6] from the eighteenth and nineteenth centuries were combined with twentieth-century sociological theories to produce political narratives and strategies for attacking the sources and agents of decline and decay. Finally, we look at the way this narrative of domination and decline is transformed into the anti-globalist narrative of the contemporary New Right. The primary focus and affective target (the enemy) of this narrative is the managerial liberal elite—the New Class that dominates modernity and that is the prime agent and beneficiary of globalization, and that is the enemy of Western civilization and the "real" national people who compose it.

## Decline: Reinscribing the Past

To understand the narrative of the New Right, we need to extend our inquiry back to the eighteenth century, to the key historical events around which modern conservatism largely defines itself: the narrative of progress initiated in the Enlightenment and the French Revolution. Despite their differences, most moderns, including liberals and Marxists, embrace historical narratives of progress. To be sure, cyclical metaphors of degeneration and decay inherited from antiquity and the Christian Middle Ages continued to circulate within visions of progress. But in most cases, these were cast as pointing to pathological symptoms that would eventually be overcome through progressive transformations toward ever more inclusive forms of political communities and the universal rule of reason.[7] Even the Romantic movement, which brought together conservatives and their radical opponents to denounce the decadence of modern life, was a reaction against the overwhelming successes of progress.[8]

The New Right, by contrast, sees the modern era as a tale of decline, error, and destruction. Although, as we will see, the New Right departs from the reactionary thinkers of the eighteenth and nineteenth centuries who clung to the ideal of an essentially medieval hierarchical society defended by landed aristocrats, the cultural pessimism of these reactionaries provided a significant contribution to the narrative of subsequent movements on the right. The cultural pessimism expressed in these views rejected the notion of progress, and developed a narrative of modernity as a movement toward terminal civilizational degeneracy.

One of the earliest and most influential exponents of this reaction was the French aristocrat and embittered royalist Arthur de Gobineau (1816–1882). Trained in languages and Oriental culture, Gobineau is widely recognized as the first racial theorist in nineteenth-century Europe.[9] Whereas earlier classical conservatives derived their attack on the Enlightenment from the wisdom of Christianity, hierarchy, and tradition, Gobineau's systematic emphasis on race was a deliberate effort to modernize the political theory of reaction by bringing it in line with the positivist scientism of the age. A close reader of Hegel, Gobineau approached human history in terms of one single universal scheme characterized by the cyclical rise and fall of civilizations, the fate of which he associated with racial composition. Although he accepted the idea of a common humanity posited by the Enlightenment, he rejected any suggestion of racial equality and progress. Developed over years of historical, anthropological, and ethnological studies, his theses rested on the completely unsubstantiated notion that races are intellectually, physically, and spiritually distinct, and that the "Aryan" (or Germanic) race was superior in intellect, beauty, and creative energy to all other races.

For Gobineau, the problem is that the global expansion of this race through commercial and military conquest inevitably led to miscegenation with inferior breeds, and thus to the slow debilitation of the Aryan race that was to him apparent in the condition of cultural decline and political decay afflicting Europe in the nineteenth century. As he put it in the *Essay on the Inequality of the Human Race* (1853–1855):

> From the very day when the conquest is accomplished and the fusion begins, there appears a noticeable change of quality in the blood of the masters. . . . Henceforth, as the nation grows, whether by war or by treaty

> its racial character changes more and more. It is rich, commercial and civilized. The needs and the pleasures of other peoples find ample satisfaction in its capitals, its great towns, and its ports; while its myriad attractions cause many foreigners to make it their home. After a short time, we might truly say that a distinction of castes takes the place of the original distinction of race.[10]

Looking across the Atlantic to America, Gobineau admired how white Europeans had historically sought refuge in the hope of renewing the vitality of their race and pursing its civilizational mission by reasserting its control over the world. The Anglo-Saxons founded this new country, asserted themselves over the natives and the other color groups and miscegenated whites from other parts of Europe, and enabled the United States to rise as the dominant power in the New World. According to Gobineau, this tremendous success on behalf of the white race was a result not of the commitments to natural rights and equality of the settlers and their successors, but rather of the willingness of these conquerors to ignore those commitments when dealing with other races.[11]

The Anglo-Saxons were the last group to defend the civilizing cause of the Aryan race. Yet even they had already advanced too far down the debilitating path of modernity to hold the fort for long. By the mid-nineteenth century, white America was already a thing of the past. Mass immigration was changing its demographic composition at such a rate that the Anglo-Saxons would soon become only one group in a wide melting pot of the races characterized by cultural degeneracy and the proliferation of violent ethnic conflicts. Gobineau saw the American experience as a more intense replay of the process of democratization and miscegenation that had already debilitated Europe. Rather than a beacon of the future, America was the latest symbol of the accelerating globalization that would bring about the end of European civilization, and with it the end of human civilization as such:

> The reunion of all these degenerated types produces and will continue to produce new ethnic disorders. Those disorders are neither unexpected nor unprecedented; they will not yield combinations that we have not already experienced (or that we could experience) in Europe [ . . . ]. This people which calls itself young is in fact the old people of Europe, less restrained by more permissive laws but just as uninspired. . . . The mere transfer from

> one place to another does not regenerate races that are already more than half-extinct.[12]

The *Essai* was largely ignored in France, where the republican tradition was strong enough to keep the forces of reaction in check. But it found a receptive audience in the newly unified Germany from the mid-1870s onward, where liberal political traditions remained weak and where rapid economic modernization and the prospect of a massifying and mechanizing "Americanization" of the German Spirit were creating deep anxieties among the Junker aristocracy and educated elites.[13] Championed by Richard Wagner's "Bayreuth Circle" of nationalist intellectuals and the influential racialist historian Houston Stewart Chamberlain (Wagner's son-in-law), Gobineau's declinist philosophy of history was soon assimilated into organicist theories of the state and other narratives of political and cultural decline developed by the emerging school of *Geopolitik* and thinkers of the so-called conservative revolution.

The conservative revolution does not refer to a clearly defined ideological project, but to a set of intellectual and political experimentations which coalesced around a radical critique of liberal modernity in Weimar Germany. Its most well-known thinkers include Arthur Moeller van den Bruck, Hans Freyer, Oswald Spengler, Carl Schmitt, and Ernst Jünge.[14] Over the past two decades or so, it has become one of the most significant events in the intellectual and historical self-understanding of the New Right in Europe and North America.[15] Unlike earlier generations of traditional conservatives who rejected the utilitarian cultural habitus of modernity in the name of an idealized pre-capitalist community of values (*Gemeinschaft*), conservative revolutionaries shared the belief that Germany's ability to influence the global balance of power depended on its ability to reconcile the romantic irrationalism of German nationalism with the innovative spirit and rationalist functionalism of modern technology and industry.

Few representatives of the conservative revolution expressed this fusion of conservatism with the forward-looking voluntarism of modernity more dramatically and influentially than Spengler, who cast the West's rise to global domination within a narrative of ascendance followed by a process of decline that grew directly out of the sources of its success. Spengler described the rise and inevitable disintegration and foreseeable end of a culture that had originated in Western and Central Europe in the Middle Ages.[16] He called this culture "Faustian." In the same way that Faust had sold his soul to the devil to increase his power, the modern West had embraced the spirit of technology to become the dominant global force. Like all great cultures in human history (Greco-Roman, Indian, Babylonian, Chinese, Egyptian, Arabian, and Mexican), Spengler argued, the "Faustian" culture of the West had experienced stages of creative beginning and energetic consolidation. Spengler reminded his readers that the great material improvement of the nineteenth century had been achieved mainly through the brutal exploitation of human and natural resources in many non-Western parts of the world. The question was whether the metaphysically exhausted civilization of the West could continue to sustain these asymmetric relations of power between nations, classes, and races.[17]

Spengler's answer to this question was no. Since the French Revolution, he argued, the West had entered an irreversible phase of degeneration that would ultimately result in its extinction. At the heart of this process of decline were the economic and cultural impacts of globalization. Spengler maintained that the masses always experience culture through the ideals and norms promulgated by a small elite of exceptional individuals, and that the only path to the creation and maintenance of greatness within and between human communities was through the principle of hierarchy: "there is a natural distinction of grade between men born to command and men born to service, between the leaders and the led. . . . In the centuries of decadence the majority force themselves to deny or to ignore it, but the very insistence on the formula that 'all men are created equal' shows that there is something here that has to be explained away."[18] Spengler believed that in our industrial age it was engineers, inventors, and commercial entrepreneurs who had to take on this important role and provide the leadership necessary to orient the amorphous masses toward long-lasting cultural goals.[19] In his eyes, however, this led directly to the "cultural catastrophe" that industrial off-shoring, the importation of foreign workers, and indiscriminate immigration were bound to generate for white supremacy:

> And then, at the close of last century, the blind will to power began to make its decisive mistake. . . . The famous "dissemination of industry" set in, motivated by the idea of getting bigger profits by bringing production into the marketing area. And so, in place of the export of finished products exclusively, they began an export of secrets, processes, methods, engineers, and managers. . . . The unassailable privileges of the white peoples have been thrown away, squandered, betrayed. . . . Where there is coal, or oil, or

> hydroelectric power, there a new weapon can be forged against the heart of Faustian Civilisation. Here begins the exploited world's revenge on its masters. The innumerable hands of the coloured races—at least as clever, and far less exigent—will shatter the economic organization of the whites and its foundations.[20]

For Spengler and many other thinkers associated with the conservative revolution,[21] globalization is an expression of the West's civilizational power *and* the cause of the decline and destruction of that power. Progressive narratives of universal history are misleading. History is a narrative of ascendance and decline, and the West has passed its apex. Unlike other historical pessimists, theirs is not a call for nostalgia. There is no escape from modernity in going backward. But there is, or at least may be, a way forward that understands the sources of the West's global greatness and the causes of its decline, and struggles against them. Bleak diagnoses are thus transformed into narratives of revolutionary energy rather than reactionary despair.

It is this synthetic, forward-looking narrative, a combination of decline and determination, that has inspired so many New Right intellectuals to mobilize the political theory of the conservative revolution. In the mission statement of Counter-Current Publishing,[22] for example, Greg Johnson declared that "history is cyclical and our present era of globalization corresponds to a Dark Age in which decadence reigns and all natural and healthy values are inverted," Yet hidden in the depths of this Dark Age are "countercurrents . . . remnants of the past Golden Age that sustains the world and serve as seeds of the Golden Age to come."[23] However, change involves more than simply waiting for the wheel of history to turn; it requires a positive alternative as well. Reactionary fatalism or traditional conservative narratives of loss and decline are insufficient. What is required is a new political theory: a vision and narrative beyond progress or decline, past or future, toward a renewed revolutionary traditionalism that can overcome globalizing modernity.[24]

New Right intellectuals and ideological entrepreneurs see it as their mission to develop such a political theory as part of an asymmetric "metapolitical" culture war against the incumbent regime of global liberal managerialism and the hybrid, amalgamated "culture" of contemporary liberal societies. In Johnson's words:

> We metapolitical radicals must think of ourselves as the vanguard of our people, as a political avant-garde. We are the ones who must summon our courage, take the risks, blaze the trails, and lead our people toward their salvation. Vanguardism must be repeatedly emphasized, because the instinct of every politician seems to do the exact opposite. Politicians are inveterate panderers and flatterers of the public mind, which unfortunately has been completely moulded by our enemies for generations. Politicians follow the people. Vanguardists seek to lead them. Politicians take public opinion as a given. Vanguardists seek to change it.[25]

## Metapolitics: Narrating the Global

The idea of narratives of the global is particularly useful for understanding how the New Right envisages this process of change. The New Right differs from many of its reactionary forebears in its rejection of anti-intellectualism and extra-parliamentary violence as means of change. Instead, it adopts a "metapolitical" strategy based on the conviction that the success of any parliamentary or revolutionary initiatives depended on the prior existence of cultural sympathies forged in the realms of education, the media, and the arts. This goal was first articulated during the 1970s by De Benoist, Faye, Venner, and other leading GRECE thinkers as "the social diffusion of ideas and cultural values for the sake of provoking profound long-term, political transformation."[26] Similarly, in the United States, "paleoconservative" thinkers argued that renewal of the American Right depended on its ability to a create its own "Middle American" counterculture. As Francis wrote in 1992:

> The main focus should be the reclamation of cultural power, the patient construction of an alternative culture within but against the regime. Rather than searching in vain for an honest presidential candidate, a Middle American Right should begin working in and with schools, churches, clubs, women's groups, youth organizations, civic and professional associations, the military and police forces, and even in the much dreaded labor unions to create a radicalized Middle American consciousness that can perceive the ways in which exploitation of the middle classes is institutionalized and understand how it can be resisted.[27]

Narratives of the global—and of globalization—have key roles in this metapolitical strategy. Here, we focus on two. First, the process of globalization is that of abstract forces causing social dislocation. It is identified with the domination of a specific social system (liberal managerialism) and particular agents (the New Class) who benefit from it materially and symbolically while damaging or even destroying the livelihoods and cultures of large parts of their own societies. The narrative seeks to craft an identifiable enemy—one who is materially exploitative, socially distant, and morally culpable. This narrative interweaving of material interest, moralized values, and resentment has been a particularly powerful part of the New Right's appeal. Second, this global narrative wraps these arguments in a wider narrative of fear and promise centering on the West itself, which is threatened by liberal managerialism and the New Class and that needs to be defended by articulating and aggressively asserting the traditional values of the West itself, including (in some guises) its racial foundations.

The concept of elite managerialism is at the heart of the New Right's narrative of the global.[28] Managerialist theory sees globalization as not just the effect of capital, but as the product of a wider twentieth-century transformation in social power toward managerial techniques and the dominance of a "New Class." By the mid-twentieth century, corporations were run by managers and governments by administrators, and both were linked to mass communications and educational institutions that shared their organizational structures and much of their underlying managerial ideology.[29]

In this view, the real driving force behind economic and cultural globalization lies not in capitalism or realpolitik as traditionally conceived by Marxists or Realists, but in the dynamics of liberal managerialism itself. Globalization is not simply an economic process, or of diverse cultural flows—it is the product of the logic of liberal rule and power, of the interests and the "utopia" underpinning liberal modernity as an epoch. The combination of the rootless cosmopolitanism of liberal elites whose expertise can be applied anywhere, their pluralist ideology, transnational capital, and borderless cultural flows are intrinsic elements of the globalizing imperatives and desires of liberalism and its proponents.

Economically, this analysis echoes many other critiques of economic globalization. Unlike other critical diagnoses of globalization, the political forces targeted by the polemics of the New Right are not those of an impersonal capitalist system of "governance without government." What is striking is the way that the New Right seeks to identify these dynamics with the advantages of specific groups—the "elites" of the New Class—and to mobilize resentment against the cultural politics of this class. For the New Right, globalization is the product of forces unleashed and controlled by the liberal "managerial" elites and the client groups they favor (migrants, certain identifiable minorities) and that in turn support them. As Alain de Benoist and Charles Champetier declare in the millennial Manifesto of the French Nouvelle Droite:

> In the process of globalization, Western civilization is promoting the world-wide domination of a ruling class whose only claim to legitimacy resides in its abstract manipulations (logico-symbolic) of the signs and values of the system already in place. Aspiring to uninterrupted growth of capital and to the permanent reign of social engineering, this New Class provides the manpower for the media, large national and multinational firms, and international organizations. This New Class produces and reproduces everywhere the same type of person: cold-blooded specialists, rationality detached from day to day realities. It also engenders abstract individualism, utilitarian beliefs, a superficial humanitarianism, indifference to history, an obvious lack of culture, isolation from the real world, the sacrifice of the real to the virtual, an inclination to corruption, nepotism and to buying votes.[30]

According to the New Right, the economic and social losers in the liberal world order are those who cannot or will not adopt or adapt to globalist imperatives. These are the "left behinds," those still tied to locality, who experience migration or cultural cosmopolitanism as a threat, as well as the "basket of deplorables" who hold on to tradition, to their inherited communities and prejudices, even as they are being eroded by globalization. These groups are disparaged as backward and bigoted, dependent, and (if they are lucky) in need of "re-skilling" by a liberal elite which is the condescending agent of their increasingly dire economic plight and that dismisses and disparages their feelings of social and cultural dislocation or alienation.

This narrative allows for hostility toward global capital without necessarily being anti-capitalist. It allows hostility toward the "managerial state" without being anti-nationalist. And it allows hostility toward subordinate groups who are portrayed as the beneficiaries of this system of power. Anti-elitism and, often, racially inscribed attacks on marginal groups are two sides of the same narrative logic.

## Narrating the Nations of the West

The second core element of the New Right's narrative of the global builds on this critique of managerial liberalism. Echoing Spengler (and even Gobineau) at times, the New Right argues that the very success of the West's "rise to globalism" is leading to the destruction of the West itself. The rationalism and pragmatist progressivism of liberal managerialism destroys substantive values and orders, including those that sustained the rise and power of the West. Liberalism's pluralism and relativism is hollowing out the necessary belief in fundamental values, and their grounding in substantive communities that are the preconditions for the success of any true culture. All that is left is empty technocracy or relativistic pluralism that leads to decadence, social fragmentation and disorder, loss of national identity, and self-confidence—in short, to decline papered over by increasingly desperate technocratic domination.

As a result of these shifts, the older, substantive identities of particular social classes, communities, and religious and ethnic groups can no longer effectively mobilize populations for collective (national) political action. Managerial liberalism's hedonistic ethics and therapeutic social practices tend to fragment societies into ever more diverse groups, each advocating their own vision, programs, and interests, inhibiting collective action and weakening the progressive state's ability to enact its promises through appeals to collective solidarity and national identity and unity. This sense of societal fragmentation and political division is conveyed most explicitly by the subjectivist language of "values" that has become so central to the ways our "postmodern" liberal democratic societies express ethical choices, public policy preferences, and visions of world order.

This situation is affecting both the nations of the West and the West itself. The inherited substance—the cultural solidarity and confidence that underpinned the West's collective power and greatness—is nearly depleted, and its massive technological prowess masks the fundamental hollowing out of Western civilization. The Enlightenment narrative remains central to the reproduction of contemporary liberal orders, but it has lost all metaphysical credibility and genuine collective appeal: "It persists by dint of force and propaganda. But in the sphere of thought, poetry, music, art or letters, this metanarrative says and inspires nothing. It has not moved a great mind for 100 or 150 years."[31] In politics, Faye argues, this has become evident in the ways in which leaders in the West increasingly rely on negative legitimation tactics to authorize their rule: "Politicians no longer say, 'Vote for us because we've got the right solutions and we'll improve your living conditions' [ . . . ]. Instead they say (implicitly), 'Vote for us, since even though we're a bunch of good-for-nothings, bunglers and bullies, at least we'll protect you from fascism.' "[32]

Echoing familiar Spenglerian themes, New Right intellectuals contend that even what was once called "the West" has also become a mere ideological abstraction sustained by a conglomerate of Atlanticist economic interests. This conglomerate is not "led" by inspiring political and cultural figures, but only "managed" according to its own expansionist regulatory imperatives.[33] NATO, argues Angelo Codevilla, has now become little more than a committee for managing the affairs serving "the interests of the transatlantic ruling class."[34]

## Beyond the Crisis

The New Right's narrative is one of crisis verging on despair. But as we discussed earlier, as followers of the conservative revolution, they see this situation as calling for the reassertion of will that can mobilize the social forces available to turn the tide. Here, their narrative becomes one of mobilization where the historical and analytic are turned to practical use. The goal, as Pierre Bourdieu might have put it, is to have the vision of the global and the principles of "di-vision" it inscribes become the guiding categories of political actors. The narrative of the New Right not only seeks to describe the conditions of the "left behinds": it seeks to make these (and other) groups conscious of those conditions, the reasons for them, and the people and forces responsible.

The combination of economic dislocation, cultural resentment, and mythic mobilization provides an opportunity to reverse this situation, and to form these groups into a newly self-conscious populist-nationalist, conservative movement that crosses the conventional lines between Left and Right. Equally importantly, it allows for the construction of that quintessentially fertile political figure: the enemy. The enemy is not an abstract "system" or "logic" of capital: it is the concrete figure of liberal managerial elites and the client groups they support.

As a narrative that combines both analysis and affect, the metapolitics of the New Right seeks to exploit the social conditions it describes to generate political change. Only by reconsidering and reasserting the values of Western nations and the West itself, supporting those groups that still embody those values, and engaging in virulent (even violent) resistance to the New Class enemy and its combination of relativism, false universalism (for instance, in empty human rights), and cosmopolitan ethic, as well as its multicultural allies, can the tide be turned. If successful, this will lead to the renaissance of a West that is powerfully solidarist, and yet *not* universalist. This is not a call for the return of the culturally or racially superior, universal West. The West lost its way into the destructive dreams of the Enlightenment and embarked on its disastrous Modern project. It needs now to rediscover the value of plurality, but doing so also (and, in fact, most importantly) entails powerfully reasserting the value of its *own* particularity: the unapologetic defense is its own historical culture(s) within the wider framework of Western civilization.

This position adopts and co-opts many (particularly postcolonial) critiques of liberalism, turning them into rationales for the "defense" of Western particularity, as well as demanding and legitimating a retreat from cosmopolitan concerns and global engagement. In international policy terms, it tends toward isolation or loose regionalism, blunt assertion of Western interests when necessary, but without universalist aspirations or rationalizations. Domestically, it calls for strong controls on immigration, and educational and cultural policies supporting particularist or traditionalist values, institutions, and organizations. There are certainly debates and disagreements over the meaning and boundaries of the West on the New Right (is Russia in or out? are Anglo-Americans European or not?), but they take place within a common narrative of the need for renewed self-assertion, valorizing local or national values and identities, including the significance of race.

## Conclusion

Narratives are not descriptions. Their structural, affective, and performative dimensions are vital. A narrative of struggle and domination, of enemies and allies, or of righteous resistance, operates in registers very different from those of "cool," reasoned dialogue or technocratic rationality. Narratives are communicative forms, and as such are tied to mediums of communication and different affective capacities within them. In a hyper-mediated world of tweets, memes, and images, narratives of enmity, outrage, and grievance, combined (as they often are) with assertions of superior virtue and resentment, take new and powerful forms. In the face of liberal relativism or technocracy, the "old Gods," as Max Weber once observed, rise again.

A focus on historical narratives of world order provides a particularly useful device for bringing out both commonalities and important divergences among this otherwise disparate constellation of views. It is a narrative that mobilizes a long history, a story in many ways of destruction and decline; but it is also a narrative that takes the political potential of narrative itself particularly seriously, stressing the importance of ideas and rhetoric in politics as vital resources for action and rebirth—a *narrative* that can provide the basis for an alternative political project. It is also a narrative that crosses the domestic/international divide, grounding its ideas in a wider vision of politics. It is neither reactionary in the sense of trying simply to reinstate an old, pre-modern order, nor purely nostalgic—it is a call to action. The New Right thus provides a powerful illustration of the construction of narratives—of narrative re-emplotment and transformation, of the links between intellectual and specifically affective dimensions of politics, and the linking of narrative and myth. It also provides an illustration of the power of narratives of the international in politics, and how these narratives reconfigure existing elements into novel, sometimes influential, and in this case, in the view of many, worrying forms.

As many critics have pointed out, the catchphrase "populism" that is often used to describe this sweeping critique it is a severely limited device. But when Steven Bannon and his international interlocutors in the (albeit stuttering) transnational right-wing "Movement"[35] in Europe and beyond speak of their desire to destroy the "administrative state" and to fight "globalizing elites" in the name of "the people," they are not simply spouting rhetorical flourishes; they are reflecting a wider sociological and political vision and narrative framing that provides a unifying analytic and strategic framework for much of the radical Right. It is this vision of the specifically "administrative" state, not the state in general (which they often want to strengthen) that they want to attack. It is also a narrative expression of that most useful of political devices: an identifiable Enemy, or more accurately, a malleable, transposable logic of enmity toward "globalizing elites" that can support a wide range of formulations, agendas, and transnationally resonating cultural strategies.

Like Gobineau, Spengler, and the thinkers of the conservative revolution, the New Right interprets globalization as a process of homogenization that comes into conflict with the survival of the West itself. More broadly, they see global liberalism as a force that "threatens not just Europeans but every unique identity on Earth."[36] What liberalism narrates as the creation of ever more inclusive forms of human solidarity, the New Right sees as the mass emulation of Western practices of overproduction and overconsumption by those who have historically been the main political victims of these practices—the dissolving of all authentic cultures into an undifferentiated humanity linked solely through markets and the virtual reality of the internet—including, crucially, that of the West itself.

## Notes

1. Such divides have provided the narrative structure of much of the field of IR throughout its history; see, for instance, Reinhold Niebuhr, *The Irony of American History* (New York: Charles Scribners's Sons, 1952); Toni Erskine and Richard Ned Lebow, eds., *Tragedy and International Relations* (London: Palgrave, 2012); Alison McQueen, *Political Realism in Apocalyptic Times* (Cambridge: Cambridge University Press, 2017).
2. See Rita Abrahamsen, Jean-François Drolet, Alexandra Gheciu, Karin Narita, Srdjan Vucetic, and Michael C. Williams, "Confronting the International Political Sociology of the New Right," *International Political Sociology* 14, no. 1 (2020): 94–107.
3. For overviews, see Mark Wegierski, "The New Right in Europe," *Telos* 98–99 (Winter 1993–Spring 1994): 55–70; Michael O'Meara, *New Culture, New Right: Anti-Liberalism in Postmodern Europe* (London: Artkos, [2004] 2013); Tomislav Sunic, *Against Democracy and Equality: The European New Right* (London: Arktos, [1990] 2011); Benjamin R. Teitelbaum, *Lions of the North: Sounds of the New Nordic Radical Nationalism* (Oxford: Oxford University Press, 2017). Influential European writers who either identify explicitly with the New Right, or whose work closely aligns with the general positions expressed by Benoist and leading New Right figures since the early 1970s, include Guillaume Faye, Charles Champetier, Tomislav Sunic, Jean-Claude Valla, Michel Marmin, Jean Haudry, Marco Tarchi, Sigrid Hunke, Luc Pauwels, Yves Christen, Pierre Le Vigan, Pierre Gripari, Christopher Gérard, Armin Mohler, Karlheinz Weissmann, Javier Ruiz Portella, and Sebastian J. Lorenz, Julien Freund, Giorgio Locchi, Gerd-Klaus Kaltenbrunner, Pierre Krebs, Pierre Vial, Robert Steuckers, and Alexander Dugin.
4. For overviews, see Paul Gottfried and Thomas Fleming, *The Conservative Movement* (Boston: Twayne, 1988); Joseph Scotchie, *The Paleoconservatives: New Voices of the Old Right* (New York: Routledge, 1999); Jean-François Drolet and Michael C. Williams, "America First: Paleoconservatism and the Struggle for the American Right," *Journal of Political Ideologies* 25, no. 1 (2020): 28–50.
5. Paul Gottfried, "Some Observations from the Man Who Created the Alt-Right," *Frontpage Mag*, August 30, 2016, http://www.frontpagemag.com/fpm/263988/

some-observations-man-who-created-alt-right-paul-gottfried [November 7, 2017]; Timothy Shenk, "The Dark History of Donald Trump's Revolt," *The Guardian*, August 16, 2016, https://www.theguardian.com/news/2016/aug/16/secret-history-trumpism-donald-trump, [September 20, 2017]. See also Michael Brendan Dougherty, "How an Obscure Advisor to Pat Buchanan Predicted the Wild Trump Campaign in 1996," *The Week*, January 19, 2016, http://theweek.com/articles/599577/how-obscure-adviser-pat-buchanan-predicted-wild-trump-campaign-1996, [October 9, 2016].

6. Darrin M. McMahon, *Enemies of the Enlightenment: The French Counter-Enlightenment and the Making of Modernity* (Oxford: Oxford University Press, 2002).
7. Reinhardt Koselleck, "Progress and Decline," in *The Practice of Conceptual History* (Stanford, CA: Stanford University Press, 2003), 227–231.
8. "European civilization's awe-inspiring power took on a quality of 'overmuchness,' a surfeit of easy wealth, social mobility, material comfort, and complacency—as well as a surfeit of change and destruction of what had come before." Arthur Herman, *The Idea of Decline in Western History* (New York: Free Press, 1997), 45.
9. After a period as personal secretary to Alexis de Tocqueville during his short term as foreign minister in 1849, Gobineau served as a diplomat in a wide variety of locations across Europe, the Middle East, and South America. His best-known work is the *Essai sur l'inégalité des races humaines*, ed. Hubert Juin (Paris: Pierre Belfond, [1853–1855] 1967). The English translation, *An Essay on the Inequality of the Human Race*, trans. Adrian Collins (London: William Heinemann, [1853–1855] 1915), is an abridged version of the original four-volume work. See also Michael D. Biddiss, *Father of Racist Ideology: The Political and Social Thought of Count Gobineau* (New York: Weybright and Talley, 1970); Herman, *The Idea of Decline*, 46–75; James W. Ceaser, *Reconstructing America: The Symbol of America in Modern Thought* (New Haven, CT: Yale University Press, 1997), 87–105.
10. Gobineau, *An Essay*, 31.
11. Gobineau, *Essai*, IV, 304–311.
12. Ibid., 313, 316–317. Authors' translation. As James W. Ceaser observes: "Perhaps, then, it was Arthur de Gobineau who was the first to speak definitively of an end to history. He surely was the first to take America out of the realm of possible dreams for the future and to incorporate it into the existing scheme of universal history. Gobineau in this sense completed Hegel's thought by foreclosing any idea of an unchartered future on a new continent." *Reconstructing America*, 105. See also Audrey Smedley, *Race in North America: Origin and Evolution of a Worldview* (Boulder, CO: Westview Press, 1993).
13. Fritz R. Stern, *The Politics of Cultural Despair: A Study in the Rise of the Germanic Ideology* (Berkeley: University of California Press, 1974), 131.
14. The conservative revolution as a concept is above all an academic construct that only really gained currency during the Cold War following the publication of Armin Mohler's influential *Die Konservative Revolution in Deutschland, 1918–1932* (Stuttgart: Friedrich Vorwerck-Verlag, 1950). For good overviews in the English language, see Roger Woods, *The Conservative Revolution in the Weimar Republic*

(New York: St. Martin's, 1996); Martin Travers, *Critics of Modernity: The Literature of the Conservative Revolution in Germany, 1890–1933* (Oxford: Peter Lang, 2001); Jeffrey Herf, *Reactionary Modernism: Technology, Culture, and Politics in Weimar and the Third Reich* (Cambridge: Cambridge University Press, [1984] 2002).

15. See the new edition of Mohler's study by Radix Press (the main outlet of the Alt-Right), and with a preface, foreword, and afterword by leading intellectuals of the contemporary French, American, and German New Right, namely Alain De Benoist, Paul Gottfried, and Karlheinz Weissman. See also Paul Gottfried, *Carl Schmitt: Politics and Theory* (New York: Praeger, 1990); Alain De Benoist, *Quatres figures de la Révolution Conservatrice allemande: Werner Sombart, Arthur Moeller van den Bruck, Ernst Niekisch, Oswald Spengler* (Paris: Association des Amis d'Alain de Benoist, 2014); Michael Minkenberg, "The New Right in France and Germany: Nouvelle Droite, Neue Rechte, and the New Right Radical Parties," in P. H. Merkl and L. Weinberg, eds., *The Revival of Right Wing Extremism in the Nineties* (London: Frank Cass, 1997); Tomislav Sunic, *Against Democracy and Equality: The European New Right* (London: Arktos [1990] 2011), 75–82; O'Meara, *New Culture, New Right*, 46–50.
16. Oswald Spengler, *The Decline of the West*, 2 vols., trans. Charles Francis Atkinson (London: Allen & Unwin, [1918/1922] 1926/1928). For general assessments, see James Joll, "Two Prophets of the Twentieth Century: Spengler and Toynbee," *Review of International Studies* 11, no. 2 (1985): 91–104; John Farrenkopf, "The Transformation of Spengler's Philosophy of World History," *Journal of the History of Ideas* 52, no. 3 (1991): 463–485; Herman, *The Idea of Decline*, 225–236.
17. Oswald Spengler, *The Hour of Decision*, trans. Charles Francis Atkinson (London: Allen & Unwin, 1934), 67–71.
18. Oswald Spengler, *Man and Technics*, trans. Charles Francis Atkinson and Michael Putman (London: Arktos, [1931] 2015), 56. Emphasis original.
19. Ibid., 68. See also Spengler, *The Decline of the West*, vol. II, 497–507.
20. Spengler, *Man and Technics*, 76. See also Spengler, *The Hour of Decision*, 218.
21. As Carl Schmitt puts it in *The Concept of the Political*, trans. George Schwab (Chicago: Chicago University Press, [1927] 2007), 94–95: "How ultimately this century should be understood will be revealed only when it is known which type of politics is strong enough to master the new technology and which type of new friend-enemy groupings can develop on this new ground." See also Hans Freyer, "Revolution from the Right," in Anton Kaes, Martin Jay, and Edward Dimendberg, eds., *The Weimar Reader* (Berkeley: University of California Press, [1931] 1994); Arthur Moeller van den Bruck, *Germany's Third Empire* (London: Arktos, [1923] 2012); Ernst Jünger, *The Worker: Dominion and Form* (Evanston: Northwestern University Press, [1932] 2017).
22. Counter-Current Publishing is one of the main outlets and ideological platforms of the North American New Right and the Alt-Right.
23. Greg Johnson, "About Counter-Currents Publishing and North American New Right," online at https://www.counter-currents.com/about/ [August 7, 2019]. This passage also bears the influence of another thinker of decline and renewal, Julius Evola.
24. See de Benoist, and particularly his support of Alexander Dugin's call for a new "fourth political theory" for the twenty-first century that can supplant the liberalism,

socialist, and nationalist theories that successively dominated the previous three. *The Fourth Political Theory*, trans. Mark Sleboda and Michael Millerman (London: Arktos Media, 2012).

25. Greg Johnson, *Toward a New Nationalism* (San Francisco: Counter-Currents, 2019), 74.
26. Guillaume Faye, *Why We Fight: Manifesto of the European Resistance* (London: Artkos Media, 2011), 190.
27. Samuel Francis, *Beautiful Losers: Essays on the Failure of American Conservatism* (Columbia: University of Missouri Press, 1994), 17.
28. See, for instance, Samuel T. Francis, *Leviathan and Its Enemies* (Washington, DC: Washington Summit Publisher, 2016); Paul Gottfried, *After Liberalism: Mass Democracy in the Managerial States* (Princeton, NJ: Princeton University Press, 2001); Alain de Benoist and Charles Champetier, *Manifesto of the French New Right in Year 2000*, online at http://www.4pt.su/en/content/manifesto-french-new-right, [February 5, 2019]; O'Meara, *New Culture, New Right.*
29. Drolet and Williams, "America First."
30. De Benoist and Charles Champetier, *Manifesto.*
31. Robert Steuckers, "Post-Modern Challenges: Between Faust and Narcissus," *North American New Right* 1 (2012): 250. Domitius Corbulo, "The Enlightenment from a New Right Perspective," *North American New Right* 2 (2017): 7–32.
32. Guillaume Faye, *Archeofuturism: European Visions of the Post-Catastrophic Age* (London: Artkos, 2010), 94).
33. Guillaume Faye, *Le système à tuer les peuples* (Paris: Copernic, 1981); Paul Gottfried, "America and the West: The Multiculturalist International," *Orbis* 46, no. 1 (2002): 145–161; Francis, *Leviathan.*
34. Angelo Codevilla, "NATO Now Serves the Interests of the Transatlantic Ruling Class," *American Greatness*, July 15, 2018. Online at: https://amgreatness.com/2018/07/15/nato-now-serves-the-interests-of-the-transatlantic-ruling-class/ [February 6, 2020].
35. Adam Nossiter and Jason Horowitz, "Bannon's Populists, Once a 'Movement,' Keep Him at Arm's Length," *New York Times*, May 24, 2019. https://www.nytimes.com/2019/05/24/world/europe/steve-bannon-european-elections-paris.html [June 9, 2019].
36. Richard Spencer, "What It Means to Be Alt-Right: The Charlottesville Statement," August 11, 2017, online at altright.com/2017/08/11/what-it-means-to-be-alt-right/ . [August 7, 2019]. See also Alain De Benoist, "Confronting Globalization," *Telos* (1996): 117–137.

# 6

# The Chinese Global in the Long Postwar

## Narratives of War, Civilization, and Infrastructure since 1945

*Rana Mitter*

In 2015, the Chinese academic and nationalist public intellectual Zhang Weiwei was given funding to establish a "China Model Development Institute." As he told the *New York Times* in June of that year, the Institute aimed to articulate the concept of *huayuquan* (话语权). Asked how he would define this term, Zhang replied: "I suggest 'Chinese discourse' or 'Chinese narrative,' or in certain contexts, 'Chinese political narrative.' It means there is a rightful place for Chinese discourse in the world."[1]

Zhang's explanation is a starting point to analyze the confluence of circumstances that has in recent years seen a growing interest in an idea of a "narrative" emanating from China. This narrative is often defined by official circles as "the China Story," with the term defined very much as a singular one, with no acceptance of variation, flaws, or contradictions. This chapter will suggest that since the first decade of the twenty-first century, China (through a combination of governmental, academic, and media discourse) has been engaged in an active production of narratives which seek to reposition the country as a strong and consequential actor within global order, as well as redefining China's own role as a shaper of norms and ideas in other countries. This program is perhaps the single most important such effort by China for some two centuries, rivaled only by the revolutionary discourse of the Mao era. Although the terms "discourse" and "narrative" (as used by Zhang) will both be relevant, the argument will concentrate on the idea of "narrative," as there is an increasingly linear and teleological element to the discourses created, making the term appropriate. The idea of China as a "global" actor is increasingly tied to a self-definition that suggests a new kind of modernization theory, while avoiding other liberal/enlightenment teleologies such as democratization.

Rana Mitter, *The Chinese Global in the Long Postwar* In: *Debating Worlds*. Edited by Daniel Deudney, G. John Ikenberry, and Karoline Postel-Vinay, Oxford University Press. © Oxford University Press 2023. DOI: 10.1093/oso/9780197679302.003.0007

However, the argument will also stress that the production of such narratives is not an innovation. Since the loss caused by imperialism to Chinese autonomy over the country's immediate geographical and cultural hinterland in the late nineteenth century, there have been many attempts to create a new narrative of Chinese presence in the global order, and, more ambitiously, of a Chinese role in shaping it. Three examples are used here, suggesting a traceable process of change over time. First comes an exploration of a relatively under-examined debate in China in the immediate postwar (post-1945) years: at this time, the prominent liberal intellectual and politician Jiang Tingfu articulated a new narrative of China that could draw on universalist norms while delineating a new identity as a culturally distinctive state, with the implication of mentorship for other emergent postcolonial nations. This geopolitical throat-clearing provided a forerunner of sorts for the better-known Maoist narrative of profound social change domestically, combined with revolutionary change abroad (which I do not explore in detail here, as it is relatively well-known), prominent in the era from the 1950s to the early 1970s. The other two cases date from the early twenty-first century, detailing two parallel narratives that are currently being used to craft a narrative that underpins China's new, largely economically defined, standing: (1) the role of China in World War II and the consequences of that role for its attitude toward regional order in Asia; and (2) the "civilizational" narrative, of which Zhang Weiwei is one advocate, which proposes simultaneously that China is a *sui generis* actor, but that it also serves as a political exemplar, in particular for Global South nations.

Overall, the production of a contemporary China narrative is still a work in progress. Despite considerable resources being invested in it at the level of the Chinese state, there is still little sense that an integrated China narrative has much valency in creating new ideational frameworks for understanding global or regional order.[2] There are partial exceptions, however, which may be a sign that there is a growing effectiveness as the narrative develops and deepens: for instance, the South Korean willingness to accept some aspects of China's redefinition of an East Asian meaning of World War II, along with the growing willingness of some actors in Africa and Asia to draw on aspects of the developmental/civilizational narrative to redefine their own polities in a way that avoids the universalizing norms of the "third wave" of democratization. The downturn in the international favorability of the US under the Trump administration may also have encouraged more global consideration of China's narrative, particularly if issues such as tackling climate change can be used to add substance to China's definition of "civilization." Yet China's hostile response to global pushback against its account of the COVID-19 pandemic has, in turn, blunted its own capacity to shape responses in the Global North.

## The Twentieth Century: Little Room for Narratives

To understand why it is remarkable that there is a distinctively Chinese narrative for discussion in the first place, it is worth recalling how long it has been since any such discourse had even a chance of significant impact. The last period during which there was a meaningful discursive universe based on norms derived from Chinese culture was perhaps the mid-nineteenth century; the time when, in the term of Joshua Fogel, China was "articulating the Sinosphere" that extended to Japan, Korea, Vietnam, and other societies that were not naturally Sinophone. During the era of high imperialism in China, from the mid-nineteenth to the mid-twentieth century, there were numerous attempts to articulate a vision of global society that drew on Chinese norms. Kang Youwei's idea of "universal harmony" in the late Qing dynasty was one that still showed confidence that Chinese-derived norms might be able to provide a robust system for social cohesion. By the 1920s, the political journalist Zou Taofen was less confident, putting forward a Confucian-Mencian-derived series of ideas that argued that Chinese ideas on an ordered society could be applied to international society despite the dominance of a more Westphalian system. By this stage, however, the dynamic that would shape Chinese thinking about the global for several decades had set in: a defensive posture in the face of difficulties.[3]

For China's thinkers through much of the twentieth century were not lacking in political ideas; but the vast majority of those ideas were articulated around the idea of mitigating or solving an existential crisis in China, not in the idea of a creating a "Sinosphere" or any putatively universalist model underpinned by Chinese ideas.[4] Japan, the most obvious case for a non-Western model of expansion (conceptual as well as military) during this period, did not seriously seek to create a politically normative version of Japanese governance. Instead it adapted the language of governance to make its colonial presence more effective, for instance by the establishment of the Confucian anti-modern idea of Wangdao ("the Kingly Way") in the client state of Manchukuo, while grudgingly allowing their wartime collaborator Wang Jingwei to define himself as a modern nationalist. While, as Chris Goto-Jones has shown, Japanese intellectuals discussed the idea of "overcoming modernity" in the thought of figures such as the philosopher Nishida Kitarō, the discourse of such thinkers was not particularly teleological (discourse rather than narrative), and made little effort to include non-Japanese actors.[5]

The nature of China's early twentieth-century crisis, culminating in the disaster of the Sino-Japanese War of 1937–1945, provided few opportunities to create a universalist idea of China's role in the region and the wider world. However, World War II did provide the first chance for the country to rearticulate its vision of a wider global community shaped by China. Chiang Kai-shek made proposals for a wider Chinese role in the postwar Asian regional order, which would involve a closer relationship with Japan and a role in Korea and Southeast Asia.[6] However, the most important element of the shift in China's global standing was perhaps the ability to create a new narrative of its own role in shaping a world to come after the end of the conflict.

Chiang certainly believed that such a narrative was necessary, even if his first attempt to articulate it was relatively inward-looking and vague on detail. In *China's Destiny*, the 1943 manifesto put out under his name, but in fact largely written by the right-wing Nationalist political ideologue Dai Jitao, Chiang argued for a version of postwar economic change that would involve drawing on the idea of "Great Harmony" (as previously proposed by Kang Youwei), while encouraging a planned economy (as advocated by Sun Yatsen).[7] Elements of these ideas would also be used by another contemporary Chinese thinker, Jiang Tingfu, to propose a broader model of China's role in the postwar world. Jiang was one of the most versatile intellectual and political figures of mid-twentieth-century China. He began his career as a historian, but was appointed in the 1930s and 1940s by Chiang successively as Chinese ambassador to the USSR, chair of the Executive Yuan of the Chinese government, chief administrator of the Chinese National Relief and Rehabilitation Administration (CNRRA), and then Chinese ambassador to the United Nations.

Jiang was a prominent figure, although he was relatively isolated because of his liberalism. Nonetheless, Jiang's thinking is suggestive in the task of assessing the formation of a Chinese narrative, because it suggests a first cut at a progression toward an autonomous, post-imperialist ability to shape the postwar order in a way that simultaneously acknowledged the constraints of a dominant universalist model of international society with the desire to portray a Chinese contribution as distinctive and steeped in values or norms that were distinct from "Western" ones.

In some areas, Jiang drew heavily on Western examples. In 1936, at a time of tremendous political vulnerability for China, Jiang had identified "warlords" and "political factions" as agents of national disunity. However, he also stressed that China needed to work "progressively toward economic unity." He cited the advantage that the United States had in operating as a single economic unit, and argued that "Europe's most advanced people have long advocated studying American examples and organizing a pan-European united country. Today's economics demand a relatively large economic unit to produce efficiency."[8] However, as was also understandable in the context of prewar China, he acknowledged the importance of nationalism, drawing on a then-current European example to make a case about China: he cited the refusal of Rhinelanders to accept exemptions on indemnity taxes, and the 90 percent vote in the 1935 Saar plebiscite in favor of return to Germany, despite French financial incentives to vote the other way in both cases. "This kind of national spirit depends on ourselves to develop it," noted Jiang. "Foreigners can't help us, and nor can they stop us."[9]

Yet Jiang also wrote about the blind worship, as he saw it, of Western learning by the Chinese "scholar-officials" in terms that would seem reminiscent of Mao Zedong some decades later. "They don't do manual labour themselves," he wrote. Furthermore, their knowledge is acquired by "reading dead books," and in particular the "dead books of westerners, who are talking about western society." Even now, Jiang did not mean to advocate some sort of return to a pre-modern Chinese discourse. Instead, in a problem that is echoed in the present day (as we shall see shortly), he aimed to reconcile the desire and belief that China had a narrative that was distinctive from that of the West, and that China could use it to reshape order at home and abroad. Yet at the same time, he had to acknowledge (at least implicitly) that any Chinese system would inevitably operate within a wider set of norms that had come from the West. Jiang was very much aware that "the West" (in the 1930s) was hardly one entity: its liberal, fascist, and communist variants were as much at odds with each other as they were with the narratives of the non-European world (particularly anti-colonialism). It was also notable that Jiang's interpretation of China was very much aware of the country's flaws (a realization lacking from the more triumphalist versions of the contemporary version of the "civilizational" discourse).

A year later, in 1937, war had broken out between China and Japan, and Jiang expanded further on the question of the "bases of national strength." He listed a variety of infrastructural and cultural factors that could affect this strength, including "political systems, school curricula, communications construction, economic development, cultural direction . . . or even the pleasures of private individuals." In tones that recalled the most radical of the May Fourth reformers, who had sought to rethink or reject Confucian norms of ethics and behavior, Jiang declared: "If morality and national strength are in the balance against each other, then it is our moral outlook that we should revise." This anti-Confucian moral stand found further grounding in his praise for Chen Duxiu, cofounder of the Chinese Communist Party who had turned to Trotskyism by the late 1930s. He praised Chen for his call for the Chinese to "become uncivilized" [*yemanhua*]: "The uncivilized person's bravery is from the flesh; he dares to do and to be. . . . [T]he civilized person's bravery," in contrast, comes only "through the mouth or the pen."[10] The contrast between "wildness" and "civilization" would be echoed in various ways in decades to come; the Cultural Revolution of the 1960s, for instance, was in large part a reaction against the idea of "civilization," as in the famous aphorism from Mao that "a revolution is not a dinner party; it cannot be so civilized." Again, there is a marked contrast with the contemporary era, where the idea of "civilization" is seen as something to embrace, not to reject as inauthentic or constrictive.

Jiang had more opportunity to put his thoughts into action in the wartime and postwar era, when his ideas were mapped onto the messy reality of post-1945 relief and rehabilitation. When Jiang wrote in 1936, China's sovereignty was still seriously compromised, and the country was at best a second-tier member of the League of Nations with little wider influence. A decade later, China was about to take up a permanent seat at the United Nations and exercised significant moral power as a mentor to other postcolonial nations. This was the hesitant but real start of a new narrative of Chinese standing both at home and abroad: no longer a humiliated semi-colonial power, but instead, a fledgling regional power with global reach (through the UN and international organizations), and a potential model for other states gaining independence from the colonial powers.

In retrospect, of course, it was the destruction of the Nationalist state in the civil war of 1946–1949 that made this particular narrative implausible in the extreme. However, even before the collapse of Chiang's regime, one should note the difficulties that emerged from the disparity between Jiang's proposals and the reality of a corrupt and chaotic government operating on the ground in China. Jiang proposed that China's reconstruction after the war should be used as an example for how other nations might tackle questions of postwar rebuilding (again, in the early twenty-first century, Chinese arguments about infrastructure and development would be a powerful part of their creation of the idea of a "China model"). Jiang attempted to address some of these contradictions in a long and detailed essay in 1947 entitled "Political Liberalism and Economic Liberalism," engaging in particular with the tensions between the two.

Jiang had no compunction about arguing that liberalism was a construct of the European Enlightenment, seeing it as the product of "a long period of struggle with feudal forces, and many bloody revolutions." "From the eighteenth century to the First World War, liberalism enjoyed 160–170 years of being the orthodoxy in thought," he argued, adding that by the early twentieth century, there was a global recognition of the dominant status of liberalism: "most peoples around the world recognized liberalism as the 'orthodox school' of culture."[11]

To demonstrate how universalist ideas could be combined with cultural specificity, Jiang discussed constitutions. He noted that in the Russian Duma in the 1905 revolution that followed the Russo-Japanese War, "they promulgated a constitution," and that the Young Turks at around the same time advocated a culture whose "most important element was liberalism." He went on:

> China and Japan, which had come up with their own cultural system, and were very different from the zone and environment of liberalism, in the early 20th century also prepared to set up a constitution, or had already done so, which planned to widen the people's freedom and the scope of the political assembly.[12]

While this statement could clearly be critiqued strongly in its details, it fitted neatly with Jiang's wider thesis that he had been developing before the war, that a normatively liberal order in the pre–World War I era was disrupted during the middle part of the century, and was, potentially, now in 1947 being restored; by implication, the establishment of a new Chinese constitution in 1946–1947 was one part of that set of changes. Jiang saw the postwar moment as one where certain political ideas could be acknowledged and appropriated for Chinese use. Thus his model of the "liberal" state really described the new welfarist, centrally planned government of post-1945 Britain under Clement Attlee, as well as that of the US that had been transformed by the New Deal. Britain's Labour Party had used free democratic means [*ziyou minzhu*] to nationalize Britain's central bank, coal mines, and railways. Examples cited included reducing the hours in the working week, organizing trade unions ("now there are even factories where you *have* to be unionized"), and the steady rise in workers' wages. When it came to factory and mining health and safety provisions, and unemployment and sickness insurance, they are such that "workers of a hundred years ago could not even have dreamed of."[13]

However, Jiang's delicate advocacy of a politically liberal and individualist politics, along with a planned/directed economy, was not only difficult to articulate in the context of a Nationalist party that was still vanguardist, and wedded to a partial democratization at best. It also fell on stony ground in the China of 1947, where the constitution was being promoted in a polity that was fast collapsing under the weight of civil war. By 1949, Mao had conquered the mainland.

Still, it is worth noting the nature of Jiang's thinking. This was, after all, the first time that China had been able to articulate a vision of its own role without making the expulsion of foreign imperialism the first-order goal. Jiang's system of thought and approach was internationalist, seeing China as part of a world system but also as capable of influencing that system. Writing in 1947, shortly after the end of the UNRRA program, Jiang proposed an argument that seemed to have the aura of Bretton Woods and the idea of economic interdependence, perhaps gathered from figures such as Sun Fo, who had had input into the meeting:[14]

> Modern scholars of economics have become more optimistic overall about the future of the world economy. They feel that with modern science, the production capacity and standards of living of the whole world can be greatly raised. They believe that one country's poverty leads directly to disaster in other countries. To put it the other way, one country's prosperity can directly affect the benefit felt by another country. Economically, this is a world of mutual coexistence and mutual prosperity. If every country's foreign policy was decided by economic factors, international cooperation would be smoothly realized.[15]

There is a poignancy about the "if" in Jiang's last sentence, as there is in his wry statement: "In my experience, friends who use addition and multiplication are much more numerous than those who use subtraction and division." He followed it with a thought that went well beyond wishful thinking: "In politics, China is plotting a transition from the politics of military force to the politics of public opinion."[16] In 1947, such a statement demanded a willfully over-optimistic view of the civil war that was clearly raging. In that year, Jiang could aspire to create a *huayuquan*, a narrative power of what a postwar China could do for Asia in the world. But the political, economic, and military situation made it painfully clear that a narrative was not sufficient in itself.

## Mao's China Narrative and After

The successors to Chiang's regime had rather more success in articulating a China-specific narrative. Mao's China was able to promote a significant revolutionary discourse with a great deal of valency in the postcolonial world. At least two different discourses, one of revolutionary violent change and one of Bandung-style non-interference and cooperation, were sometimes in conflict, but helped to shape an idea of China as a global actor, albeit one whose political power far exceeded its economic one. Many postcolonial nations in Asia and Africa drew on Maoist ideas, as well as insurgent movements such as the Naxalites in India. However, this was more a discourse than a narrative; other than a broad sense of changing global order, it was never entirely clear what the new world would look like, not least since China still aspired to re-enter the existing global order (which it did in 1971 by taking the China seat at the United Nations). The revolutionary discourse became even less prominent when the need for reconstruction after the Cultural Revolution changed China's priorities. Zhou Enlai's articulation of Mao's Theory of the Three Worlds at the United Nations in 1974 provided a new view of China's relations with the world, but also marked a step away from an articulated and holistic vision of what that global vision might be. It also coincided with a period of serious retrenchment at home, underpinned by Deng Xiaoping's idea of "the Four Modernizations."

The 1970s and 1980s marked a time of relative Chinese absence from visions of global order. Domestic political concerns meant that China's attention turned inward, albeit for rather different reasons from the 1930s.

Cultural visions of the 1980s were much more turned toward drawing on models drawn from a neoliberal West (and reformist communist bloc)—as Julian Gewirtz has shown, China's economic reformers at the time drew from figures as varied as Alec Cairncross, Milton and Rose Friedman, and Janos Kornai.[17] The seminal television documentary *River Elegy* (*Heshang*) contained a strong thesis that China needed to embrace the "Blue Ocean" rather than the "Yellow River" to revive its national culture. By implication, it was the US that was the inspiration for a post–Cultural Revolution China. However, this particular vision of economic and cultural liberalization ended with the 1989 Tiananmen crisis, and the fall of Chinese Communist Party (CCP) general secretary Zhao Ziyang.[18]

The year 1989 also proved to be a major obstacle in the Chinese aim of articulating a global narrative. After the killings in Tiananmen Square, the country was regarded as an international pariah, or at best an anomaly, particularly as the same year saw the fall of Europe's communist regimes and a widespread sense that there would be a "third wave" of democratization. The 1990s saw China seeking to re-enter international society by offering few vetoes at the UN (not obstructing the 1991 Gulf War, for instance), and beginning to rebuild its presence with events such as the holding of the 1995 UN Women's Conference near Beijing. However, this period did not see a clear articulation of a Chinese vision of global engagement. Instead, there was an enthusiasm to enter international institutions and networks that gave China prestige (in 2001, China entered the World Trade Organization and also won the right to the Beijing Olympics in 2008), rather than creating or altering those institutions in any major way. During this period, however, China continued to post very high annual growth rates, paving the way for the next phase of development of the idea of the global. The economic basis that had been lacking in all previous articulations of a China narrative was at last plausible.

That plausibility was strengthened by the 2008 economic crisis, which marked a turning point for China's vision of itself in the global community. The Western world appeared to be on the brink of a major economic disaster, possibly rivaling that of the 1930s. At the same time, the Chinese decision to use aggressive credit creation to boost their own economy proved successful in preventing their growth rate from slowing down at a time when many of China's export markets were going into recession. (By the mid-2010s, the results of this policy were causing the Party leadership serious headaches, but that would not become apparent for some years.) At the time, the Chinese leadership became much bolder about the idea that China's aim should no longer be merely to seek membership, even privileged membership, of the existing global order. Instead, it should seek to bolster its now undoubted economic power by seeking to create a new model of Chinese engagement with the world in which "Chinese" views would be more evident and a narrative of a rising Chinese presence in the world would emerge.

## Sources of the New Narrative

However, even if post-2008 China had the economic basis to articulate a new narrative, it was still hampered by a much longer-standing reality: the linguistic and discursive universe within which China could operate was heavily constrained by the norms of Western-derived, putatively universalist political language. In recent years, there have been stimulating academic experiments in trying to subvert the dominance of such language: one example is the political scientist Leigh Jenco's work *Changing Referents*, which argues for the idea of *qun* as a term that could be used to describe various types of "grouping."[19] Within China itself, the political thinker Jiang Qing (no relation to Mao's former wife) has put forward the idea of a "Confucian" constitutional order that would abandon flat democratic norms for a reconstituted form of humane Confucian hierarchy. Yet although Jiang is well-known and has influence, official circles are wary of associating themselves with his ideas; and in reality, he is an unusual figure with little input into the formation of official policy.[20] The dilemma identified by Frantz Fanon and a range of other postcolonial intellectuals, that political liberation does not provide liberation from the linguistic and conceptual structures spread by imperialism, remains a trap within which Chinese discourse and narratives are still confined. The Sinosphere will not return.

The discursive opportunities to reinvent the Chinese narrative, even within the repertoire of modern political thought, have also been limited by the way in which certain narratives of China's engagement and shaping of global discourse have become politically unhelpful or illegitimate. The most obvious of these narratives is China's role as a revolutionary actor in the Cold War. For much of the period from the 1950s to the early 1970s, Mao's China proposed a role for itself as part of a global discourse that was inflected in ways that differentiated itself significantly from dominant discourses from the West and the Soviet Union: based in the Third World (Global South), based on technology and agricultural developmental self-sufficiency; and dedicated to a transformative revolutionary violence (at a time when the USSR sought stability more than ideological revolutionary change).

These ideas are no longer as potent as they were half a century ago. In the contemporary world, there is little enthusiasm for an explicitly revolutionary state in international order. The idea of being a "global" actor, on the other hand, is clearly central to a discourse of international cooperation and stability, and China has made itself central to that language. There was much discussion of Chinese president Xi Jinping's declaration at Davos in January 2017 that China would become a champion of free trade, a veiled rebuke to the protectionist rhetoric of then president-elect Donald Trump. This, however, was a statement of faith (at least, purported faith) in the existing international system, rather than an attempt to redefine its narrative.

Yet there is still the potential for a reinvention of a Chinese narrative, or narratives in the plural. In the 1990s, much Chinese political discourse was more purely rejectionist (and more non-teleological, with no sense of narrative projection): an example of this would be the bestselling *Zhongguo keyi shuo bu* (1996; *China Can Say No*), a nationalist tract based on a Japanese original (*The Japan That Can Say No* by Ishihara Shintaro and Akio Morita) that was as much a near-nihilist riposte to the outward-looking narrative of *Heshang* as it was a rebuke to the foreign powers (particularly the US) whose sins against China were detailed in its pages.[21]

In the first decade of the twenty-first century, China's ability to offer an economic model has been part of the construction of a more positive narrative, albeit one where the Chinese role is regarded as distinctive and countercultural: the Chinese economist Justin Yifu Lin titled his book, which has positive assessments of China's economic policies, *Against the Consensus* (although Lin himself served as chief economist of the World Bank and therefore made a rather anomalous exemplar of anti-establishment thinking).[22] We see here (for instance, in Lin's other work), the beginnings of a discourse of China as mentor for economics and infrastructural development, just as Jiang Tingfu had hoped Nationalist China might be in the 1940s.

One product of the Chinese desire to establish a new definition of itself within world order is its embrace of global historical narratives in which the Chinese role is made more explicit. The voyages of the Ming-dynasty admiral Zheng He have been made part of a new narrative in which there is a putative connection between the outward-looking (and supposedly nonviolent) explorations in the early modern era and the global engagement of contemporary China. This link between the historical, cultural, and economic can also be seen in the official discourse of the New Silk Road ("One Belt One Road") where historical tropes are used to recall a partly mythicized period when Chang'an (now Xi'an) stood at the center of a major Eurasian trading network. However, the discursive work that needs to be done on this idea has not yet progressed very far. One reason is that "ownership" of the discourse is not exclusively Chinese. The internalization of "Western" discourses of international society in the post-1945 world has been deep and long lasting. The effects of a discourse that is only a few years old, that is largely driven by Chinese material interests, and that has powerful opponents within the region (for instance, Japan) are not yet very clear.

## The Reinvention of Wartime

In contrast, another revised narrative has gained rather greater depth over the past two decades: Chinese efforts to create an alternative discourse of the post-1945 world in which China's wartime experience plays a much greater role. Summed up very briefly, this discourse, which has developed since the first decade of the twenty-first century, turns on the idea of China as an actor in a global anti-fascist alliance. Its logic runs as follows: The dominance of the United States in Asia is a product of its role in fighting in the Pacific in World War II, which gave it the political clout, combined with its economic strength, to reshape the region. By this logic, China should also be able to take up a leading role in the region, since China also made huge sacrifices (10 million or more dead, 100 million refugees, and the holding down of over half a million Japanese troops) in the war.

This narrative has overshadowed, but not eliminated, the previous narrative: that China's war against Japan was almost entirely a product of the CCP's resistance to Japan and leadership of the Chinese population. This version made the Chinese narrative a purely domestic one, in which neither political rivals (the Guomindang), foreign actors (US, USSR, Britain), or indeed collaborators with Japan played any significant role.

As a result, historiography in China has been turned in directions that are favorable to this narrative, a shift from the national to the international. The term "global" is applied largely to the nature of the war itself, as an "anti-fascist" war in which China is projected as having played a significant part. A turbulent first decade of the new century exposed how much of the "unfinished business" of 1945 remained ripe for resolution. In particular, the rise of China during the presidency of Hu Jintao (2002–2012) showed that there were plenty of areas in which the 1945 settlement in Asia had been essentially inadequate.

As a consequence, in the mid-2010s, China and Japan, the two powers in the region with the most unreconciled view of their mutual conflict, drew on clashing interpretations of their World War II experience. Japanese right-wingers spoke in ever-louder tones about a revisionist view of Tokyo's imperial wars in Asia in the 1930s and 1940s. The Japanese revisionist view is shared by only one section of the Japanese public, although that grouping does include prominent politicians in the ruling Liberal Democratic Party. It is almost entirely domestically directed, and is vigorously opposed by liberal elements within Japan itself. There is no significant external constituency that is supportive of the idea that Japan's aggression in Asia prior to 1945 should be reassessed in overall positive terms.

China, in turn, produced a revisionist argument about its role during the war: the promotion of China as a country that played a highly significant international role in the ultimate defeat of the Japanese empire in 1945, and now deserved to reap the benefits of its sacrifices. There is a significant domestic audience in China for the idea that the country should be given more credit for its contribution to the defeat of Japan in 1945 and that this acknowledgment of China's wartime sacrifice should help bolster contemporary ideas of Chinese identity. But unlike the revisionist Japanese discourse, the Chinese rediscovery of their wartime history is intended to have an internationalist element. However, it shares a problematic element with the Japanese discourse: it is based on political rather than historical assumptions. The Chinese desire to recast their wartime contribution in the eyes of the world goes against the grain of the politics of the Mao era, as it makes some attempt to restore the reputation of the Chinese Nationalists under Chiang Kai-shek, and acknowledges that without the efforts of (mostly Nationalist) armies to hold down some 750,000 or more Japanese troops, the history of East Asia might have been very different. But it is only in recent years that the Nationalist contribution has been given due credit on the Chinese mainland.[23]

The rehabilitation of the Nationalists is not a product of a desire for historical accuracy, however. The current Chinese government is keen to take the more positive elements of Nationalist resistance to Japan (previously rarely mentioned) during the war and draw on them to create a new narrative of the war for current geopolitical needs. Most of the Western world paid little attention to the seventieth anniversary of the Cairo Conference, which fell in November 2013. But in China and Taiwan, it was noted with interest. The 1943 Cairo Conference was the only conference of World War II where China was treated as an equal Allied power with the US and Britain (not the USSR, which was neutral in the war against Japan). For decades, this was not mentioned in Chinese textbooks because of the unfortunate historical reality that the Chinese leader who represented China at Cairo was not Mao Zedong but Chiang Kai-shek. But the new, grudging tolerance of Chiang in the mainland means that it is now possible to use Cairo to demonstrate a wider point, that China was on the side of the Allies at the most crucial moment for civilization in the past century.

However, it is also clear that the "meaning" of Cairo is being heavily oriented toward contemporary Chinese views of the Asia-Pacific settlement. The Cairo Declaration stated, "It is their purpose that Japan shall be stripped of all the islands in the Pacific which she has seized or occupied since the beginning of the first World War in 1914, and that all the territories Japan has stolen from the Chinese, such as Manchuria, Formosa, and The Pescadores, shall be restored to the Republic of China." It also added the statement that Japan should "be expelled from all other territories which she has taken by violence and greed."[24]

Chinese news media reported extensively that this formulation gave the authority of international law to Chinese claims over the Diaoyu/Senkaku islands. In the early 2010s, disputes had arisen over these eight small uninhabited rocks in the East China Sea. To the Japanese, they were known as the Senkaku; the Chinese referred to them as the Diaoyu (in Taiwan, the Diaoyutai). However, the Chinese interpretation showed the fluid nature of the way in which they used the legacy of World War II in pressing their claims. The first part of the Cairo Declaration does not name the Diaoyu islands explicitly, and since they were designated as Japanese in 1895, they do not fall under the "since 1914" clause.

To add to the complexity, the Ma Ying-jeou administration then in power on Taiwan made it clear that it supported the idea that the islands should return to Chinese sovereignty. But since the Cairo Declaration explicitly demands that the territory should return to "the Republic of China," this opens up a new area of confusion in which the Taipei government, not Beijing, might be considered the rightful inheritor of the Chiang regime on the mainland. In addition, in Taiwan there has been lively debate over the validity of the Cairo Declaration as a legal document, as opposed to a statement of intent. Taiwan's public sphere is much freer than China's, and there have been significant voices that have doubted Ma's reading of sovereignty over the islands.[25]

The eruption of this dispute in the present era shows how the freezing of the Cold War in postwar Asia prevented the creation of multilateral organizations and treaties that might have created a stable framework in the region. China notes, correctly, that the 1952 San Francisco Treaty, which was supposed to mark the final settlement of the war in Asia, excluded the People's Republic. But the reasons for this exclusion draw blame onto both actors in the dispute. The United States refused to recognize Mao's regime, excluding an emergent power from helping define an overall settlement in the region. And China, with Stalin's support, backed up North Korea in its attack on South Korea, making a settlement with the United States close to impossible. The most recent reshaping of the narrative, however, bypasses much of this Cold War history and instead creates a linear connection between the decisions of Nationalist China in the mid-1940s and the PRC government today.

A recent change to the new narrative of wartime China is a chronological one: the official adoption in January 2017 of the idea that China's war against Japan lasted not eight years (from the Marco Polo Bridge incident in 1937 until 1945) but fourteen (from the invasion of Manchuria in 1931). School textbooks were expected to reflect the new interpretation by the spring of 2017, with further emphasis on the role of the CCP, but also on China's role as part of the battlefield against "global anti-fascism."[26] The "fourteen-year" interpretation owes some of its origin to the long-standing concept in Japanese (mostly liberal) historiography of a *jyugonen no senso* (fifteen-year war) over the same period, and was actually quite commonplace in academic scholarship in China during the early 2000s. However, the official adoption of the concept by the state emphasized the importance of a revised narrative for two, at first seemingly divergent, goals: an emphasis on Japanese aggression in the *longue durée*, and the continuing desire to portray China as an internationalist, cooperative actor in the war against fascism, with a clear implication that China's role in the past is similar to its role in the present. So far, it is fair to say that China's revisionist account of its own wartime narrative as part of a wider revisionism has had more impact domestically than abroad; yet China's viewpoint has some standing in places such as South Korea which have not yet managed to achieve full reconciliation with Japan.

## China as "Civilizational State"

The term "narrative" is particularly appropriate in yet another example of the struggle to create a new framework through which China can express its global vision to the wider world. This is the case made by Zhang Weiwei, who runs the China Institute at Fudan University (established in 2015). Zhang has declared: "We have to have our own narrative. There is a Western narrative—mainstream views in the Western media about China which are not accurate and are sometimes very misleading. We have a track record now."[27] It is in this context that he writes about the need for a new *huayu quan* (话语权), or "discursive power," that will allow China to express its worldview in an effective way in a world of rival global discourses.[28]

Zhang's work has become one of the relatively well-known articulations of the idea of a new Chinese "civilizational discourse." It sits among other articulations, including that of Jiang Qing, mentioned earlier, and Daniel A. Bell, who argues that the Chinese government might be seen, in ideal form, as operating on the basis of meritocracy (as opposed to liberal democracy) in selecting talent.[29]

Zhang has explained his aims as follows:

> Discourse is crucial for any country, especially for a superlarge and fast-changing country like China, whose rise has global implications and provokes questions and suspicions. To my mind, the country should face them squarely and explain itself clearly and confidently to its own people and to the outside world. This calls for new narratives, new in content as well as in style. China has its own official political discourse ranging from the party's doctrines to China's foreign policy statements. But it's also true that such a discourse is not easily understandable to non-Chinese, or even to many Chinese. It requires knowledge of China's political context. For instance, the "scientific outlook for development" is a concept crucial for China's own development and for unifying the ideology of the party's rank and file, but it is hardly understandable to non-Chinese.[30]

The narrative of the "civilizational school" makes certain assumptions about China as an international actor, with a role in international society that is explicitly normative. The norms that China claims to espouse, in this model, include but are not limited to:

- the idea of China as a state that does not intervene in other countries' affairs: a rejection of the "responsibility to protect" (R2P) doctrine, but also a partial revisiting of a longer discourse of "non-interference" dating back to the Cold War;
- China as a developmental mentor, providing infrastructural assistance for other developing countries, without the bureaucracy or "irrelevant" norms (for instance, adherence to universalist human rights regimes);
- rejection of a "Washington consensus" (generally defined as neoliberal versions of economic shock therapy).

In *The Civilizational State* (*Wenmingxing guojia*) (2017), Zhang proposes changes in political norms that would come with the idea of a "civilizational state" using the China model. Thus, he argues for the idea of "a changing model: from 'democracy as the only system of government' to 'good government vs bad government.' "[31] Zhang also argues for a "farewell" to "westcentrism" (*xifang zhongxinzhuyi*):

> At the heart of western discourse [*huayu*] is "westcentrism" or "eurocentrism." This claims that European civilization is outstanding, representing the "ultimate stage of human civilization." However, the swift rise of the "China model" has dealt a severe blow to [this] and the idea of "the end of history." People from this country have drawn springs of confidence from history and the present day, calling on China to create a systemic force and cultural force for the rise of a 'civilizational state.' "[32]

Again, Zhang's argument stands in contrast to the codewords used in *Heshang* (*River Elegy*). The program spoke of China abandoning the "yellow river" (the waterway symbolizing an inward-looking parochialism and cruelty) and instead looking to the "blue water," that is, across the Pacific. Very much a product of discourses of the late Cold War, the program included phrases such as "it is industrial civilization! It is calling to us!" Zhang's work is typical of the turn toward a much more nationalistic culture, celebratory of Chinese civilization as a means of understanding wider questions of culture and governance.[33] Zhang has continued to have influence: in June 2021, he is reported to have given a speech to the Politburo about the need to create a "good China story."[34]

However, the work of the "civilizational" school suffers from a major problem with generalizability, a difficulty that is generated by its essentially political, rather than analytical origins. The "China Model," as Zhang (for one) proposes it, is simultaneously an argument that China is *sui generis*, as a large civilizational state, unsuited either to political or economic (neo-) liberalism, but is also a "model" for other states, particularly non-Western ones in Africa and Asia. (The "civilizational school" has been less enthusiastic to embrace the neo-revolutionary discourse of the Chavez or Morales type in South America.) This has led to an opposition of stylized visions of the "West" against a supposedly clearly defined Chinese "civilization" or China "story." In this version of the division between the two sides, liberal/pluralist states and entities in the Global South fail to make much of an appearance (India, Brazil, South Africa, etc.), and other categories ("Africa") are used to conceal difference through a broad-brush definitional approach.

The model that Zhang and others put forward is largely shaped by political goals, and (unlike Jiang Tingfu's earlier articulations) has almost no negative assessments of contemporary China. However, it is useful to consider it as a political phenomenon, because it reflects a much wider sense in China, and also among some other Global South actors in particular, that there is still a discursive hegemony from the "West" that fails to accommodate difference in any meaningful way. The most egregious examples of Chinese domestic human rights abuses (notably the crackdown on media, lawyers, and academics under Xi Jinping) have obscured a wider reality: that progress toward democratization is no longer regarded as an inevitable norm, even if it is a dominant one, in many parts of the Global South, and indeed in some parts of the Global North also.

There is, of course, a path dependency that the "civilizationists" do not tend to stress in advocating their "model"; namely, that once a population is awarded wider individual civil rights, it is much harder to reverse that situation. So, it would be implausible to go to Brazil or Taiwan and suggest that they end or curtail civil liberties as the price of economic growth. On the other hand, the Turkish AK government has done something similar to this during its rise to power, as the Turkish civil sphere has withered away, a move underpinned by repeated AK majoritarian victories. (Also, Putin's Russia removed direct election for provincial governors in the early 2000s, and Russia, Poland, and Hungary have at different levels restricted norms on freedom in the public sphere that had emerged in the 1990s, in the latter two cases while embedded in EU and ECHR membership). Nor is it implausible to argue that countries whose civil society and economy have been damaged by the policies of austerity and neoliberalism might choose alternative models or narratives.

## Conclusion

There has never been only one "China story," despite the efforts of today's Communist Party to promote the idea of a unitary narrative of China's rise and exemplary status with regard to other countries and societies. However, there are themes that have emerged as constants in the wider development of a China narrative in the postwar era. The prewar China discourse is significantly different since it was inevitably inflected by the need to regain full Chinese sovereignty and to counteract the many threats to China from within and outside. The year 1943, the date when the old system of extraterritoriality for foreign powers ended, marks the conclusion of that older discourse and the emergence, instead, of a narrative: the idea of China as a country with its own sense of progression that is written within more universalist norms, but inflected by its own experience (as an underdeveloped, relatively poor, non-Western state). Jiang Tingfu and Mao Zedong had rather different political views, to put it mildly, but they both shared the idea that industrial and agricultural reconstruction combined with a sense of national destiny could be a powerful combination that might inspire both China and other countries. That viewpoint is not a huge distance away from the narrative of China's rise conveyed today by China's development experts and diplomats in places as far apart as Ethiopia, Cambodia, and Pakistan. The challenge now for China is to design an endpoint for the narrative which can compete with what they would regard as the discredited teleology of a liberal-pluralist "end of history."

## Notes

1. https://cn.nytimes.com/china/20150615/c15zhangweiwei/en-us/?mcubz=1.
2. On Chinese use of propaganda in the contemporary era, see Anne-Marie Brady, *Marketing Dictatorship* (Lanham, MD, 2008).
3. See Joshua Fogel, *Articulating the Sinosphere* (Cambridge, MA, 2009); on Zou Taofen, see Rana Mitter, "The Individual and the International 'I': Zou Taofen and Changing Views of China's Place in the International System," *Global Society* 17, no. 2 (2003).
4. William Callahan, *China: The Pessoptimist Nation* (Oxford, 2009).

5. Christopher Goto-Jones, *Political Philosophy of Japan* (Abingdon, UK, 2005).
6. Xiaoyuan Liu, *A Partnership for Disorder: China, the United States, and Their Policies for the Postwar Disposition of the Japanese Empire, 1941–1945* (Cambridge, 1996).
7. Chiang Kai-shek, *Zhongguo zhi mingyun* [China's Destiny] (Chongqing, 1943).
8. "Lun guoli de yuansu" [The basis of national strength, November 16, 1938], in *Jiang Tingfu wenji* [Collected essays of Jiang Tingfu], hereafter JTFWJ, 651.
9. "Lun guoli," 651, 652.
10. "Lun guoli," 645, 646.
11. "Zhengzhi ziyou yu jingji ziyou" [Political freedom and economic freedom, April 26, 1947] in JTFWJ, 661.
12. "Zhengzhi ziyou," 661.
13. "Zhengzhi ziyou," 664, 665.
14. Eric Helleiner, *Forgotten Foundations of Bretton Woods; International Development and the Making of the Postwar Order* (Ithaca, NY, 2014).
15. "Mantan zhishi fenzi de shidai shiming" [Discussing the mission of this era of intellectuals, June 16, 1947], JTFWJ, 674.
16. JTFWJ, 674.
17. Julian Gewirtz, *Chinese Reformers, Western Economists, and the Making of Global China* (Cambridge, MA, 2017).
18. Su Xiaokang and Wang Luxiang, *Deathsong of the River* (Ithaca, NY, 1991).
19. Leigh Jenco, *Changing Referents: Learning across Space and Time in China and the West* (Oxford, 2016).
20. Jiang Qing, *A Confucian Constitutional Order: How China's Ancient Past Can Shape Its Political Future*, trans. Edmund Ryden, ed. Daniel A. Bell and Ruiping Fan (Princeton, NJ, 2013)
21. Zhang Xiaobo, et al., *China Can Say No: Political and Emotional Choices in the Post Cold-War Era* [Zhongguo keyi shuo bu: lengzhan hou shidai de zhengzhi yu qinggan jueze] (Beijing, 1996).
22. Justin Yifu Lin, *The Quest for Prosperity* (Princeton, NJ, 2012) and *Against the Consensus* (Cambridge, 2013).
23. Rana Mitter, *China's Good War: How World War II Is Shaping a New Nationalism* (Cambridge, MA, 2020).
24. Cairo Communique: the text and a reproduction of the original document can be found at: http://www.ndl.go.jp/constitution/e/shiryo/01/002_46/002_46tx.html; see also Mitter, *China's Good War*, ch. 6.
25. See, for instance, Wu Sihua, Lu Fangshang, and Lin Yongle, eds., *Kailuo xuanyan de yiyi yu yingxiang* [The significance and impact of the Cairo Declaration] (Taipei, 2014).
26. http://www.scmp.com/news/china/policies-politics/article/2060939/chinas-education-ministry-extends-timeline-war-against.
27. https://www.forbes.com/sites/sarahtilton/2015/10/30/zhang-weiwei-talks-about-his-new-think-tank-u-s-china-relations-and-why-he-loves-bhutan/#276761a82aee.
28. https://sinosphere.blogs.nytimes.com/2015/06/12/q-and-a-zhang-weiwei-on-why-china-will-succeed-under-the-communist-party/?mcubz=1&_r=0.

29. Daniel A. Bell, *The China Model: Political Meritocracy and the Limits of Democracy* (Princeton, NJ, 2015).
30. https://sinosphere.blogs.nytimes.com/2015/06/12/q-and-a-zhang-weiwei-on-why-china-will-succeed-under-the-communist-party/?mcubz=1&_r=0.
31. See ch. 6, Zhang Weiwei, *Wenmingxing guojia* [The civilizational state] (Shanghai, 2017).
32. Zhang, *Wenmingxing*, 156.
33. Geremie Barme, "To Screw Foreigners Is Patriotic: China's Avant-Garde Nationalists," in Jonathan Unger, ed., *Chinese Nationalism* (Armonk, NY, 1996).
34. https://uscnpm.org/2021/06/09/who-is-zhang-weiwei/.

# 7

# Narrating India in/and the World

## Colonial Origins and Postcolonial Contestations

*Itty Abraham*

A hallmark of Indian foreign policy under Prime Minister Narendra Modi has been the active redefinition of India from a secular nation-state to the contemporary manifestation of a great civilization, or as it is often termed, "civilization-state."[1,2] In a recent study, Ian Hall argues that Modi seeks to be a "transformational leader" whose vision is to ground Indian foreign policy "in Hindu nationalist ideology. . . . [leading to a] foreign policy shaped by [India's] civilizational ethos."[3] While these are accurate characterizations of Modi's effort to redefine India's international personality, this is not the first time that "civilization" or variations on that term have been used to describe the foundations of its foreign policy. Indeed, as we shall see below, its original usage takes us back to before India was a sovereign state, although the ascribed meaning of civilization in the nineteenth century was somewhat different from its current, post-Huntington, usage. What remains consistent is the association of the term with a hierarchical world order and embedded implications of cultural superiority.

Being acknowledged as a civilization-state is not all that marks India's new foreign policy orientation. Modi has made outreach to India's estimated 30 million-strong diaspora a distinct feature of his tenure, holding as many as fifteen sold-out rallies at iconic venues including New York's Madison Square Garden, London's Wembley Stadium, and Sydney's Olympic Park, before Covid-19 ended his global travels. On September 22, 2019, 50,000 overseas Indians packed Houston's NRG stadium to greet him in a mass rally that received global media attention. Modi was joined on stage by the US president, both Texas senators, and a US congressional delegation in a remarkable show of bipartisan political support. Modi's Houston rally was a spectacle, but not a surprise. His political party, the Bharatiya Janata Party (BJP), has always considered ties with India's diaspora of great importance, in marked contrast

Itty Abraham, *Narrating India in/and the World* In: *Debating Worlds.* Edited by Daniel Deudney, G. John Ikenberry, and Karoline Postel-Vinay, Oxford University Press. © Oxford University Press 2023.
DOI: 10.1093/oso/9780197679302.003.0008

to India's other national political party, the once-dominant Indian National Congress, which ruled the country continuously from India's first elections in 1951 until 1977.

Narratives of India's external relations are channeled along two vectors: the underlying *ideas and beliefs* that shaped India's interactions with the world beyond its borders, summarized here as "India and the World"; and, the planetary spread of *people of Indian origin* and changes in their imagined relations with the homeland, or "Global India," to use Latha Varadarajan's apt term.[4] The discursive origins of these two narratives lie in events and conditions preceding formal sovereignty, meaning that these narratives are imposed on long-term tendencies and structural forces foundational to external relations.

Narratives are stories based on what Cornelius Castoriadis has called social "imaginaries." Drawing on Jasanoff and Kim's interpretation of his work, social imaginaries are defined here as world-envisioning technologies that engender collective interpretations of social reality.[5] They constitute a "reservoir of norms and discourses, metaphors and cultural meanings out of which [elite] actors build their policy preferences . . . they articulate feasible futures." Not surprisingly then, there is no single imaginary that captures the entirety of the social context in question, in this case external relations. Further, stories based on these imaginaries—narratives—are contested from both within and without. Narratives of India and the World (India as civilization-state) and Global India (India as diaspora) coexist and overlap and may even be contradictory at times. Taken together, these narratives cannot be analytically reduced into a singular and uniform "foreign policy."[6] Rather, if competing narratives are understood as stories seeking dominance, what is conventionally termed "foreign policy" should be seen as the outcome of discursive and political *struggles* over which narrative(s) should be dominant.

India and the World is composed of narratives of the identities, representations, values, and principles that the country stands for as an international actor. The dominant narrative of India's international personality has moved from a struggle for recognition as an independent state (the colonial period) to an oppositional engagement with an unequal and hierarchical international order (the postcolonial period) to mimicry and conformity with great power behavior. Global India, by contrast, is constituted by narratives of the shifting boundaries of the Indian nation. In a world defined by, ideally, the territorial coincidence of nation and state, the global dispersion of people of Indian origin becomes an anomaly to understand

and explain. Global India's narratives have ranged from deep concern over the condition of India's overseas populations during the colonial period to careful distance during the early years of independence to a renewed engagement today on entirely new terms. In other words, the spatial and conceptual boundaries of the nation as well its preferred identity have both changed radically over the past two centuries. These changes are manifested in and explained by changing narratives.

## India and the World

"Civilization" has always been a deeply contested term in international discourse. It demands consideration of what it means to be "civilized," a term that has international legal significance as well as cultural and humanist meaning,[7] even as it marks a "standard": a political measure of the global standing, contributions, and achievements of a cultural zone or country in the modern world order.[8] The term is most directly contested in struggles against being identified as "uncivilized," as much of the world was characterized until the era of decolonization.[9] The term thus marks—simultaneously—difference as well as universality.[10]

India was no exception to this immanent duality. A central theme of India's relations with the world are built around this term—to be seen as one of the world's great civilizations and to be considered as civilized as anyone else. The centuries-long struggle to affirm civilizational standing and to overturn perceptions of its lack would shape profoundly India's international personality and domestic politics. This chapter's starting point is to argue that the colonial-era debate over India's alleged civilizational lack constitutes the intellectual foundation of how postcolonial Indian elites continue to see themselves in the world. Following a brief exegesis of the civilization debate, it spells out how the deployment of civilization-talk as a means of colonial subjugation engendered two contrasting narratives.

The first imaginary, manifested as an "Indic territorial" narrative, is fundamentally a defensive vision of the country, requiring the protection of a sacred geobody always vulnerable to foreign threat and invasion. The second imaginary, elaborated as an "Asian cosmopolitan" narrative, argues for an equal and democratic world order not shaped by materialism and military power (seen as Western values). The Indic territorial narrative explains post-imperial continuities in regional affairs, while the Asian cosmopolitan narrative leads to the call for a just and democratic world order. Both narratives exist simultaneously, each engendering different foreign policy practices. Hence, shifts in Indian foreign policy are better understood as changing combinations of these civilizational narratives and their corresponding practices. And that is exactly what Modi's foreign policy innovations represent—namely, a new synthesis of old narratives. Due to the radical anxiety underlying the urge to claim India's civilizational status, however, familiar associations are turned on their head. Instead of the "fact" of a great civilization engendering the imperative of becoming a great power, the opposite is true: achieving strategic autonomy proves that India is a great civilization.

## British Orientalism and Liberalism

The origins of "civilization" as a conceptual ground from which to understand India's relations with the world lie in the late eighteenth and nineteenth centuries, beginning with the British Orientalist tradition and subsequent intersections with colonial ethnology and governance.[11] The historian Thomas Trautmann offers two simple images to help understand the political implications of classical philology, the intellectual foundation of the Orientalist tradition, identifying the tree (and its branches) as one heuristic scaffolding of this tradition, the other being the staircase.[12]

Initially, the image of the tree held sway. The first generation of Orientalists, William Jones and Henry Thomas Colebrook, followed by Friedrich Max Müller, professor of Sanskrit at Oxford, seeking to understand the linguistic affinities between Sanskrit and European languages, posited a common "Indo-European" root language from which "branch" languages as different as Hindi, Persian, the Romance languages, and German originated. For Müller, the morphological similarities of dispersed languages would be explained by the migration paths of a common people to different corners of the globe. The term "Arya" (a self-referential term for "us") would become a racial category, the "Aryans," the first speakers of the root Indo-European language.[13] And (to summarize a huge body of scholarship), "by century's end a deep and lasting consensus was reached respecting India . . . that Indian civilization was produced by the clash and subsequent mixture of light skinned civilizing invaders (the Aryans) and dark skinned barbarian aborigines (often identified as Dravidians)."[14] In the "tree" schema, no language was seen as inherently superior or more advanced than another. Notwithstanding, this discourse would lead to tropes of invasion and racial difference, mediated by skin color, becoming naturalized as powerful foundations of Indian elite self-understanding.

The staircase image owes its roots to British liberal critics of Jones and his fellow Orientalists, most notably James Mill, father of John Stuart. The senior Mill, author of the "hegemonic" *History of British India* (1817), saw in India all the failings of a decayed civilization.[15] These views would be amplified and made a global commonsense by other Western scholars, notably the German philosopher Hegel, who "held . . . that only the civilizations of the Near East had a major contribution to make to world, that is Western, civilization."[16] For the Mills, Hegel, and others who followed in their tradition—including, it should be remembered, Karl Marx and Max Weber—India's civilizational failings would include a "dream-like" metaphysics, asymptotic to reason; an irrational social structure built around caste; the village as the center of social life; and despotic kingship as the natural form of politics. These and other figures of backwardness gave proof to the belief that world civilizations could be ordered in hierarchical terms, captured by the image of the staircase. Needless to say, Europe stood on a much higher step than did other civilizations. India may have been the object of discussion but imperial-era orientalism (in the sense used by Edward Said) "defined Europe and capitalism as much as it did India."[17] It should be noted that the staircase metaphor would go on to shape the modern social sciences profoundly, most perniciously in the form of modernization theory and development studies.[18]

Faced with "the conundrum of a dark-skinned people with an ancient civilization,"[19] a further shift needed to take place before liberalism, the defining "progressive" ideology of the nineteenth century, could be used to justify imperialism.[20] Trautmann argues that a key figure in the transformation of linguistic similarities into racial difference was James Cowles Pritchard, a (now forgotten but typically Victorian) medical doctor, philologist, and Quaker. The central thrust of Pritchard's early writings was to argue that "civilization was a *cause* of race," with higher civilizations evolving into lighter skinned people.[21] Pritchard would translate philological discourse into racialism, buttressing the claims of James Mill and his followers that India represented a lower stage of civilization. Darkness of skin was now coterminous with backwardness of civilization. The final plank in this transformation was laid by the colonial official and legal scholar Henry Maine, expressing his belief that while India and Britain might belong the same "family of mankind," Indian civilization had been "arrested at an early stage of development."[22]

At the risk of sounding overly functionalist, in retrospect it is not difficult to see British debates over India's civilizational status as prologue to the justification of empire. As Uday Singh Mehta shows, Mill and his liberal followers were engaged in a bitter struggle with the Orientalists who expressed "admiration for the civilizations of the East."[23] What was at stake for the liberals, in arguing that higher stages of civilization corresponded to greater progress on a human scale, was to determine the form of rule most appropriate for the colony. A grave danger of considering respectfully any evidence of Indian philosophy and culture, in their view, was an inappropriate form of governance being applied to the country. James Mill would write, "if [the British government] have conceived the Hindus to be a people of high civilization, while they have in reality made but a few of the earliest steps in the progress to civilization," it would lead to disaster, for "no scheme of government can happily conduce to the end of the government, unless it is adapted to the state of the people for whose use it is intended."[24] Civilization, far from being the universal patrimony of human endeavors, had become the cause and explanation for difference across and within human societies.

The point of reviewing this seminal nineteenth-century debate, in however cursory a manner, are its political legacies. It is difficult to underemphasize the extent to which orientalist conceptions of India shaped modern Indian thinking during and after the colonial period.[25] Their power is shown by how closely Indian reactions would hew to grounds established by the charge that India was both uncivilized and lacked a true civilization as measured by universalist standards.

The need to respond to the alleged failings of India as understood by the British Orientalists and their liberal counterparts would become a leitmotif of Indian colonial and nationalist thought through the nineteenth and twentieth centuries. Broadly speaking, the image of the tree would profoundly shape Indian visions of themselves, while the staircase would become the starting point for contesting India's place in the world. Philologists seeking to explain the common origins of languages in Europe and India would come to normalize a historiography structured by invasion and racial difference, shaping a territorial vision of India as a sanctified and spatially distinct Hindu homeland. Nineteenth-century British liberals seeking to establish that Western civilization was superior to all others and that alleged civilizational backwardness could justify imperial rule would lead to a counter-claim that Indian civilization was unique and superior to its Western counterpart, characterized by spirituality, non-material values, and a harmonious balance with nature.[26] These origins, combined with imperial geopolitics and the work of French Orientalists, shaped intertwined discourses of "civilization" that continue to resonate in India today. They have led to both a defensive and inward-looking vision that reduces India to a Hindu state, the "Indic territorial" narrative; as well as a cosmopolitan variant that sees Indian civilization as an expression of Asian cultural difference,[27] the "Asian cosmopolitan" narrative.

## A National History of "Invasion"

The "first generation" of responses to British claims of civilizational backwardness included social reform movements, often glossed as early nationalist thinking.[28] Criticisms of Indian civilization as characterized by social decay and despotism would lead to efforts to modernize the Indian family and especially its treatment of women, as well as multiple calls to reform and eliminate caste as a central ordering principle of Indian society.[29] These defensive reactions would be joined by active contestations of India's alleged civilizational lack. As Gyan Prakash shows, another response was to assess ancient Indian philosophy and Vedic texts in terms drawn from modern science. Through this anachronistic move, Indian intellectuals offered a robust challenge to the charges of unreason levied by colonial detractors. The central problem, as the nationalists saw it, was the restoration of a brilliant past through modern reinterpretation of ancient texts: "to identify a body of ancient knowledge that conformed to modern scientific truths and methods," thereby reclaiming Orientalist knowledge in the justification of a modern nation through the valorization of ancient "Hindu science."[30] The willingness to acknowledge or to contest the "backwardness" of Indian social orders would be explained in terms of a decline of Indian civilization from a prehistoric golden age to its current debased form. In responding to British dismissals, history would become both the explanation of current backwardness and the source of future resurrection.

Adopting a meta-narrative of historical decline from glorious origins required an explanation that did not self-indict Indian civilization. This was provided by the trope of invasion.[31] A wide swath of Indian opinion, from cosmopolitan liberals to advocates of Hindu nationalism, would contest the significance and meanings of different invasions, but none would disagree with a periodization of national history as punctuated by foreign invasion. The oldest invasion was the Aryan entry in India and defeat of the indigenous Dravidians, as Orientalist philology appeared to suggest, while the most recent was the arrival of the British empire by sea.[32] In between, there would be invasions by the Greeks, Kushans, Sakas, Huns, and many others. By far the most narratively pernicious, however, were the multiple incursions of the second millennium CE, which would lead to centuries of Muslim rule of "Hindu" India—Khiljis, Tughlaks, and Lodhis, capped by the pre-colonial Mughal Empire. For those who saw India as a Hindu state, the decline of India from its past glory to the present would be attributed to the Muslim invasions of the "medieval" period;[33] hence the true meaning of postcolonial nationalism was the restoration of a Hindu order. Even for cosmopolitans such as Nehru, the turning point in Indian history would be the invasion of Mahmud of Ghazni, seeking only to pillage and loot, unlike earlier generations of "barbarian" invaders who had assimilated into a superior Indian civilization (not unlike Chinese accounts of their own past).[34] In response, Indian civilization would retreat into a shell, "stagnation grew and all avenues of growth were stopped": in short, civilizational decline.[35]

From these discursive origins would come the crystallization of the contemporary view that India was occupied by two nations with incommensurable loyalties, beliefs, and practices, one Hindu and the other Muslim. Religious affiliation would, with the coming of electoral politics, intersect with the idea of majorities and minorities, making India a Hindu nation for all political persuasions.[36] For cosmopolitan liberals, religious difference aside, there was no reason to assume an inherent antipathy be tween these religious communities. Secular nationalism would supersede communal differences, following the removal of colonialism and the consolidation of a modern rational and scientific state. For the advocates of a Hindu nation, by contrast, there could be no meeting of these two worlds. Hindus and Muslims had always been separate people ,requiring each to have their own nation. Thus, as Gyan Pandey usefully explains, not only was religious communalism a form of nationalism, shaped by "colonialist knowledge," "the *historical* character of communalism (or nationalism) [would] come after the *historical* character of the past has been established.[37] This weaponization of history as political discourse continues well into the present.

If history would become a critical site of struggle and contestation with significant contemporary implications, geography too had its place, in the form of determining India's national and territorial boundaries. Orientalist scholarship (now including British and French scholars) and imperial geopolitical ideas played a critical role in setting the initial terms that would then be reinterpreted and recast in other registers by Indian intellectuals and strategic thinkers.

## Indic Territorial: Contained and Expansive National Geographies

The trope of invasion was predicated on and amplified by the spatial imagination of India as a geobody uniquely blessed by a benevolent nature.[38] In this spatial vision, India was rendered discursively as a naturally contained geophysical entity bordered in the north by the high mountains of the Himalayan ranges and surrounded by protective seas in the south.[39] Violations of this territory through invasion would become doubly damaging for its implication of desecration of a sacred space, rendered as a national homeland for the Hindus. K. M. Panikkar, historian and diplomat, would be the most eloquent in normalizing this spatial vision as productive of a distinct geopolitical imaginary, but he was working on well-trodden ground.[40] The special character of Indian territory was already a powerful motif in both imperial and nationalist writings, albeit in different registers. From Lord Curzon, viceroy of India at the beginning of the twentieth century who would develop the idea of the imperial frontier, to widely circulating cultural representations of India as "Bharat Mata" (Mother India)—the nation as goddess—an ideologically potent visual image of India as a mapped territory had become normalized by the end of the nineteenth century.[41]

Sumathi Ramaswamy emphasizes the importance of the visual image at this moment, arguing that the "scientific map form" had become the dominant template against which competing visions of the nation had to be measured. "Mother India's body thus functions as a microcosm of the nation's plural religious history, even as it is used to signal what can—and cannot—be included in its ample fold. Her cartographed form is pictured to suggest that members of India's diverse religious communities are co-dwellers of the Indian geobody, but some more intimately than others."[42] This territorialized vision of India, amplified and widely circulated through mass-produced images, would work to naturalize the idea of India as a sacred space and as primarily a Hindu homeland. Indic thought drawing on the distinctiveness of this territorial space would breed a politics of defensive inwardness, leading its proponents to see the outside as always a source of threat and danger, hence advocating radical self-reliance.[43]

Along with the geobody and the cartographic map, there is another significant geographical inheritance to contend with as well. French Orientalists working at the turn of the nineteenth century, notably Sylvain Lévi, Jean Przyluski, and Jules Bloch, would introduce the idea of a so-called Greater India.[44] Their expansive conception of India as the origin of a unique and advanced civilization spreading eastward would become extremely influential and remains highly resilient. Combining a number of methods and sources of evidence from textual and cultural analysis to archaeological fieldwork, French scholars would develop their thesis that Southeast Asian empires and cultural practices from dance to music were deeply shaped by Indic origins, hence the term, Greater India. This line of thought would become immensely popular and expanded upon by eminent Indian historians such as R. C. Majumdar and Kalidas Nag, Lévi's student, who, along with others, would go on to found the Greater India Society.

What made the idea of Greater India particularly appealing, Susan Bayly explains, was its ability to subvert the received wisdom of British Orientalists and offer a very different picture of Indian civilization.[45] Far from being passive and reactive, this vision allowed its proponents to propose that India had always been a dynamic place, spreading its unique wisdom and civilization to the east without recourse to arms, through means we would now call "soft power," namely, the inherent attractiveness of Indian ideas and culture. Unlike Islamic and European empires that had forced their way into India, Indic civilization, comprising both Hindu and Buddhist thought and practices, was willingly received and assimilated from "Angkor to Borobudur," from the Cham of Vietnam to Java's Majapahit empire. Symptomatically, a review of Phanindranath Bose's *The Hindu Colony of Cambodia* (1927) would propose, "India also had its Napoleons and Charlemagnes, its Bismarcks and Machiavellis. But the real charm of Indian history does not consist in these aspirants after universal power, but in its peaceful and benevolent Imperialism. . . . [Indians used] the weapons of their superior culture and religion [to bring] the world under their sway."[46] For these intellectuals and their followers, Greater India's "cultural colonization" would extend peacefully through Burma, Cambodia, Vietnam, Java, and Bali, and on to China and Japan.

## India as an Asian Civilization: A Cosmopolitan Vision

The Indian writer and intellectual Rabindranath Tagore would offer a far less parochial vision of a pan-Asian sensibility in his writings and dialogues with Japanese and Chinese scholars during his numerous visits to eastern Asia. His vehement rejection of nationalism and patriotism—"the Nation is the greatest evil for the Nation"—would lead to fierce disagreements with his Japanese and Chinese hosts and marked his distance from more extreme proponents of Indian nationalism back at home.[47] In sharp contrast with the masculinist and aggressive imaginary typical of those who equated Indian civilization with a Hindu ethos, Tagore's views offered a view of Asian commonality through metaphors of fraternity that tied together premodern Asia from Mesopotamia to Japan. When it came to defining Asian difference, characterized by Rustom Bharucha as a form of self-orientalization, Tagore would represent "Asian" civilization in essentialist terms that highlighted its opposition to values associated with the West—"not political but social, not predatory and mechanically efficient but spiritual and based upon all the varied and deeper relations of humanity."[48]

Tagore was adamant that modernization, which he saw in terms of technological materialism, was not the same as modernity, which was universal and free of imitation. Copying Western materialism and the Western path to development would be akin to, in his acidic phrase, "dressing our skeleton with another man's skin."[49] Asian civilization's objective, if one can call it that, was to have the self-confidence to articulate its own modernity, independent of external influences, in a mode expressive of its own singular genius, including morality, aesthetics, and spiritualism.[50]

Tagore's message would be repeated and amplified across Asia, most memorably at the historic Asian Relations Conference, held in New Delhi in April 1947. This conference, held on the verge of decolonization, is significant for a number of reasons, not least its wide representation of participants from across Asia and Oceania.[51] Its spirit can be captured by Jawaharlal Nehru's opening comments: "Asia, after a long period of quiescence, has suddenly become important again in world affairs . . . the old imperialisms are fading away . . . and we look at each other again and meet as old friends long parted." For Nehru, whose vision would shape India's foreign policy for the rest of the century, two additional themes needed emphasis. The first was India's geopolitical centrality to the Asian region, "the meeting point of western and northern and eastern and southern Asia," from where it had been influenced by and shaped the rest of Asia; the second was Asia's special place in international relations, "there can be no peace unless Asia plays her part." He would go on to add, "we have arrived at a stage in human affairs when the ideal of that 'One World' and some kind of a world federation seems to be essential . . . [with] the countries of Asia cooperating together for that larger ideal."[52]

Conference president Sarojini Naidu's soaring opening speech would develop the theme that a free Asia would save the world from itself. "Asia [has] always stood for . . . the common ideal of peace. Not the peace of negation, not the peace of surrender, not the peace of the coward, not the peace of the dying, not the peace of the dead, but the peace, militant, dynamic, creative of the human spirit which exalts." And, "what will Asia do with her renaissance? . . . through compassion, love and forgiveness shall the world be redeemed."[53] All too aware of the imminence of Asian decolonization, speaker after speaker would make the case that an independent Asia would have to return to its true civilizational origins in order not to fall into and replicate the sins of Western materialism and aggression. Asia was represented as the source of the world's greatest religions, a geo-cultural region that had always treated the rest of the world as equals without discrimination on the basis of race or religion, unlike the imperial West.

This view of Asian civilization as shared by cosmopolitans such as Nehru and Tagore was shaped above all by the image of the staircase. While India had been assigned by colonial discourse to the lowest steps of world civilization as a decayed and degenerate body, their critique sought to revise that hierarchy and raise India to the highest reaches of the staircase. For them, Indian civilization was distinguished from and superior to Western thought due to a deep morality, emergent from the peaceful and spiritual essence of Indian civilization.

This view would be complemented by a vision of India that drew on the combined legacies of British and French Orientalists, taking shape in the form of a distinct identity and a powerful spatial imaginary. India was the homeland of the Hindu civilization and race, the sacred space of which had been invaded repeatedly from the north and west. It would assimilate some invaders but others, notably Muslims, could not be incorporated into the body of the nation except as a civilizational and political minority. Looking outward, India's relations with the world were marked by expansion and influence by means other than force. While southern India had shaped profoundly the cultures of regions as far away as Indonesia, it has done so through the force of attraction, not via military power as European imperialism had done. Global influence through the projection of spiritual and cultural power was a sign of India's difference. Both cosmopolitans and Hindu nationalists saw national sovereignty as inseparable from a restoration of India's place in the inner circle of global powers; they differed, however, on the means to do so. Both would agree that sovereignty would only be complete when the universality of Indian civilization was globally acknowledged.

## Asian Civilizational Difference and World Order

Nehru would address the Constituent Assembly in 1949, saying, "What does independence consist of? It consists fundamentally and basically of foreign relations. That is the test of independence. All else is internal autonomy. Once foreign relations go out of your hand, into the charge of someone else, to that extent and in that measure, you are not independent."[54] This statement comes as no surprise. The first leader of a newly sovereign postcolonial country, in "someone else's charge" for the past century, could hardly be expected to think otherwise, one would think.

Yet, turning from rhetoric to practice, given Nehru's categorical assertion of the need for independence in foreign policy, it is all the more remarkable that India's early participation in the United Nations would be characterized by a willingness to *dilute* its hard-won sovereignty in the interests of promoting peace among states. This apparent contradiction can only be understood as an expression of the power of the Asian cosmopolitan narrative.

The extent and meaning of Nehru's support for "One World," in the phrase popularized by Wendell Wilkie, have long been disputed.[55] First mentioned in the Quit India resolution in 1942, at the peak of World War II, the Congress Party explicitly invoked a world federation as the only means by which "future peace, security and ordered progress of the world" would become possible.[56] Nehru would invoke One World and its synonyms, "world government" and a "world federation of states," repeatedly during the next decade. "I have no doubt that a World Government must and will come, for there is no other remedy for the world's sickness. The machinery for it is not difficult to devise. It can be an extension of the federal principle, a growth of the idea underlying the United Nations, giving each national unit freedom to fashion its own destiny according to its genius but subject always to the basic covenant of a World Government."[57]

Priya Chacko offers an apposite reading of Nehru's One World formulation by situating it in relation to civilizational discourses and lessons learned from earlier failures of interstate organizations.[58] The postwar world, Nehru felt, was shaped by a "psychology of fear," best captured by a phrase in the UNESCO preamble that he would often repeat: "wars begin in the minds of men."[59] Fear was compounded by global interdependence, making fear a universal condition. Drawing on Gandhi, he would emphasize that in order to overcome fear, it was crucial to pay attention to the *means* by which it was produced. Fear, he argued, was generated by and embedded in arms races, alliances between states, military bases on foreign soil, and colonial rule of one people by another, among other familiar features of contemporary international relations. Hence, those instruments of fear would have to be removed before positive change could be expected to come about. India would oppose adamantly various causes of fear: the superpower arms race, military alliances, foreign military bases, and colonialism. The foundation of world government to come was the United Nations. In furtherance of this objective, not only would India support the entry of as many countries as possible into the UN, making it a truly global organization, it would submit its own bilateral disputes to this forum to be adjudicated by the power of world opinion.

Nehru has never been forgiven by Indian political opinion for taking the Kashmir conflict to the UN, forever internationalizing a "domestic" dispute.[60] Yet this action remains the best proof of how he hoped the UN would evolve into a world government. By submitting this dispute to the global body, Nehru's decision was shaped by his desire to prove by example his beliefs about the necessity of world government, joined by confidence that the Indian case was stronger than their opponent's. He would be proved wrong on the latter front, not least because he underestimated the force of the British foreign office working against the Indian position, to the extent of even surprising the US.[61] Even this considerable setback would not make India lose its faith in the UN. In the following years, India would work actively to conciliate warring parties during the early years of the Cold War, especially in Asia, most notably through its chairmanship of the Korea Armistice Commission and involvement in multiple Indochina peace negotiations. The desire to use the UN as a constructive base to remove the instruments of global fear would include supporting the creation of institutions to advance general disarmament and reducing the threat of nuclear war through a ban on nuclear testing. With the advantage of hindsight, it is impossible not to be struck by how actively India was involved in international issues that it had no immediate or direct interest in, beyond what it saw as the pursuit of international peace.

In their classic study, Heimsath and Mansingh capture the essence of this approach to the UN and the Cold War in the following terms: India had great faith in "face-to-face encounters among principal policy makers . . . [that] could elicit that essential rationality, even humanness that political relations conducted at a distance always managed to obscure." As a result, India was most likely to support UN resolutions that led "to talks between contending parties . . . rather than those specifying particular solutions offered by one side."[62] Priya Chacko has theorized this approach as a "politics of friendship," a direct legacy of the cosmopolitan view of Asian civilizational difference. She argues that Nehru drew on Buddhist and Jain precepts to foreground the importance of direct dialogue in overcoming the inevitable differences of individual points of view. From her exposition, it becomes clear that friendship can be relevant even if a country is not directly involved in a dispute. In such cases, the path to peace is predicated on not taking sides with one or another warring party, allowing for the possibility that "friendly" intervention might make it possible for the parties in dispute to find a way out of their mutual disagreements. More generally, a politics of friendship—"a voluntary emotional attachment that grows from recognition of interdependence and translates into a commitment to a common project"—enable the emergence of "common values," leading eventually to "the possibility of moral transformation in world politics."[63] The most significant effort in seeking to transform these ideals into practice would be the agreement on five principles of mutual coexistence, or *Panchsheel*, that India and China would sign in 1954.[64]

The decline of a politics of friendship and corresponding willingness to dilute Indian sovereignty in the interests of world peace would begin from the end of the 1950s. It could be said to have definitively ended in 1974, when India exploded a "peaceful nuclear device." Directly and indirectly, China was the proximate cause of this turnaround. The Panchsheel agreement was, for Nehru, a direct expression of his faith in the possibility of friendship for international peace. The greatest chance of good relations between India and China, the most consequential bilateral relationship in Asia in his view, would be improved by "making it more and more difficult progressively for the other country to break trust." His hope was that by making it "a little more dangerous for the other party to break away from the pledges given," China would fear the reputational costs of violating international agreements and, with time, would come to value the importance of good relations with India. Cognizant of the risks involved (and there were many contemporary criticisms of this agreement), Nehru would argue that it was better not to be tied down by fear. "Surely it is better, with nations as much as individuals, to hope for and expect the best, but at the same time to be prepared for any eventuality."[65]

This faith would end with China's military intervention against India in 1962. This Chinese action would revive two deep-rooted tropes of Indic civilizational discourse—invasion by a foreign force and violation of sacred territory—to end the politics of friendship as international behavior. In response to the charge of being unprepared, military expenditures would rise and the imperative of protecting India's borders would become elevated to the highest levels of national security. No government could risk showing flexibility on territorial disputes for fear of being charged with a lack of patriotism. In 1974 India would conduct an underground nuclear test, offering evidence of nuclear weapons capability to the world. While China was not the proximate cause of this test, Chinese nuclearization in 1964 had led to an intense public debate in India about the need to follow suit, in effect engendering an arms race in the region, given Pakistan's likely response.[66] The politics of friendship had been turned on its head. With a politics of fear now defining India's international relations, the cosmopolitan legacy of civilizational thinking had been replaced by the Indic vision: a re-territorialized vision of the country as a vulnerable geobody. This would translate into expressions of national sovereignty and self-interest that would increasingly take on a narrower and more inflexible cast.

India's relations with the world were shaped by complex intersections of discrete narratives. While the overarching imperative of searching for respect and recognition from the world as a universal civilization remained fixed, the respective influence of each narrative would vary. In the early years of independence, cosmopolitan Asian thinking would combine with imperial geopolitics to shape Indian behavior. In succeeding decades, the balance between cosmopolitanism and an inward-looking and defensive Indic belief system would tilt toward the latter, with a re-territorialized vision of India as a Hindu homeland eventually becoming national common sense. In the immediate "neighborhood" of South and Southeast Asia, imperial geopolitics and Greater India, the idea of India as a benign imperial power, would hold sway for much longer. Only occasionally and briefly would cosmopolitan beliefs affect relations with India's neighbors. Coming to the present, the Indic territorial narrative has shrunk still further into *Hindutva*, a majoritarian view that relegates religious minorities and civilizational others to the margins of domestic society.

## Global India

During the nineteenth and twentieth centuries, overseas Indians were mostly resident in European imperial territories and Dominions, not only the British Empire, but also the metropoles and African and Caribbean colonies of the French and Portuguese empires.[67] Overseas Indians could be divided into a number of functional categories, of which the most numerous were indentured workers and their descendants, but including also seamen, pilgrims, merchants and traders, civil servants, convicts and exiles, and soldiers serving in the imperial army.[68] Not all overseas Indians stayed abroad permanently. There was a regular circulation of men, women, and families between India and places abroad, leading to traces of the global becoming visible and not unfamiliar, even in "remote" villages, by the end of the nineteenth century.[69] With advances in global transport technologies and communication links and the growth of a small middle class in India by the end of the nineteenth century, overseas residents began to include small numbers of students, as well as intellectuals and political activists, based in metropolitan safe havens in Germany, France, Japan, and the US. These latter figures would become vital nodes in global networks of anti-colonial agitators with political allegiances ranging all the way from transnational communism and socialism to exclusivist conceptions of Hindu nationalism.[70]

## Ambivalence toward the Diaspora

Following World War I, New Delhi could be said to control an "informal empire" ranging from the Gulf of Aden to Singapore, an enormous region across which the Indian rupee was the dominant currency and Indian military force maintained imperial order.[71] This power would exacerbate intra-imperial tensions when a newly emboldened but far from sovereign Government of India demanded to send officials and representatives to the Dominions to assess for themselves the conditions of overseas Indians. V. S. Srinivasa

Sastri would be appointed an official emissary of the Indian Government to Australia, New Zealand, and Canada to look into the well-being of Indian immigrants in 1922. Later, he would become the first "Agent" of the Indian Government in South Africa from 1927 to 1929, effectively Indian High Commissioner to an autonomous Dominion within the British Empire. Protecting the interests and rights of overseas Indians had become important enough to constitute an autonomous foreign policy for India within the Empire.[72]

For all this genuine effort to protect overseas Indians, India's relations with its diaspora began to change from this moment onward. While on the one hand, public and political concerns about the treatment of overseas Indians would be expressed ever more fervently, Indian politicians were moving away from seeing overseas Indians as legitimate citizens of the territorial homeland and increasingly calling on the diaspora to remain in their adopted homelands and to accommodate themselves to the terms laid down by host countries.

This mixed message would be reinforced by political leaders in visits to overseas Indian communities. Even as the Congress Party would draw an explicit connection between the condition of overseas Indians and independence for territorial India, Congress leaders would also be careful to qualify the extent of a "right of return" for the diaspora. Thus, the president of the Indian National Congress in 1926, Srinivasa Iyengar, would say, "The status of Indians abroad . . . depends inevitably on the status of Indians in their own land; and the *Swaraj* (freedom) for India depends in its turn on the brave and unfaltering spirit of our kith and kin across the seas."[73] Yet just a few years earlier, prominent Indian National Congress leader Sarojini Naidu had expressed the ambivalence of India's relationship with overseas Indians (not to mention deep paternalism toward black Africans). In her presidential address to the East African Congress in Mombasa in 1924, she would state bluntly, "East Africa is one of the earliest legitimate territories of the Indian nation . . . the legitimate colony of the surplus of the Great Indian nation."[74] Shortly afterward, traveling in South Africa, she would mark the limits of diasporic solidarity with the homeland, calling on overseas Indians to see their primary allegiance to their African neighbors: "Do not turn your eyes to India. You are nearer to the black man who looks to you more trustingly [*sic*] . . . you are citizens of an Africa which can never be only white."[75]

Jawaharlal Nehru, head of the Congress Overseas Department, whose visits to Southeast Asia in the 1930s had been greeted with rapturous public meetings with overseas Indians and deep suspicion by colonial authorities, would explain to the Indian Constituent Assembly why overseas Indians had no permanent claim to the protection of the Indian state. While acknowledging that overseas Indians could opt for Indian "nationality," he was in favor of them remaining in their countries of residence and adopting local citizenship. Nehru would make clear that as long as they remained overseas, India's interest in them would be "cultural and humanitarian, not political," noting "we cannot protect any [overseas Indians'] vested interests which injure the cause of the country they are in." Ruminating that the "vitality" of Indian immigrants was a constant source of anxiety in their host countries, Nehru would reiterate that host states had the right to make decisions that were in their own national interests: "We advise our countrymen to put up with those difficulties." Unfair treatment of Indians would be met with official protest, but "even then we protest in a friendly way; we do not issue threats."[76] In short, notwithstanding decades of official and popular concern about overseas Indians, the emerging policy of newly independent India was to turn its back on its diaspora. Postcolonial India's fledgling relations with the rest of the world were far more important to nurture than the protection of its overseas populations who had made the struggle for Indian independence a global affair.

The perigee of this turnaround came with Idi Amin's sudden decision to expel Asians from Uganda in 1972.[77] Overnight, tens of thousands of people of Indian origin, both Hindu and Muslim, would be forced to leave the country, leaving their substantial assets behind. India's third prime minster, Indira Gandhi, would make clear that this forcibly displaced population was not her country's concern. In her view, since most Ugandan Asians were British overseas subjects, it was to the UK that they should turn for help and aid, not India. In response to appeals for support, Gandhi would reply that she did not want India to become a "dumping ground" for this overseas population. In the end, India would absorb just a few thousand Ugandan Indians, with the remaining tens of thousands finding refuge in the UK, Canada, and Australia.

A complete transformation of India's diaspora policy would take official shape in 2000. Under the BJP government, led by Atal Behari Vajpayee, a commission was set up under the chairmanship of a senior party leader, the lawyer and diplomat M. L. Singhvi, to review India's diaspora policy. Seeking to replicate the model of massive overseas Chinese investment in the homeland following Deng Xiaoping's economic reforms, commissioners traveled around the world and interviewed scores of overseas Indians to gauge their views of India and to consider how the government might respond to their concerns.[78] A major recommendation of the report was to recommend the modification of India's citizenship laws, carving out new categories of non-resident Indian, namely, the Person of Indian Origin (PIO), which was later followed by the Overseas Citizen of India (OCI). The policy change was carefully crafted to prevent the millions of Muslims who had fled India during the Partition and after to regain Indian citizenship.[79] The Diaspora report recommended offering this new category of national membership only to citizens of well-to-do countries in North America, Europe, and Southeast Asia.

This exclusion led to a strong reaction from overseas Indians in the Caribbean and elsewhere in the Global South, who saw in this action a disavowal of their history as the unwanted descendants of indentured labor. Some years later, under a Congress government, this restriction would be removed, and all overseas Indians and their spouses and families would become eligible for the OCI classification. A Ministry of Overseas Indian Affairs would be created in 2004, institutionalizing India's new view of its diaspora: Global India.

The global Indian diaspora is a telling manifestation of India's engagement with the modern world order. From the mid-nineteenth century, the colonial Indian government would engender deep divisions within the British Empire through its forceful demands for greater respect and protections for its overseas residents. This politically resonant concern would end with the onset of Indian independence. For the next four decades, India would turn its back on the diaspora, effectively drawing a clear boundary between the country and its overseas nationals. This policy of careful distance would change beginning from the 1980s. At this moment the global Indian diaspora was no longer represented by the descendants of indentured laborers as it once was, but by successful middle-class professionals who had emigrated to First World countries and had become wealthy. Reconnecting with the diaspora began from the desire to attract material resources and foreign investment, as China had successfully done; however, this policy turnaround also reveals conspicuous national fault lines of both class and caste.

## Bringing the Diaspora Home

What explains these reversals in India's relations with its diaspora? From the mid-nineteenth century onward, Indian political leaders and the Indian public were deeply troubled by the harsh conditions facing Indians abroad, placing the colonial government under constant pressure to protect them. This pressure would lead to the beginnings of an autonomous foreign policy in the colonial state, including vis-à-vis the interests of the imperial government, an anomalous situation, to put it mildly. The diaspora responded in kind, using their safe havens and foreign platforms to agitate against colonial rule in varieties of ways, making the struggle for Indian independence a global affair. Yet, with independence, India would turn away from its diaspora in the interests of building better relations with postcolonial host countries by reducing fears of dual loyalties among overseas Indians. India would encourage the diaspora to stay in their countries of residence, adopt local citizenship, and not assume any right of return.

Beginning in the 1980s, the policy of disavowal began to change. By the turn of the twentieth century, India had rediscovered its diaspora and was now actively seeking ways of encouraging them to invest in their homeland. This revivification of the diaspora was driven, in the first instance, by economics: the desire to emulate the Chinese experience of receiving huge foreign investment from overseas populations. But there is more. Social, cultural, and political factors significantly shaped this turnaround as well.[80]

The first "wave" of overseas Indians, dating back to the 1830s, was dominated by impoverished lower-caste populations who ended up in the plantation economies of the colonial world. By contrast, the second wave of overseas migrants, beginning in the 1960s, were composed primarily of well-educated upper-caste and middle-class families who had emigrated to the West. While both cohorts left the country primarily in order to improve their material conditions, more recent emigrants were also shaped by the decline of inherited social privilege in a rapidly democratizing India.

The change in diaspora policy was an effort to re-insert privileged overseas Indians into the body of the Indian nation, now rendered as a Hindu space. This was a move to celebrate the diaspora's achievements overseas and at the same time to offer a rebuttal to the domestic critique of the Hindu social order as inherently exclusionary and hierarchical. In crude summary, the economically successful Indian in the Global North was the kind of figure an emerging power wanted to be associated with, not the descendant of an indentured laborer, typical of the Indian diaspora in the Global South. If upper-caste Indians could succeed abroad, despite lacking cultural and social capital in their new homes, it offered new ammunition to the conservative argument that the Hindu caste hierarchy reflected inherent ability ("merit" in local political parlance), rather than being merely an attribute of social inheritance.[81] In addition, as Modi's Houston rally emphasized, this overseas population was increasingly becoming a valuable resource in India's relations with the great powers. The enduring contradiction in this desired vision of national "insiders without" remains the toiling bodies of Indian migrant workers in the Gulf, lacking rights and respect at home and abroad, but still a major source of remittances and foreign exchange in India's contemporary political economy.[82]

## Conclusion

Struggles over civilizational imaginaries have not ended in India. With the rise of the BJP as a national political force, and especially under the leadership of Narendra Modi, India has actively redefined itself from a secular nation-state to the contemporary political manifestation of a great civilization. This civilizational state embodies the dominance of the Indic territorial imaginary over the Asian cosmopolitan vision, producing a defensively oriented and territorially insecure Hindu majoritarian state where Muslims and other alleged civilizational inferiors are assigned permanent inferior status.

In its external manifestation, two factors should be noted. First, what Modi seeks to achieve is a new synthesis of these foundational civilizational imaginaries. The Indic territorial narrative remains firmly in place, now joined by a *Hindutva* variant of the Asian cosmopolitan vision. This current mutation of the latter narrative retains claims to spiritual and cultural superiority, but eschews any talk of pacifism or global moral orders. Tagore's influence has waned, replaced by the allegedly benign imperialism of the Greater India Society. Second, the *excess* of civilization-talk in Modi's India only goes to highlight its perceived absence: in short, constant repetition indexes radical doubt. Where is the global status that accompanies civilizational status? Why is India's world rank not universally and unequivocally recognized? Anxiety is the subtext of the renewed and repeated claims to civilizational status.

What the acolytes of Hindutva appear not to realize is that civilization is not a neutral or purely descriptive term, but political language that has always sought to rank and exclude on a global scale. It may be claimed by many, but is awarded by few. While the search for maximum strategic autonomy in foreign affairs appears to follow from the "fact" of India as a great civilization, the reverse is true. The only unimpeachable evidence of India being a great civilization will be attaining genuine autonomy in foreign affairs. The impossibility of this latter end is why elite anxiety can never be assuaged.

## Notes

1. My thanks to the organizers and participants in the "Contested Narratives of the Global" workshops for their thoughtful and patient suggestions. I am grateful for comments received on earlier versions of this essay from Kanti Bajpai, Priya Chacko, Ian Hall, Amit Julka, and Sankaran Krishna
2. Kate Sullivan de Estrada and Rosemary Foot, "China's and India's Search for International Status through the UN System: Competition and Complementarity," *Contemporary Politics* 25, no. 5 (2019): 567–585. https://doi.org/10.1080/13569775.2019.1621718.
3. Ian Hall, *Modi and the Reinvention of Indian Foreign Policy* (Bristol: Bristol University Press, 2019).
4. Latha Varadarajan, *The Domestic Abroad: Diasporas in International Relations* (New York: Oxford University Press, 2010).
5. Sheila Jasanoff and Sang-Hyun Kim, "Containing the Atom: Sociotechnical Imaginaries and Nuclear Power in the United States and South Korea," *Minerva* 47, no. 2 (2009): 119–146.
6. Itty Abraham, *How India Became Territorial: Foreign Policy, Diaspora, Geopolitics* (Stanford, CA: Stanford University Press, 2014).
7. Antony Anghie, *Imperialism, Sovereignty and the Making of International Law* (Cambridge: Cambridge University Press, 2007).
8. Gerrit W. Gong, *The Standard of "Civilization" in International Society* (Oxford: Clarendon Press, 1984).
9. Lydia He Liu, *The Clash of Empires: The Invention of China in Modern World Making* (Cambridge, MA: Harvard University Press, 2004).
10. Talal Asad, *Formations of the Secular: Christianity, Islam, Modernity. Cultural Memory in the Present* (Stanford, CA: Stanford University Press, 2003).
11. "Orientalist" is now intimately associated with Edward Said's critique of "Orientalism," his term for a hegemonic worldview that sees the non-west through essentialized markers of civilizational inferiority and cultural lack (Said 1994). In this chapter I distinguish orientalism (Said) from Orientalist scholarship, referring to the Indological tradition which "discovered" and celebrated ancient Indian thought and scriptures, especially Sanskrit texts. I use lower case to refer to Said's critical use of the term, orientalist, and upper case to refer to the philological tradition of scholarship, Orientalist.
12. Thomas R. Trautmann, *Aryans and British India* (Berkeley: University of California Press, 1997), 8.

13. For a careful discussion of how *Arya* moved from Indology to become the Aryan ideology of the National Socialists in Germany, see Sheldon Pollock's essay, "Deep Orientalism?" (Pollock 1993).
14. Trautmann, *Aryans and British India*, 4.
15. Quotation from Ronald B. Inden, *Imagining India* (Oxford: Blackwell, 1990), 45.
16. Inden, *Imagining India*, 51.
17. David Ludden, "Orientalist Empiricism: Transformations of Colonial Knowledge," in Carol Breckenridge and Peter van der Veer, eds., *Orientalism and the Postcolonial Predicament: Perspectives on South Asia* (Philadelphia: University of Pennsylvania Press, 1993), 268.
18. Frederick Cooper and Randall Packard, eds., *International Development and the Social Sciences: Essays on the History and Politics of Knowledge* (Berkeley: University of California Press, 1997).
19. Trautmann, *Aryans and British India*, 224..
20. Uday Singh Mehta, *Liberalism and Empire: A Study in Nineteenth-Century British Liberal Thought* (Chicago: University of Chicago Press, 1999).
21. Trautmann, *Aryans and British India*, 171 (emphasis in the original).
22. Thomas R. Metcalf, *Ideologies of the Raj*, The New Cambridge History of India (Cambridge: Cambridge University Press, 1995), 66; Kavita Philip, *Civilizing Natures: Race, Resources, and Modernity in Colonial South India* (New Brunswick, NJ: Rutgers University Press, 2004).
23. Mehta, *Liberalism and Empire*, 89.
24. Quoted in Mehta, *Liberalism and Empire*, 91.
25. Carol Breckenridge and Peter van der Veer, eds., *Orientalism and the Postcolonial Predicament: Perspectives on South Asia* (Philadelphia: University of Pennsylvania Press, 1993).
26. Prasenjit Duara, *The Crisis of Global Modernity: Asian Traditions and a Sustainable Future* (Cambridge: Cambridge University Press, 2015). https://doi.org/10.1017/CBO9781139998222.
27. Prasenjit Duara, "The Discourse of Civilization and Decolonization," *Journal of World History* 15, no. 1 (2004), http://www.historycooperative.org/cgi-bin/justtop.cgi?act=justtop&url=http://www.historycooperative.org/journals/jwh/15.1/duara.html.
28. Sumit Sarkar, *Modern India: 1885–1947* (Delhi: Macmillan, 1983).
29. Lata Mani, "Contentious Traditions: The Debate on Sati in Colonial India," *Cultural Critique*, no. 7 (1987): 119–156. https://doi.org/10.2307/1354153.
30. Gyan Prakash, *Another Reason: Science and the Imagination of Modern India* (Princeton, NJ: Princeton University Press, 1999), 91, 98–99.
31. Romila Thapar, *The Past as Present: Forging Contemporary Identities through History* (Chicago: University of Chicago Press, 2019). https://www.press.uchicago.edu/ucp/books/book/distributed/P/bo38690227.html.
32. Kavalam Madhava Panikkar, *India and the Indian Ocean: An Essay on the Influence of Sea Power on Indian History* (London: G. Allen & Unwin, 1962).
33. Metcalf, *Ideologies of the Raj*.

34. Prasenjit Duara, *Rescuing History from the Nation: Questioning Narratives of Modern China* (Chicago: University of Chicago Press, 1997).
35. Jawaharlal Nehru, *Glimpses of World History: Being Further Letters to His Daughter Written in Prison, and Containing a Rambling Account of History for Young People*, first US edition (New York: John Day, 1942), 182.
36. Arjun Appadurai, *Modernity at Large: Cultural Dimensions of Globalization* (Minneapolis: University of Minnesota Press, 1996).
37. Gyanendra Pandey, *The Construction of Communalism in Colonial North India* (Delhi: Oxford University Press, 1990), 6, 22.
38. Thongchai Winichakul, *Siam Mapped: A History of the Geo-Body of a Nation* (Honolulu: University of Hawaii Press, 1997).
39. Itty Abraham, *How India Became Territorial: Foreign Policy, Diaspora, Geopolitics* (Stanford, CA: Stanford University Press, 2014).
40. Kavalam Madhava Panikkar, *Geographical Factors in Indian History* (Delhi: Bharatiya Vidya Bhavan, 1969).
41. Peter John Brobst, *The Future of the Great Game: Sir Olaf Caroe, India's Independence, and the Defence of Asia* (Akron, OH: University of Akron Press, 2005); Ramaswamy, Sumathi. *The Goddess and the Nation: Mapping Mother India*. Durham, NC: Duke University Press, 2010).
42. Ramaswamy, *The Goddess and the Nation*, 51.
43. Christophe Jaffrelot, *The Hindu Nationalist Movement and Indian Politics: 1925 to the 1990s: Strategies of Identity-Building, Implantation and Mobilisation (with Special Reference to Central India)* (London: C. Hurst, 1996).
44. Susan Bayly, "Imagining "Greater India": French and Indian Visions of Colonialism in the Indic Mode," *Modern Asian Studies* 38, no. 3 (2004): 703–744.
45. Bayly, "Imagining "Greater India."
46. Quoted in Bayly, "Imagining "Greater India," 712..
47. Quoted in Rustom Bharucha, *Another Asia: Rabindranath Tagore and Okakura Tenshin* (Delhi: Oxford University Press, 2006), 82.
48. Bharucha, *Another Asia*, 79.
49. Quoted in Bharucha, *Another Asia*, 89.
50. Ashis Nandy, *The Illegitimacy of Nationalism: Rabindranath Tagore and the Politics of Self* (Delhi: Oxford University Press, 1994).
51. A. Appadorai, *Asian Relations: Being Report of the Proceedings and Documentation of the First Asian Relations Conference, New Delhi, March–April, 1947* (New Delhi: Asian Relations Organization, 1948); Itty Abraham, "From Bandung to NAM: Non-Alignment and Indian Foreign Policy, 1947–65." *Commonwealth & Comparative Politics* 46 (2008), https://doi.org/doi:10.1080/14662040801990280.
52. Appadorai, *Asian Relations*, 21–23.
53. Appadorai, *Asian Relations*, 28–29.
54. Quoted in Charles Herman Heimsath and Surjit Mansingh, *A Diplomatic History of Modern India* (Bombay: Allied, 1971), 58.
55. Priya Chacko, *Indian Foreign Policy: The Politics of Postcolonial Identity from 1947 to 2004* (London and New York: Routledge, 2012), 46–48.

56. Manu Bhagavan, *The Peacemakers: India and the Quest for One World* (Delhi: HarperCollins, 2012), 17–18.
57. Jawaharlal Nehru, *India's Foreign Policy: Selected Speeches, September 1946–April 1961* (Delhi: Publications Division, Ministry of Information and Broadcasting, Govt. of India, 1961), 183.
58. Chacko, *Indian Foreign Policy*.
59. Nehru, *India's Foreign Policy*, 165.
60. Sisir Gupta, *Kashmir: A Study in India-Pakistan Relations* (Bombay: Asia Publishing House, 1966), 448–453.
61. Prem Shankar Jha, *The Origins of a Dispute: Kashmir 1947* (Delhi: Oxford University Press, 2003).
62. Heimsath and Mansingh, *A Diplomatic History of Modern India*, 91.
63. Chacko, *Indian Foreign Policy*, 55.
64. Antony Anghie, "Bandung and the Origins of Third World Sovereignty," in Luis Eslava, Michael Fakhri, and Vasuki Nesiah, eds., *Bandung, Global History and International Law* (Cambridge: Cambridge University Press, 2017), 535–551.
65. Heimsath and Mansingh, *A Diplomatic History of Modern India*, 192–193.
66. Itty Abraham, *Making of the Indian Atomic Bomb: Science, Secrecy and the Postcolonial State* (London: Zed Books, 1998); George Perkovich, *India's Nuclear Bomb: The Impact on Global Proliferation* (Berkeley: University of California Press, 1999).
67. Brij Lal, Peter Reeves, and Rajesh Rai, eds., *The Encyclopaedia of the Indian Diaspora* (Singapore: Editions Didier Millet, 2006).
68. Sugata Bose, *A Hundred Horizons: The Indian Ocean in the Age of Global Empire* (Cambridge, MA: Harvard University Press, 2006).; G. Balachandran, "Circulation Through Seafaring: Indian Seamen, 1890–1945," in *Society and Circulation: Mobile People and Itinerant Cultures in South Asia, 1750–1950* (Delhi: Permanent Black, 2003), 89–130; T. N. Harper, "Singapore, 1915, and the Birth of an Asian Underground," *Modern Asian Studies* 47, no. 6 (2013): 1782–1811; Sunil S. Amrith, *Migration and Diaspora in Modern Asia* (Cambridge: Cambridge University Press, 2011).
69. Amrith, *Migration and Diaspora in Modern Asia*; Itty Abraham, "Germany Has Become Mohammedan: Insurgency, Long-Distance Travel and the Singapore Mutiny, 1915," *Globalizations* 12, no. 6 (2015): 913–927.
70. Harald Fischer-Tiné, "Indian Nationalism and the 'World Forces': Transnational and Diasporic Dimensions of the Indian Freedom Movement on the Eve of the First World War," *Journal of Global History* 2, no. 3 (2007): 325–344, https://doi.org/10.1017/S1740022807002318; Fredrik Petersson, *International Communism and Transnational Solidarity: Radical Networks, Mass Movements and Global Politics, 1919–1939* (Leiden: Brill, 2016), https://www.academia.edu/31660856/International_Communism_and_Transnational_Solidarity_Radical_Networks_Mass_Movements_and_Global_Politics_1919_1939_Leiden_Brill_2016_; Maia Ramnath, *Haj to Utopia: How the Ghadar Movement Charted Global Radicalism and Attempted to Overthrow the British Empire* (Berkeley: University of California Press, 2011).
71. James Onley, "The Raj Reconsidered: British India's Informal Empire and Spheres of Includence in Asia and Africa," *Asian Affairs* 40, no. 1 (2009): 44–62.

72. Vineet Thakur, *India's First Diplomat—V. S. Srinivasa Sastri and the Making of Liberal Internationalism* (Bristol: Bristol University Press, 2021).
73. Lal, Reeves, and Rai, eds., *Encyclopaedia of the Indian Diaspora*, 83.
74. Herbert Luthy, "India and East Africa: Imperial Partnership at the End of the First World War," *Journal of Contemporary History* 6, no. 2 (1971): 55–85.
75. Goolam Vahed, "Race, Empire, and Citizenship: Sarojini Naidu's 1924 Visit to South Africa," *South African Historical Journal* 64 (June 2012): 319–342; 337, https://doi.org/10.1080/02582473.2012.671353.
76. Nehru, *India's Foreign Policy*, 127–129.
77. Anirudha Gupta, "Ugandan Asians, Britain, India and the Commonwealth," *African Affairs* 73, no. 292 (1974): 312–324.
78. India, Ministry of External Affairs, "Report of the High Level Committee on the Indian Diaspora. Chairman L. M. Singhvi," New Delhi: Indian Council of World Affairs, 2001.
79. Abraham, *How India Became Territorial.*
80. Latha Varadarajan, *The Domestic Abroad: Diasporas in International Relations* (New York: Oxford University Press, 2010); Devesh Kapur, *Diaspora, Development, and Democracy: The Domestic Impact of International Migration from India* (Princeton, NJ: Princeton University Press, 2010); Abraham, *How India Became Territorial.*
81. Ajantha Subramanian, "Making Merit: The Indian Institutes of Technology and the Social Life of Caste," *Comparative Studies in Society and History* 57, no. 2 (2015): 291–322. https://doi.org/10.1017/S0010417515000043.
82. Deepak Nayyar, *Migration, Remittances, and Capital Flows: The Indian Experience* (Delhi: Oxford University Press, 1994).

# 8

# Inequality, Development, and Global Distributive Justice

*Jeremy Adelman*

## Introduction

In recent years there has been a revival of development thinking. Particularly after the financial shock of 2008, the retreat of globalization since 1989, and the rise of challengers from the Chinese Belt-and-Road project to the spread of nationalisms and *ressentiments* worldwide, the idea that the world economy should be rescued from world bankers and Western technocrats (and technologies) has gained ever more currency. Indeed, development advocates have stormed back onto the stage, often proclaiming newfound virtues of state authority, after having been pushed aside by the triumph of neoliberalism, a credo that proclaimed the need for all societies to relinquish their dreams of an alternative order and their national or regional exceptionalist narratives. There is a temptation to treat our moment as a break from the past, a rupture after nearly two centuries of European and North American, generally "liberal," ascendancy and hegemony.

This chapter will argue that there was always a counterpoint narrative of and about the West and its claims to provide the coordinates for world integration—through empire and its successor, the assemblage of international organizations that emerged in the interwar years and formed the "Bretton Woods" family after 1945. In its heyday, the dominant story went something like this: free trade, open borders, and commercial peace reinforce each other; societies that embraced reciprocal ties with others are societies that prospered and saw their liberal institutions reinforced. Many of the chapters in this volume plumb the makings and assumptions of this narrative under the broad mantle of liberal internationalism. It has justified, in a variety of incarnations, a gamut of market-based systems of convergence. Free traders in the 1840s, advocates of a return to financial and trading

Jeremy Adelman, *Inequality, Development, and Global Distributive Justice* In: *Debating Worlds.* Edited by Daniel Deudney, G. John Ikenberry, and Karoline Postel-Vinay, Oxford University Press. © Oxford University Press 2023.
DOI: 10.1093/oso/9780197679302.003.0009

orthodoxy after 1918, the hobbled defenders of open borders in the 1930s, and the champions of the Bretton Woods arrangements may have varied in their nationalities, institutional commitments, and social backing. But they shared one thing in common: faith in markets to dissolve conflicts, to uplift trading partners, and even to close the gap between haves and have-nots.

But just as the convergence story has had its ebbs and flows, so too has a contrary narrative. It has been a powerful counter-current to the uplifting plotlines about the rewards from market convergence. The counterpoint to the free-market story is premised on the idea that integration does not automatically bring convergence; it sets some societies back. Integration, in effect, yields stratification; indeed, for some narrators and spinmeisters, integration required hierarchy and the wielding of asymmetrical power in order to buoy commercial interdependence. In response to the calls for free trade and open borders, the dissenters have called for policies and institutions that redistributed what the market so unfairly apportioned; commercial integration produced divides instead of erasing them. This was the international developmental narrative, one that enjoyed deep appeal among Westerners and Resterners. Indeed, the development narrative erased the lines between the two camps even as it—somewhat paradoxically—pointed to the inequalities and injustices of the divides that separated Resterners and Westerners.

Critics called for distributive justice at a global scale. They did so by summoning stories about capitalism and markets that did not conform to the pieties of free trade and the virtues of structural adjustment. Indeed, the international development narrative was at times tangled up with socialist and welfarist narratives of expanding rights at the national scale. International development and national welfare had common parabolic arcs, rising in the late nineteenth century, reinvented and repurposed in a Cold War contest. This chapter covers that arc, from the origins of the narrative that global integration produces a problem of falling behind, of having to conform increasingly to a history being made by other peoples located in other places, starting in the 1890s and ending with the anti-colonial imaginary of the early 1960s.

In so doing, this essay challenges inferences that there is something altogether new about the anti-Western or counter-liberal spinners today. What is new, however, is that the development narrative is no longer mainly about the Third World or postcolonial dreaming. We live in a moment of great inversion. How did a narrative that was once identified with the peripheries of the world economy storm the metropolitan cores? The recent globalization and its disenchantments have had the effect of spreading a narrative that was once a view from and about the periphery. We find as much, if not more, fear about falling behind in what were once the centers of the world economy, like the United States and Europe—and sentiment that has fueled homegrown resentments and backlashing, as Karoline Postel-Vinay catalogues in the Conclusion to this volume. But it is important to underscore this role-reversal act. No sooner did the erstwhile Third World—most notably but not only China (Modi's India proclaims itself unique, Vladimir Putin's Russia is presented as a moral economy capable of defying Western markets, and Islamist financial leaders have their own integrative projects)—close the gap than the old winners in Europe and America turned their backs on the narrative they had once championed. The champions of anti-globalization are more likely to be found among nationalists of the West to defend the West than among Resterners. We might ask ourselves whether late globalization has flipped the storytelling habits, whether it will be the Global South that champions market internationalism while it is Europe and the United States that recoil, worry, and search for alternatives to falling behind?

## Shadow

Long before this inversion, development became a way to understand and explain emergent global divides—and a prescription for how to tackle them by redistributing power and resources. The international development narrative was concerned about the terms of world integration, but in a way that was not satisfied with its inequalities. The origins of narratives about international distributive justice can be traced back to when poverty ceased to be seen as part of a natural order, when thinkers began to see that misery was not necessarily bequeathed by God, the fates, or nature; it could be man-made. The debate became more heated with the birth of trade unions, socialists, and progressive reformers in the nineteenth century. Alfred Marshall would declare in 1890 that ridding poverty "gives economic studies their chief and their highest interest." Thereafter, the rise of welfare and social democracy were closely entwined. No longer was the story of indigence or poverty reduced to the work of inhuman or timeless forces.[1]

It was in the latter half of the nineteenth century that arguments about injustice became a concern of the dynamics between societies. The spasm of imperial expansion highlighted the disparities between the haves and have-nots. American marines and German troops found themselves plodding through tropical forests in the Philippines and Namibia, with ethnographers and photographers in tow, to pursue villagers and guerrillas who had different ideas of governance and property than the scientific conquistadors. New methods and ideas about settlement closely aligned with racialized doctrines of social difference and civilization. Nitobe Inazo, the Japanese born-again agricultural economist, for instance, redeployed terms like "colony" and "colonization" to depict how Tokyo's new empire should view its new possessions like Korean and Taiwan, whose "natives" could be corralled to work for God's plan for Japan. Along the way, a technocratic elite had to be trained in a new field for a new age, "colonial policy studies" rolled out for the country's new Western-modeled institution of learning, the Imperial University of Tokyo—which became the standard-bearer for Japan. At the start of each teaching day, Nitobe would write on the blackboard, "Colonization is the spread of civilization."[2]

There were many, from Buenos Aires to Bombay, who embraced integration as the path to civilization. Some saw it as the ticket to progress and internalized many of the scientific models of racial differences to explain their struggles to keep up. When Kang Youwei visited Hong Kong in 1879, he marveled at the orderly bustle of the British outpost. Perhaps the interlopers had figured out how to turn China into a precinct of modern capitalism and breathe new life into the decaying empire? Alarmed at the widening gap between the modern West and an ancient kingdom, this Confucian reformer was an important figure in mentoring a generation that would make development a centerpiece of their crusade for the periphery. Among his most important disciples was Liang Qichao. Liang was aware of the Western shadow. Coming from Guangdong province, where commercial, financial, and missionary penetration into China was most intense, he steeped himself in Western texts, then traveled to Beijing in 1895 to sit for his exams. That year, the shock of the loss to Japan in the first Sino-Japanese War (1894–1895) sparked the immediate realization that the world had decisively changed from the comforts of Sinocentrism. "The defeat in 1895, loss of Taiwan, and two hundred million taels in reparations awoke our nation from its four-thousand-year-long dream," he proclaimed. Likening China to the Ottoman Empire, he coined the term *dongfang bingfu*—"sick man of Asia"—as an epithet. In Shanghai, he founded a newspaper called *Xiwu Bao*—"Chinese Progress"—to celebrate the virtues of industrialization and education and to circulate the gospel of Social Darwinism to promote a "science of group strength" to overturn backwardness.[3]

The flurry of wars and conquests at the end of the 1890s sharpened the stratification between winners and losers. It began to seem as if the narrative of progress was pulling out of sight, beyond access to those who sought to modernize by emulating or borrowing. Liang himself began to feel that the world was being carved up by the powerful at the expense of the powerless. In the wake of the Boxer Rebellion and another round of humiliating treaties, Liang authored a bitter diatribe, "On the New Rules for Destroying Countries," cataloguing the fates of Poland, India, and Egypt at the hands of capitalists. "To those who claim," intoned Liang, "that opening mining, railroad, and concessionary rights to foreigners is not harmful to the sovereignty of the whole, I advise you to read the history of the Boer War." In 1902, he published a counterfactual utopian novel set in the year 2062, *The Future of New China*, which begins during the fiftieth anniversary of the late Qing Reform in Shanghai and the celebration of the World Expo.[4] The year before, Dadabhai Naoroji, an early Indian nationalist and newspaper editor who became the first Indian member of the British Parliament (representing the London constituency of Finsbury for the Liberal Party in the 1890s) published *Poverty and Unbritish Rule in India*. The work was a sensation; it questioned the presumption that Britain was in India to instill order and create wealth *for* the colony. Advocating a "drain" theory of Indian finances, Naoroji catalogued the many ways in which financial and commercial rules sucked wealth from the colony.[5]

So it was that by World War I there was a distinct sense that integration of the world's parts had created greater world disparities. The spectacle of interventions and repressions in Asia, Africa, and Latin America cast a pall on the storyline that "backward" societies could keep up with—even catch up with—the trailblazers by adapting their scripts.

## Year Zero

World War I and the Great Depression kicked the legs out from under what was left of old liberal convictions about civilization and scientific ordering. The year 1919 was Year Zero for the idea of development if only because it pulled the veil back on the injustices of the global order and triggered a worldwide search for alternative narratives to European integration. A wave of revolt circled the world. In Mexico, *agraristas* defended a new conception of rural wealth, laid the foundations for nationalizing their oil and mining rights, and made life miserable for American troops dispatched to restore order. Anarchists and syndicalists rose up from Buenos Aires to Shanghai. In April 1919, clashing with police in Punjab led to the Amritsar Massacre and the spread of the Non-cooperation Movement. A month later, anti-imperialist demonstrators took to the streets of Beijing to protest the transfer of German concessions in Shandong and founded the May Fourth Movement. Embittered by the postwar deal, Sunni, Shia, and working-class Iraqis rose up against British mandate authorities to demand Arab sovereignty. Northern Kurds did the same. There emerged a sense that social injustice was constitutive of the world economy, neither an accidental byproduct of integration nor a holdover of an earlier era.

If Europeans could plunge the world into ruin and reclaim privileges afterward, then, it stood to reason, perhaps the welfare of peripheral peoples would be better served by charting other pathways, reasons, and narratives of global integration. Ever since, there has been a furious debate about whether the have-nots would be better off as part of the global order or free of it.

What could not be rolled back was the acknowledgment that fundamental inequities were at stake and needed to be remedied. A good example of how economic integration created the need for distributive justice was Sun Yat-sen, the father of Chinese republicanism. Outraged by the humiliation of China at the hands of self-anointed great powers, and disappointed by the treatment of the struggling Republic at the treaty discussions at the end of the war, he sat down in Canton in 1921 to map out what we would now call a "strategy" for Chinese development. His manifesto, *The International Development of China*, argued that his country "is now prey of militaristic and capitalistic powers—a greater bone of contention than the Balkan Peninsula." In a sense, he turned J. A. Hobson's theory of imperialism on its head. If Hobson had argued that the problems of capitalism in the metropole drove potentates in London, Berlin, and Washington to subject "inferior races" to their will and create empires that careened to war, Sun insisted that the creation of backwardness and inferiority in peripheries was what threatened world peace. By creating have-nots in an interdependent world, empires produced weak links in the chain of integration. Sun was the first to connect development of the peripheries to global peace and security; without a solution to "the China Question," another war was inevitable. While advanced countries were deep into a "second industrial revolution," China could not enter the first, he argued. Because of the ways in which outsiders imposed treaties on a feeble state, China, like many other parts of the world, was out of sync with modernization; the planet's progress had integrated parts but put them onto fundamentally different paths. Whereas Europe and America proceeded through stages of progress—stadial models were gaining increasing currency—others were sliding through the opposite sequence, into backwardness. Global integration had, Sun argued, created a battle over time, a divergence of narratives about interdependence—the world was becoming more fused and polarized at the same time.[6]

If Sun and others worried about the ways in which international integration fractured societies, some observers began to see that integration created an illusion of internal divides, a separation of times between the modern and the backward. Was it possible that integration created backwardness as part of becoming modern, part of the world economy? The Peruvian Marxist José Carlos Mariátegui noted that the merging of Andean peasants into the modern world economy as producers of maize or metals hardly dismantled old vestiges. Rather, it gave them a new lease. This was an important insight: Mariátegui observed the cunning ways in which global integration relied upon and reinforced older versions of organizing societies. Backwardness was not a relic; it was a creation of progress itself. Institutions like mines and plantations that relied on a gamut of coerced labor systems bounced back. Ancient Andean, feudal, and modern systems overlapped and interlinked—which yielded the illusion of pulling the country forward while watching it drift backward. "The elements of three different economies coexist in Peru today," he noted in the late 1920s. "Underneath the feudal economy inherited from the colonial period, vestiges of the indigenous communal economy can still be found in the sierra. On the coast, a bourgeois economy is growing in feudal soil; it gives every indication of being backward, at least in its mental outlook." The development of the capitalist economy, he went on, was entrusted "to the spirit of the fief."[7] The advent of market forces, the penetration of foreign capital, and the rise of modern cities did not automatically tear down the leftovers of the old world; it recombined them for modern purposes. In Europe, capitalism dissolved feudalism; in Peru, capitalism revitalized it.

With the growing awareness that integration created new hierarchies, coupled with the unsettling effects of World War I and doubts about liberal capitalism's ability to resolve social conflicts, we see the beginnings of "development" as a solution that relied on a different historical imaginary, one that argued that not all societies had to share the same narrative in order to advance, they did not all have to conform to the same script for modernization. Redrafting narratives of how societies could survive or thrive in an interdependent world—even though this was admittedly still a faint idea—pointed to correcting international flows.

## Malthusian Shadow

Then came the Depression. The Wall Street crash and the buckling financial system crumpled the confidence in the old order and the familiar, if fatigued, narrative of the commercial peace. The collapse unleashed a plethora of competing narratives to fill the gap. There was the naked neo-Mercantilist reaction: a spasm of coercive integration, which seemed to harden the view that wealth of one society required exploitation of another. Even wealthy societies like Argentina felt screws tightening. The 1933 Roca-Runciman Pact, which brazenly favored British importers of beef over Argentine exporters, brought the tensions to a surface. When news arrived in Buenos Aires of the terms, the economist Ernesto Malaccorto thundered that the deal was a "betrayal of Argentina." Indeed, the bare neomercantilism of the 1930s spawned more explicit calls for redistribution. In Argentina, the furious "Meat Debate" catalyzed economic nationalism. In steps, Argentina adopted policies aimed at stanching the outflow of wealth. By 1943, Central Bankers in this paragon of export-led prosperity were calling for "inward-directed growth." A technical term, this would soon become a political slogan and graffiti as anti-imperialism gathered strength under the mantle of Peronism.[8] Nehru railed against British exploitation. "The only way to right [injustice and exploitation] is to do away with the domination of any one class over another," he told an audience in Lahore in 1920. "The exploitation of India and other countries," he exclaimed in *Whither India?*, "brought so much wealth to England that some of it trickled down to the working class and their standard of living rose."[9] Accusations that the international order punished primary exporters led to charges of global injustice and a sense that development in the peripheries required more than turning inward. It required reversing the geographic flow of resources.

Echoing the neo-Mercantilist turn was a revival of a Malthusian narrative about how poverty was a trap. Laced with biological and evolutionary anxiety, neo-Malthusians insisted that the poor would consume the green shoots of prosperity and development and would condemn the have-nots to a vicious cycle. The shadow of race would never be far away from the story, as backwardness became associated with phenotype, so that entire people were made to carry the traits of their self-induced misfortunes. If China, for instance, were to re-hinge to industrial modernity, she needed do something about what many considered to be internal obstacles stuck in archaic times and falling further behind. One effect was a rush to organize "backward" societies into calculable categories of peoples. The idea was to make communities commensurable and thus capable of reform in order to integrate them. Chen Changheng's *A Treatise on Chinese Population* echoed some Malthusian angst about China's plague of people. But the US-trained economist also argued for statistical analysis to inform state intervention to curb the reproduction of the wrong sort of citizens. He set a tone. The fever for surveying reached its height in the late 1920s; between 1927 and 1935, a generation of social science (*shehui kexue*) was summoned to conduct no less than 9,000 surveys in the drive to create social facts about China to put the country on the path to progress.[10] One French administrator in Indochina worried that it was premature to grant to private citizens full freedom of economic action in such a backward, agrarian society. Instead, it "will have to submit its economy to a firm discipline to avoid seeing it founder in chaos."[11] In 1938, the Carnegie Corporation enlisted the Swedish economist Gunnar Myrdal to come to the US to study "the Negro Question" with this spirit in mind. But it is worth reminding ourselves the degree to which Chen Changheng's Malthusianism was shared. Myrdal's own 1938 Godkin Lectures upheld the practice of rational birth control, to prevent people in misery from passing it on by cutting off the number of heirs. "Today," he argued, "the problem is how to get a people to abstain from not reproducing itself."[12] Reversing the pernicious effects of global backwardness meant national integration of uneven parts, starting by making them visible, calculable, and harmonizing them into one, national, temporality—creating a modern nation-state was the condition for striking better deals in the nasty, competitive, one-upmanship that was gripping trade and migration policy worldwide.

There is something ironic in this interwar moment of inward-oriented change as a condition for outward recovery. It coincided with the malaise and then breakdown of the world economic order. Just as some social scientists rounded on local peoples as the source of the problem, the world around them collapsed.

## Time Machines

But the collapse, and the growing tensions of empire, did eventually force a change in the narrative. The general crisis of the world economy demolished the faith in voluntary models of integration and betterment. As a result, the 1930s was the decade that brought the first calls for international redistribution as a necessary component of national growth, that without policies and institutions that reversed the hemorrhaging of resources from the "periphery"—a term that the Argentine economist Raúl Prebisch, often seen as the founder of "dependency theory," began to use in his private correspondence by 1940—the periphery was doomed to slide further behind. The brazen use of state power in Europe and the United States to strike better bilateral deals at the expense of trading partners, and the example of domestic structural reforms in Italy and the American New Deal, revealed both the need to assert powers of one's own on the international stage and the need for new deals at home.[13]

If 1919 was Year Zero for spotlighting global injustice and the 1930s cleared the way for a wave of defection from the liberal trading order, World War II provided a new global moment for redistributive justice.

Calls for redistribution did not come from the old core or the emerging hegemon of the world economy. In fact, Latin American leaders had petitioned through the 1930s for the creation of a lending institution to invest in countries suffering from capital shortages. With the outbreak of the war in 1939, Latin American finance ministers met in Panama to create an Inter-American Financial and Economic Advisory Committee to inch the notion forward. By 1940, there was a draft. Harry Dexter White of the US Treasury even endorsed the concept at a meeting in Rio in January 1942. The 1943 Hot Springs conference took on food and agricultural issues and the challenge of creating international institutions designed to promote freedom from want. The point is: the pressure to embrace development was coming from outside the charmed circle of statesmen and social scientists we usually suspect of thinking globally for everyone else. Lest the powerful forget, as Mahatma Gandhi noted in a letter to the American president that summer, the promises "sound hollow, so long as India, and for that matter, Africa are exploited by Great Britain, and America has the Negro problem in her own home."[14]

One site for conflict over redistributive justice was the hotel at Bretton Woods in 1944 where the postwar economic architecture was supposed to be hammered out. American officials like White and Henry Morgenthau, swayed by Latin American pressures, were already on board the idea of lending institutions that did more than "reconstruct" but also got into the "development" business. When Morgenthau presented the first drafts of the International Monetary Fund (IMF) and the International Bank for Reconstruction and Development (IBRD) to Roosevelt in May 1942, he argued that the institutions were necessary "to supply the huge volume of capital that will be needed abroad for relief, for reconstruction, and economic development essential for the attainment of world prosperity and higher standards of living." White pushed for a Bank that would "help stabilize the prices of essential raw materials and other important commodities" and floated an "International Commodity Stabilization Corporation to stabilize the price of important commodities." He even endorsed the support of infant industries in the periphery to help poor countries out of their lot. At Bretton Woods, Morgenthau announced that "poverty, wherever it exists, is menacing to us all." But the pressure was coming mainly from Latin American entreaties, from Indian and Chinese delegates, and especially the envoy from Mexico, the vocal Eduardo Suárez.[15]

As the war came to a close, there was thus a split between rival models of the world economy—between a restoration of the multilateral, free-market, re-convergence with tweaks to stabilize it, and a developmental order thickened with institutions that would protect primary exporters from being drained of rents and earmark resources for them to diversify and industrialize. Latin American and Indian economists in particular, soon to be joined by others from Africa and Asia, made the case for the latter. What emerged from the New Hampshire hotel is well known; it was *not* an architecture for development. The defeat of the idea of an International Trade Organization that would ensure price floors for primary producers, and an International Bank for Reconstruction *and* Development which took the latter as seriously as the former, left a bitter taste among those who hoped for a different postwar than the one that staggered out of 1918.

As a constituent moment, 1945 reset the terms of interdependence. There was a choice between reframing the narrative about markets as machines for closing the gap between societies, and redistributive drive to make sure the have-nots got at least their share of global rents. The decision had important consequences. Bretton Woods, in short, set up the postwar economic architecture; it also revealed a fault line that became a battle zone in the years to come as development offered a language to contest the partitioning and governing of global wealth. It pushed the language of development and narrative about the need for redistribution more fully into the vocabulary of anti-colonialism.

## Catching Up

The idea of development quickly positioned itself at odds with the emerging concept of multilateralism in the US and Europe. It did so for one important reason: the struggle *against* European empires was fueled by the search *for* development. For colonies to stay under their old mantles was to be condemned to falling further behind. Narratives of progress diverged sharply after 1945. India's independence in 1947 was a political event with intellectual consequences. Some British and American observers vexed about the country's global alignment as Nehru drew from the Soviet planning model to accelerate history and the passage from a rural society to an industrial economy; after all, he had served as a national planner to the Congress Party since the 1930s. Free from London, a National Planning Commission got more rein that its colonial predecessor (called the National Planning Committee—which goes to show that the rage for planning had imperial, and pre-war, precedents). The point, as far as the eventual head planner, the physicist Prasanta Mahalanobis, was concerned, was to reverse the hemorrhaging of resources from the colony to the metropole by becoming a new manufacturing power bristling with its own heavy-metal plants. By coupling statistics with steel, Indian social scientists could effect a fundamental change in the global economic geography and interrupt centuries of one-sided accumulation under the aegis of colonialism.[16] If British authorities once imagined themselves bringing modernity to the periphery, Indians imagined themselves reversing the damage and misery. These were two utterly discordant narratives of the future.[17]

Development was increasingly seen, then, as an enterprise devoted to one part of the world—the have-nots—at the expense of another part—the haves. Justice took on an explicitly redistributionist mien, and its claims acquired more antagonistic features. To challenge deep-seated norms, rules, and institutions, it fell to national planners, the new heroes of the story, to punch through the entrenched hindrances. The liberal mien had rested on notions of flexibility, substitutability, and curves upon which to plot the workings of some interchangeable, free-flowing system, tweakable and adjustable to keep the equilibrium. When it came to what would soon become called the "Third World," the assumptions had to be flipped. Gunnar Myrdal pointed to "the rising revolt in underdeveloped countries themselves which is the active force in demolishing the barriers of opportunistic ignorance in our minds." He called this "the Great Awakening," a moment that inaugurated "a new phase in the struggle for equality" as people became more aware of injustices at a new, global, scale. At the core of the Great Awakening was the spread of developed countries' "inherited ideal of equality of opportunity" to the underdeveloped. Poorer lands were seeing themselves less as backward and more as deprived. The trouble was, out in the peripheries and colonies, getting to equal opportunity on a global scale meant "world revolution." The issue for Myrdal was whether it would be a peaceful revolution or a violent one.[18]

In the peripheries, social scientists joined forces with the planner; sometimes the two became one. Fresh from the New Deal, war, and reconstruction, it was an alliance that made sense. It also brought the piecemeal connections between domestic backwardness and international inequality into view. No one framed this coalition better than the Argentine economist Raúl Prebisch and an entourage of social scientists at the new United Nations Economic Commission for Latin America (CEPAL). By the mid-1940s, Prebisch had turned on his earlier faiths in liberal internationalism, not because he'd become more radical but because he'd become more sober; he felt the rules and organizational defaults of the trading system punished primary exporters and siphoned wealth from peripheries to cores. "To resist subordination of the national economy to foreign movements and contingencies," he noted in a 1943 manuscript, "we must strengthen our internal structure and achieve an autonomous functioning of our economy." The prose was rather bloodless, but he was making explicit the linkage between relationship between domestic divides and international inequities.

In 1945, Prebisch started to refer to the plights of the "periphery" in letters to friends, an indication of how the vocabulary was starting to label global injustice.[19] By then, Washington had scotched any idea of an inter-American development bank and the Truman administration wanted nothing of the hotheads questioning the global economic principles of Bretton Woods. Congress, meanwhile, was gearing up to reject the 1948 International Trade Organization. In the CEPAL offices in Santiago, an unsure and frustrated Prebisch poured his frustrations into *The Economic Development of Latin America and Its Principal Problems*, a declaration of discontent against the global economic order. Though couched in technicalities about elasticities of demand and business cycles, the normative purpose came through; all the slights from Washington were now bearing fruit in a mélange of objective data and righteous anger. Not only were primary exporters stuck in a historic rut and condemned to diminishing rewards for their staples, but unequal exchange would fossilize them there. In effect, the past was a kind of prison.

If Prebisch and his predecessors once thought that international integration was the key to breaking out of poverty, the CEPAL Manifesto argued the reverse. The only solution was to turn inward, to reap the rents that once flowed out from agrarian societies to industrial powers. Now, it was the international system that had to change as a condition for the improvement of its social parts.

Dreaming about development involved a quest for models, metaphors, and alternative narratives. These were the glory years of social scientific self-confidence in the capacity to shape the planet's order to abstract models of time; metaphors practically dropped from the trees. Big pushes, takeoffs, great leaps forward—the 1950s brimmed with temporal metaphors of man-made human change. They shared a similarity. Prebisch's Brazilian colleague, Roberto Campos, called this a "structural" diagnosis. Structural problems demanded structural solutions because, left on their own, peripheral societies would fall further behind. Nothing short of structural change would reverse the course and close the gap between advanced and backward nations.

American social scientists did not stand by as the rest of the world explored narratives about how societies close gaps, catch up, or even leap ahead. After all, they were fresh from a successful war and an idealized New Deal. Many looked up to American-style planning as a model for the rest. The Rockefeller Foundation treated it as a potential foundation for a Chinese New Deal. Indeed, China offered to American social scientists a "laboratory" which they had lacked "where experiments can be carried out in controlled conditions." It would not be the only time China would be the test tube for someone else's human trials. To the Tufts economist Eugene Staley, American dams (and finance) could serve as a model for intervention in poorer countries as a way to neutralize totalitarianism.[20] Staley coined the term "modernization theory" to denote an understanding of historical time that liquefied peripheral arguments about development as a race against time. Whereas Sun Yat-sen and Mariátegui conjoined archaic and modern features that reinforced the other, and Prebisch argued that integration progress was doomed to grind peripheries into perpetual behindness, modernization theorists insisted that the timeline of change in Europe could be replicated elsewhere—and should not be rejected elsewhere. Development meant mastering time in order to accelerate it.

A social science in this key had special appeal for Americans, or for Europeans transplanted to a land of optimistic bravura. At the apex of its global influence and in the wake of a war that demolished the confidence in European modernity, American social science was flush with assurance. The American Miracle could be rendered less miraculous: it could be stylized for export, stripped of its redemptive, exceptionalist storyline to fit a universal plot. In a fit of optimism, the advocates of modernization insisted that all good things go together: growth begets democracy, and democratic life creates the right environment for sustained growth.

It was a creed ripe for muscular intellectuals disposed to export the confidence in their models; indeed, one might argue that it was *the* great American intellectual export. The ultimate goals of development, noted Walt W. Rostow, wunderkind of the new confidence, to an audience, were "psychological and political."[21] One of the hubs of this kind of thinking, the Center for International Studies at MIT, opened a branch in New Delhi in 1955 to persuade Indian social scientists and policymakers of the wisdom of modernization. Shortly thereafter, MIT brain-trusters unveiled "A Proposal" for an aid policy for India, aimed to win friends and stymie enemies. But, they warned, it could easily backfire, lest the accelerated change unleash the demons "inherent in the awakening of formerly static peoples."[22] From that hub came Rostow's *The Stages of Economic Growth: A Non-Communist Manifesto*, a book that quickly earned a kind of Talmudic status and went through twelve printings in its first five years. It was a distillate of Rostow's understanding of the industrial revolution, mixed with lessons about how to shake traditional societies from their timeless lethargy. Tradition, he argued, immunized societies from science and denied them the rewards of its application; tradition prevented villagers from upgrading their roads, thwarted productivity, and condemned them to a perpetual cycle of diminishing returns. Determined to turn Malthus on his head, Rostow aimed to show a way out of the darkness, for the poor "to enjoy the blessings and choices opened up by the march of compound interest."[23]

Once it became imaginable that one could master history and accelerate it, whatever humility was left dissolved into an impatience of astounding proportions. Paradoxically, just as intellectuals thought they had found the clues to arranging time, leaders began to feel as if the clock was running out. Brazilian president Juscelino Kubitschek (aka JK) summoned the country to a pace of "Fifty Years Progress in Five," a drive to cover the country with spider webs of roads and cables—including deep into Amazonia. In 1958, construction of the "road of the jaguar" began to open a causeway into the forests from the coast. Opened to fanfare in 1960, the "caravan of integration" opened the *terra devolutas*, unsurveyed lands, to privatization; between 1959 and 1963, 13.4 million acres of land in the state of Pará were privatized. The scramble for the Amazon and its systematic deforestation was on.

If Brazil could make headlong progress, why not the rest of Latin America? Frustration with the pace of reform at the global scale prompted the ambitious American politico John F. Kennedy to call in 1958 for *Operation Pan-America* to uplift the region in concert with more borrowing and more control over export rents. By luring foreign investors into domestic industries, pouring money to open highways to hinterlands, and erecting towering modernist icons out of the wilderness of the plains of central Brazil, JK was the emblem of "development*alism*" (as it was now called, having become an ism of its own).[24] Later that year, Milton Eisenhower toured Latin America and returned arguing that Washington could assuage the creeping North-South tensions by embracing more of the developmental ideas coming from the South. The menace of the Cuban Revolution helped to snap the pieces together in the form of Kennedy's Alliance for Progress. Instead of Truman's now anemic-seeming technical assistance, there was "aid" and support for domestic redistributive justice (agrarian reform, education, tax reform). Kennedy's signature was to call this a "peaceful revolution," though the redistributive connotations of creating a transnational welfare regime was clear enough. "I have called on all the people of the hemisphere," noted Kennedy, in a nod to North-South interdependence, "to join in a new Alliance for Progress—Alianza para Progreso—a vast cooperative effort, unparalleled in magnitude and nobility of purpose, to satisfy the basic needs of the American people for homes, work and land, health and schools—*techo, trabajo y tierra, salud y escuela*." (As far as I can tell, this was the first time Spanish words came from the mouth of an American president.) The fate of the American economy was now tethered to others in a "massive planning effort which will be at the heart of the Alliance for Progress."

Where the euphoria to compress years into quintiles really took off was not where liberal capitalists refined modernization ideas, but where comrades revamped Marxist ones. What the master-planners of capitalism dreamed up was nothing compared to the development utopias of Party chiefs. In 1957, Nikita Khrushchev announced at a gathering of world party leaders at a congress to celebrate the fortieth anniversary of the October Revolution that the Soviet Union was committed to eclipsing American industrial output in fifteen years. Not to be outdone, and frustrated that China was still inching after one Five Year Plan, Mao's proclamation of a Great Leap Forward to outdo British industrial output in fifteen years, only to plunge much of China back into the stone age. In the hype, the missile scientist Qian Xuesen waxed "How High Will Grain Yields Be?" in *China Youth Daily* to convince doubters of the promise of "Sputnik" expectations. Mao began to rethink his own fevered projections: surpassing the UK may take only two or three years, "especially in steel production." As it became clear that any advance on the industrial front required better carts—without railroads or trucking, "cartification" was the aim—making ball bearings gained urgency for home factories. "Every household a factory, every home ringing with a ding-dong sound" was the slogan. Though the output was useless, *People's Daily* celebrated national "bearingification" as a monumental breakthrough. Meanwhile, "right deviationists" and "degenerate peasants" blamed for tripping progress were rounded up; reports of local food shortages were dismissed as "temporary crises." Thirty million people starved to death in three years in humanity's worst manufactured famine.[25]

## Discontents

Faced with narratives that promised so much change in so little time, it was inevitable that the redistributionist narratives would soon face a reckoning.

It is worth noting that not everyone looked upon developmentalism with such outsized expectations. Not everyone subscribed to a version of history as stylized steps and compressed timelines. There were skeptics, like Alexander Gerschenkron, Albert O. Hirschman, and P. T. Bauer. Even as modernization theory was taking off, Alexander Gerschenkron, the Russian-born doubter, noted that the half-truth of stagist history concealed an awkward other half—"that is to say, in several very important respects the development of a backward country may, by the very virtue of its backwardness, tend to differ fundamentally from that of an advanced country." How useful can any partial truth be?[26] Gerschenkron's colleague, Albert O. Hirschman, watched development schemes in Colombia close up in the 1950s. The experience made him more, not less, concerned about the convictions of the money doctors and their clients, who considered poor people as simpler folk and their societies mired in inertia, waiting for a big push to hurry them into the modern world. To Hirschman, it did not require that all good things come together in order to make any good thing happen; trying to manufacture such an ideal scenario was likely, he felt, doomed to disappoint.[27]

We face a basic paradox: while the apostles of modernization encountered more criticism from colleagues on the Left and the Right, and the cataclysmic example of mass starvation in China should have given pause, the 1960s saw development reach its zenith. The United Nations declared it the "Development Decade." American foundations rushed to support work in the Third World. The World Bank became a full-throated global development agency devoted to recycling member contributions to build dams, railways, factories, and ports around Asia, Africa, and Latin America.

Yet, many were starting to question the underlying assumptions of development-talk altogether. As de-colonization spread, and Third Worldism grew more radical, the appeals to more structuralist criticisms of the model of interdependence—market convergence leavened with some aid and lots of talk—disenchantment spread.

The Martiniquian psychiatrist Frantz Fanon was among the first to call attention to the hypocrisy of developmentalism and its sibling anti-colonialism. After serving in North African hospitals, he invoked the acidic words of an unnamed "Senegalese patriot" disenchanted with the promises of the poet-president Senghor: "We asked for the Africanization of the top jobs and all Senghor does is Africanize the Europeans." Fanon's prose dripped with disdain, especially for the intellectuals who rid colonies of their European masters while having assimilated the colonizer's culture, and so authoring a kind of "self-hatred that characterizes racial conflict in segregated societies." *Les Damnés de la terre*, written in Fanon's dying months, from April to July 1961, sliced through the mist of development's false hopes. "The Third World," he concluded, "must start over a new history of man which takes account of not only the occasional prodigious theses maintained by Europe but also its crimes, the most heinous have been committed at the very heart of man, the pathological dismembering of his functions and the erosion of his unity, and in the context of the community, the fracture, the stratification and the bloody tensions fed by class, and finally, on the immense scale of humanity the racial hatred, slavery, exploitation and, above all, the bloodless genocide whereby one and a half billion have been written off."[28]

The malaise shifted development and global redistribution from the solution to becoming the problem. It became an exhibit of the "perversity thesis"—when purposive action to help winds up hindering. The ideas of development and welfare would soon become prime targets for this style of argument. When it came to development, it was Hirschman's colleague, the Harvard political scientist Samuel Huntington, who would burnish his credentials as one of America's Cassandras by dismantling modernization theory. Hirschman and Huntington forked in striking ways. Economic and social change, Huntington warned, could fuel expectations of the teeming masses in Asia, Africa, and Latin America and lead to more, not less, impatience and radicalization. The core of the problem was that the theorists had never understood that social or economic change required political order as a necessary condition. Huntington ripped away what was left of the notion that the Third World could follow History laid out by the First. Unlike in Western liberal or Eastern communist regimes, development unfolded in "debile political systems." The effort to uplift the poor had drowned fledgling political systems. Americans, and the multilateral institutions they pulled along, were only too eager to project their own "happy history" onto societies not as blessed by customs and norms of modernity. The fundamental assumption that political stability would follow economic growth was not just wrong; it was ruinous. The results were, for Huntington, catastrophic. In contrast to the faith that all good things go together, Huntington concluded that when it came to development, all bad things go together. What was needed was "an organizational imperative," effective authority to tutor new political subjects out of their traditional ways before giving them new liberties. "In the modernizing world he controls the future who organizes its politics." Many saw this type of argument as a justification for authoritarian rule.[29]

As with the unwinding consensus around national welfare, confidence in modernizing development was coming apart. Even the promises of more radical redistribution seemed threadbare. In 1964, Edmundo Desnoes struck a less defiant, more resigned tone in his novel, *Memories of Underdevelopment*. Echoing Dostoevsky's prose of doubt and isolation, Desnoes' rendition of development uprooted his protagonist, Sergio, without giving him new ground. Far from living in Marxist or modernizationist certainties about phases and stages, Sergio wanders Havana in a state of limbo. Underdevelopment has become a state of mind. If Mariátegui had once imagined an integrated time of ancient and modern, a revolutionary Cuba dedicated to transcending the past with development leaves Sergio sighing: "the truth is I feel washed out, sad with my new liberty-solitude."[30]

So it was that the scientific certainties about progress unraveled even as the travails of the Third World became more, not less, visible. This was already apparent before the UN development decade was halfway through. By the 1970s, for a growing chorus of those finding fault with the world, the nub was not so much inequality as the precepts of what it meant to be modern and prosperous. It was not a coincidence that in the same year that brought the final withdrawal of US forces from Vietnam that the words "climate warming" made their debut. The new vocabulary of constraint and limits accented the man-made crux of the problem, not nature's fetters. What is more, the limits were not posed by Traditional Man that had obsessed the neo-Malthusian rural reform from the 1930s. They were the result of the very actor who, Marx predicted, was supposed to transcend necessity: Modern Man. History, thanks to our capacity to mold the planet to our consumption needs, had bent the curve of necessity back to where we started. Development, instead of freeing humanity from nature, took us to the cliff where we had to choose either to conserve or risk the future of the planet. Under these circumstances, it became harder to raise the flag of development as a model of global redistribution. As Hirschman noted in a kind of epitaph on the field that had done better than the object of its study, time had caught up with the discipline of development economics.[31]

Developmentalism as distributional justice did not go down without a fight. After all, the problems of poverty had not gone away. In fact, the critique of the fundamental injustices of the world order grew in intensity. It emboldened OPEC countries to hike oil prices in the name of recirculating rents away from Western consumers to Third World producers. In this scheme, development in the periphery required renegotiating the terms of global transactions in a more assertive, unilateral way than was ever envisioned by the economists of CEPAL who, for all their worries about unequal trade, wanted multilateral solutions. These, like the General Agreement on Trade and Tariffs, the Bretton Woods twins, and clubs like the IMF's Committee of Twenty, were seen as the guardians of an order that tilted in favor of the haves. Aid was a band-aid. The World Bank in particular was singled out as the commanding height of development to keep the world unfair. In 1973, the Non-Aligned Countries met in Algiers and adopted an Action Programme calling for a "New International Economic Order" (NIEO) as the only way to remedy the problems of underdevelopment.

The NIEO advocates wanted new rules and more democratic membership of global institutions to reflect the postcolonial order of 1973 and not the postwar order of three decades earlier. They wanted structural reforms less for undoing domestic obstacles than redressing what were seen as entrenched global asymmetries. The irony, of course, is that few things demolished the bloc of underdeveloped countries more than the embourgeoisement of sultanates and the growing debt of oil importers in the Third World.

Reformists also hung on; there was one last stab at a heroic counter-narrative as the neoliberal juggernaut was starting to gather strength in the 1980s. Consider the *Report of the Independent Commission on International Development Issues*. Better known as *North-South: A Programme for Survival*, or the Willy Brandt Report for its chair, it doubled as a manifesto for the survival of the species and one of the last of its own species. Thereafter, the world would get no more such clarion calls (the Millennium Development Goals is better known for its thematized, local, campaigning than for its global insights). The Brandt Report did break new ground, however. It coupled the cause of redistribution to the Third World to another—disarmament. This is why development was a matter of survival. Citing the resources funneled into weaponry, the commissioners argued that the world had to choose, again rather apocalyptically, between "destruction or development." The money being spent on "arming ourselves to death" could mitigate hunger, disease, and reduce the sources of international conflict which, the report insisted, had roots in global maldistribution. Even an otherwise sympathetic social democrat like Gunnar Myrdal saw that such "a massive transference of capital to developing countries" was "rather futile." By 1980, the whole aid business was under assault for propping corrupt, rent-seeking (a term that was catching on at the time) governments and for supporting more consumption on the periphery than capital formation.[32] On the heels of Margaret Thatcher's election and on the eve of Ronald Reagan's, the timing could not be worse. The second OPEC spike was starting to create serious problems within the developing bloc. Then, in the summer of 1982, the Mexican finance minister announced to a convention of world financiers at the World Bank-IMF summit in Toronto that his country was unable to pay its debts. For the rest of the 1980s, the idea of redistribution got buried by a global debt crisis which had the opposite effect: redistributing rents from peripheries to financial institutions in the core.

One of the paradoxes of the Brandt Report is that while it may have been a pipe dream, it was the first document to my knowledge that used the term "globalization"—though what was meant was an acknowledgment that interdependence required seeing how development, redistribution, and curbs to the global arms trade were of a piece in making global prosperity and security.

That narrative, however, ceded to a different understanding of the term "globalization." The decade that gave us the Washington Consensus, structural adjustment (with another flip in the use of a word), and a return to market fundamentalism also gave us a return to an older narrative about how much the "West" had to tutor the Rest. Nineteenth-century stadial thinkers believed in progress as a narrative that all societies had to converge upon; modernizers like Rostow gave it new meaning. Ever since, the social sciences have recycled the idea that the first modernizers cornered the market on lessons about how to do it. Hernando De Soto, the Peruvian economist who gained fame for extolling the virtues of Latin America's swollen informal sector, joined the parade to unmask, reveal, disclose the secrets of the world—though this rendition was to accent the mysteries of the plot, one by one revealing the clues to readers with a solution to the *roman policier* put together in the final act. To his credit, it was the poor who concerned De Soto, and it is for the have-nots that he believes knowledge should be summoned. But if development has stumbled, it is because it failed to see that the mystery of capital was that everyone should be a capitalist, regardless of creed or culture—indeed, regardless of their capacities. The Rest simply need to be more like the West and see everyone as a potential possessive individualist. This was, he concluded, "the only game in town."[33]

## Conclusion

By the end of the century, like socialism, development became an all-but-extinct species to explain the conjunction of inequity and integration—at least as a way of postulating that interdependence and inequality were inextricably connected. The two followed similar parabola, fading out with the waning faith in collective solutions to common problems. As things now stand, we lack a systemic way to explain how integration and inequality are entwined. This has given way to a chronic case of equality pessimism and a fog about how to reckon with the connections between capitalism and distribution. Development talk, in effect, once accomplished both an analytical and a moral purpose.

In its absence, we have a strange incoherence. On one hand, there is the blood-boiling indignation of a Naomi Klein—and a silent fury about increasing concentrations of wealth and power and the near-universalization of the struggle to keep up with the one-percenters. In the wake of the Occupy movement and the spreading criticism of financial capitalism, this kind of despair about any kind of capitalist future gripped critics' imaginations.[34] In the other corner is development as "community service," as if the chasm that separates the privileged from the poor would close if we could just send more students to build houses in Honduras and divas to Africa. Faced with the complexity of the world and the inadequacy of our explanations, who can blame those who retreat to the simple narratives that we have too many devils and not enough angels?[35]

Faced with the vacuum in the West and the loss of confidence in the bravura of liberalism and capitalism in their wellsprings, development has returned. And has become globalized—in the sense that the champions of redistribution can be found everywhere, north and south, east and west. But being everywhere to justify bulking up state muscles in the service of national or regional advancement makes it more incoherent, a kind of grab-bag of disenchantments and retreadings of resentments from the humiliation of nineteenth-century treaties with China to Donald Trump's fables about how American cosmopolitans gave away the store when they designed the World Trade Organization; the new development consensus, if it can be called that, shares one feature: it claims to break with everything that has come before, to restore justice, but this time bereft of the world-making vision that had been a throughline of the narratives from the late nineteenth century. Development now is less a narrative framing for global justice and too often than a way to redeem national zero-sumism; it has taproots in old arguments about global integration, but it requires forgetting them.

## Notes

1. Gareth Stedman Jones, *An End to Poverty? A Historical Debate* (New York: Columbia University Press, 2004); Samuel Fleischacker, *A Short History of Distributive Justice* (Cambridge, MA: Harvard University Press, 2004).
2. Alexis Dudden, "Nitobe Inazo and the Diffusion of a Knowledgeable Empire," in Adelman, ed., *Empire and the Social Sciences: Global Histories of Knowledge* (London: Bloomsbury, 2015).

3. Orville Schell, *Wealth and Power: China's Long March to the Twenty-First Century* (New York: Random House, 2013), 95; Pankaj Mishra, *From the Ruins of Empire: The Intellectuals who Remade Asia* (New York: Farrar, Straus & Giroux, 2012), 142–143.
4. Mishra, *From the Ruins of Empire*, 159.
5. Eric Helleiner, "Economic Nationalism as a Challenge to Economic Liberalism? Lessons from the 19th Century," *International Studies Quarterly* 46, no. 3 (August 2002): 307–329; Helleiner, *The Neomercantilists: A Global Intellectual History* (Ithaca, NY: Cornell University Press, 2021), especially Section 3.
6. Sun Yat-sen, *The International Development of China* (Shanghai: Commercial Press, 1920).
7. José Carlos Mariátegui, *Siete ensayos de interpretación de la realidad peruana* (Lima: Biblioteca Amauta), 24–25.
8. Edgar J. Dosman, *The Life and Times of Raúl Prebisch, 1901–1986* (Kingston and Montreal: McGill-Queens University Press, 2008), 102, 160.
9. Jawaharlal Nehru, "Whither India?" (1933), in *India's Freedom* (London: Unwin Books, 1962), 21.
10. Tong Lam, *A Passion for Facts: Social Surveys and the Construction of the Chinese Nation-State, 1900–1949* (Berkeley and Los Angeles: University of California Press, 2011), 3, 44.
11. Jean de la Roche, "French Indo-China's Prospective Economic Regime," Institute of Pacific Relations, 9th Conference, Hot Springs, VA, January 1945.
12. Gunnar Myrdal, *Population: A Problem for Democracy* (Cambridge, MA: Harvard University Press, 1940), 20.
13. Kiran Klaus Patel, *The New Deal: A Global History* (Princeton, NJ: Princeton University Press, 2016).
14. Elizabeth Borgwardt, *A New Deal for the World: America's Vision for Human Rights* (Cambridge, MA: Harvard University Press, 2005), 8–9, 118–121; Eric Helleiner, "The Development Mandate of International Institutions: Where Did It Come From?" *Studies in Comparative International Development* 44 (2009): 189–211. For a recent retreading of the familiar story of titans creating the world order, see Benn Steil, *The Battle of Bretton Woods: John Maynard Keynes, Harry Dexter White, and the Making of a New World Order* (Princeton, NJ: Princeton University Press, 2013).
15. Helleiner, *Forgotten Foundations of Bretton Woods: International Development and the Making of the Postwar World* (Ithaca, NY: Cornell University Press, 2014), 197–199.
16. Stephen Clarkson, *The Soviet Theory of Development: India and the Third World in Marxist-Leninist Scholarship* (Toronto: University of Toronto Press, 1978).
17. Nikhil Menon, *Planning Democracy: Modern India's Quest for Development* (New York: Cambridge University Press, 2022).
18. Gunnar Myrdal, *Rich Lands and Poor* (New York: Harper & Bros., 1957), 7, 128–129.
19. Dosman, *The Life and Times of Raúl Prebisch*, 180–181, 214.
20. David Ekbladh, *The Great American Mission: Modernization and the Construction of an American World Order* (Princeton, NJ: Princeton University Press, 2010), esp. 63–71, 162, 213.

21. Cited in David C. Engerman, "West Meets East: The Center for International Studies and Indian Economic Development," in Engerman et al., eds., *Staging Growth: Modernization, Development, and the Global Cold War* (Amherst: University of Massachusetts Press, 2003), 199
22. Ibid., 203, 210.
23. W.W. Rostow, *The Stages of Economic Growth: A Non-Communist Manifesto* (New York: Cambridge University Press, 1960), 6
24. Susana Hecht and Alexander Cockburn, *The Fate of the Forest: Developers, Destroyers, and Defenders of the Amazon* (London: Verso, 1989), 100–101
25. Yang Jisheng, *Tombstone: The Great Chinese Famine, 1958–1962* (New York: Farrar, Strauss and Giroux, 2008), xviii–xxi, 77.
26. Alexander Gerschenkron, "Economic Backwardness in Historical Perspective," (1952) in his *Economic Backwardness in Historical Perspective: A Book of Essays* (Cambridge, MA: Harvard University Press, 1962), 7.
27. Bauer, "Remembrance of Studies Past: Retracing First Steps," in G. Meier and D. Seers, eds., *Pioneers in Development* (New York: Oxford University Press, 1984), 32–33.
28. Frantz Fanon, *The Wretched of the Earth* (New York: Grove, 2004), 10, 68, 232, 238.
29. Samuel Huntington, *Political Order in Changing Societies* (New Haven, CT: Yale University Press, 1968), 1, 4, 460–461.
30. Edmundo Desnoes, *Memorias del subdesarrollo* (Havana, 1965), 14.
31. Hirschman, "The Rise and Decline of Development Economics," in his *Essays in Trespassing: Economics to Politics and Beyond* (New York: Cambridge University Press, 1981), 1–23.
32. Report of the Independent Commission on International Development Issues, *North-South: A Programme for Survival* (Cambridge, MA: MIT Press, 1980), 13; Gunnar Myrdal, "International Inequality and Foreign Aid in Retrospect," in Meier and Seers, eds., *Pioneers in Development*, 163.
33. Hernán De Soto, *The Mystery of Capital: Why Capitalism Triumphs in the West and Fails Everywhere Else* (New York: Basic Books, 2000).
34. Naomi Klein, *This Changes Everything: Capitalism vs. the Climate* (New York: Simon & Schuster, 2014).
35. For an effort to keep alive some principles of radical egalitarianism after socialism, see Samuel Bowles, *The New Economics of Inequality and Redistribution* (New York: Cambridge University Press, 2012). For the latest campaign, see http://www.globalpovertyproject.com/.

# 9

# The Great Schism

## Scientific-Technological Modernity versus Greenpeace Civilization

*Daniel Deudney*

### Prometheus Unbound

Any discussion of the contested imaginaries of the modern and the global across the past several centuries must give central attention to the rise of modern science and technology, and its accompanying narratives. What fundamentally distinguishes the past several centuries is the great amplification and acceleration of human activities, empowered and transformed by science-based technological innovation. Scientific-technological modernity (STM) emerged in a particular place and time, but has spread like an inexorable explosion to disrupt and remake pretty much everything, everywhere on this planet. STM has powerfully remade the world because societies following its path have been spectacularly successfully in generating power and wealth, the pursuit of which have propelled and shaped human activity in every place and time. Because it has been so elementally successful, the fate of virtually every other unit of human life, from the micro to the macro, has hinged on how they have negotiated their relationships with the products of science-based technology and its powerful worldview. While the human world remains ferociously divided in innumerable ways, it is materially connected, interdependent, and vulnerable in historically unprecedented ways that stem straightforwardly from the spread of STM. In terms of its overall impact, the program and progress of STM greatly exceed that of any other religion, ideology, or program in modern history.

From its outset, STM has had a very distinctive, and lavishly developed, discursive imaginary and narrative. This imaginary has inspired, informed, and guided its expansion, and in turn has further expanded and developed as successes—and problems—have unfolded. In its original early modern

Daniel Deudney, *The Great Schism* In: *Debating Worlds*. Edited by Daniel Deudney, G. John Ikenberry, and Karoline Postel-Vinay, Oxford University Press. © Oxford University Press 2023. DOI: 10.1093/oso/9780197679302.003.0010 formulations, the essentials of this civilizational narrative were simple: the advance of scientific knowledge would produce a cascade of technological innovations which would enable humanity to master nature for its benefit, unleashing steady progress and elevations in the human condition. The future would be radically unlike the past and present. This vision of "tooltopia," of the Earth and society remade for Man, assumed traditional ways of life and worldviews, based on ignorance and superstition, would wither away, replaced by an Age of Reason. Its sturdy foundation would be a full and proper reading of the Book of Nature, not supernatural revelation. Tooltopia, its prophets proclaimed, would be a secular utopia, a City of Man.[1]

From its inception, and at every stage of its unfolding, contestations involving the ideas and projects of STM have been numerous and often far-reaching in their stakes. These contestations—the focus of this chapter—have been both external—between STM and its predecessors—and internal to it. Before exploring the major axes of these contestations, a brief glance at the main features of STM is useful.

## The Civilization of Scientific-Technological Modernity

The juggernaut of STM emerged out of the great scientific revolution in Europe in the long seventeenth century. This revolution had complex roots, and many practitioners and visionaries.[2] But something close to the Ur moment of STM can be found in two keys moves made by the English statesman and philosopher Francis Bacon.[3] First, and perhaps most consequentially, Bacon, in *The New Organon* and other works, crystallized a new mode of acquiring knowledge, one which he claimed would generate much more reliable knowledge of the natural world. This method would be systematically empirical and experimental, "torturing nature to reveal her secrets." Second, in his utopian *New Atlantis*, Bacon sketched the scope of technological transformations within human reach.[4] His new path to knowledge would enable humanity to "effectuate all things possible" and enable the progressive "elevation of the human estate," the expansion of "human empire" which would, after a long process, eventually produce an "instauration," or return, to an approximation of the mythical Garden of Eden of limitless abundance, health, and well-being.

Both the Scientific Revolution and its Enlightenment offspring were pan-European movements, with many local flavors and variations.[5] This visionary narrative was echoed and amplified by a widening network of theorists, publicists, and activists across the long nineteenth century, and robustly embedded in vernacular culture.[6] Progress, rooted in steadily improving science and technology, became the distinguishing touchstone of this protean and dynamic new civilization. Across the twentieth century, the new science and this attractive vision of technological improvement became globally pervasive. A rolling cascade of new reliable knowledge about nature was assembled by growing numbers of scientists, equipped with ever more powerful instruments, in all parts of the world.[7] The "republic of science" was from its outset international and is now among the most fully global of social formations. The knowledge-standards of modern science, while not unchallenged, are pervasive in countries everywhere. And this in turn has enabled a vast engine of technological innovation whose deployment has remade the human condition and much of the Earth.

Beyond its exceptional practical successes, the narrative and imaginary of STM differs from earlier civilizational narratives in four major ways.

The first defining feature of STM is the central role it accords modern natural science as a source of reliable knowledge. Modern science starts with a complete skepticism toward all forms of knowledge based on authority and tradition. Instead, only empirical observation can generate reliable knowledge. Much of the energy of early STM was directed at debunking and subverting claims of miracles and supernatural intervention. Instead, reliable knowledge can be found in the Book of Nature, which is accessible, with the right methods, by everyone everywhere. Eventually, this method promises full understanding—and thus the potential control and direction—of nature, humanity, and society.

Second, STM has been from its inception an extreme Humanism, making human improvement the appropriate measure of all things. STM aims for the betterment of all humanity, not the worship of God, not the fulfillment of tradition, and not the adoration of nature. This powerful progressive Humanist imaginary developed even further in the wake of the Darwinian revolution, with new expectations and aspirations for radical improvements in the biological fabric of humanity itself, the prospect of "supermen" resulting from scientifically based and technologically enabled biotechnologies, and even some approximation of apotheosis.[8]

Third, STM has a distinctive, thoroughly instrumental, view of nature and its relation to humanity. Unlike its predecessors who generally sought harmony with nature or viewed animated nature as sacred, STM had a starkly binary cosmology, with a sharp divide between the human and the natural, and a firm commitment to the human conquest and mastery of nature. The Earth, indeed the cosmos, is merely raw material for the expansion and elevation of human empire. While all societies, whatever their cosmologies, have used (and abused) nature in varying degrees, empowered modernity has reconstructed local, regional, and increasingly global landscapes.

Fourth is the emphasis placed on futurity, on envisioning futures radically unlike the past and present. At its core, the temporal narrative of STM is about what has not happened, but could be made to happen. Starting with Bacon's *New Atlantis*, much of this future imaginary has been in the form of "science fiction," which is the distinctive literature of this civilization. STM is radically revolutionary in its ambition. As its relentless outpouring of knowledge and capabilities unfolded, the project of "futurism" and questions of "where things are headed" have become developed, contentious, and practically important.[9]

## Contesting Scientific-Technological Modernity

Over the course of its march to world-historical influence, the path of STM has been marked by three defining sets of clashes, each quite different from the others, but often temporally overlapping and intermingling.

First, stretching from its inception to the present, has been the clash between the narratives and worldviews of STM and those of religion-centered civilizations which everywhere preceded it, and which it challenged everywhere. The first iteration of this contestation was between STM and the traditional civilization of Latin Christendom, a clash which has defined the course of European history across the modern era. It was in the course of this collision of worldviews that the distinctive and fundamental features of STM first emerged. Subsequent iterations of this clash, unfolding on a global scale, have occurred as non-European traditional civilizations have been forced to succumb, adapt, or emulate in response to the relentless imperial, colonial, and mercantile pressures from the expansive Europeans empowered by the early fruits of STM.

The second great front of contestation, beginning in full in the nineteenth century, is about which forms of social, economic, and political organizations are best suited to unlock the cornucopia of modern empowerment and abundance while coping with its distinctive problems. The initial answer to the social-political question was some form of enlightened despotism, which then gave way in the later eighteenth century to the view that liberal, capitalist, and democratic forms were especially suited to the opportunities and problems associated with the new material civilization. But by the mid-nineteenth century, this rough consensus within the Party of Progress was shattered by the rise of socialist alternatives which claimed to be better equipped to realize the new potentials and address the unforeseen problems that industrial modernity produced. Later joined by alternatives from the authoritarian right, this axis of contestation continues to play out in modern societies everywhere.

The third great contestation—the focus of this chapter—is much more recent, beginning in full in the middle years of the twentieth century, and is much more consequential in its implications. The idea that riding the tiger of technological development might turn out poorly for humanity had been part of the conversation about STM across the nineteenth century. But in the mid-twentieth century, with the development of nuclear weapons of mass destruction and the growing magnitude of human degradation of the planet's biospheric life-support system, basic doubts about the trajectory of STM have become central to the worldwide conversation about the overall human situation. As awareness and understanding of these technogenic perils of planetary scope have grown, a new and fateful axis of fundamental contestation has emerged, one so basic in its stakes as to amount to a great schism within the party of STM itself. On one side are those who want to double down and accelerate technological advance; on the other side are those who want to significantly restrain and redirect it.

## The Planetary Age, Civilizational Catastrophe, and the End of History

Over the past three-quarters of a century, the clashes among alternative political modernities have been increasingly overshadowed by the prospect of civilizational annihilation from nuclear war and biospheric destruction. By the middle years of the twentieth century, the potency of destructive technologies produced by human ingenuity, particularly nuclear weapons, and the extent of human damage to the planet's habitability by burgeoning human populations equipped with industrial-era energy, production, and transportation technologies have become so great as to begin to call into question the survival of modern civilization, and even the human species. These ominous new developments have triggered another major, and particularly fateful, front of fundamental contestation over the trajectory and consequences of STM.

The middle years of the twentieth century, particularly the rough decade between the mid-1940s and mid-1950s, should be recognized as a major juncture in human and Earth history, the beginning of the Planetary Age. Enormous—and sometimes sudden—leaps in human technological capabilities, and the resulting alterations in the relationship of human activities and the Earth, signal the beginning of a new historical epoch. Macrohistorians thus commonly delimit major epochs in world history, such as the Stone Age, the Agricultural Revolution, and the Industrial Revolution, as major new technologies emerge and transform all aspects of human affairs. By these metrics, the middle years of the twentieth century can claim milestone status in the largest scale of the human story, because of the emergence of the very real possibilities of nuclear apocalypse and catastrophic environmental collapse, which have radically altered the survival prospects of the human species. In addition to the first nuclear and thermonuclear explosions (1945 and 1952) and the beginning of the "great acceleration" in fossil-fueled economic expansion (~1950), these years also witnessed the beginnings of the "space age" with the first human activities beyond the planet's atmosphere in "outer space" (1942 and 1957), the first mapping of the DNA codes governing all life (1953), and the first reprogrammable electronic digital computer (1953). And many geologists designate these years as the beginning of the "Anthropocene" as a distinct period in the geological history of the planet Earth. Fortunately for human capacities to cope, the pace with which these technological developments have matured and have been deployed varies greatly, with two—nuclear weapons and biospheric degradation—leading the way.

The middle years of the twentieth century also should be recognized as an epochal juncture in human history because for the first time in its quarter million year existence, humanity has equipped itself with artifacts plausibly capable of producing complete human extinction.[10] Human societies have always conjured various "end times," brought about by divine or natural processes, but only over recent decades has anthropogenic annihilation of the human species become a practical possibility, and thus of concern for politics. Disasters at every scale of human organization, from the family to great empires, have been a recurrent feature of human life from its outset. Great empires have fallen, and nations, states, and entire peoples have disappeared, destroyed by wars, great plagues, or environmental abuse. But what is novel about the planetary era of human Earth history is that such mega calamities now threaten the *entirety* of civilization and the *entirely* of humankind. Over recent decades, this dark and full "end of history" has increasingly rivaled and eclipsed progressive Enlightenment visions of universal peace, freedom, and prosperity, the cosmopolitan "city of man." This development is reflected in the increasing supremacy of dystopian imaginaries in popular culture. The contestations among rival alternative modernities were about how to achieve utopia, or some practicable best of all possible worlds. But the new choices and disputes of the planetary age concern the avoidance of extreme dystopias, ones latent in the very instrumentalities promising to elevate the human estate.

These ominous possibilities, and their bleak futurity, have triggered widespread and consequential contestation along a largely novel axis of debate, one centered on alternative imaginaries, visions, and programs concerning human-technology and human-Earth relations. Although fatefully connected to every aspect of every dimension of human affairs, contestations about technology and the planet's life support system are novel in their focus on the problematic features of the relationship between human activities and nature, rather than on competing social models and systems operating within a shared commitment to STM. They are also novel in the significance they attach to the "global," and increasingly the "planetary," as primary spatial realities. In many ways the issues of planetary techno- and eco-politics now so practically salient in human affairs, and so vigorously contested, are civilizational in character, about the trajectory, limits, and alternatives to the civilization of STM and its aspiration to elevate the human estate by progressively harnessing and refashioning nature.

From the "ban the bomb" movements of the 1950s to the contemporary "Extinction Rebellion," narrative contestations over the nuclear and environmental fate of humanity and the Earth have defined an important and novel part of world politics. These debates about human-material relations have been entangled in great power international political conflicts, debated vigorously in the mass media and across many intellectual disciplines, and voiced by leading scientists, technologists, public intellectuals, and journalists. They are embodied in popular political movements spanning from the neighborhood to the global scale. And these debates remain thoroughly unresolved, suggesting that the new planetary politics has just begun.

The specter of nuclear and ecological mega-disasters has opened a great schism *within* STM, between those who want to accelerate and double-down on its humanity-elevating and Earth-conquering program, and those who want to restrain and redirect the juggernaut of human technological deployment. These critics seek to create what, for lack of a better label, can be called "greenpeace civilization," or scientific-technological Earth modernity (STEM). They seek an overall human arrangement as unlike previous iterations of modernity as STM is unlike its traditional civilizational predecessors.[11] This narrative contestation between STM and its nascent STEM successor increasingly shapes disputes about choices within ever larger domains of human activity, and gives the discursive landscape of the last near-century its distinctive character.

## Technology Out of Control

The practical reason STM was so successful was its innovative and potent technology. And technology is the reason STM is faced with a civilizational crisis, and a new rival. In a nutshell, the technologies empowering humanity have unintended consequences and potentials for great disasters. As awareness of these problems has grown, the optimistic modernist story of limitless progress through scientific and technological advance has come to be rivaled and sometimes overshadowed by a much more pessimistic, even apocalyptic, vision of the trajectory of the modern project rooted in doubts about human abilities to control technology.[12] Premonitions of technological wizardry leading to disasters are extremely old, dating back at least to ancient agricultural societies.[13] With the Industrial Revolution, dark anticipations became increasingly widespread, in works such as Mary Shelley's *Frankenstein* and Karel Capek's *R.U.R.* Perhaps machines, becoming ever more capable and interconnected, were the next step in the evolution of life, destined to dominate and eventually eliminate humanity, as Samuel Butler warned.[14] The contours of the future, H. G. Wells announced in his famous 1902 lecture, "The Discovery of the Future," were difficult to discern but would surely be unlike the past or the present, and definitely included disasters of new types and magnitudes.[15]

In the ghastly world wars, industrial genocides, and totalitarian tyrannies of the mid-twentieth century, technological advances empowered barbarism on a new scale, undermining the simple modernist faith that more capable tools are a straight path to human betterment.[16] Rather, technological advance has produced a cornucopia of double-edged swords, with amplified possibilities for both progress and disaster. New horsemen of the anthropogenic apocalypse have ominously appeared on the human horizon of possibility, starting with nuclear weapons and rampant environmental decay, and followed by rouge genetic engineering, total surveillance despotism, and runaway artificial intelligence.

At the heart of the new contestations over techno- and eco-affairs is a debate over the civilization of STM, its relationship with species survival prospects, and the birthing, through thought and action, of its possible successor. "Must destruction be our destiny?," the title of a popular book from the 1940s asked.[17] Or can humanity radically reconfigure its relationship with potent technologies and the vulnerable Earth? How much must be changed? Are major changes in human identities needed to support the political and economic arrangements required for human survival? Does survival require abandoning the state-system, capitalism, industrialism, high-consumption lifestyles, or can more reformist measures suffice?

## Between One World and None

Since before recorded history, humans have been killing each other, often in great slaughters. All primary human groups have placed great value on the effective mastery of violence. Long before the emergence of modern science, innovations in the technologies of killing have shaped the rise and fall of nations and empires. But innovation in killing tools, while often immensely consequential, was slow and haphazard. With the rise and spread of STM, the pace of military technological innovation has greatly accelerated. Across the nineteenth century, the Industrial Revolution brought chemical high explosives, steel guns, steam-powered ships, railroads, and telegraphs. These lethal innovations propelled the industrial states to further superiority over pre-modern societies, while also greatly increasing the lethality of war among developed countries.[18]

As new destructive capabilities poured forth, anticipations of vastly more potent tools of war, and anxious consideration of their implications, also poured forth, much of it in popular science fiction, adding to the darkening futurity of modernity.[19] In response to doubts about the benefits of this kind of "progress," optimists insisted, as one political economist pithily put it, that "war would kill war."[20] Making war more terrible would ensure that war would become too destructive to be a rational activity, and it would, like other vestiges of pre-modern times, wither away and eventually disappear.

But others were less sanguine about the capacity of long-established human institutions to rationally phase themselves out. The more common anticipation was that increasingly destructive wars would destroy civilization, a view bolstered by the relentless arms racing of the great power states and the massive devastations of "the Great War" (1914–1918). But more immediately operative than such broad anticipations was the hope—and fear—among governments that some new military technological innovation would provide a decisive military capability to whatever state first acquired it.[21] These pervasive anticipations have fueled the creation of vast and lavishly funded military scientific and technological complexes aggressively pushing every possible frontier of knowledge for better death tech.

More than any other development, the new ability to "split the atom" in the early 1940s was the crucial juncture in humanity's technological progress, moving civilizational obliteration and human extinction from the realm of vague speculation into real possibility. "The Bomb" was the offspring of rapid progress in the science of physics during the first decades of the century. Albert Einstein's simple equation $E = mc^2$, published in 1922, revealed the possibility of technologically unleashing the immense energies latent in atomic nuclei. The idea of exploiting these natural phenomena to make weapons of unprecedented destructive power had been recognized by Frederick Soddy in 1911, and H. G. Wells had forecast the invention of what he called an "atomic bomb" in his 1914 novel, *The World Set Free*.[22]

By the outset of World War II, these possibilities were understood by members of the international scientific community of physicists, who warned governments that a shatteringly decisive weapon might be developed. Well aware of the ability of new weapons based on new scientific principles to decisively alter the military balance, governments took these warnings seriously, and all the major combatants (except China) investigated these possibilities. But only the United States, with its Manhattan Project, allocated sufficient resources to actually build a bomb. In the late summer of 1945, in the waning weeks of the war, the United States tested and then dropped atomic bombs on two Japanese cities, Hiroshima and Nagasaki, definitively beginning the nuclear age.[23] The Soviet Union soon followed, testing a nuclear device in 1949.[24] And a few years later, in 1953, an even more fearsome weapon, the hydrogen bomb, or thermonuclear weapon, capable of unleashing thousands of time more energy, was tested and then deployed.[25] The new weapons were *millions* of times more powerful than those based on chemical explosives. In the global Cold War, some 120,000 nuclear weapons were fabricated.[26] At their peak around 1970, the "superpower" arsenals contained some six tons of TNT equivalent for every human on the planet.

Having been produced in a secret archipelago of laboratories and industrial facilities, the first atomic bombs were a complete surprise to general publics everywhere. But news of their capabilities was quickly and widely disseminated.[27] U.S. President Truman gave a nationally radio-broadcast speech announcing them in the most solemn and sober terms. *The New Yorker* magazine published an extended article by John Hersey, soon released as a small, best-selling book, *Hiroshima*, which graphically described the horrors of the bomb's effects.[28] And the US government even published a short book, the Smyth Report, outlining the scientific principles behind the bomb.[29]

That nuclear weapons were unprecedentedly destructive was indisputable. But what were their implications for humanity, and for international politics? Was humanity doomed? Was world government of some sort necessary? Or could these weapons somehow be employed, like all others before them, as useful instruments of international military rivalry? Buckminister Fuller observed that Hiroshima meant humanity had begun taking its final exam.[30] But what were the correct answers? Even before their actual invention, such questions had been posed and a wide range of very different, sometimes sharply clashing, answers proffered. Debates between different schools of nuclear thought have raged, unresolved, across the nuclear age, making for a clash of fundamentally clashing narratives about this momentous capability.[31]

Views of the prospects and appeals of abandoning violence-based world orders and establishing some form of world government have varied enormously.[32] On one side, "nuclear one worlders," strong globalists, and world federalists, following in the steps of H. G. Wells and others, saw some form of world government as vital for civilizational survival.[33] For these thinkers, the need to establish world government was the inevitable consequence of the rise of intense levels of interaction and interdependence, particularly of violence, on a worldwide scale. All the reasons why governments were established in the past now pointed to the need for world government. But advocates differed on whether a world government should be configured as a classic state, enlarged in size, or as a more circumscribed union or confederation.[34]

On the other side of this debate, a vastly larger group has viewed world government as unnecessary, practically impossible, and a menace to freedom. Even modest steps toward international cooperation and institution-building are viewed as dangerous steps onto a slippery slope toward world totalitarian government. Despite the apparent need for post-anarchic worldwide governance of some sort, the world, far from unifying, has been politically fragmenting. Creating even modest international cooperative institutions has become extremely difficult, and no significant movement supports creating world government.

In many ways, the great debate on the nuclear age began in full among the nuclear scientists in the hidden alcoves of the Manhattan Project.[35] The largest body of these scientists concluded that the transcendent power of the bomb required entirely new approaches to international politics, and specifically the control of this technology by an international organization, or even a world government.[36] They also decided that they had the unique ability—and responsibility—to move public opinion and governments toward their solutions. For these ends they established lobbying organizations, and launched a public education journal, *The Bulletin of the Atomic Scientists*. Leading physicists, starting with Albert Einstein, spoke extensively and pointedly about the need for radical changes in world politics. In the 1950s, in the wake of the Russell-Einstein Manifesto of 1955, the atomic scientist movement became transnational, with the establishment of the Pugwash organization, which included leading American, Soviet, and European physicists. The ancient task of "speaking truth to power" was now organized and globally networked—and conducted with mass media megaphones.

Scientists had long been advisers to princes and publics, but the atomic scientist movement took an unprecedented further step, in banding together to publicize and promote policy alternatives challenging the prerogatives and agendas of governments on a strategically paramount weapon and its enabling technology. Thus was born "public interest science," a model that in subsequent decades was widely emulated by other scientists from other disciplines.[37] In the middle years of the twentieth century, scientists were widely revered as authoritative voices across the modern world, especially in the Soviet Union, whose ideology gave exalted status to scientists and engineers as the avant garde of technological modernization. The fact that the leaders of scientific progress were not extolling some new advance for human well-being, but rather warning of the grave dangers of new deployed technologies, marked a watershed development in the civilizational trajectory of STM.

For a brief few years, the scientists' agenda for international control of atomic technology was at the center stage of international politics. In 1946 plans developed by the atomic scientists, known as the Baruch Plan, were publicly debated in the new United Nations Committee on Atomic Energy.[38] But by the 1950s, hope for these initiatives had been largely dashed by the rising Soviet-US rivalry. As both countries raced to deploy nuclear arsenals in the 1950s, prospects for any major arms control and disarmament appeared dim.

But in the later 1950s a new, quite unexpected, source of opposition to nuclear weapons emerged, stemming from the health effects of the radioactive "fallout" produced by nuclear tests in the atmosphere. That nuclear explosions would produce lingering radioactive material had been theoretically anticipated, and empirically observed in the ruins of Hiroshima and Nagasaki. But this novel feature of these weapons was powerfully conveyed to global audiences in the wake of giant hydrogen bomb explosions in the South Pacific. These tests dispersed many tons of highly radioactive material into the atmosphere and oceans, and radiation was soon detected everywhere on the planet by scientists equipped with sensitive monitoring instruments. As it became widely understood that even the *testing* of these behemoth bombs posed a public health threat, public opinion polls registered widespread alarm, and anti-nuclear organizers, particularly in the United States and Europe, seized upon this threat to push for test bans.[39] A particularly politically influential lesson in the planetary scope of the nuclear peril was the discovery of radioactive material, mainly Strontium 90, in the teeth of infants. Asking mothers to send fallen baby teeth to their laboratories, scientists measured their radioactive content, and their reports were widely covered in the media. These concerns, combined with the sobering encounter with the possibility of nuclear war during the Cuban Missile Crisis of 1962, led the US, USSR, and UK to sign the Limited Test Ban Treaty in 1963, which banned nuclear testing in the atmosphere, the oceans, and outer space.[40]

Despite these and other arms control measures, the superpowers continued to expand and modernize their nuclear arsenals, and other countries developed nuclear weapons. Public opinion vacillated between fear of nuclear war and fear of adversaries with nuclear weapons. Since the 1960s, official thinking about nuclear weapons has been dominated by the idea of deterrence, the notion that nuclear war can be avoided if states maintain nuclear military forces of sufficient size and character to absorb a first blow and then retaliate with devastating force. This would make nuclear attack suicidal and thus, it is reasoned, very unlikely. But within this deterrence school, debate rages about whether small "minimum deterrent" arsenals, or large "extended deterrence" ones capable of carrying out a wide range of missions, are needed. And there is fundamental disagreement about whether deterrence is an acceptable permanent way to avoid major war, or a risky short-term expedient until deep arms control can be realized.[41] And some even question what all the fuss is about.[42]

## The Fate of the Earth and Nuclear Zero

Both the great debate over nuclear weapons and world order, and international nuclear politics, took unexpected directions in the 1970s and 1980s. The notion that a full-scale nuclear war would end civilization, and perhaps humanity, had been widely voiced, but the causal mechanisms by which human extinction might result had never been illuminated. During the 1960s, as atmospheric scientists began researching the effects of industrial pollutants on the stratospheric ozone layer, they realized that the detonation of a large number of nuclear weapons and the resultant mega fires might so degrade the ozone layer as to render the planet uninhabitable for higher forms of life, including humans, and trigger general ecosystem collapse.[43] This momentous discovery was followed in the early 1980s with the realization that vast quantities of soot injected into the atmosphere from the mass burning of cities would also have major planet-wide environmental effects, in the form of what was dubbed "nuclear winter"—the severe reduction of the planet's temperature caused by the reduction of sunlight reaching the Earth's surface.[44]

The discovery of these planetary environmental fragilities meant that both the winners and losers of a nuclear war—and everyone else as well—would also be destroyed, a radical novelty in the annals of warfare. These discoveries also meant that the stakes of a nuclear war were vastly increased, to encompass the real possibility of human extinction, and thus the fates of vast numbers of unborn humans who would never come into existence. During the carnage of World War I, the French leader Georges Clemenceau had famously observed that war had become too important to be left to the generals. With the fate of the Earth and humanity now at stake, war has become too important to be left to states.

These findings were widely publicized during a time of growing international tension. Powerful philosophical reflections on the prospects of human extinction were provided by *The New Yorker* writer Jonathan Schell in *The Fate of the Earth*, a book which was translated into nearly two dozen languages and sold millions of copies. A vividly realistic feature-length movie, *The Day After*, was aired on prime-time American television. The public was becoming aware of these ominous realities during a period of heightened Soviet-American tension and nuclear arms buildup, known as the Second Cold War. Further fueling the flames of public alarm, the administration of President Ronald Reagan was particularly belligerent rhetorically, and cavalier in dismissing the dangers of nuclear war.[45] The result of this confluence of developments was an immense eruption of popular anti-nuclear activism in the United States and Western Europe. Fearing electoral backlash, the Reagan administration quickly backtracked and embraced arms control.[46]

Then, quite unexpectedly, long marginalized radical nuclear one wordlist narratives returned and helped catalyze major political change. The new reformist Soviet leader Mikhail Gorbachev and Reagan, meeting in Reykjavik in 1986, discovered they both desired to move rapidly toward the abolition of nuclear weapons, a policy option far outside the mainstream of official nuclear thinking in both their countries. The nuclear threat to civilization was so great, they reasoned, that major change in international relations was urgently needed to lower the risk of war and enable major disarmament measures. Reagan, it turned out, had been an advocate of nuclear disarmament during his early career as a labor organizer in Hollywood, and had long peppered his anti-Soviet speeches with calls to eventually abolish nuclear weapons.[47] Gorbachev came to his nuclear abolitionism through an updating of Soviet Marxism that replaced the previously paramount "class interest" with a "human species interest" jeopardized by nuclear war and environmental degradation.[48] Radical nuclear disarmament thinking also reached across the Iron Curtain of Soviet information controls through the transnational networks of nuclear physicists operating since the 1950s.[49] This nuclear narrative helped end the Cold War, and its objectives were significantly realized in the major nuclear disarmament agreements that were the centerpiece of the diplomatic settlement of this global conflict.

Despite this unexpected important step forward, the nuclear "Sword of Damocles" still hangs ominously over civilization, and has in important ways become more dangerous over the past three decades. The terrorist attacks in the fall of 2001 highlighted the possibility of "non-state actors" acquiring nuclear weapons and destroying a major city, a vector of attack not readily subject to deterrence, or easily defended against.[50] The anthrax bioweapons attacks, which were eventually traced to a disgruntled scientist working within the US bioweapons complex, pointed to another form of vulnerability to weapon of mass destruction (WMD) attack. Compared to nuclear weapons, bioweapons were potentially available to even more actors and even more difficult to defend against, or even to reliably link to their perpetrators. In short, the ability to wreck massive levels of destruction was slowly leaking into the hands of actors the size of gangs, posing a type of security threat which societies had never before encountered.[51]

Looking at these developments as part of the progressive unfolding of STM clearly suggests that the cornucopia of technological advances anticipated to elevate the human estate is very much a mixed bag. Advancing technology is a double-edged sword, capable of bringing both great betterment and great ruin. The narrative of progressive STM confronts the sobering fact that humanity, for all its progress in so many spheres over the past few centuries, has built, at immense cost, a planet-spanning apparatus to nearly instantaneously obliterate civilization, and perhaps doom the entirety of humanity for all time. The fact that the great debate on nuclear weapons and world order remains so unresolved, and perhaps unresolvable, is also a sobering indicator of the limited ability of human inquiry to provide adequate answers to practical questions of the highest importance.

## Biospheric Degradation and Environmentalism

The second major locus of far-reaching new contestation between STM and STEM is the natural environment and the effects of human activities on it. Although the technologies and features of the Earth in play are vastly varied and complex, the newly vulnerable and contested Earth emerges from a quite simple source: the collision between the seemingly unstoppable force of STM and a seemingly immovable, but finite and fragile object—the planet Earth.

The roots of environmentalist thinking trace to the beginnings of industrial modernity. The early counter-Enlightenment movement of Romanticism emphasized the aesthetic and spiritual value of untrammeled nature, and viewed the relentlessly expanding mercantile and industrial society with alarm and suspicion.[52] In 1864, the American diplomat George Perkins Marsh, in *Man and Nature*, sketched a melancholic critique of the human damage to the environment, and its dangerous implications for the future of civilization.[53] By the early twentieth century, the damaging effects of the burgeoning Industrial Revolution on landscapes and wildlife, and air and water, were increasingly recognized, and stimulated extensive measures to reduce pollution, conserve natural resources, create parks, and protect wildlife.[54] Usually fiercely resisted by powerful business interests, these early reforms were enacted due to the efforts of popular environmental organizations, the Progressive movement, and the New Deal. In Germany, a "back to nature" movement was a prominent part of popular culture in the early twentieth century, and was part of the conservative nationalism and anti-modernism of the Third Reich.[55] This period also witnessed the emergence of "ecology" as a scientific discipline, the conceptualization of the "biosphere," and the discovery of the powerful role of trace gases in regulating the planet's temperature.[56]

But it was only in the middle years of the twentieth century that widespread concern over environmental destruction became a prominent part of contestation over the trajectory of STM.[57] The rapid growth unleashed in the advanced industrial democracies after World War II did much to alleviate the class conflicts plaguing industrial societies, but it had the unintended but powerful effect of calling into question the ecological sustainability of modern prosperity.[58]

By all accounts, a watershed event in the emergence of modern environmentalism was the 1962 publication of *The Silent Spring* by the American biologist Rachel Carson.[59] The focus of Carson's work was narrow, but the implications were broad. She documented the unanticipated environmental harm caused by the insecticide DDT. Produced in enormous quantities and sprayed in large campaigns to suppress the mosquitoes which transmitted malaria to humans, DDT was widely hailed as a triumph of modern technology against an ancient scourge. Once introduced to nature, however, DDT did not degrade. It became increasingly concentrated as it made its way up the food chain, disrupting the reproduction of many species of birds. Among them was the bald eagle, the American national symbol, which was pushed to near extinction in large parts of the United States.

Alarming signs of environmental destruction were increasingly visible.[60] Industrial chemicals, produced in volume and dumped into the environment, were linked to cancers and birth defects in humans. Fertilizers, which boosted food production, flowed into rivers and lakes, stimulating luxuriant growth of algae and suffocating fish life. Large quantities of oil from a malfunctioning offshore well off the coast of southern California fouled its popular beaches and killed large numbers of birds. The air in the Los Angeles basin was thick with petrochemical "smog" resulting from gasoline-burning automobiles. The Cayuga River, emptying into Lake Erie by Cleveland, was so polluted with industrial effluents that it caught fire, destroying a bridge. The industrial smokestack, a modernist icon of progress and prosperity, evolved into an emblem of ecological threat and danger to public health. Hydroelectric dams and river development projects, icons of high modernism from the 1930s through the 1950s, were increasingly seen as ecological disasters.[61]

In response to these problems, environmental movements have emerged everywhere over the past half century.[62] In the Western parliamentary democracies, Green Parties have emerged to contest elections from the local to the national level. A UN organization has been established, and numerous treaties and regimes have been established, with greatly varying effectiveness, to deal with different environmental problems. Natural and social science research on environmental problems has rapidly expanded. In the wealthy countries, considerable progress has been achieved, at considerable cost. In the United States, the Clean Air Act, over its 50 years of operation, has cost some $65 billion to implement, with some $2 trillion in benefits. More than 90 percent of acid rain has been reduced. Environmental impact reviews are now routinely conducted for major projects. Many dams, pipelines, refineries, and power plants have been halted due to resistance from environmental activists. But in poor and developing countries, environmental conditions have deteriorated steadily, due to lax regulation and the headlong effort to escape crushing poverty and modernize. And the worst off, in both developed and developing countries, continue to bear the brunt of pollution, floods, and droughts.

These alarming developments triggered an extremely broad, diverse, and far-reaching debate, which continues unresolved to the present, over the civilizational implications of the collision between industrial societies and the planetary biosphere. For many, the assaults on the biosphere could no longer be viewed as a series of incidental events, to be remedied with modest adjustments, but were unmistakable indicators that something very fundamental had gone wrong and that major changes were necessary. Eco-Marxists looked to capitalism as the essential problem, and argued that only socialism could adequately address the problems.[63] But this promise was undermined by the terrible environmental record of "actually existing socialism" in the Soviet Union and Communist China.[64] Others looked to better market incentives to stimulate innovation and more efficient and rational uses of natural resources.[65] For some, human population growth, surging from two billion in 1930 to over five billion in 1970, was an underlying culprit, to be remedied with aggressive population-stabilization measures.[66]

Many "green religion" thinkers leveled basic critiques at Western rationalism and monotheism, and sought to revive pre-modern pagan and indigenous religions and create new forms of Earth religion and spirituality.[67] Some indicted the anthropocentricism of modernity and sought to endow other species, as well as inanimate objects and landscapes, with rights.[68] Some, such as the *Limits to Growth* study released in 1970 by a group of researchers from the Club of Rome, argued that the high-consumption lifestyles long viewed as the goal of modern society were no longer sustainable and had to be replaced by a new frugality.[69] Such thinking led to notions of a "steady state economy" not dependent on growth.[70] But this necessary reduction in consumption would, others argued, require authoritarian government and undermine the foundations of modern liberal democracy.[71] Ideas of "intergenerational equity" were advanced and debated.[72] Some indicted the instrumentalism of modernity and modern science itself as the root cause of the problem, and raised doubts about the ability of science to fully grasp the vast complexity of the biosphere and the myriad life forms composing it. But others claimed that more and better science was needed, and that a recognition of a new scientific object, the Earth System, was essential. From this scientific proposition, some claimed that the Earth as a whole was itself a living organism, dubbed Gaia, after the ancient Greek goddess of the Earth.[73] Eco-feminists attributed ecological destruction to oppression of women and the feminine, and proposed "gyn-ecology" as a remedy.[74] Others looked to wholesale transformations of consciousness as a motor for change. Some expected a mental revolution to result from wide viewing of the Whole Earth photographs, pictures of the Earth taken from outer space, an unexpected spin-off of the space programs of the 1960s.[75] Others, such as the Earth First! network, pursued direct action to slow the machine, with "ecotage" and "monkeywrenching."[76]

The response of modern societies to the cascade of environmental problems has ranged from the grossly inadequate to the remarkably successful. One particularly important success is the global response to the depletion of stratospheric ozone. Chlorofluorocarbons (CFCs) are new chemicals invented in the early twentieth century. Widely marketed under the trade-name Freon, CFCs found extensive use in air conditioning systems and as spray can propellants. But in the 1970s, a small group of atmospheric chemists realized that CFCs posed an imminent threat to the planetary life-support system. The great commercial appeal of CFCs was that they did not interact chemically or easily break down. But released into the atmosphere, CFCs gradually drifted to the stratosphere, where they were broken down by solar ultraviolent (UV) radiation, releasing the CFCs' highly reactive components, which rapidly gobbled up the naturally occurring "ozone layer." This ozone blocked most of the sun's UV rays from reaching the surface of the planet. Studies indicated that, if left unchecked, this ozone depletion would result in much higher skin cancer rates and eventually render blind all organisms with eyes, thus posing a catastrophic threat to humanity and the biosphere.

Reaction to these alarming possibilities was quick and decisive. Even before there was evidence of actual depletion of the ozone layer, the US in 1977 banned all use of CFCs in spray cans. Then, after the discovery of a hole in the ozone layer over Antarctica, all the major producing countries agreed, in the 1983 Montreal Protocol, to rapidly phase CFCs out of almost all uses.[77] This success story results from the availability of substitutes, the small number of producers, the robust consensus among scientists about the problem, and the severity of the prospective harms. While this is in many ways the paradigm case of successful planetary environmental regulation, it is also a sobering reminder of the extremely complex ways in which seemingly benign technological advances can have unanticipated catastrophic environmental consequences.

Another front of contestation has been over the use of nuclear energy to generate electricity. During the 1950s, the use of nuclear energy for power production was advanced by many as a major technological advance, due to the immense amounts of energy which could potentially be produced. Governments in both the developed and underdeveloped world saw nuclear power plants as icons of advanced modernity and poured resources into the creation of an industry to build and operate nuclear plants and produce nuclear fuel. Nuclear visionaries spoke of building "cities of the second sun" which would offer abundant and cheap electrical energy to sustain prosperity long after fossil fuels reserves were exhausted.[78]

In the late 1960s, a powerful environmental backlash against nuclear power emerged to contest the construction of further nuclear power plants. Critics argued that nuclear power plants were potentially subject to devastating accidents in which large quantities of lethal radioactive material could be released, contaminating large areas, sickening and killing millions. Accidents at Three Mile Island in Pennsylvania (1979), Chernobyl in Ukraine (1986), and Fukushima in Japan (2011) seemed to confirm these fears. Opposition was also kindled over the puzzle of what to do with the extremely long-lived wastes from nuclear power plants, which would have to be kept isolated for tens of thousands of years, a time horizon far beyond conventional policymaking. Others pointed out that the fissile material associated with nuclear plants might be diverted by terrorists to make nuclear weapons. But more important for the practical fortunes of the nuclear industry, local groups opposed to the siting of nuclear plants near their communities were quite effective in slowing and stopping many nuclear projects. Such "not in my backyard" (NIMBY) opposition was particularly successful in political systems in which local governments had significant decision-making roles, but less so in more centralized political systems. Nuclear plants were also very expensive and time-consuming to construct, further retarding the industry's growth. Critics since the 1960s have viewed nuclear power as the quintessential "technological misfire," and opposition to nuclear energy has been a central feature of the modern environmental movement.

## Climate Change and the Anthropocene

Even more central to the rise of environmental concern and the growth of fundamental critiques of STM is climate change. Over the past half century, scientific understanding of the atmosphere and changes in climate across deep historical time has rapidly advanced. A powerful driver of the planet's overall temperature is the strength of the "greenhouse effect" caused by trace quantities of gases, most notably carbon dioxide and methane, which absorb infrared (heat) energy radiating from the surface of the sun-warmed planet. Evidence is strong that several of the major mass extinction events which have punctuated the history of complex life over the last half billion years were the result of the emission of carbon dioxide from extended volcanic eruptions.[79]

Over the past two centuries, and especially since the "great acceleration" of energy-intensive growth after 1950, the burning of fossil fuels, especially coal and oil, has increased the level of carbon dioxide in the atmosphere by some 20 percent, from 360 parts per million (ppm) to about 425 ppm. As a result, global average temperatures have increased by about one degree Celsius. The last time the planet was this warm, several million years ago, the global ocean was some 55 feet higher. Rising average temperatures also produce more frequent and severe storms, more prolonged and severe droughts, melting glaciers and thinning sea ice in the Arctic, changes in meso-scale weather and ocean circulation patterns (such as the monsoons and the Gulf Stream), large-scale melting of the permafrost in the vast belt of lands around the Arctic Ocean, and mass dislocation and extinction of wildlife.[80]

There are also alarming indications of looming "positive feedbacks," in which warming releases more greenhouse gases from the enormous natural sinks in the oceans, soils, and permafrost.[81] Runaway climate change, pushing average temperatures up several degrees, would produce the horror of "Hothouse Earth" in which all the planet's ice would eventually melt, raising sea levels by some 275 feet. Agriculture would largely collapse, and most of the planet would be too hot for human activities. To register the significance of these immense alterations of the planet by recent human activity, many geologists designate the beginning of a new epoch in Earth history, the Anthropocene, the "age of man." Efforts to prevent these outcomes are commonly referred to as "saving the planet," but what is actually at stake is the human habitability of the planet.

Over the past half century, as these scientific understandings emerged, and as the effects of climate change started to be felt, concern over climate change has emerged everywhere as an increasingly important political, economic, and social issue, as well as triggering far-reaching debates about STM and its trajectory. Across these decades, the conclusions of climate science have been extensively politicized. Powerful and wealthy corporate interests have spread misinformation and climate "denialism."[82] Because the political power of producers is so extensive, and because the use of fossil fuel sources of energy is so basic to the operation of modern society, as well as the aspirations of poor counties to develop economically, efforts to actually scale back the production of greenhouse gases have been unsuccessful overall, and the total quantities of such gases produced have continuously and relentlessly grown. A first international agreement, the Kyoto Protocol, was modestly ambitious, and largely unsuccessful. A second effort, culminating in the Paris Climate Convention of 2012, was considerably more ambitious, aiming to largely de-carbonize the world economy by 2050, and cut back some 50 percent by 2030. This effort is also off to a slow start, and the realization of these goals is increasingly slipping out of reach.

But there are important marks of progress. There have been spectacular declines in the cost of wind and solar photovoltaic renewable energy systems. High-quality electric vehicles are rapidly penetrating commercial markets. Every economic sector, from residential construction and agriculture to shipping, aviation, and heavy industry, is the site of major sustainability innovations and initiatives. The problem is rapidly getting worse, and important and probably irreversible thresholds for action are rapidly approaching. But there now exist, in at least functioning prototype form, successful alternative energy systems, which if universally employed would largely solve the climate crisis. Public awareness of climate change is rapidly increasing everywhere, and is particularly strong among younger generations.

As these developments have unfolded, the contestations over civilizational environmental fundamentals, beginning in the 1960s, have become even more pronounced, radical, and urgent. Climate change has joined nuclear war as a comprehensive civilizational challenge, posing deepening doubts about the overall trajectory of STM and the human future. Dystopian "cli-fi" (climate science fiction) has exploded in popularity. All of the doubts raised about environmental degradation in relation to the major aspects of the contemporary world, from the state-system, capitalism, and industrialism, to mass prosperity, excessive humanism, technology, and religious beliefs, have become sites for renewed and intensified contestation. Sometimes these recent contestations explicitly continue earlier lines of argument and dispute, but in others new labels for old ideas obscure continuities.

There are important differences between the first and new climate-centered environmentalism. Most notable is a new sense of unity and priority, with climate change assuming the role of the environmental problem of problems, in contrast to the great heterogeneity of different environmental problems in play in earlier decades. Also different is the near disappearance of human population stabilization efforts as a front in environmentalist activism. This is in part because the growth of human population has slowed, and in part because earlier efforts to lower rates of human reproduction are widely seen as abusive of basic human rights.[83] The early period was shadowed by expectations that higher-grade fossil fuels would soon be exhausted, while the climate-centered period labors under the reality of abundant new supplies brought into reach by advancing technologies of extraction.

Also different, nuclear power has a much more positive status within climate-change environmentalism. While many environmentalists still oppose nuclear power, others embrace nuclear energy as an important potential contributor to de-carbonization.[84] In the face of the severe disruptions guaranteed to result from climate change, the risks of nuclear energy are seen by increasing numbers of environmentalists as much less problematic. However, this partial change in attitudes has yet to significantly reverse the prospects of the nuclear industry, especially in Europe, where anti-nuclear attitudes have taken on dogmatic certainty among the surging Green movements and parties.

## The New Technopolitical Spectrum of Contestation

As a final step in this exploration of the newly contested trajectory of STM, it is useful to consider the ways in which the emergence of super-violence capabilities and biospheric degradation is producing a new axis of contestation within, and against, STM. The great contestations within STM between the Left, the Center, and the Right, between socialism, liberal democratic capitalism, and authoritarianism and fascism, still represent an indispensable framework for understanding the principal alternatives for organizing societies to take advantage of the opportunities of modernity and respond to its new problems. But for thinking about planetary-scope super-violence and eco-catastrophe, this conceptual spectrum is inadequate. To grasp these realities and register the spectrum of emergent contestation about them, a different framing is needed.

Views of technology fall along a five-segment spectrum, stretching from *Promethean technophiles*, *techno-optimists*, *cautious Soterians*, and *Friends of the Earth* to *Luddite technophobes*. They differ in many ways, three of which are most important: on the overall human prospect, the value of technology, and human relations to nature and the Earth. Although labels for these different schools of thought are not fully settled, this spectrum of clashing narratives and worldviews has increasingly come to supplement the older Left-Center-Right political spectrum.

Most bullish are the hypermoderns, the Prometheans, for whom utopia is within reach and some approximation of apotheosis is eventually likely.

Technology is white magic, leading to radical progress, and its development should be accelerated. "Science is the only news," and "failure of nerve is the greatest sin." Prometheans have complete confidence in the knowledge produced by science and technology. Present humanity is transitional, to be succeeded by a transhuman or superhuman species surpassing humanity's many limitations. Nature and the Earth are merely raw material to be completely reconfigured. Society and politics are flimsy obstacles, to be flung aside and preferably replaced with a comprehensive technocratic enlightened despotism.

The techno-optimists hold considerably more moderate versions of the same pro-technology worldview.[85] They see perpetual progress as probable. They are highly optimistic that technological advances will be overwhelmingly positive and that negative effects can be readily identified and corrected, usually with more technology. Environmental problems can be fixed with "ecological modernization" to produce a "good Anthropocene." Nature and the Earth should be mastered and exploited, and humanity should be gradually enhanced with bio- and cyber-technology. Most social and political problems can be solved with technical fixes, and technological misfires can be solved with different and better technologies. Many techno-optimists embrace technocracy, but others, particularly American techno-optimists, embrace radical libertarian and total free market arrangements. They have very high, but not complete, confidence in scientific and technological knowledge.

Sitting in the middle of the spectrum are the Soterians (named after Soteria, the Greek goddess of safety, preservation, and deliverance from harm).[86] Soterians believe humanity is doomed without capable steering. Whether technologies benefit or harm depends on foresight and steerage capacity. They believe that nature and the Earth should be used, but within limits. But the control of nature is difficult. While acknowledging the difficult-to-change "crooked timber of humanity," Soterians believe that steady, although potentially reversible, progress can be achieved with better education, knowledge, and institutions. While greatly valuing natural science, they are pragmatists, looking to practical experience as a vital source of knowledge. Soterians favor deceleration to make better decisions. The greatest sin is hubris. The vital information needed for successful steering is difficult but possible to obtain. Soterians identify various syndromes of human-technology interaction making steerage difficult, justifying regulatory restraints and even selective relinquishments. Technology, while a human product, is partly uncontrollable and opaque. The deep arms control and disarmament answer to the nuclear question is Sotarian because it emphasizes the likelihood of accidents and inadvertent escalation stemming from complexity and speed, and seeks to "lengthen the fuse" to allow more time for deliberative decision-making.[87]

The Friends of the Earth hold moderate versions of an Earth-centered worldview. They advocate "de-growth" for environmental sustainability. They see only probable eventual doom for humanity and impose high burdens of proof on the introduction of any new technology in the form of stringent "precautionary principles." Nature should be treated with respect and care, and extensive restraints on humans are needed. They favor checks and balances, stakeholder vetoes, and public accountability in social and political arrangements and are conservative of traditions. Their presumptive caution is anchored in the conviction that both nature and human affairs remain significantly opaque to humans.

At the far end of the spectrum are the Luddite technophobes, for whom the overall prospect is surely doom. Technology is black magic, the source of existential miseries and environmental catastrophes. Luddites worship nature, whole and holy, as the source of all value. Embracing "posthumanism," they want to subsume or terminate humanity to protect the Earth and its teeming nonhuman inhabitants. They embrace small-scale social and political arrangements, oppose further technological development and economic growth, and see techno-administration as a source of alienation and oppression. They are deeply suspicious of science and its claims of authoritative knowledge, but completely confident in their intuitions.

One emerging locus of contestation of considerable interest and importance is over "geo-engineering," a recently coined term to describe measures to intervene in the Earth's climate system, not to reduce emissions, but to otherwise compensate for the buildup of greenhouse gases and global heating.[88] Several dozen distinct geo-engineering schemes have been proposed, many of which are sure to prove ineffective or impractical. But others, such as the injection of sulfate particles into the stratosphere to deflect incoming solar radiation, appear to be quite feasible and affordable to undertake. Advocates of this scheme, a variety of solar radiation management (SRM), are confident that such injections will significantly alter global temperatures because such measures essentially mimic naturally occurring stratospheric sulfate injections produced by some volcanic eruptions. Others propose to seed the oceans with critical nutrients to stimulate plant growth, which would draw carbon dioxide out of the atmosphere, and then sequester it as the plants die and fall to the deep ocean floor.

Although no geo-engineering scheme has ever been attempted at scale and only the most rudimentary tests have been conducted, geo-engineering has already evoked extremely strong opposition on numerous grounds.[89] Critics insist that manipulating the planet's geo-physical systems in such ways is very likely to produce unanticipated effects, and cannot be realistically tested in a fully meaningful way without conducting such schemes at scale. Others point out that geo-engineering schemes, to the extent they are effective, amount to the creation of a "planetary thermostat." Who, acting on behalf of whose interests, will make decisions on the suitable level for it to be set? Despite these and other significant doubts, problems, and criticisms, research is slowly but surely beginning, and geo-engineering is attracting support from those who see it as a potential substitute for the costly reductions in fossil fuel use. Many advocates insist that geo-engineering should only be used as a last-ditch effort, a "plan B" for emergency implementation if efforts to reduce emissions fail or strong positive feedback mechanisms begin to kick in.

A central anticipation of Prometheans and, to a lesser extent, techno-optimists is that human expansion beyond the Earth into "outer space" will become increasingly feasible, and will be enormously transformative in many positive ways. Such anticipation has been a central theme of science fiction since the later nineteenth century and permeates global popular culture. "Space expansionism" has been powerfully articulated and propagated by some of the leading scientific-technological intellectuals, such as the German-American rocket engineer Wernher von Braun, the American planetary scientist and science educator Carl Sagan, the British astrophysicist Stephen Hawking, and most recently, the billionaires Elon Musk and Jeff Bezos. Like hydroelectric complexes and nuclear power, space programs are iconic steps in the path of modern progress. The space futures imaginary has become extremely elaborate and detailed since the mid-twentieth century, when the first steps in making humanity a space-faring species took place, in Nazi Germany, Soviet Russia, and Cold War America. The full aim of this visionary imaginary is to fill the orbital space of this planet with massive infrastructures and build human settlements of increasing size on an essentially limitless number of worlds, in this solar system and then far beyond.

The technological imaginary visionary of space expansionism is conceptually interesting because it builds its case by pointing to the many problems shadowing the human present and future on the Earth.[90] Space advocates point out that "all our eggs are in one basket," the vulnerable and fragile Earth, thus jeopardizing the long-term survival of humanity. The brief for big space is a thus a mirror for Earth's problems. If nuclear-tipped long-range missiles are a menace, then missile interceptors should be built in orbit.[91] If the Earth needs large quantities of clean energy, then giant solar collectors, "solar power satellites," should be built.[92] If the Earth is running out of accessible mineral resources, then the asteroids, many of which are thought to contain large quantities of metal, should be mined.[93] If the Earth is getting too hot, then giant solar shades should be built around the planet.[94] If industrial processes are damaging the ecology of the Earth, then polluting industry should be relocated to the vast and lifeless voids of outer space.[95] If the Earth is running out of habitat for its burgeoning human population, then giant canister space colonies should be constructed with lunar and asteroidal material.[96]

What is striking about these glittering technological imaginaries is the vast gulf between conceptualization and implementation. The space activities glass is very large, but it is almost entirely empty. Advocates believe, perhaps correctly, that technological advances will soon start closing this gap, leading to a cascade of space activities of progressively greater magnitude and importance. If these anticipations are realized, a series of great debates about these steps and their actual desirability are likely to ensue, pitting the most cherished projects of the Prometheans against extensions of the more cautious technopolitical approaches.[97]

Finally, taking into consideration the perils of super-violence and eco-catastrophe, and lines of dispute over technopolitics, where does this leave STM? Are the different sides across this yawning schism over basic questions still within STM? Or has a fundamental alternative of STEM now emerged? Many on the "slow, halt, and reverse" side of the technopolitical spectrum who are strongly antagonistic to the actual trajectory of STM call into question its fundamental assumptions, its core "operating manual." Given the magnitude of these differences, and the extremely wide array of alternative arrangements, at all scales, and in all domains, which have emerged at the margins of STM, it is appropriate to recognize that these alternative worldviews and ways of proceeding constitute a civilization-grade global narrative phenomenon, an emergent "greenpeace civilization."

Whether humanity's ride on the tiger of technological innovation will end poorly in various mega-catastrophes, or carry humanity to the stars, remains to be determined. But what is certain is that humanity—and the fate of the Earth—now, and probably for the indefinite human future, hinge on making the right choices in the deployment and regulation of the empowerments brought by STM, for better or worse.

## Notes

1. Mary Midgley, *Science as Salvation: A Modern Myth and Its Meaning* (London: Routledge, 1992); and David F. Noble, *The Religion of Technology: The Divinity of Man and the Spirit of Invention* (New York: Penguin, 1999).
2. David Wootton, *Inventing Science: A New History of the Scientific Revolution* (New York: Harper, 2015).
3. Jerry Weinberger, *Science, Faith, and Politics: Francis Bacon and the Utopian Roots of the Modern Age* (Ithaca, NY: Cornell University Press, 1985).
4. Francis Bacon, *New Atlantis*, ed. A. B. Gough (Oxford: Blackwell, 1915).
5. For a recent synoptic account, see Anthony Pagden, *The Enlightenment and Why It Still Matters* (Oxford: Oxford University Press, 2013).
6. Hiram Caton, *The Politics of Progress: The Origins and Development of the Commercial Republic, 1600–1835* (Gainesville: University of Florida Press, 1988).
7. David S. Landis, *The Unbound Prometheus: Technological Change and Industrial Development in Western Europe from 1750 to the Present* (Cambridge: Cambridge University Press, 1969); and Thomas P. Hughes, *American Genesis: A Century of Invention and Technological Enthusiasm, 1870–1970* (New York: Penguin, 1989). Humphery Jennings, *Pandaemonium, 1660–1886: The Coming of the Machine as Seen by Contemporary Observers* (New York: Free Press, 1985).
8. Elise Bohan, *Future Superhuman* (Sydney: University of New South Wales Press, 2022).
9. I. F. Clarke, *The Pattern of Expectation: 1644–2001* (New York: Basic Books, 1979); Peter Bowler, *A History of the Future: Prophets of Progress from H. G. Wells to Isaac Asimov* (Cambridge: Cambridge University Press, 2017); and Jenny Andersson, *The Future of the World: Futurology, Futurists, and the Struggle for the Post-Cold War Imagination* (New York: Oxford University Press, 2018).
10. Sir Martin Rees, *Our Final Hour: A Scientist's Warning* (New York: Basic Books, 2003); Nick Bostrom and Milan M. Cirkovic, eds., *Global Catastrophic Risks* (Oxford: Oxford University Press, 2008); and Toby Ord, *The Precipice: Existential Risk and the Future of Humanity* (New York: Hachette, 2020).
11. For a brief sketch, see Daniel Deudney and Elizabeth Mendenhall, "Green Earth: The Emergence of Planetary Civilization," in Sikina Jinnah and Simon Nicolson, eds., *New Earth Politics: Essays from the Anthropocene* (Cambridge, MA: MIT Press, 2016), 43–72.

12. Langdon Winner, *Autonomous Technology: Technics-out-of-Control as a Theme in Political Thought* (Cambridge, MA: MIT Press, 1977); and Edward Tenner, *Why Things Bite Back: Technology and the Revenge of Unintended Consequences* (New York: Knopf, 1996).
13. Adrienne Mayor, *Gods and Robots: Myths, Machines and Ancient Dreams of Technology* (Princeton, NJ: Princeton University Press, 2018).
14. George Dyson, *Darwin among the Machines* (New York: Basic, 1997).
15. H. G. Wells, "The Discovery of the Future," *Nature* 65 (1902): 326–331; Mark R. Hillegas, *The Future as Nightmare: H. G. Wells and the Anti-Utopians* (New York: Oxford University Press, 1967); and Simon J. James, *Maps of Utopia: H. G. Wells, Modernity, and the End of Culture* (Oxford: Oxford University Press, 2012).
16. Ira Katznelson, *Desolation and Enlightenment: Political Knowledge after Total War, Totalitarianism, and the Holocaust* (New York: Columbia University Press, 2003).
17. Harrison Brown, *Must Destruction Be Our Destiny?* (New York: Simon & Shuster, 1946).
18. Daniel Headrick, *Power over Peoples: Technology, Environment and Western Imperialism 1400 to the Present* (New York: Oxford University Press, 2010).
19. I. F. Clarke, *Voices Prophesying War, 1783–1984* (Oxford: Oxford University Press, 1966); and Nigel Calder, ed., *Unless Peace Comes: A Scientific Forecast of New Weapons* (London: Allan Lane, 1968).
20. The Italian Gerolamo Boccardo, cited in Edmund Silberner, *The Problem of War in Nineteenth Century Thought* (Princeton, NJ: Princeton University Press, 1946), 117.
21. For military utopianism, see H. Bruce Franklin, *War Stars* (New York: Oxford University Press, 1988).
22. H. G Wells, *The World Set Free* (London: Macmillan, 1913).
23. Richard Rhodes, *The Making of the Atomic Bomb* (New York: Simon & Schuster, 1986).
24. David Holloway, *Stalin and the Bomb: The Soviet Union and Atomic Energy, 1939–1956* (New Haven, CT: Yale University Press, 1994).
25. Richard Rhodes, *Dark Sun: The Making of the Hydrogen Bomb* (New York: Simon & Schuster, 1995).
26. Harold A. Feiveson, Alexander Glaser, Zia Mian, and Frank von Hippel, *Unmaking the Bomb: A Fissile Material Approach to Nuclear Disarmament and Nonproliferation* (Cambridge, MA: MIT Press, 2014).
27. Paul Boyer, *By the Bomb's Early Light: American Thought and Culture at the Dawn of the Atomic Age* (New York: Pantheon, 1985).
28. John Hersey, *Hiroshima* (New York: Knopf, 1946).
29. Henry DeWolf Smyth, *Atomic Energy for Military Purposes: A General Account of the Development of Methods of Using Atomic Energy for Military Purposes, 1941–1945* (Princeton, NJ: Princeton University Press, 1945).
30. R. Buckminster Fuller, *Operating Manual for Spaceship Earth* (Carbondale: Southern Illinois University Press, 1969).
31. For the inability to resolve the nuclear debate empirically, see Matthew Connelly et al, "'General, I Have Fought Just as Many Nuclear Wars as You Have': Forecasts, Future Scenarios, and the Politics of Armageddon," *American Historical Review* 117, no. 5 (December 2102): 1431–1460.

32. Mark Mazower, *Governing the World: The History of an Idea* (London: Allan Lane, 2012).
33. H. G. Wells et al., *The Idea of a League of Nations* (Boston: The Atlantic Monthly Press, 1919); W. Warren Wager, *H. G. Wells and the World State* (New Haven, CT: Yale University Press, 1961); John S. Partington, *Building Cosmopolis: The Political Thought of H. G. Wells* (Aldershot, UK: Ashgate, 2003). For the immediate postwar period, see Wesley T. Wooley, *Alternatives to Anarchy: American Supranationalism since World War II* (Bloomington: Indiana University Press, 1988); Or Rosenboim, *The Emergence of Globalism: Visions of World Order in Britain and the United States, 1939–1950* (Princeton, NJ: Princeton University Press, 2017); Rens van Munster and Casper Sylvest, *Nuclear Realism: Global Political Thought during the Thermonuclear Revolution* (London: Routledge, 2015).
34. Daniel H. Deudney, "Anticipations of World Nuclear Government," ch. 9 in Deudeny, *Bounding Power: Republican Security Theory from the Polis to the Global Village* (Princeton, NJ: Princeton University Press, 2007).
35. Robert Gilpin, *American Scientists and Nuclear Weapons Policy* (Princeton, NJ: Princeton University Press, 1962).
36. Eugene Rabinowitz, ed., *Minutes to Midnight: The International Control of Atomic Energy* (Chicago: Bulletin of Atomic Scientists, 1959).
37. Joel Primack and Frank von Hippel, *Advice and Dissent* (New York: Free Press, 1975).
38. Joseph Lieberman, *The Scorpion and the Tarantula: The Struggle to Control Atomic Weapons, 1945–1949* (Boston: Houghton Mifflin, 1970); and Lenice N. Wu, *The Baruch Plan: U.S. Diplomacy Enters the Nuclear Age* (Washington, DC: Government Printing Office, 1972).
39. Toshihiro Higuchi, *Political Fallout: Nuclear Weapons Testing and the Making of a Global Environmental Crisis* (Stanford, CA: Stanford University Press, 2020).
40. Robert Divine, *Blowing on the Wind: The Nuclear Test Ban Debate, 1954–1960* (New York: Oxford University Press, 1978).
41. Daniel Deudney, "The Great Debate: The Nuclear-Political Question and World Order," ch. 23, in Alexandra Gheciu and William Wohlforth, eds., *The Oxford Handbook on International Security* (New York: Oxford University Press, 2018), 334–349.
42. John Mueller, *Atomic Obsession: Nuclear Alarmism from Hiroshima to Al-Qaeda* (New York: Oxford University Press, 2009).
43. National Academy of Sciences, *Long-Term Worldwide Effects of Multiple Nuclear-Weapons Detonations* (Washington, DC: National Academy Press, 1975).
44. Paul R. Ehrlich, Carl Sagan, Donald Kennedy, and Walter Orr Roberts, *The Cold and the Dark: The World after Nuclear War* (New York: W. W. Norton, 1984); and Lawrence Badash, *A Nuclear Winter's Tale: Science and Politics in the 1980s* (Cambridge, MA: MIT Press, 2009).
45. Robert Scheer, *With Enough Shovels: Reagan, Bush, and Nuclear War* (New York: Random House, 1982).
46. David Cortright, *Peace Works: The Citizen's Role in Ending the Cold War* (Boulder, CO: Westview, 1993); and Jeffrey W. Knopf, *Domestic Society and International*

*Cooperation: The Impact of Protest on US Arms Control Policy* (Cambridge: Cambridge University Press, 1998).

47. Paul Lettow, *Ronald Reagan and His Quest to Abolish Nuclear Weapons* (New York: Random House, 2005); and James Mann, *The Rebellion of Ronald Reagan: A History of the End of the Cold War* (New York: Viking, 2009).
48. Stephen Shenfield, *The Nuclear Predicament: Explorations in Soviet Ideology* (London: Routledge & Kegan Paul, 1987).
49. Matthew Evangelista, *Unarmed Forces: The Transnational Movement to End the Cold War* (Ithaca, NY: Cornell University Press, 1999).
50. Walter Laquer, *The New Terrorism: Fanaticism and the Arms of Mass Destruction* (New York: Oxford University Press, 1999).
51. Richard A. Falkenrath, Robert D. Newman, and Bradley Thayer, *America's Achilles Heel: Nuclear, Biological and Chemical Terrorism and Covert Attack* (Cambridge, MA: MIT Press, 1998).
52. Leo Marx, *The Machine in the Garden: Technology and the Pastoral Ideal in America* (New York: Oxford University Press, 1964).
53. George Perkins Marsh, *Man and Nature* (Cambridge, MA: Harvard University Press, [1864] 1967).
54. Samuel P. Hays, *Conservation and the Gospel of Efficiency: The Progressive Conservation Movement, 1890–1920* (Cambridge, MA: Harvard University Press, 1959); Samuel P. Hays, *Beauty, Health, and Permanence: The Environmental Movement in the United States from 1945 to 1985* (Cambridge: Cambridge University Press, 1987); and Douglas Brinkley, *Rightful Heritage: Franklin Delano Roosevelt and the Lands of America* (New York: HarperCollins, 2016).
55. Frank Uekoetter, *The Green and the Brown: A History of Conservation in Nazi Germany* (Cambridge: Cambridge University Press, 2006).
56. Vladimer Vernadsky, *The Biosphere*, complete annotated edition (Springer-Verlag, 1996); and Spencer R. Weart, *The Discovery of Global Warming* (Cambridge, MA: Harvard University Press, 2003).
57. Hayward Alker and Peter Haas, "The Rise of Global Ecopolitics," in Nazli Choucri, ed., *Global Accord: Environmental Challenges and International Responses* (Cambridge, MA: MIT Press, 1993).
58. For landmark overviews, see William L. Thomas, ed., *Man's Role in Changing the Face of the Earth* (Chicago: University of Chicago Press, 1956); and B. L. Turner, W. C. Clark, R. W. Kates, J. F. Richards, J. T. Mathews, and W. B. Meyer, *The Earth as Transformed by Human Action* (Cambridge: Cambridge University Press, 1990).
59. Rachel Carson, *The Silent Spring* (New York: Knopf, 1962); and Thomas R. Dunlap, *DDT: Scientists, Citizens, and Public Policy* (Princeton. NJ: Princeton University Press, 1981).
60. J. R. McNeill, *Something New under the Sun: An Environmental History of the Twentieth Century* (New York: W. W. Norton, 2001).
61. M. Taghi Farvar and John P. Milton, eds., *The Careless Technology: Ecology and International Development* (New York: Natural History Press, 1972).

62. John McCormick, *Reclaiming Paradise: The Global Environmental Movement* (Bloomington: Indiana University Press, 1989); and Robert Falkner, *Environmentalism and Global International Society* (Cambridge: Cambridge University Press, 2021)
63. Ted Benton, ed., *The Greening of Marxism* (London: Guilford Press, 1997); McKenzie Wark, *Molecular Red: Theory for the Anthropocene* (London: Verso, 2015).
64. Murray Feshbach and Alfred Friendly, Jr., *Ecocide in the USSR: Health and Nature under Siege* (New York: Basic, 1992); and Judith Shapiro, *Mao's War against Nature: Politics and the Environment in Revolutionary China* (Cambridge: Cambridge University Press, 2001).
65. Paul Hawken, Amory Lovins, and R. Hunter Lovins, *Natural Capitalism: Creating the Next Industrial Revolution* (Boston: Little, Brown, 1999).
66. Paul and Anne Ehrlich, *The Population Bomb* (New York: Ballentine, 1968); and Garrett Hardin, *Living Within Limits: Ecology, Economics and Population Taboos* (Oxford: Oxford University Press, 1993).
67. Lynn White, Jr., "The Historic Roots of Our Ecological Crisis," *Science* 155 (1967): 1203–1207; Max Oelschlaeger, *Caring for Creation: An Ecumenical Approach to the Environmental Crisis* (New Haven, CT: Yale University Press, 1994); Bron Taylor, *Dark Green Religion: Nature Spirituality and the Planetary Future* (Cambridge, MA: MIT Press, 2009).Franke Wilmer, *The Indigenous Voice in World Politics* (Newbury Park, CA: Sage, 1993).
68. Aldo Leopold, *A Sand County Almanac* (Oxford: Oxford University Press, 1949); Christopher Stone, *Should Trees Have Standing? Toward Legal Rights for Natural Objects* (Los Altos, CA: William Kaufman, 1974); Roderick Nash, *The Rights of Nature: A History of Environmental Ethics* (Madison: University of Wisconsin Press, 1989).
69. Duane Elgin, *Voluntary Simplicity* (New York: William Morrow, 1981).
70. Herman Daly, *Steady State Economics* (San Francisco: W. H. Freeman, 1977); and Herman E. Daly and John B. Cobb, Jr., *For the Common Good: Redirecting the Economy toward Community, the Environment and a Sustainable Future* (Boston: Beacon Press, 1989).
71. Robert Heilbroner, *An Inquiry into the Human Prospect* (New York: W. W. Norton, 1974);William Ophuls, *Ecology and the Politics of Scarcity: Prologue to a Political Theory of the Steady State* (San Francisco: W. H. Freeman, 1976).
72. Edith Brown Weiss, *In Fairness to Future Generations: International Law, Common Patrimony, and Intergenerational Equity* (New York: Transnational Publishers and United Nations University, 1988).
73. James Lovelock, *Gaia: A New Look at Life on Earth* (New York: Oxford University Press, 1979).
74. Irene Diamond and G. F. Orenstein, eds., *Reweaving the World: The Emergence of Ecofeminism* (San Francisco: Sierra Club Books, 1990); and Carolyn Merchant, *Earthcare: Women and the Environment* (London: Routledge, 1996).
75. Robert Poole, *Earthrise: How Man First Saw the Earth* (New Haven, CT: Yale University Press, 2008).
76. Martha F. Lee, *Earth First! Environmental Apocalypse* (Syracuse, NY: Syracuse University Press, 1995); and Dave Foreman, *Confessions of an Eco-Warrior* (New York: Harmony Books, 1991).

77. Edward A. Parson, *Protecting the Ozone Layer: Science and Strategy* (New York: Oxford University Press, 2003); and Karen Litfin, *Ozone Discourse: Science and Politics in Global Environmental Cooperation* (New York: Columbia University Press, 1994).
78. Glenn T. Seaborg and William R. Corliss, *Man and Atom: Building a New World through Nuclear Technology* (New York: E. P. Dutton, 1971); and Gerald Garvey, *The City of the Second Sun* (Lexington, MA: Lexington Books, 1977).
79. Peter Brannen, *The Ends of the World: Volcanic Apocalypses, Lethal Oceans, and Our Quest to Understand Earth's Past Mass Extinctions* (New York: HarperCollins, 2017).
80. Elizabeth Kolbert, *Field Notes from a Catastrophe: Man, Nature and Climate Change* (New York: Bloomsbury, 2005); John S. Drysek, Richard B. Norgaard, and David Schlosberg, *Climate Challenged Society* (Cambridge: Cambridge University Press, 2013).
81. Fred Pierce, *With Speed and Violence: Why Scientists Fear Tipping Points in Climate Change* (Boston: Beacon Press, 2007); David Wallace-Wells, *The Uninhabitable Earth: Life after Warming* (New York: Duggan Books, 2019).
82. Clive Hamilton, *Requiem for a Species: Why We Resist the Truth about Climate Change* (London: Earthscan, 2010); and Naomi Oreskes and Erik M. Conway, *The Merchants of Doubt* (New York: Bloomsbury, 2010).
83. Matthew Connolly, *Fatal Misconceptions: The Struggle to Control World Population* (Cambridge, MA: Harvard University Press, 2008).
84. William Sweet, *Kicking the Carbon Habit: Global Warming and the Case for Renewable and Nuclear Energy* (New York: Columbia University Press).
85. Stewart Brand, *Whole Earth Discipline: An Ecopragmatist Manifesto* (New York: Penguin, 2009).
86. Clive Hamilton, *Defiant Earth: The Fate of Humans in the Anthropocene* (Oxford: Polity, 2017).
87. Jonathan Schell, *The Abolition* (New York: Knopf, 1984); Jonathan Schell, *The Gift of Time: The Case for Abolishing Nuclear Weapons Now* (New York: Henry Holt, 1998); Beatrice Fihn, "The Logic of Banning Nuclear Weapons," *Survival* 59, no. 1 (February–March 2017): 43–50; Harold A. Feiveson, ed., *The Nuclear Turning Point: A Blueprint for Deep Cuts and De-altering of Nuclear Weapons* (Washington, DC: Brookings, 1999); and George Schultz, Steven Andersen, Sidney D. Drell, and James Goodby, eds., *Reykjavik Revisited: Steps Toward a World Free of Nuclear Weapons* (Stanford, CA: Hoover Institute Press, 2008).
88. For advocate accounts, see Oliver Mortin, *The Planet Remade: How Geoengineerng Could Change the World* (Princeton, NJ: Princeton University Press, 2015); David Keith, *A Case for Climate Engineering* (Cambridge, MA: MIT Press, 2013).
89. Clive Hamilton, *Earthmasters: The Dawn of the Age of Climate Engineering* (New Haven, CT: Yale University Press, 2013).
90. Robert Zubrin, *Entering Space: Creating a Spacefaring Civilization* (New York: Jeremy P. Tarcher & Putnam, 1999); Michel van Pelt, *Dream Missions: Space Colonies, Nuclear Spacecraft, and Other Possibilities* (New York: Springer, 2017).
91. Jerry Pournelle and Dean Ing, *Mutual Assured Survival* (New York: Bean Enterprises, 1984); and Ben Bova, *Assured Survival* (Boston: Houghton Mifflin, 1984).
92. Peter E. Glaser, "Solar Power from Satellites," *Physics Today* (February 1977): 30–38; John Mankin, *The Case for Space Solar Power* (Houston: Virginia Edition, 2014).

93. John S. Lewis and Ruth A. Lewis, *Space Resources: Breaking the Bonds of Earth* (New York: Columbia University Press, 1987).
94. Edward Teller, "Sunscreen for Planet Earth," *Wall Street Journal*, October 17, 1997; H. S. Hudson, "A Space Parasol as a Countermeasure against Greenhouse Effect," *Journal of the British Interplanetary Society* 44 (1991): 139–144.
95. G. Harry Stine, *The Third Industrial Revolution* (New York: G. P. Putnam's Sons, 1975).
96. Gerard O'Neill, *The High Frontier* (New York: William Morrow, 1977).
97. For this debate, see Daniel Deudney, *Dark Skies: Space Expansionism, Planetary Geopolitics and the Ends of Humanity* (New York: Oxford University Press, 2020).

# Conclusion

## Many Worlds and the Coming Narrative Dilemma

*Karoline Postel-Vinay*

In late February 2022, after the launch of Russia's unprovoked attack on Ukraine, President Volodymyr Zelensky shed his suit and tie for a soon-to-be iconic khaki t-shirt and became overnight the most powerful voice of the liberal world order narrative. He became ubiquitous on the digital international scene, addressing the European Parliament and the United States Congress, the Japanese Diet and the Israeli Knesset, using different repertoires to convey the same message: at stake were both the survival of a free and open society against the aggression of a rogue authoritarian state, and the preservation of the international rule of law and other basic liberal international principles.[1] It took an extraordinary turn of events—not so much the Russian invasion that was expected at least by the United States, but the fierce Ukrainian resistance that was not—to transform an improbable stand-up comedian turned president of a country with limited clout into the vibrant champion of a global narrative that only yesterday was the hallmark of Western powers. By comparison, in societies of Europe and North America the liberal international narrative has looked somewhat fragile. How can that be? The threat of annihilation explains the clarity and strength of Zelensky's narrative, which itself reflects the spirit of the Ukrainian resistance. But in the West, and despite a strong rally of public opinion in support of Ukraine, the long-term vitality of the liberal narrative and its impact on international organizations seem uncertain. Inward-looking populism and marked indulgence, if not fascination, for authoritarianism are still running strong within Western societies. This trend preceded Russia's invasion of Ukraine and will likely outlast it. The French presidential elections that took place in April 2022, while war crimes were being committed by the Russian Army in Mariupol, eventually ended with the reappointment of the outspoken advocate of liberal internationalism Emmanuel Macron, but also with the rise,

Karoline Postel-Vinay, *Conclusion* In: *Debating Worlds*. Edited by Daniel Deudney, G. John Ikenberry, and Karoline Postel-Vinay, Oxford University Press. © Oxford University Press 2023. DOI: 10.1093/oso/9780197679302.003.0011 not the decline, of extremist parties that had consistently showed sympathy for leaders such as Vladimir Putin. Nor did the staging in Ukraine of Putin's worldview prevent the re-election of pro-Moscow leaders in Hungary and in Serbia. Meanwhile, on the other side of the Atlantic, the political forces that, since the election of Donald Trump, contributed to the erosion of the global liberal narrative are clearly still well and alive. The story of the Ukrainian resistance has undoubtedly re-energized the bigger story of the liberal international order. But will this boost have a durable impact? This question raises at least three different issues.

It first raises the issue of narrative power as such. How do narratives of the global emerge and become dominant? Few narratives have acquired the planetary influence that liberal internationalism gained after the end of the Cold War. The end of the bipolar conflict, but also new "hot" conflicts, accompanied its ascent. Soon after the fall of the Berlin Wall, the war in former Yugoslavia broke out and the United Nations Security Council (UNSC) voted unanimously in favor of intervention. In contrast with the Ukrainian situation of 2022, the rallying call for action in the Balkans in 1991 truly illustrated liberal internationalism at work. Earlier that same year, and less than a year before the collapse of the Soviet Union, the UN-led intervention in the Persian Gulf, although not supported by a unanimous UNSC vote, did bring together the former foes of the Cold War, inspiring president George H. W. Bush to hail the onset of a "new world order." Whether this new order was a US-centered unipolar moment or not, it signaled the triumph of a narrative that was not the exclusive property of the US, but shared by millions of citizens who had pushed for the advent of liberal democracy in Latin America, East Asia, and Eastern Europe during the 1980s. In other words, if the rise and dominance of the liberal internationalism narrative did reflect a change of balance of power, it also pointed to the attractiveness of the narrative itself. Two decades later, one might therefore argue that doubts or outright distaste expressed within Western societies for the liberal narrative should not necessarily lead to the disappearance of its global influence. Narratives of the global are not bound by a specific space, and it is precisely this spatial plasticity that gives them lasting influence. For example, as Michael Cox points out in Chapter 2 of this volume, the Soviet-inspired global narrative of anti-capitalism survived the breakup of the USSR: its force is still manifest, with renewed tropes, in the twenty-first-century narratives of de-growth, de-globalization, and environmental justice.[2] So likewise, even if the post-1989 US-led world order weakens dramatically, the liberal internationalism narrative it has sustained will most probably survive. To a certain extent, there is a decoupling of narrative power from geopolitical power.

Hence the second issue raised by the Ukrainian resistance story is ownership. Volodymyr Zelensky and his team might not "own" the liberal internationalism narrative in the way the US and its allies did in the decade following the Cold War, but they outsmarted the skepticism expressed in the West toward that narrative. The relationship between narrative power and geopolitical power is not straightforward because the former entails complex and unstable agency. This volume presents a diversity of state and non-state actors whose role as narrators of global stories does not follow a predictable pattern. Sometimes important international actors lack narrative power. Japan, as Kei Koga and Satori Katada argue in Chapter 4, never showed a willingness to produce a narrative of global significance, even when, as the world second largest economy, it was seen, wrongly, as a challenge to the United States' international predominance. There could not be a bigger contrast than with China, which has been engaged under Xi Jinping's leadership, as Rana Mitter notes in Chapter 6, in an active production of narratives aiming at global influence. From the perspective of the Global South, standing at the periphery is not incompatible with access to narrative power, as Jeremy Adelman shows in Chapter 8 in his discussion of the rise of the idea of development and the making of the long-lasting narrative of global distributive justice. Important narratives of the global have been written outside the core of geopolitical power, albeit often in response to scripts disseminated by this core. What matters then is not only who are the narrators, but also how they take ownership of their narratives.

The way in which the Ukrainian resistance storytellers unequivocally embraced the narrative of liberal international order in its most idealistic, post-1989 version, exposes by comparison a problem of consistency on the side of the Western powers that originally promoted this narrative. The 1990s witnessed the formation of a "happy globalization" story where economic and political integration along liberal terms seemed almost boundless. This optimism carried beliefs that were, in the following decades, contradicted by events, such as 9/11, or trends that have now been well identified.[3] Yet these beliefs also had structural defaults of their own. The urge to include all countries in the liberal internationalism project came along with shortsightedness and de facto compromises. In 2000, when the European Union was still made of fifteen countries, most of them old democracies, the idea of working with the newly elected Austrian far-right leader Jörg Haider was unfathomable for most member states: two decades later, and with thirteen additional members, this intolerance has become impractical with the growing presence of illiberal components in the Union. On a larger scale, the leaders of the liberal international order took at face value the rhetoric of "spin dictators"[4] who govern illiberal regimes with the apparel of modern moderates, but whose endgame is rarely the establishment of liberal democracy. Like the Davos World Economic Forum that welcomed Vladimir Putin just a year before he launched his military attack on Ukraine, Western institutions of global regulation have tended to put aside the possibility, despite available evidence, of "spin dictators" becoming plain old-fashioned dictators. Such an approach might have been inspired by the wishful thinking that somehow authoritarian leaders could be part of the liberal family, or by a calculated bet, or realist preference, for effective governance. At any rate, the Ukraine disaster has been an indication of the potential cost—including for global regulation—of focusing on the technicality of government to the detriment of the political standards of liberal internationalism.

Yet the complexity of global problems and their sheer planetary scale are here to stay and will require some form of world order to tackle them. For lack of alternatives, that order might remain the liberal international one, but their main supporters will have to choose, as John Ikenberry has argued, between a "small and thick" or a "large and thin" version of it[5]: one that focuses on the Western democracies of the Cold War and their allies, or one that is inclusive of a more diverse and bigger number of globalization stakeholders. The "large and thin" interpretation of liberal internationalism sustained the launching of the first G20 Summit in 2008, which seemed then better fit to address new global challenges, as opposed to the G7, or even the G8 (when Russia was part of it), which looked like a quaint legacy of the 1970s. The confidence in the possibility of broad and heterogeneous participation in global governance under the banner of liberal internationalism was such that the discarding of the G8 and its replacement by the G20 were seriously contemplated in 2009. This idea was abandoned when widening divergences between G20 members, notably around the Syrian civil war, made the G7 appear as an indispensable discussion space for liberal democracies. Meanwhile, the G20 remained the necessary forum for global regulation and in fact a laboratory for a world order that is far more disparate than the one envisioned by the globalist imagination of the 1990s.[6] In that sense, the "small and thick" and "large and thin" versions of liberal international order already coexist through the G7 and G20, as well as within most UN agencies. Yet in the long run this coexistence might trigger a growing discrepancy of narratives where the thick version of liberal internationalism is still recognizable as a story of moral and political progress, and the thin version resembles the diary of day-to-day crisis management (from pandemics to environmental catastrophes).

It has been argued that in the United States, conservatives tell stories whereas liberals do not.[7] Donald Trump and his supporters produced the sweeping cultural narrative of retrieving a fantasized lost paradise that would remodel America, while the Democrats were putting forward data, statistics, and technical solutions to rebuild the country. The former were responding to an assemblage of emotions—anger, fear, nostalgia, and disenchantment—when the latter were addressing a complex equation of needs and interests. The single-minded search for competent government by liberal institutions would explain the source of their faltering narrative power. This argument has been made about the "narrative problem" of the European Union, whose functionalist legacy has transformed it into a remarkably efficient tool for regional integration and regulation but a soulless technocracy prone to populist criticism.[8] Liberal Europhiles have also lamented that the Union lacked a narrative, or rather a renewed narrative,[9] as the powerful story of peace and reconciliation of the early days of European integration is inevitably fading away. The global liberal internationalism narrative was also fed by auspicious war endings: they provided stories of one-world-ism that accompanied the establishment of the League of Nations after the Great War, the UN after World War II, and the renewal of global governance institutions after the Cold War. As with the EU, the momentum created by the actual events ebbed away, and new realities—such as the rise of non-Western powers with different priorities—called for a renewal of the liberal narrative. Does the EU's struggle with its own narrative search provide an indication for the challenge that the liberal internationalism narrative is facing on a larger scale? Has too much focus on competent government and neutral technology indeed produced the story-less liberal? Would that explain then the rise of identity politics in North America, and to a lesser extent in Europe, in which liberals have been increasingly involved? As Charles Tilly has demonstrated, societies require narratives that are constantly negotiated and renewed.[10] In the realm of world politics, that entails the continual adjustment of global narratives to the changing plurality of the international scene. This adjustment has proved, so far, to be an uphill battle for narrators of liberal internationalism.

While the liberal international narrative has been struggling to reinvent itself, other narratives of the global have emerged. One important feature of this new scene is the rise of non-Western civilizational narratives. This evolution comes across several chapters of this volume, notably the discussions of present-day China and India. The use of the civilization repertoire is, however, not unprecedented. In fact, the Western-defined notion of civilization has inspired many of the pan-nationalist movements of the late nineteenth century, in particular Pan-Asianism as well as Pan-Islamism, which Cemil Aydin presents in Chapter 3 of this volume.[11] Today the growing assertiveness of civilizational narratives on the international scene goes in par with novel geopolitical considerations, albeit not along the lines of the "clash of civilizations" theory.[12] The scramble for putting back together the former Soviet Union since the 1990s has gradually produced a distinct narrative of civilizational grandeur that Vladimir Putin and his entourage have displayed along with the successive invasions of Russia's neighbors. Until 2022, the governments of the Western world reacted with notable restraint to the new civilizational powers' claims to territorial influence and subsequent initiatives: Russia's invasion of Crimea, India's takeover of Kashmir, and China's military buildup on the South China Sea's islands and stronghold on Hong Kong triggered negative comments or limited economic sanctions at best. The most advanced Western intelligence assessed that Ukraine would be taken over in a matter of days in February 2022 without much reaction anywhere in the world. Yet the Ukrainian resistance was immediately and vehemently expressed through all possible ways, including quasi-performance (Ukrainian civilians throwing makeshift Molotov cocktails at heavy Russian tanks), and this time the geopolitical consequences of Russia's civilizational project caught the attention of a wider international public opinion and of Western governments and their allies. The possibility of a Chinese invasion of Taiwan has now moved from a hypothesis commonly dismissed as implausible to a scenario closely studied by a large defense community. The change of perception also reveals a stronger awareness of the far-reaching programmatic dimension of some of the current civilizational narratives.

Yet civilizational narratives are not by definition potentially bellicose and not even nationalistic at their core. In the second half of the nineteenth century, modern reformists from Japan, Korea, and China found in the notion of Pan-Asianism resources to build both new national narratives and a common discourse on regional identity and solidarity that eventually survived the Pacific War and was partly recycled at the time of the 1955 Bandung Conference.[13] In Chapter 7, Itty Abraham discusses the long trajectory of the Indian narrative that involved major shifts from the cosmopolitan space envisioned by Rabindranath Tagore to the ethnicized "civilization-state" put forward by Narendra Modi. Early Pan-Islamism, as Cemy Aydin reminds us, was in practice a platform of claims and demands for the improvement of the rights of Muslims within European empires that would mitigate the notion of white/Christian supremacy, and to assert the equality of existing Muslim states in international law. Europe had then a civilizational discourse of its own, encapsulated by the highly hierarchical notion of "standard of civilization"[14] that divided the world between those who had acceded to an all-encompassing modernity (from steamships and railways to sea bathing and Western-style clothing) and those who had not. In that sense, there is a plausible genealogy that links the old non-Western civilizational narratives to the most recent ones, following a thread of encounters with the Western world, eventually leading, albeit neither uniformly nor systematically, to expressions of anti-Westernism. They have yielded tropes of humiliation, some long-lasting and elaborated, such as in China's "century of humiliation" narrative, some fuzzier but nevertheless efficient, as in the Russian civilizational narrative.[15]

*Ressentiment*, or resentment, is paradoxically a common theme to some of the rising civilizational narratives of the non-Western powers and the radical conservative narratives of the West discussed by Jean-François Drolet and Michael Williams in Chapter 5 of this volume. What is similar indeed is the use of a collective emotion that is all the more compelling in that it not only nurses a plot but participates in the very process of emplotment, or *mise en intrigue*, as Paul Ricoeur called it. Emplotment, or the transformation of disparate historical events into a structured script, is more precisely a story with a moral, providing its narrators with a powerful political resource.[16] But what distinguishes Western and non-Western narratives fed by floating feelings of humiliation and anger is actual history. The contestation of liberalism within the West that can be traced back to the reaction against the rise of the Enlightenment is entirely a Western story. Experiences of collective humiliation in the non-Western world that generated expressions of anti-Westernism refer to a completely distinct set of events and therefore might lead to criticism of liberal internationalism, but not necessarily so and not always exhaustively. Anti-Western rhetoric does not systematically translate into a thorough critique of the liberal international order; again, the G20 shows that Westernophobia is compatible with at least a "large and thin" version of liberal internationalism. In other words, if there is a threat to the dominance of the liberal internationalism narrative it is fueled by anti-liberal narrators—whether Kim Jong-un or Donald Trump, or their common stagecraft—but not by the rise in itself of non-Western civilizational narratives.

Since the end of the Cold War, the narrative of liberal internationalism has dominated the codes of global governance. Those codes look sufficiently established to endure a relative decline of the liberal international narrative, as the emergence of new narratives have not yet prevented cooperation around crucial global issues in various domains, such as finance, health, or the environment. Is that a fragile balance between several forces that will not last longer than the interregnum? Or is the coexistence of a universalistic liberal narrative with civilizational narratives sustainable? It has been argued that taking into account the voices of the new civilization-states will not undermine the liberal international order, but rather reinvigorate the international scene with stronger pluralism.[17] Whether the Ukrainian situation is a temporary aberration or, on the contrary, inaugurates a new era of violent confrontations will give more or less weight to this argument. But even without speculating about possible new wars, the coexistence of two different types of narratives of the global does not seem entirely self-evident. It might lead to a fundamental dilemma, which could be defined, borrowing from education theories, as the pluralist dilemma:[18] finding a balance between the fair representation of pluralities and the necessity of a common social contract. Pluralism is a constant demand of communities, and its increase on the international scene is manifest. Yet what is implicit in the argument for global pluralism is the existence of a meta-narrative. None of the present major civilization-states narratives aims at a complete isolation from globalization (not even the narrative that sustains Russia's invasion of Ukraine, which again, was expected by Moscow and Western powers alike to be obtained with little reaction[19]). The assumption then is that particularistic narratives can be part of a *grand récit*, as Jean-François Lyotard defined it:[20] a grand narrative that is essential for the legitimation of institutions and more specifically, from an international relations perspective, institutions of global regulation.

This is where lies not only the main success, but also the failure of the liberal international narrative, in the sense that it has become both an essential agenda-shaper and a major contestation-crystallizer on a global scale. This paradoxical situation carries some of the baggage of the liberal narrative's historical trajectory. The eighteenth-century constellation of ideas and visions called liberalism encountered internationalism in the nineteenth century, along with the planetary expansion of European power. Hence "liberal internationalism" became the title of a meta-narrative that conflates globalization with a legacy of European ideas, values, and visions. This conflation today obscures two realities: first, that globalization has thrived well beyond the realm of liberal democracies; and second, that liberal democracies, although still concentrated in the West, have been established elsewhere in the world. Yet it is a compelling conflation, nurtured in the West as much as in the so-called Rest. The numerous discussions of Eurocentric understandings of the expansion of international society point to the lasting influence of Western-centrism in the management of global issues.[21] The less abundant academic literature on "Occidentalism" illuminates symmetrically the long history of essentialization of the West by non-Western societies and how it can impact international affairs.[22] Despite those intellectual resources, deconstructing the conflation of the liberal international narrative that was originally written in the West, with the representation of today's globalization, whether celebrated or contested, might prove arduous. It does, however, complicate the challenge of producing a functioning meta-narrative for global cooperation.

This challenge is twofold. It first entails retrieving universalism from a Westernized interpretation of the liberal narrative. The claim to universalism has been crucial in the promotion of transnational narratives around and within global institutions. The emergence of transnational narratives of women's rights in the late nineteenth century was undoubtedly supported by a Western repertoire of liberal ideas, reflected in the early feminist movements of Meiji Japan, among others.[23] But those narratives eventually gained a life of their own and grew within the framework of global institutions such as the UN: as Laura Shepherd has argued, there is an intrinsic global logic to the very fabric of the women's rights narrative as it plays out in issues such as peace and security.[24] The same universal substrate and its expression in global institutions were crucial for the deployment and recognition of the Global South narrative of distributive justice. One can argue, of course, that the civilizational narratives of Pan-Asianism and Pan-Africanism played an essential role in the formation of the "Bandung spirit" and the original Third World narrative, but their impact on the global agenda would have been quite different without the framework of universal organizations such as the UN agencies. By comparison, an entity such as the BRICS (Brazil-Russia-India-China-South Africa) Forum, although calling for the revival of the "Bandung spirit" story, did not manage to provide a similarly powerful narrative, nor did it yield the same scope and level of cooperation. The room for an African civilizational narrative within the new context of civilization politics is also less obvious.[25]

Second, the challenge of producing a functioning meta-narrative entails retrieving liberal pluralism from today's globalization. Liberal internationalism now coexists with illiberal internationalism within the sphere of global governance: the figure of the "spin dictator" mentioned earlier is a metaphor for this new coexistence. The shift from "spin" to plain dictatorship can create disruptions in the web of flux that feeds globalization. Calls for a return to Realpolitik, such as those made regarding Ukraine, could mitigate those disruptions and save specific national interests as well as, broadly speaking, global connectivity. The push for Realpolitik would also reinforce the juxtaposition of rival civilizational narratives and hence "provincialize," as Dipesh Chakrabarty would put it,[26] the liberal international narrative. It could even bring it back to a core element of its cultural construction, the idea of a coherent "Anglosphere" analyzed by Duncan Bell in Chapter 1 of this volume. The notion of a common destiny of English-speaking nations has in practice constituted an asset in the shaping of the post-1945 liberal cooperation framework, but it also weakens the liberal international narrative's claim to universalism. The potential provincializing of the liberal narrative is a far cry from the globalism it promoted in the 1990s and that accompanied the "happy globalization" that saw the birth of the millennial generation and its promise of pluralism.[27] Likewise, the move toward strong civilizational narratives—including liberal ones such as the vision of European sovereignty[28]—seems to herald the onset of a narrative of globalism that offers essentially lip service to pluralism. It might rather lead to a competition of claims and global pursuit of narrative power, an evolution that Xi Jinping and his team have in a sense already theorized through the slogan *huayuquan*, or "speak and be heard"—often translated as discursive or narrative power, and referring specifically to China's right to exert influence on world politics. A heightening battle of narratives on the international stage could transform the liberal pluralism project, which at some point informed globalism, into a wasteland. However, a wasteland can be a good starting point to thoroughly reconsider narratives that can make sense of today's global interconnectedness. Such a project goes beyond the immediacy and polarization of identity politics, and its aim is not an assessment of the "rise and fall" of grand narratives. It begins rather, as this volume proposed to do, by a historically informed appreciation of past and present narratives of the global as a way to sketch out the contours of our imaginaries and our expectations of a unifying pluralism.

## Notes

1. Volodymyr Zelensky, *War Speeches I: February–March 2022* (Berlin: LM Verlag, 2022).
2. Walden Bello, *Deglobalization: Ideas for a New World Economy* (London: Zed Books, 2002), Serge Latouche, *Le Pari de la Décroissance* (Paris: Fayard, 2006). For a discussion, see, inter alia, Neera M. Singh, "Environmental Justice, Degrowth and Post-Capitalist Futures," *Ecological Economics* (September 2019).
3. See, inter alia, Rebecca Adler-Nissen and Ayse Zarakol, "Struggles for Recognition: The Liberal International Order and the Merger of Its Discontents," in David Lake, Lisa Martin, and Thomas Risse, eds., "Challenges to the Liberal International Order: International Organization at 75," *International Organization* (Spring 2021).
4. Sergei Guriev and Daniel Treisman, *Spin Dictators: The Changing Face of Tyranny in the 21st Century* (Princeton, NJ: Princeton University Press, 2022).
5. G. John Ikenberry, "The End of Liberal International Order?," *International Affairs* (January 2018).
6. Karoline Postel-Vinay, *Le G20, laboratoire d'un monde émergent* (Paris: Presses de Sciences Po, 2011); English translation: *The G20: A New Geopolitical Order* (New York: Macmillan, 2013).
7. David Ricci, *Why Conservatives Tell Stories and Liberals Don't: Rhetoric, Faith, and Vision on the American Right* (New York: Routledge, 2016).
8. Hartmut Behr, "Technocracy and the Tragedy of EU Governance," *Journal of Contemporary European Research* (May 2021), Richard McMahon and Wolfram Kaiser, "Narrative Ju-jitsu: Counter-Narratives to European Union," *Journal of Contemporary European Studies* (July 2021).
9. Kalypso Nicolaïdis and Robert Howse, "'This Is My EUtopia . . .': Narrative as Power," *JCMS: Journal of Common Market Studies* (December 2002); Mary Kaldor, Mary Martin, and Sabine Selchow, "Human Security: A New Strategic Narrative for Europe," *International Affairs* (March 2007).
10. Charles Tilly, *Stories, Identities, and Political Change* (Lanham, MD: Rowman & Littlefield, 2002).
11. See also Cemil Aydin, "Beyond Civilization: Pan-Islamism, Pan-Asianism and the Revolt against the West," *Journal of Modern European History* (September 2006).
12. The abundant debate and critique provoked by Samuel Huntington's thesis has evolved through time and world events, but still points to problems linked to the use of cultural determinism as its main framework. See, for example, Paul Barker, ed., *The Clash of Civilizations Twenty Years On* (Bristol: E-International Relations Edited Collections, 2013).
13. Sven Saaler and Christopher Szpilman, eds., *Pan Asianism: A Documentary History*, Vol. 1, *1850–1920* (New York: Rowman & Littlefield, 2011).
14. Gerrit Gong, *The Standard of "Civilization" in International Society* (Oxford: Clarendon Press, 1984).
15. William Callahan, "National Insecurities: Humiliation, Salvation, and Chinese Nationalism," *Alternatives* (March 2004), Sergey Radchenko, "'Nothing but

Humiliation for Russia': Moscow and NATO's Eastern Enlargement, 1993–1995," *Journal of Strategic Studies* (September 2020).

16. Paul Ricoeur, *Time and Narrative* (Chicago: University of Chicago Press, 1984). See also Hayden White, "The Value of Narrativity in the Representation of Reality," *Critical Inquiry* 7, no. 1 (1980): 5–27. On the use of narratives of humiliation in the West, see, inter alia, Alexandra Homolar and Georg Löfflmann, "Populism and the Affective Politics of Humiliation Narratives," *Global Studies Quarterly* (March 2021).
17. Amitav Acharya, "The Myth of the 'Civilization State': Rising Powers and the Cultural Challenge to World Order," *Ethics & International Affairs* (July 2020). More generally on the merits of a civilizational approach to the understanding of international relations, see Gregorio Bettiza, "Civilizational Analysis in International Relations: Mapping the Field and Advancing a 'Civilizational Politics' Line of Research," *International Studies Review* (March 2014).
18. Brian Bullivant, *The Pluralist Dilemma in Education: Six Case Studies* (Sydney: Allen & Unwin, 1981).
19. The joint Russia-China communiqué of early February 2022 is significant in this regard: it can be read from the perspective of liberal internationalism as a threatening, or darkly farcical, depiction of democracy promotion, but it is also the self-portrait of two powers that consider themselves, and de facto are, major players in global connectivity. See "Joint Statement of the Russian Federation and the People's Republic of China on the International Relations Entering a New Era and the Global Sustainable Development," February 4, 2022.
20. Jean-François Lyotard, *La Condition Postmoderne* (Paris: Editions de Minuit, 1979). English translation: *The Postmodern Condition: A Report on Knowledge* (Minneapolis: University of Minnesota Press, 1984).
21. Inter alia, John Hobson, *The Eurocentric Conception of World Politics: Western International Theory, 1760–2010* (Cambridge: Cambridge University Press, 2012), Turan Kayaoglu, "Westphalian Eurocentrism in International Relations Theory," *International Studies Review* (June 2010).
22. Meltem Ahiska, "Occidentalism: the Historical Fantasy of the Modern," *South Atlantic Quarterly* (April 2003), Katalin Miklóssy and Pekka Korhonen, eds., *The East and the Idea of Europe* (Newcastle upon Tyne: Cambridge Scholars, 2010).
23. Barbara Molony, "The Quest for Women's Rights in Turn-of-the-Century Japan," in Barbara Molony and Kathleen Uno, eds., *Gendering Modern Japanese History* (Cambridge, MA: Harvard University Press, 2005).
24. Laura Shepherd, *Narrating the Women, Peace and Security Agenda: Logics of Global Governance* (Oxford: Oxford University Press, 2022).
25. Paul-Henri Bischoff, Kwesi Aning, and Amitav Acharya, eds., *Africa in Global International Relations: Emerging Approaches to Theory and Practice* (London: Routledge, 2015). The Chinese Belt and Road Initiative in Africa, in particular, is a game-changer in Sino-African relations: see Chris Alden and Daniel Large, *New Directions in the Study of Africa-China Relations* (London: Routledge, 2017).
26. Dipesh Chakrabarty, *Provincializing Europe: Postcolonial Thought and Historical Difference* (Princeton, NJ: Princeton University Press, 2007).

27. Stella M. Rouse and Ashley D. Ross, *The Politics of Millennials: Political Beliefs and Policy Preferences of America's Most Diverse Generation* (Ann Arbor: University of Michigan Press, 2018).
28. Bart M. J. Szewczyk, *Europe's Grand Strategy: Navigating a New World Order* (London: Palgrave Macmillan, 2021).

# Index

*For the benefit of digital users, indexed terms that span two pages (e.g., 52–53) may, on occasion, appear on only one of those pages.*

Figures are indicated by an italic *f* following the page number


Abbott, Lyman, 40–41
Abduh, Muhammed, 87–88
Abe Shinzo, 134–36
Abraham, Itty, 20–21, 276–77
Adelman, Jeremy, 21, 273
Afghani, Jamaluddin al-, 88–89
*Against the Consensus* (Lin), 173
Ahmad, Khurshid, 107–8
Algeria and Pan-Islamism, 85, 97–98, 102–3, 104–5
Ali, Abdullah Yusuf, 80–81
Ali, Muhammed, 97, 112n.25
Alt-Right movement, 144
Amin, Idi, 202
Anglo-American Committee (1898), 35–36
Anglo-American League (1898), 35–36
Anglo-American Union (1896), 35–36
Angloworld
  Anglo-union proposal for, 28–29, 31–33, 34–44, 48–50
  Brexit and, 17, 28–29, 49–50
  British Empire's future and, 29–43, 44–45, 46–47, 48–49
  CANZUK and, 49–50
  capitalism and, 41, 44
  citizenship and, 34–35, 37–38, 41, 44, 45
  civilizational narratives and, 30–32
  Cold War and, 43–44, 46, 48
  debates over future of, 31–32
  definition of, 28–29
  emergence of, 28–30
  European Union and, 28–29, 49–50
  federalism and, 31–33
  *fin de siècle* discourse on, 29–31
  Germany and, 31, 39–40
  globalization and, 29–30, 33
  Greater Britain proposed for, 29–35, 37, 40–41, 42
  imperialism and, 38, 46–47
  Industrial Revolution and, 29–30, 33
  interwar years and, 41–42
  Japan and, 137
  liberal democracy and, 41, 44
  models proposed for, 32, 41–45
  nationalism and, 33–34, 38–39
  overview of, 17, 28–29, 50, 280
  Pan-Islamism and, 29–30
  racial narratives and, 30–31, 33–35, 37–41, 43, 45, 48–49
  return of, 47–50
  Round Table movement and, 34, 41
  Russia and, 30–31
  September 11th attacks and, 48
  superiority narratives and, 17, 29, 33, 38–39, 45, 48–49
  UN and, 28–29, 45–46
  United Kingdom and, 44, 48–50
  United States and, 29, 32, 33–42, 44–46, 47
  universalism and, 40–41, 44–45, 46–48
  universal peace through union of, 40–41, 45, 47–48
  Venezuelan boundary dispute and, 35–36
  Western civilization and, 29, 43–44, 49–50
  world government and, 41–47
  World War I and, 41, 42, 45
  World War II and, 42–43, 46–47
Anthropocene Age, 1–2, 241, 257, 260
Appadurai, Arjun, 34–35
Arab-Israeli War (1973), 106–7, 109–10
Aras, Tevfik Rüştü, 98–99

Argentina, economic policies in, 218
Asali, Shukri al-, 92
Asian financial crisis (1997-1998), 134–35
Aso Taro, 134–35
Atatürk, Mustafa Kemal, 102–3
Atlantic Union (1901), 35–36
Attlee, Clement, 168–69
Aydin, Cemil, 18, 275–77

Bacon, Francis, 237, 239
Balfour, Arthur, 37–38
Balkan Wars (1912-1913), 94–95
Bandung Conference (1955), 101–2, 276–77, 279–80
Bannon, Steven, 157
Barakatullah, Muhammad, 91–92
Barker, Ernest, 31–32
Baruch Plan (1946), 248
Bayly, Susan, 193
Befu, Harumi, 119
Bell, Daniel A., 178
Bell, Duncan, 17, 280
Bennett, James, 48–50
Berlin Wall, 1, 48, 272–73
Bernstein, Leonard, 1
Bezos, Jeff, 262
Bharatiya Janata Party (BJP) (India), 184–85, 202–3, 205
Bharucha, Rustom, 194
Bialer, Seweryn, 79n.73
Blair, Tony, 28–29, 48
Bloch, Jules, 193
Blunt, Wilfred, 90
Borrell, Josep, 3–4
Bose, Phanindranath, 193
Bourdieu, Pierre, 155
Brazil and development narrative, 225–26
Bretton Woods system, 19–20, 169, 211–12, 220–22, 223–24, 230–31
Brexit, 2, 17, 28–29, 49–50
BRICS (Brazil-Russia-India-China-South Africa) Forum, 279–80
British Empire
  British Commonwealth reimagining of, 41–42
  debate over future of, 29–43, 44–45, 46–47, 48–49
  federalism and, 31–32
  Greater Britain proposal and, 29–35, 37, 40–41, 42
  India and, 187–90, 200–1, 203
  interwar period and, 41–42
  Pan-Islamism and, 80–81, 85, 90, 93, 100–1, 102–3
  threat of democratization to, 31
  United States relationship with, 35, 37, 42
  World War I and, 41
  World War II and, 42–43
Brown, Gordon, 28–29
Bush, George H. W., 272–73
Bush, George W., 48
Butler, Samuel, 243

Cairncross, Alec, 170–71
Cairo Conference (1943), 175–77
Camp David Accords (1978), 106–7, 109–10
Campos, Roberto, 224
CANZUK (Canada, Australia, New Zealand, and the United Kingdom) federation proposal, 49–50
capitalism
  Angloworld and, 41, 44
  China and, 214, 216–17
  development narrative and, 217–18, 226–27
  distributive justice and, 212, 232–33
  environmentalism and, 253–54
  free trade and, 13–14, 49–50, 135–36, 173, 211–12, 221
  India and, 188
  Japan and, 120, 134
  narratives of the global and, 10–11, 12, 13–14, 16, 272–73
  Orientalism and, 188
  Pan-Islamism and, 104–6
  radical conservatism and, 152
  Soviet Union, as enemy of, 61, 62–64, 67, 69–70, 74–75, 226–27, 272–73
  STM and, 244, 253–54, 258, 259
Carnegie, Andrew, 38–39, 40–41
Carr, E. H., 42, 58–59, 65–66
Carson, Rachel, 252
Carter, Jimmy, 70
Castoriadis, Cornelius, 185

CCP (Chinese Communist Party), 174, 177, 181
Ceaser, James W., 159n.12
CEPAL (UN Economic Commission for Latin America), 223, 230–31
Chacko, Priya, 197, 198
Chakrabarty, Dipesh, 280
Chamberlain, Houston Stewart, 148
Chamberlain, Joseph, 32, 37
Chamberlain, Neville, 63–64
Champetier, Charles, 152–53
Chatham House (International Institute of International Affairs), 42
Chen Changheng, 218–19
Chen Duxiu, 167
Chiang Kai-shek, 165, 167–68, 175–76
China
  Boxer Rebellion in, 215
  Cairo Conference and, 175–77
  capitalism and, 214, 216–17
  CCP in, 174, 177, 181
  century of humiliation in, 276–77
  China Model narrative in, 162, 179–81
  civilizational narratives and, 162–64, 167, 178–81
  civil war in, 167–68
  climate change and, 163–64
  Cold War and, 172–73, 177
  Confucianism in, 164–65, 167, 172
  Cultural Revolution in, 167, 170
  democratization and, 162–64, 169, 171, 180
  development narrative and, 214–17, 219, 224–25, 226–27
  disputed island claims of, 176–77, 275–76
  economic development and, 166, 167, 170–73
  end of history and, 179, 181
  Enlightenment narrative and, 168
  environmentalism and, 253–54
  Four Modernizations in, 170
  global economic crisis of 2008 and, 171–72
  Great Leap Forward in, 226–27
  *huayuquan* and, 162, 170, 280
  imperialism and, 163, 164, 165–66, 169, 172
  India and, 198–99
  Japan and, 124, 135–36, 174–75
  liberal democracy and, 162, 168–69, 282n.19
  Mao's narrative of, 162–63, 167, 169, 170–72, 181
  Marxism and, 73
  May Fourth movement in, 167, 215–16
  modernity and, 15–16, 164–65, 218–19
  nationalism and, 128, 166
  nuclear weapons and, 199
  Ottoman Empire and, 214
  outward-looking perspective in, 173–74
  overview of, 19–20, 162–64, 181
  Qing dynasty in, 164
  reform era in, 170–71
  rehabilitation of Nationalists in, 175–76
  reinvention of wartime in, 174–77
  Sino-Japanese War of 1894-1895, 120–21, 126, 214
  Sino-Japanese War of 1937-1945, 165, 167, 177
  Sinosphere claims about, 164–65, 172
  sources of new narrative in, 172–74
  Soviet Union and, 71–72, 73
  Taiwan and, 176–77, 180–81, 275–76
  Tiananmen crisis in, 170–71
  Trump and, 173
  twentieth century narratives of, 164–70
  UN and, 167
  United States and, 1–2, 170–71, 173, 224–25
  universalism and, 94, 163–66, 168, 172, 181
  Western civilization and, 15–16, 166, 171–72, 173–74, 178, 179–80
  World War II and, 163–64, 165, 174–77
  WTO membership of, 1, 171, 233
*China Can Say No (Zhongguo keyi shuo bu)* (Zhang), 173
Chinese Communist Party (CCP), 174, 177, 181
Churchill, Winston
  Anglosphere and, 28–29, 48–50, 55n.68
  citizenship and, 55n.68
  Cold War and, 42–43
  narratives of the global and, 4
  Soviet Union and, 65

citizenship
  Angloworld and, 34–35, 37–38, 41, 44, 45
  India and, 201–4
  Pan-Islamism and, 85, 91
  racial narratives and, 37–38
civilizational narratives. *See also* Western civilization
  Angloworld and, 30–32
  Asian difference in civilization and, 194, 196–200
  China and, 162–64, 167, 178–81
  clash of civilizations in, 21–22, 81–82, 85, 94–95, 98–99, 275–76
  development narrative and, 213–14
  India and, 184, 186–88, 190–91, 193, 195–200, 205, 276–77
  Japan and, 118, 128–29
  Ottoman Empire and, 84–85, 86–87, 90, 94–95, 96–97, 99–100
  overview of, 1–3, 9–10, 12–13, 15–16, 275–78, 279–80
  Pan-Islamism and, 81–83, 84–85, 86–87, 88–89, 91, 93–101, 105–6, 107, 110–11, 276–77
  radical conservatism and, 146–47
  STM and, 236–39, 241–43, 263
  uncivilized contrasted with civilized in, 31–32, 37, 84–85, 87–88, 96–97, 118, 167, 186, 189
Clemenceau, Georges, 249–50
climate change
  causes of, 257
  China and, 163–64
  denialism about, 257–58
  development narrative and, 230
  feedback loops and, 257
  narratives of the global and, 1–2, 3–4
  renewable energy and, 258
  STM and, 240–43, 249–50, 256–59
Codevilla, Angelo, 155
Cold War
  Angloworld and, 43–44, 46, 48
  arms treaties in, 69
  Berlin Wall in, 1, 48, 272–73
  China and, 172–73, 177
  as conflict between ways of life, 66
  Cuban missile crisis in, 69, 248
  development narrative and, 212
  India and, 197–98
  Japan and, 117–18, 122–24, 131–33
  liberal democracy and, 2, 71, 278
  narratives of the global and, 2, 272–73, 274–75, 278
  NATO and, 68
  Pan-Islamism and, 101, 102–4, 105–10
Colebrook, Henry Thomas, 187–88
colonialism, 18, 41–42, 82–84, 88–89, 102–6, 186, 191, 194–95, 197. *See also* imperialism
*Cominform* (1947), 68
communism, 1, 58, 59, 103–4, 118, 200. *See also* Marxism
Communist Party of the Soviet Union (CPSU), 62, 68
Confucianism, 164–65, 167, 172
Congress of Vienna, 84–85
Conquest, Robert, 28–29, 49–50
conservatism, radical. *See* radical conservatism
Council on Foreign Relations, 42
Covid-19 pandemic, 3–4, 21, 184–85
Cox, Michael, 17–18, 272–73
Crawford, Nita, 6–7
Cuban missile crisis (1963), 69, 248
Curtis, Lionel, 34, 46–47

Dai Jitao, 165
Davis, Muriam Haleh, 85–86
De Benoist, Alain, 143–44, 151, 152–53
decline narratives, 143, 145–51, 157, 190–91
decolonization, 18, 41–42, 102–6, 186, 194–95. *See also* imperialism
democratization, 2, 14, 15, 31, 115–16, 126–27, 147, 162–64, 169, 171, 180. *See also* liberal democracy
Deng Xiaoping, 19–20, 170, 202–3
Derrida, Jacques, 7
Desnoes, Edmundo, 229–30
De Soto, Hernando, 232
Deudney, Daniel, 21–22, 29–30, 46
Deutsch, Karl, 44
development narrative. *See also* Industrial Revolution
  Argentina and, 218

backwardness and, 216–17, 218–19, 223, 227–28
Brazil and, 225–26
Bretton Woods system and, 220–22, 223–24
capitalism and, 217–18, 226–27
China and, 214–17, 219, 224–25, 226–27
civilizational narratives and, 213–14
climate change and, 230
Cold War and, 212
disarmament and, 231
distributive justice and, 212, 213, 216–17, 220–21, 222–23, 226, 233, 273, 279–80
free trade and, 211–12, 221
globalization and, 211–13, 231–32, 233
Great Depression and, 215–16, 218
IBRD and, 220–21
IMF and, 220–21, 230–31
imperialism and, 216–17, 218
India and, 215–16, 218, 222, 225
integration and, 214, 217, 224–25
International Trade Organization proposal and, 223–24
Japan and, 213–14
Latin America and, 226, 232
liberal democracy and, 211–12, 223, 226–27
modernity and, 216–18, 224–25, 226–27, 228, 229
nationalism and, 218
neo-Malthusian narrative and, 218–19, 230
neo-Mercantilism and, 218–19
origins of, 213–15
overview of, 211–13, 232–33
racial narratives and, 213–14, 219, 228
reckoning of redistributionist narratives and, 227–31
redistributive justice and, 220–23, 226–27, 229–32, 233
Soviet Union and, 226–27
Taiwan and, 213–14
Third World and, 212–13, 222–23, 228–31
UN and, 228, 230
United States and, 218–20, 223–26, 230
universalism and, 225, 233
Western civilization and, 211–13, 232
World War I and, 215–16, 217–18
World War II and, 220
Dilke, Charles, 33, 37, 39–40
distributive justice, 212, 213, 216–17, 220–21, 222–23, 226, 232–33, 273, 279–80
Dos Passos, John Randolph, 38–39
Doyle, Michael, 47–48
Drolet, Jean-François, 19, 277–78
Du Bois, W. E. B., 30–31
Dulles, Allen, 78n.54
Dulles, John Foster, 45–46

economics. *See* capitalism; communism; development narrative; globalization; Marxism
Egypt and Pan-Islamism, 84–85, 89, 99, 100, 105–6, 108–10
Einstein, Albert, 45–46, 245, 247
Eisenhower, Milton, 226
end of history, 102, 179, 181, 241–42
Enlightenment narrative
China and, 168
overview of, 7, 11, 277–78
radical conservatism and, 145–46, 154–56
STM and, 237–38, 241–42, 251–52
environmentalism, 242, 251–56, 258–59
Ersoy, Mehmet Akif, 87–88
Europe. *See* imperialism; Western civilization
European Recovery Program, 67
European Union (EU)
Angloworld and, 28–29, 49–50
Brexit from, 2, 17, 28–29, 49–50
narratives of the global and, 3–4, 273–74, 275

Falk, Richard, 46
Fanon, Frantz, 172, 228
Faye, Guillaume, 151, 154–55
Ferguson, Niall, 48–49
Feuerbach, Ludwig, 7
Finnemore, Martha, 6–7
Fogel, Joshua, 164
Foucault, Michel, 7

France
  Japan and, 124, 126, 127
  Pan-Islamism and, 84–85, 87–88
  radical conservatism and, 143–44, 148, 149, 152–53
Francis, Sam, 144, 151
Free and Open Indo Pacific (FOIP) initiative, 135–36
Freeman, Joseph, 76n.27
free trade, 13–14, 49–50, 135–36, 173, 211–12, 221
Freud, Sigmund, 7
Friedman, Milton, 170–71
Friedman, Rose, 170–71
Fukuyama, Francis, 71, 73
Fukuzawa Yukichi, 126
Fuller, Buckminster, 246

G7 Summit, 274–75
G20 Summit, 274–75, 277–78
Gagarin, Yuri, 69
Gandhi, Indira, 202
Gandhi, Mahatma, 20–21, 197, 220
Germany
  Angloworld and, 31, 39–40
  Japan and, 126, 127, 128
  Nazi Germany, 58, 63–64, 65, 262
  radical conservatism and, 143–44, 148
  Soviet Union and, 63–65
  STM and, 251–52
Gerschenkron, Alexander, 227–28
Gewirtz, Julian, 170–71
Gladstone, W.E., 86–87
global climate change. *See* climate change
global government, 41–47, 117, 196–98, 246–47
globalization
  Angloworld and, 29–30, 33
  development narrative and, 211–13, 231–32, 233
  happy globalization, 273–74
  Industrial Revolution and, 29–30
  liberal democracy and, 1, 19, 273–74, 278–80
  narratives of the global and, 1, 10–11, 19, 273–75, 278–80
  Pan-Islamism and, 82, 90, 91
  pluralism and, 280
  radical conservatism and, 143, 147, 149, 150, 152–53, 156–58
  STM and, 237–38, 239–40
global modernity, 2–3, 4, 5–6, 8, 9–11, 13–14, 19
global narratives. *See* narratives of the global
Global South, 15–16, 21, 163, 179–80, 203, 204–5, 212–13, 273, 279–80
Gobineau, Arthur de, 146–48, 154, 157–58, 159n.9
Gorbachev, Mikhail
  decline of Soviet Union and, 72
  narrative of Soviet Union changed by, 17–18, 59–60, 71–73
  nuclear weapons and, 250
Goto-Jones, Chris, 164–65
government. *See* liberal democracy; Marxism; world government
grand narratives, 7, 81, 99, 280
Great Depression, 62–63, 128–29, 215–16, 218
Greater Britain proposal, 29–35, 37, 40–41, 42
Greater East Asian Co-Prosperity Sphere, 137–38
Greek war of independence (1821-1832), 84–85
Grew, Joseph, 98–99
*Groupement de recherché et d'etudes pour la civilisation européenne* (GRECE), 143–44, 151

Haider, Jörg, 273–74
Halid, Halil, 91
Hall, Ian, 184–85
Hanotaux, Gabriel, 87–88
Harper, Stephen, 48
Harrison, Benjamin, 36–37
Hartley, Livingston, 43–44
Hawking, Stephen, 262
Hayek, Friedrich, 65–66
Hegel, G. W. F., 146, 188
Heimsath, Charles Herman, 198
Helsinki Accords (1975), 70
Hersey, John, 246

Herz, John, 46
*Heshang (River Elegy)* (television documentary), 170–71, 173, 179
Hibiya incendiary incident (1905), 126
Hirschman, Albert O., 227–28, 229, 230
Hitler, Adolf, 4, 63–64
Hobhouse, L. T., 31–32
Hobson, J. A., 31–32, 216–17
Howard, John, 28–29, 48
Hu Jintao, 174–75
Hunter, William, 87
Huntington, Samuel, 81–82, 184, 229, 281n.12
Hutchins, Robert M., 45–46
Huxley, Aldous, 45–46

Ibrahim, Abdurreşid, 88
IBRD (International Bank for Reconstruction and Development), 220–21
Ikenberry, John, 274–75
IMF (International Monetary Fund), 220–21, 230–31
imperialism
  Angloworld and, 38, 46–47
  anti-imperial efforts against, 64, 69–70, 218
  China and, 163, 164, 165–66, 169, 172
  development narrative and, 216–17, 218
  India and, 85, 185–86, 188, 194–96, 205
  Japan and, 115–16, 124, 125, 126–27, 129–30
  narratives of the global and, 13–14, 16
  Pan-Islamism and, 81–90, 91–92, 94, 96, 100–1, 105–6, 109–11
  Soviet Union and, 64, 69–70
India
  ambivalence toward diaspora from, 200–3
  Amritsar Massacre in, 215–16
  Asian cosmopolitan narrative in, 186–87, 189–90, 194–96, 205, 276–77
  Asian difference in civilization and, 194, 196–200
  BJP in, 184–85, 202–3, 205
  bringing diaspora home to, 203–5
  British Empire and, 187–90, 200–1, 203
  capitalism and, 188
  China and, 198–99
  citizenship and, 201–4
  civilizational narratives and, 184, 186–88, 190–91, 193, 195–200, 205, 276–77
  Cold War and, 197–98
  colonialism and, 186, 191, 194–95, 197
  decline narrative and, 190–91
  decolonization in, 185–86, 191, 194–95, 196–97
  development narrative and, 215–16, 218, 222, 225
  diaspora from, 184–85, 200–5
  Greater India concept in, 193, 199–200, 205
  Hindu-Muslim relations in, 80–81, 85, 97, 191, 205
  *Hindutva* in, 199–200, 205–6
  imperialism and, 85, 185–86, 188, 194–96, 205
  Indian National Congress in, 184–85, 201
  Indic territorial narrative in, 186–87, 189–90, 192–93, 199, 205
  invasions of, 190–92
  Kashmir conflict in, 197–98, 275–76
  liberal democracy and, 187–90
  modernity and, 194
  nationalism and, 190–91, 194, 200
  nuclear weapons and, 197–98, 199
  Orientalism and, 187–92, 193, 195–96
  origins of, 187–88
  overview of, 20–21, 184–86, 205–6
  Pan-Islamism and, 80–81, 85, 94, 100
  partition of, 102–3
  racial narratives and, 187–88, 189–90
  rebellion of 1857 in, 85
  superiority narratives and, 184, 189–90, 191, 193, 195, 205
  Uganda expelling overseas Indians, 202
  UN and, 196–98
  United Kingdom and, 202
  United States and, 225
  universalism and, 94, 186, 189, 195–96, 199–200, 205
  Western civilization and, 188–90, 194
  world government and, 196–98

Industrial Revolution. *See also* development narrative
  Angloworld and, 29–30, 33
  globalization and, 29–30
  global politics developed in, 29–30
  Japan and, 115, 117–18, 120–21, 125
  modernity and, 12–13
  narratives of the global and, 6, 12–13
  Soviet Union and, 60
  STM and, 241, 243, 244, 251–52
inequality, 2, 3–4, 21, 128, 137–38, 223, 230, 232
Inoue Kaoru, 126–27
International Bank for Reconstruction and Development (IBRD), 220–21
International Institute of International Affairs (Chatham House), 42
International Monetary Fund (IMF), 220–21, 230–31
international relations (IR) scholarship, 6–7, 35, 46, 66, 103–4, 278
Inukai Tsuyoshi, 128–29
Iran and Pan-Islamism, 99, 102–3, 105–7, 108–10
Islamism. *See* Pan-Islamism
Israel and Pan-Islamism, 102–3, 106–7, 108–10
Italy and the Ottoman Empire, 94–95, 98–99, 100–1
Iyengar, Srinivasa, 201

Japan
  Angloworld and, 137
  assimilation and, 125–27, 129–30, 133, 137
  capitalism and, 120, 134
  China and, 124, 135–36, 174–75
  civilizational narratives and, 118, 128–29
  Cold War and, 117–18, 122–24, 131–33
  democratization and, 115–16, 126–27
  development narrative and, 213–14
  disputed island claims and, 176
  Dodge line in, 122
  as between East and West, 115–16
  economic development of, 117–18, 120–23, 121*f*–22, 123*f*, 132–34, 136
  Edo period in, 120
  financial bubble in, 134–35
  fluctuating nature of, 115, 117–18, 120–24, 130–31, 137–38
  FOIP initiative in, 135–36
  France and, 124, 126, 127
  Germany and, 126, 127, 128
  Greater East Asian Co-Prosperity Sphere and, 137–38
  Gulf War and, 123–24, 134–35
  imperialism and, 115–16, 124, 125, 126–27, 129–30
  Industrial Revolution and, 115, 117–18, 120–21, 125
  inequality and, 128–29, 137–38
  Korea and, 125–29
  League of Nations and, 128
  Manchurian Incident and, 129
  Meiji period in, 18–19, 115, 119–26, 129–30, 131, 137
  militarization of, 120–22, 122*f*, 125, 129–31
  modernity and, 115–20, 131, 136, 164–65
  Monroe Doctrine and, 127–28
  nationalism and, 117, 119–20, 133, 134
  *nihonjinron* in, 115–16, 118–20
  nuclear weapons and, 122–23
  opening of, 115–16, 124
  overview of, 18–19, 115–16, 136–38
  pacifism of, 132–33
  post-war Americanization of, 131–32
  racial narratives and, 128–29, 130–31, 137–38
  Reiwa period in, 18–19, 115, 120–24
  Russo-Japanese War of 1904-1905, 91, 92, 120–21, 126, 168
  September 11th attacks and, 134–35
  Sino-Japanese War of 1894-1895, 120–21, 126, 214
  Sino-Japanese War of 1937-1945, 165, 167, 177
  superiority narratives and, 118, 133
  Taiwan and, 120–21, 214
  *tenno-sei* system in, 115–16, 125, 129–30
  theoretical implications from narratives of, 137–38
  twenty-first century narrative of, 134–36

UN and, 132, 134–35
uniqueness narratives in, 115–16, 118–19, 129–31, 132–34, 136–38
United Kingdom and, 121–22, 127, 131, 137
United States and, 119, 127–28, 131–34
universalism and, 115–16, 117, 118–19, 130–32, 134–35, 136–37
value-based diplomacy and, 134–36
Western civilization and, 125–27, 129–30, 133, 137
world government and, 117
World War I and, 127
World War II and, 121–22, 129–31, 175
Yoshida Doctrine in, 117–18, 119, 131
Jasanoff, Sheila, 185
Jenco, Leigh, 172
Jiang Qing, 172, 178
Jiang Tingfu, 19–20, 163, 165–69, 180, 181
Johnson, Greg, 144, 150–51
Jones, William, 187–88

Kaneko Kentaro, 127
Kang Youwei, 164, 214
Karakoç, Sezai, 105–6
Katada, Saori, 18–19, 273
Kato Taka-aki, 126–27
Kemal, Namik, 87
Kennan, George, 66
Kennedy, John F., 45–46, 226
Kennedy, Paul, 71
Kerr, Philip (Lord Lothian), 41
Khan, Aga, 80–81
Khan, Sahibzada Aftab Ahmad, 80–81
Khilafat movement, 80–81, 93, 97–99
Khomeini, Ruhollah, 109–10
Khrushchev, Nikita, 67, 68–70, 71, 226–27
Kim, Sang-Hyun, 185
Kim Jong-un, 277–78
Kissinger, Henry, 70
Klein, Naomi, 233
Koga, Kei, 18–19, 273
Koizumi Jun'ichiro, 134–35
Konoe Fumimaro, 130
Korea and Japan, 125–29
Kornai, Janos, 170–71
Kosygin, Nikolai, 71
Kubitschek, Juscelino, 225–26
Kupchan, Charles, 110
Kyoto Protocol (1997), 257–58

Lansing-Ishii Agreement (1917), 127
Latin Christendom, 10, 12, 239
Lausanne Treaty (1923), 81–82, 98–100
League of Nations, 91, 93, 100–1, 128, 129, 167, 275
Lenin, Vladimir, 4, 17–18, 61, 62, 64–65, 69–70, 93
Leninism, 60, 63–64, 67, 73, 74
Lévi, Sylvain, 193
Lewis, Bernard, 81–82, 103–4
Liang Qichao, 214–15
liberal democracy
Angloworld and, 41, 44
China and, 162, 168–69, 282n.19
Cold War and, 2, 71, 278
counter-narratives to, 14–15
democratization and, 2, 14, 15, 31, 115–16, 126–27, 147, 162–64, 169, 171, 180
development narrative and, 211–12, 223, 226–27
globalization and, 1, 19, 273–74, 278–80
India and, 187–90
as meta-narrative, 278–80
modernity and, 13–14
narratives of the global and, 1–2, 13–15, 272–80
origins of, 13–14
pluralism and, 154, 278, 280
racial narratives and, 15
radical conservatism's targeting of, 145, 150
Russia and, 282n.19
Soviet Union contrasted with, 59–60, 70
STM and, 254
universalism and, 1–2, 279–80
Western civilization and, 13–14, 277–79
Libya and Pan-Islamism, 94, 98–99, 101
Limited Test Ban Treaty (1963), 248
*Limits to Growth* (Club of Rome), 254
Lippman, Walter, 43–44
Lyotard, Jean-François, 7, 278

MacArthur, Douglas, 131
Macron, Emmanuel, 271–72

Mahalanobis, Prasanta, 222
Mahan, Alfred, 36–37
Mahmud of Ghazni, 190–91
Maine, Henry, 188
Majumdar, R. C., 193
Malaccorto, Ernesto, 218
Manchurian Incident (1931), 121–22, 129
Mansingh, Surjit, 198
Mao Zedong
  Cairo Conference and, 175–76
  China narrative of, 162–63, 167, 169, 170–72, 181
  Cold War and, 172–73, 177
  Great Leap Forward of, 226–27
  narratives of the global and, 19–20
  *Red Book* of, 83–84
  Western civilization and, 166
Mariátegui, José Carlos, 217, 224–25, 229–30
Marsh, George Perkins, 251–52
Marshall, Alfred, 213
Marshall Plan, 68
Marx, Karl, 7, 14, 17–18, 61–62, 64, 73, 188
Marxism, 9–10, 14, 60, 61–62, 63–64, 73, 253–54. *See also* communism
Ma Ying-jeou, 176–77
McCain, John, 47–48
McKinley Tariff (1890), 32
Mehta, Uday Singh, 189
Meiji Restoration, 18–19, 115, 119–26, 129–30, 131, 137
Mill, James, 188–89
Mitter, Rana, 19–20, 138, 273
Miyazawa Ki'ichi, 132–33
modernity. *See also* scientific technological modernity
  China and, 15–16, 164–65, 218–19
  development narrative and, 216–18, 224–25, 226–27, 228, 229
  global modernity, 2–3, 4, 5–6, 8, 9–11, 13–14, 19
  India and, 194
  Industrial Revolution and, 12–13
  Japan and, 115–20, 131, 136, 164–65
  liberal democracy and, 13–14
  narratives of the global and, 1, 2–3, 4, 5–7, 8–16, 17–18, 19, 276–77
  Pan-Islamism and, 82–83, 85, 105–6
  radical conservatism and, 145, 146, 147, 148–49, 150, 152
  resistance against, 15–16
  Soviet Union and, 62–64
  STM and, 240–42, 254
  Western civilization and, 11–14
Modi, Narendra, 184–85, 186–87, 204–5, 212–13, 276–77
Monroe Doctrine, 127–28
Montagu, Edwin, 80–81
Monypenny, W. F., 34
Morgenthau, Hans, 46, 60–61
Morgenthau, Henry, 220–21
Muir, William, 87
Müller, Friedrich Max, 187–88
Musk, Elon, 262
Myrdal, Gunnar, 218–19, 222–23, 231

Nag, Kalidas, 193
Naidu, Sarojini, 195, 201
Nakasone Yasuhiro, 133
Naoroji, Dadabhai, 215
narratives of the global. *See also* civilizational narratives; development narrative; Enlightenment narrative; racial narratives; superiority narratives
  capitalism and, 10–11, 12, 13–14, 16, 272–73
  clashes between, 3–4
  climate change and, 1–2, 3–4
  Cold War and, 2, 272–73, 274–75, 278
  Covid-19 pandemic and, 3–4
  debunking of narratives and, 7–8
  definition of, 4–6
  environmentalism and, 5–6
  European Union and, 3–4, 273–74, 275
  globalization and, 1, 10–11, 19, 273–75, 278–80
  grand narratives and, 7, 81, 99, 278, 280
  imperialism and, 13–14, 16
  Industrial Revolution and, 6, 12–13
  interdependence of planet and, 3–4, 16–17
  liberal democracy and, 1–2, 13–15, 271–80
  modernity and, 1, 2–3, 4, 5–7, 8–16, 17–18, 19, 276–77
  nationalism and, 2, 15–16

nuclear weapons and, 3–4
overview of, 1–16, 271–73
performative aspects of narratives and, 5–6, 9–10
*ressentiment* and, 277–78
road maps for present volume on, 16–22
scholarship on, 4, 6–10
task of mapping new realities in, 2, 3–4
universalism and, 1–2, 3–4, 10–12, 15, 279–80
Western civilization and, 1–3, 10–17, 275–78
world politics and, 4–6
narratology, 6–7
Nasser, Gamal Abdel, 106–7, 108–9
nationalism
Angloworld and, 33–34, 38–39
China and, 128, 166
development narrative and, 218
India and, 190–91, 194, 200
Japan and, 117, 119–20, 133, 134
narratives of the global and, 2, 15–16
Pan-Islamism and, 83–84, 100, 102, 104, 107, 108–9
radical conservatism and, 144
Soviet Union and, 62
NATO (North Atlantic Treaty Organization), 43–44, 68, 74, 102–3, 155
Nazi Germany, 58, 63–64, 65, 262
Nehru, Jawaharlal, 20–21, 190–91, 194–95, 196–99, 201–2, 218, 222
neo-Malthusianism, 218–19, 230
neo-Mercantilism, 218–19
"New International Economic Order" (NIEO), 230–31
Nietzsche, Friedrich, 7
*nihonjinron*, 115–16, 118–20
Nishida Kitarō, 164–65
Nitobe Inazo, 213–14
Nixon, Richard, 70
North Atlantic Treaty Organization (NATO), 43–44, 68, 74, 102–3, 155
*North-South: A Programme for Survival* (Willy Brandt Report), 231–32
nuclear weapons
China and, 199
India and, 197–98, 199
Japan and, 122–23
narratives of the global and, 3–4
Soviet Union and, 68, 245–46
STM and, 240–44, 245–51, 256
United States and, 245–46
Nuri, Celal, 95

Obama, Barack, 47–48
Occidentalism, 278–79
Oliver, F. S., 47
Ollman, Bertell, 61
Orientalism
capitalism and, 188
definition of, 206n.11
India and, 187–92, 193, 195–96
Ottoman Empire and, 86–87
Pan-Islamism and, 86–88, 103–4
types of, 206n.11
Ottoman Empire
Balkan Wars and, 94–95
Bolshevik Revolution and, 96–97
Bulgarian insurrections of 1876 in, 86
China and, 214
civilizational narratives and, 84–85, 86–87, 90, 94–95, 96–97, 99–100
international law and, 95–96
Italy and, 94–95, 98–99, 100–1
jihad proclamation and, 95–96
Orientalism and, 86–87
self-strengthening reforms in, 86
Sèvres Treaty and, 96–97
superiority narratives and, 96–97
World War I and, 94, 95–96

Pakistan and Pan-Islamism, 99, 102, 107
Palestine and Pan-Islamism, 85, 100, 102–3, 106–7, 108–10
Pan-Africanism, 81–82, 103, 279–80
Pan-Asianism, 29–30, 81–82, 275–77, 279–80
Panikkar, K. M., 192
Pan-Islamism
Algeria and, 85, 97–98, 102–3, 104–5
Angloworld and, 29–30
Balkan Wars and, 94–95
Bandung Conference and, 101–2
British Empire and, 80–81, 85, 90, 93, 100–1, 102–3
capitalism and, 104–6
citizenship and, 85, 91

Pan-Islamism (*cont.*)
civilizational narratives and, 81–83, 84–85, 86–87, 88–89, 91, 93–101, 105–6, 107, 110–11, 276–77
Cold War and, 101, 102–4, 105–10
colonialism and, 82–84, 88–89, 102–6
as counter-narrative, 85, 87–88, 107, 110–11
coupling geopolitical power with narratives in, 93–101
decolonization and, 101–6
disunity of narratives preceding, 82–84
Egypt and, 84–85, 89, 99, 100, 105–6, 108–10
emergence of, 81–90, 94
end of history and, 102
France and, 84–85, 87–88
globalization and, 82, 90, 91
Greek war of independence and, 84–85
imperialism and, 81–90, 91–92, 94, 100–1, 105–6, 110–11
India and, 80–81, 85, 94, 100
interwar period and, 100–1
Iran and, 99, 102–3, 105–7, 108–10
Israel and, 102–3, 106–7, 108–10
Khilafat movement in, 80–81, 93, 97–99
Libya and, 94, 98–99, 101
modernity and, 82–83, 85, 105–6
Muslim intellectual defense of Islam and, 86–88
nationalism and, 83–84, 100, 102, 104, 107, 108–9
Orientalism and, 86–88, 103–4
Ottoman Empire and, 80–81, 84–85, 86, 94–99
overview of, 18, 80–82, 110–11
Palestine and, 85, 102–3, 106–7, 108–10
problem space of narratives of, 82–90
racial narratives and, 81–82, 85–86, 89, 92, 101–2, 110–11
refashioning of narratives in, 106–10
reforming imperial world through power of narratives and, 90–93
rights claims in narratives of, 88–89, 90
Saudi Arabia and, 99, 101, 102–3, 106–7, 109–10
self-determination and, 80–81, 91, 96–97, 99–101, 102–3
superiority narratives and, 82–83, 86–88, 89, 91, 96–97, 99–100
Third World and, 103, 104–6, 109–10
Turkey and, 80–82, 97–100, 102–3
UN and, 102–3, 107–8
United States and, 100–1
universalism and, 80–81, 82–83, 91–92, 93–94, 98–99
Western civilization and, 81–83, 87–88, 91, 99–100, 105–6, 107, 108
women's rights and, 89
World War I and, 93, 94
World War II and, 100–1
Paris Climate Convention (2012), 257–58
Paris Peace Conference (1919), 18, 81–82, 93, 96–97, 128
Pilgrims Society (1902), 35–36
pluralism, 154, 278, 280
Postel-Vinay, Karoline, 212–13
Prakash, Gyan, 190
Prebisch, Raúl, 220, 223–25
Princeton Project on National Security, 47–48
Pritchard, James Cowles, 188
progress. *See* development narrative; Enlightenment narrative; globalization
Przyluski, Jean, 193
Putin, Vladimir
civilizational narratives and, 82–83, 275–76
liberal democracy and, 271–72
Soviet Union and, 74–75
Ukraine invasion of, 3–4, 74, 82–83, 137, 271–72, 273–74, 278

Qian Xuesen, 226–27

racial narratives. *See also* superiority narratives
Angloworld and, 30–31, 33–35, 37–41, 43, 45, 48–49
citizenship and, 37–38
development narrative and, 213–14, 219, 228
India and, 187–88, 189–90
Japan and, 128–29, 130–31, 137–38
liberal democracy and, 15

overview of, 13–14, 15–16
Pan-Islamism and, 81–82, 85–86, 89, 92, 101–2, 110–11
patriotism and, 37–38, 39–40
radical conservatism and, 146–47, 152, 153, 155–56
United States and, 38–39
radical conservatism
Alt-Right movement and, 144
beyond the crisis and, 155–56
capitalism and, 152
civilizational narratives and, 146–47
cyclical conception of history and, 145–46, 150
decline narrative and, 143, 145–51, 157
democratization and, 147
Enlightenment narrative and, 145–46, 154–56
France and, 143–44, 148, 149, 152–53
Germany and, 143–44, 148
globalization and, 143, 147, 149, 150, 156–58
"left behinds" and, 153, 155
liberal democracy as target of, 145, 150
managerialism and, 150, 152–54, 155
metapolitics and, 150–56
modernity and, 145, 146, 147, 148–49, 150, 152
narrative mobilization and, 144, 150, 156–58
nationalism and, 144
origins of, 143–44
overview of, 19, 143–45, 156–58
paleoconservativism and, 144, 151
racial narratives and, 146–47, 152, 153, 155–56
reemergence of, 143
relativism and, 154–57
superiority narratives and, 146, 155–57
United Kingdom and, 144
United States and, 144, 147
universalism and, 150, 155–56
Western civilization and, 145, 148–50, 152–53, 154–58
Ramaswamy, Sumathi, 192–93
Reagan, Ronald, 59, 71, 72, 73, 231, 250
redistributive justice, 220–23, 226–27, 229–32, 233
relativism, 154–57
Renan, Ernest, 87
Rhodes, Cecil, 39–41
Rhodes Trust, 39–40
Ricoeur, Paul, 277–78
Risse, Thomas, 6–7
*River Elegy (Heshang)* (television documentary), 170–71, 173, 179
Roberts, Andrew, 48–50
Roca-Runciman Pact (1933), 218
Rockefeller Foundation, 224–25
Roosevelt, Franklin D., 4, 220–21
Roosevelt, Theodore, 37, 127
Rostow, Walt W., 225, 232
Russell-Einstein Manifesto (1955), 247
Russia. *See also* Soviet Union
Angloworld and, 30–31
Crimean invasion of, 275–76
legacies of Soviet Union in, 59, 60, 73–75
liberal democracy and, 282n.19
patriotism and, 74
revolution in, 58, 61, 64–65, 168
Russo-Japanese War of 1904-1905, 91, 92, 120–21, 126, 168
Ukraine invasion of, 3–4, 74, 82–83, 137, 271–72, 273–74, 278
Rustow, Dankwart, 103–4

Sagan, Carl, 262
Said, Edward, 206n.11
SALT agreement, 69
SALT II agreement, 69
Samuelson, Paul, 77n.44
San Francisco Treaty (1952), 177
Sartre, Jean Paul, 104–5
Saud, Faisal bin Abdulaziz al-, 108–10
Saudi Arabia and Pan-Islamism, 99, 101, 102–3, 106–7, 109–10
Schell, Jonathan, 250
scientific technological modernity (STM)
Anthropocene era and, 256–59
atomic power and, 256, 259
Baruch Plan and, 248
biospheric degradation and, 251–56
capitalism and, 244, 253–54, 258, 259
civilizational narratives and, 236–39, 241–43, 263

scientific technological modernity (STM) (*cont.*)
  climate change and, 240–43, 249–50, 256–59
  contesting of, 239–40
  distinctness of, 238–39
  emergence of, 237–38
  end of history and, 241–42
  Enlightenment narrative and, 237–38, 241–42, 251–52
  environmentalism and, 242, 251–56, 258–59
  Friends of the Earth view on, 259, 261
  futurism and, 239
  geo-engineering and, 261–62
  Germany and, 251–52
  globalization and, 237–38, 239–40
  greenpeace civilization and, 243, 263
  humanism and, 238
  Industrial Revolution and, 241, 243, 244, 251–52
  liberal democracy and, 254
  Luddite techophobe view on, 259, 261
  main features of, 237–39
  militarization and, 244–46
  modernity and, 240–42, 254
  new technopolitical contestation of, 259–64
  nuclear weapons and, 240–44, 245–51, 256
  overview of, 21–22, 236–37, 263–64
  Planetary Age and, 241–42
  progress and, 237–38, 239–40, 244–45
  Promethean technophile view on, 259–60, 262, 263
  public interest science and, 247–48
  religious challenges to, 239
  renewable energy and, 258
  Soterian view on, 259, 260–61
  space expansionism and, 262–63
  superiority narratives and, 244
  techno-optimist view on and, 259, 260
  terrorism and, 250–51
  world government and, 246–47
  World War I and, 245, 249–50
  World War II and, 245–46
Seeley, J. R., 33, 34
Senghor, Léopold Sédar, 228
September 11th attacks, 48, 134–35, 273–74
Sèvres Treaty (1919), 96–97
Shepherd, Laura, 279–80
Shidehara Kijuro, 127–28
Shimonoseki Treaty (1895), 126
Singhvi, M. L., 202–3
Soddy, Frederick, 245
Soviet Union. *See also* Cold War
  Afghan war of 1979-1989, 71–72, 106–7
  authenticity of ideologues in, 61–62
  capitalism as enemy of, 61, 62–64, 67, 69–70, 74–75, 226–27, 272–73
  central planning in, 65–66, 71, 222
  China and, 71–72, 73
  collapse of, 1, 59–60, 71, 73
  CPSU in, 62, 68
  debt of, 71–72
  decline of, 72
  development narrative and, 226–27
  enemies of the people in, 62
  environmentalism and, 253–54
  forgotten successes in, 60
  Gorbachev changes narrative in, 71–73
  imperialism and, 64, 69–70
  Industrial Revolution and, 60
  inequality in, 62
  legacies of, 59, 60, 73–75
  Leninism in, 60, 63–64, 67, 73, 74
  liberal democracy contrasted with, 59–60, 70
  limits of peaceful coexistence and, 68–70
  living standards in, 69
  Marxism and, 60–64, 73
  modernity and, 62–64
  nationalism and, 62
  Nazi Germany and, 63–65
  nuclear weapons and, 68, 245–46
  overview of, 17–18, 58–60
  repression in, 61–63
  revolution of 1917 and, 58, 64–65
  role of ideas in, 60–61
  Sputnik launched in, 69
  Third World and, 58–59, 69–70, 71
  Western civilization and, 58–60, 65, 74
  Western intellectual support for, 62–64
  World Peace Council and, 77n.43
  world revolution and, 61–62
  World War I and, 65
  World War II and, 63–67, 74

Spanish-American War (1898), 35–36
Spengler, Oswald, 148–50, 154, 155, 157–58
Srinivasa, V. S., 200–1
Staley, Eugene, 224–25
Stalin, Josef
  Cold War and, 67, 68
  death of, 68, 69
  enemies of the people under, 62
  Leninism and, 64–65
  Marxism and, 64
  secret speech on, 68
  World War II and, 65, 67
Stead, W. T., 39–41
Steffens, Lincoln, 62–63
Stimson, Henry L., 45–46
STM. *See* scientific technological modernity
Streit, Clarence, 43–44, 47–48
Suárez, Eduardo, 220–21
Sun Fo, 169
Sun Yat-Sen, 93–94, 216–17
superiority narratives. *See also* racial narratives
  Angloworld and, 17, 29, 33, 38–39, 45, 48–49
  India and, 184, 189–90, 191, 193, 195, 205
  Japan and, 118, 133
  Ottoman Empire and, 96–97
  overview of, 12–13
  Pan-Islamism and, 82–83, 86–88, 89, 91, 96–97, 99–100
  radical conservatism and, 146, 155–57
  STM and, 244
Suzuki Kentaro, 126

Tagore, Rabindranath, 194–95, 276–77
Taiwan
  China and, 176–77, 180–81, 275–76
  development narrative and, 213–14
  disputed island claims and, 176–77
  Japan and, 120–21, 214
technological development. *See* development narrative; Industrial Revolution; scientific technological modernity
Thatcher, Margaret, 28–29, 48, 49–50, 72, 231
Third World, 58–59, 69–70, 71, 103, 104–6, 109–10, 212–13, 222–23, 228–31
Tocqueville, Alexis de, 50, 159n.9
Todorov, Tzveten, 23n.12
Toynbee, Arnold, 105–6
Trautmann, Thomas, 187, 188
Treaty of Sèvres (1919), 96–97
Treaty of Shimonoseki (1895), 126
Truman, Harry, 66, 67, 223–24, 226, 246
Trump, Donald, 2, 47–48, 144, 163–64, 173, 233, 271–72, 275, 277–78
Turkey and Pan-Islamism, 80–82, 97–100, 102–3

Ukraine, Russia's invasion of, 3–4, 74, 82–83, 137, 271–72, 273–74, 278
UN Committee on Atomic Energy, 248
UN Economic Commission for Latin America (CEPAL), 223–24, 230–31
United Kingdom (UK). *See also* British Empire
  Angloworld and, 44, 48–50
  Brexit in, 2, 17, 28–29, 49–50
  India and, 202
  Japan and, 121–22, 127, 131, 137
  radical conservatism and, 144
United Nations (UN)
  Angloworld and, 28–29, 45–46
  China and, 167
  development narrative and, 228, 230
  environmentalism and, 253
  India and, 196–98
  Japan and, 132, 134–35
  liberal democracy and, 275
  Pan-Islamism and, 102–3, 107–8
United States. *See also* Cold War
  Angloworld and, 29, 32, 33–42, 44–46, 47
  British Empire's relationship with, 35, 37, 42
  China and, 1–2, 170–71, 173, 224–25
  development narrative and, 218–20, 223–26, 230
  environmentalism and, 253
  India and, 225
  Japan and, 119, 127–28, 131–34
  New Deal in, 168–69, 220, 223, 224–25
  nuclear weapons and, 245–46
  Pan-Islamism and, 100–1

United States (*cont.*)
  racial narratives and, 38–39
  radical conservatism and, 144, 147
  World War I and, 42
  World War II and, 42–43, 67
United World Federalists (1947), 45–46
universalism
  Angloworld and, 40–41, 44–45, 46–48
  China and, 94, 163–66, 168, 172, 181
  development narrative and, 225, 233
  India and, 94, 186, 189, 195–96, 199–200, 205
  Japan and, 115–16, 117, 118–19, 130–32, 134–35, 136–37
  liberal democracy and, 1–2, 279–80
  narratives of the global and, 1–2, 3–4, 10–12, 15, 279–80
  Pan-Islamism and, 80–81, 82–83, 91–92, 93–94, 98–99
  radical conservatism and, 150, 155–56
  Western civilization and, 279–80
Universal Races Congress (1911), 92
Usborne, Henry, 45–46
USSR. *See* Soviet Union

Vajpayee, Atal Behari, 202–3
Varadarajan, Latha, 185
Venezualan boundary dispute (1895-1896), 35–36
Venner, Dominuque, 143–44, 151
von Braun, Wernher, 262

Wagner, Richard, 148
Waldstein, Charles, 38–39
Wang Jingwei, 164–65
Washington Naval Conference (1921-1922), 121–22, 128
Weber, Max, 156–57, 188
Weiss, Thomas, 46
Wells, H. G., 33, 45, 243, 245, 246
Wendt, Alexander, 46
Western civilization
  Angloworld and, 29, 43–44, 49–50
  anti-Westernism and, 276–78
  backlash to modernization in, 14–15
  China and, 15–16, 166, 171–72, 173–74, 178, 179–80
  contestation of narratives in, 11–13, 14–17
  development narrative and, 211–13, 232
  India and, 188–90, 194
  Japan and, 125–27, 129–30, 133, 137
  Latin Christendom narrative challenged in, 12
  liberal democracy and, 13–14, 277–79
  modernity and, 11–14
  narratives of the global and, 1–3, 10–17, 275–78
  overview of, 10–16
  Pan-Islamism and, 81–83, 87–88, 91, 99–100, 105–6, 107, 108
  radical conservatism and, 145, 148–50, 152–53, 154–58
  recession of, 1–2
  Soviet Union and, 58–60, 65, 74
  universalism and, 279–80
Westphalian system, 117, 118, 129–30, 164
White, Arthur Silva, 36–37
White, Harry Dexter, 220–21
White Man's burden, 48–49, 107
Williams, Michael, 19, 277–78
Willkie, Wendell, 45–46, 196
Wilson, Woodrow, 65, 80–82, 93, 96–97
Wilsonianism, 96–97
women's rights, 89, 279–80
World Bank, 134, 173, 211, 228, 230–31
World Economic Forum, 273–74
world government, 41–47, 117, 196–98, 246–47
World Orders Model Project, 46
World Peace Council (WPC), 77n.43
World Trade Organization (WTO), 1, 171, 233
World War I
  Angloworld and, 41, 42, 45
  British Empire and, 41
  development narrative and, 215–16, 217–18
  Japan and, 127

Ottoman Empire and, 94, 95–96
Pan-Islamism and, 93, 94
Soviet Union and, 65
STM and, 245, 249–50
United States and, 42
World War II
Angloworld and, 42–43, 46–47
British Empire and, 42–43
China and, 163–64, 165, 174–77
development narrative and, 220
Japan and, 121–22, 129–31, 175
Pan-Islamism and, 100–1
Soviet Union and, 63–67, 74
STM and, 245–46
United States and, 42–43, 67
Wright, Richard, 101

Xi Jinping, 73, 173, 180, 273, 280

Yamagata Aritomo, 125, 126–27
Yeats, William Butler, 73
Yifu, Justin, 173

Zelensky, Volodymyr, 271–72, 273
Zhang Weiwei, 162, 178–79, 180
Zheng He, 173–74
*Zhongguo keyi shuo bu (China Can Say No)* (Zhang), 173
Zhou Enlai, 170
Zou Taofen, 164